EDUCATING DEAF STUDENTS IN A MULTICULTURAL WORLD

EDUCATING DEAF STUDENTS IN A MULTICULTURAL WORLD

Kathee Christensen, Editor

San Diego, CA

Educating Deaf Students in a Multicultural World

Manufactured in the United States of America
Published by DawnSignPress

Library of Congress Control Number upon request.

ISBN-13: 978-1-58121-028-6

6130 Nancy Ridge Drive
San Diego, CA 92121
858-768-0428 VP • 858-625-0600 V • www.dawnsign.com

Contents

Dedication

Dedicated to Sage Ann, Kellan Clay and their Grampaw

Acknowledgments

In my opinion, this book is a testament to perseverance! It was three years in the making. All of the chapter authors demonstrated profound patience and professionalism. For this I am grateful to each one of them.

Throughout the process of editing this book, I have had support from so many friends and colleagues. Kathleen Kaiser and Ron Richardson were consistent with encouragement. Amy Malcolm shared creative ideas from the field, and my former graduate students were ready and willing to share stories from the "real world" of the classroom. I am especially proud that four of my former graduate students are contributors to this book.

Of course nothing could be done without Joe Dannis and DawnSignPress's support. A special thank you to our thoughtful editor, Rebecca Ryan, whose expertise informed each page.

Thank you to my husband, Ben, who was my partner in Trilingual Education, as well as my soul mate in life. Thanks for my children, Kyra and Chip, who consistently demonstrate respect for diversity in the way they live their lives and raise their children.

I am hopeful that this book will impart a sense of history, a sense of culture and an understanding of the dynamic force of multiculturalism that impacts the Deaf World.

–Kathee Christensen, Editor

Section I:
Reflections

CHAPTER 1

From Cultural Knowledge to Cultural Knowing: An Introduction

KATHEE MANGAN CHRISTENSEN, Ph.D.
Professor Emerita, San Diego State University

"The limits of my language mean the limits of my world."
–Ludwig Wittgenstein

INTRODUCTION

This is a book about culture. Specifically, it is about the cultures found within the Deaf Community—the People of the Eye. With the exception of one chapter, the authors of the chapters in this book write about Deaf people as members of a Visual Culture. The word Deaf, spelled throughout the book with a capital D, encompasses all persons who use vision as their **primary** sensory mode of communication. This definition is not about degrees of hearing. It is not a negative definition that places an emphasis on "loss." Rather it defines a culture based on the subtleties of vision, with or without the additional support of auditory input. We are addressing, from a cultural perspective, the world of people who first and foremost SEE, LOOK, and INTERPRET their everyday environment. They may or may not use hearing aids, cochlear implants, speechreading techniques, or spoken language, but all of them hold one thing in common. They depend on vision as their primary, most salient means of understanding and interpreting the world around them.

Within the Deaf World, there are cultural variations. Deaf children, typically, are born to Hearing parents. In addition, their parents may be members of a culture other than mainstream White Hearing individuals. Some Deaf children, roughly 10% or fewer, have Deaf parents. Parents, whether Deaf or Hearing, represent a variety of ethnic, racial, and cultural identities, some of which overlap. In this case, a Deaf individual may identify him/herself as multicultural and bilingual or multilingual. The purpose of this book is to explore the complexity of diverse identities within the larger Deaf World.

There is one chapter that takes a different approach to culture in the greater Deaf World. That chapter addresses the community of individuals who are Deafblind. Some Deafblind people are born with limited sight and hearing. Others acquire Deafblindness later in life. Deafblind infants meet the world with curiosity that is satisfied most directly through the senses of touch, smell, and taste. These senses are the foundation upon which communication is based. Those who acquire Deafblindness later in life can use prior life skills and experiences to make sense of the world in which they currently live. The communication options are diverse and depend on the unique situation of the individual. For example, Deaf people who become Blind may use touch to communicate through an adaptation of American Sign Language (ASL). Blind people who become Deaf may learn to use touch and signed language to communicate. In all instances, the cultural environment becomes a complex interaction of sensory information destined to create and strengthen communication linkages.

As stated previously, this book examines the diverse communities that thrive within the Deaf World. The focus is on culture and an inherent respect for cultural diversity. As we look within the Deaf community and consider the overlapping cultural circles, we see basic similarities and vast differences that exist. We cannot make generalizations. The Deaf World is diverse and growing. The experience of each individual Deaf person is unique. The experience of Deaf individuals who identify with multiple cultural groups is complex. The authors of this text explore this diversity and complexity with respect and understanding.

OVERVIEW

In 2000, I edited a book for DawnSignPress entitled *Deaf Plus: A Multicultural Perspective*. It was a collection of chapters by a diverse group of authors, all of whom cared deeply about the apparent marginalization of Deaf individuals who were members of underrepresented ethnic and racial groups. Now, 17 years later, it is time to reflect on what has been accomplished in this area, what new energy and resources have been expended on the behalf of diversity in education of Deaf People, and what innovative approaches are on the horizon.

Terminology used throughout this book is intended to reflect change and demonstrate respect for all persons. Ethnic and cultural terms change over time and within groups. All of the chapter authors have chosen terminology that, in their experience, most closely represents a population and an environment that they know well. The authors come from diverse backgrounds and bring personal perspectives gained from a wealth of experience in a variety of professional settings. Their messages shine light on areas often overlooked (e.g., Deafblind individuals) and often marginalized (e.g., educational interpreters in diverse settings). They expand boundaries and demonstrate ways in which various groups of Deaf individuals intersect.

The present book is divided into three sections: I. Reflections, II. Reactions, and III. Re-Visions.

The first section, **Reflections**, reminds us of pioneering work in the area of multicultural issues, work that has been done by individuals such as Robert Davila, Oscar Cohen, and Roz Rosen and by organizations such as the National Association of the Deaf. We reflect upon groundbreaking steps that have been taken. To paraphrase Isaac Newton (1643–1727), we stand on the shoulders of those giants who came before us.

Section II, **Reactions**, describes recent programs that grew from an awareness of the needs of Deaf individuals from diverse backgrounds. This section represents reactions to the lack of programs for these Deaf people and documents some of the progress that has been made since the year 2000.

Section III, **Re-Visions**, looks ahead to greater development in the areas of technology, social justice, and innovative research methodology. This section includes overlooked and underserved populations, specifically the Deaf Lesbian Gay Bisexual Transgender (LGBT) community and the growing community of Deafblind individuals here and abroad. Our intent is to enlarge the discussion of multicultural issues within the Deaf population, reframe social justice, and re-envision education for traditional, as well as diverse and nontraditional groups.

CULTURAL KNOWLEDGE AND CULTURAL KNOWING

There is a difference between *cultural knowledge* and *cultural knowing*. A person can take American Sign Language courses, for example, and be given high grades. That person could also enroll in a course or two in Deaf Culture and learn about Deaf people from a variety of perspectives. Do the courses and high grades ensure that, on completion, the student will possess *cultural knowing*? The deaf poet, Willard Madsen, has written: "What is it like to 'hear' a hand?/ You have to be deaf to understand." The final lines of his poem ask: "What is it like to comprehend,/ Some nimble fingers that paint the scene,/ And make you smile and feel serene,/ With the "spoken word" of the moving hand,/ That makes you part of the world at large?" What Madsen alludes to is **cultural knowing as mutual understanding**. When a Hearing person understands how a Deaf person might feel in the "world at large" that can trigger a move away from fact-based cultural knowledge and toward human understanding or cultural knowing. And, in like manner, when a Deaf or Hearing member of the majority culture can see into the situation of Deaf individuals from diverse ethnic backgrounds, a deeper level of cultural knowing can occur. Barriers must be removed to allow exposure to new realities.

From that exposure, new understanding and new consciousness can develop. Madsen's question might be rephrased: "What is it like to 'hear' the accent of an unfamiliar hand? A moving hand that paints a scene from an entirely different Deaf culture?"

All too often, a culture is defined by outsiders who study an indigenous people as "other" (Geertz, 1995). In recent years, it has been increasingly the case that Deaf individuals have reacted against the tendency of cultural definition by outsiders. The term *audist* is used in the Deaf World and beyond to describe those persons who hold "the notion that one is superior based on one's ability to hear or to behave in the manner of one who hears" (Humphries, 1977, p.12). Deaf Culture is currently defined by what is positive, what is valued, from an "insider" perspective (Lane, Hoffmeister, & Bahan, 1996; Padden & Humphries, 1988). Holcomb (2013) analyzes the various segments of the Deaf community with an eye toward diversity. He reflects on the history of Deaf culture and the evolving field of Deaf Studies, right up to the present day of technological innovation.

Recent progress in understanding and respecting Deaf Culture, overall, has been a proud accomplishment. As an example, witness growth in university and college programs across the United States that offer ASL in Departments of Modern Languages and offer courses in Deaf Culture. In addition, it is noteworthy that Deaf persons have attained success in a variety of professional areas, such as theatre, film and television, educational leadership, journalism, and sports. Glass ceilings have been cracked, if not broken, in these areas. However, the situation of Deaf individuals from diverse ethnic and racial backgrounds has not been studied often or in depth, from a multicultural framework. The intersection of cultures in the Deaf World is rich, fertile ground for meaningful ethnographic research. For example, Granda and Stoudt (Chapter 14) take their considerable cultural knowledge and apply it to knowing (understanding) a Deaf youth from Mexico now living in the United States. Cultural knowing is revealed in several ways, beginning with the decision to use materials from the subject's native culture to transition his innate understanding from one culture and language (Spanish) to new cultures and languages (ASL and English).

Throughout this book, readers are challenged to think about the condition of Deaf children from families whose home language and culture differ from the majority. For example, some children may have immigrated to the United States with their families or may have been born in the United States after their families arrived. Their families may or may not have legal status as U.S. citizens and, most likely, have come to the United States to find a better life for their children. Deaf children in this situation face challenges that include communication at home, access to their heritage language, access to the sign language of their native culture, access to American Sign Language, and access to English language and literacy. These challenges have a profound impact on the lives of these Deaf children and their families. Recent data indicate that the majority of Deaf children in the United States come from homes where languages other than English or ASL are used (GRI, 2010). In light of these findings, it is logical to believe that a multilingual approach should be a major focus of programs that prepare teachers, interpreters, administrators, and other related professionals who work with the Deaf population. In this book, Hearing and Deaf authors from diverse ethnic and racial backgrounds share their research, their personal experiences, their cultural knowledge, and, most of all, their cultural knowing.

REFLECTIONS

Text books and courses in Deaf Culture frequently overlook the contributions of Deaf people of color or others who have worked to pave the way for a better education for Deaf children. By way of introduction to this section on Reflections, I would like to contribute a short summary of just a few cultural icons from the Black and Black Deaf communities.

William Holland (1841–1907) was an ex-slave born to an African-American slave mother and a white father, Captain Bird Holland. Captain Holland bought his son's freedom and sent him to Oberlin College for his education. William Holland, a biracial Hearing man with great concern for all children in his home state of Texas, established what was called the Texas Deaf, Dumb and Blind Institute for Colored Youth in 1887. Later the school expanded to include Hearing orphans. You could say that this was the first bilingual–bicultural program with the Hearing orphans learning to sign and becoming interpreters for their Deaf peers (Tabak, 2006)!

William C. Ritter (1872–1952) established the Virginia School for the Colored Deaf and Blind in Hampton in 1909. In 1930, Gallaudet College conferred an honorary doctorate on W.C. Ritter for his work with Black Deaf children. Despite this honor, Gallaudet administrators continued to refuse admission to graduates of Ritter's school (Burch, 2002).

Andrew Foster (1925–1987) was the first Black Deaf student to earn a Bachelor of Arts degree at Gallaudet University. He went on to earn two Master's degrees and served as a missionary to Ghana where he opened the first school for the Deaf on the continent of Africa. He was awarded an honorary doctorate from Gallaudet in 1970.

Otis Massey was the second Black Deaf student to graduate from Gallaudet in the early 1950s. He was hired as a teacher at the school founded by William Holland and immediately became a role model and mentor for his students. He was the only teacher at the time who signed fluently (Tabak, 2006).

Jeremiah Germany was probably the third Black Deaf graduate of Gallaudet. I added his name to the list for personal reasons. When I was a young child living on the campus of the Michigan School for the Deaf in Flint where both of my parents worked, Jeremiah was a star player on the football team that my father coached. His kindness to me, a little child who enthusiastically attended all the MSD football games, made Jeremiah my first Deaf hero. After graduation from Gallaudet, Jeremiah went on to have a successful career as a teacher. He was one of the founders of the New Jersey Association of the Deaf in 1967.

In more recent years, **Glen Anderson** was the first Black Deaf individual to earn a doctorate. He received his degree in 1982 from New York University. Glen's contributions to the field of Rehabilitation and Counseling have been enormous, and he has mentored and encouraged many Deaf individuals to earn advanced degrees.

Of course there are many other cultural icons from a variety of ethnic and racial backgrounds. To include them all would necessitate another book. Perhaps that is a measure of progress, of sorts.

The authors of Chapter 2 need no introduction. Robert R. Davila and Oscar P. Cohen are pioneers in the field of human rights for Deaf people. Davila has been an example, a mentor, and an advocate throughout his life for Deaf Hispanic individuals. Cohen was among the first to conduct research, write articles, and develop programs for Black Deaf students. Davila and Cohen draw upon a rich cache of personal experiences to relate, through a one-on-one interview conducted at Cohen's home, a remarkable story of challenge and success.

Rosen, in Chapter 3, provides a synthesis of ideas on Deaf culture and what it means to be Deaf. She broadens the discussion of ASL by using the inclusive term "`sign language users." This term places the focus on fluency and cultural knowing instead of hearing status. Rosen uses the concept of *intersectionality* as a vantage for consideration of the validity, vitality, and value of Deaf individuals within the broader framework of several human rights movements. Her discussion of the historical practice of segregating oral and signing Deaf students by designating separate buses and separate entrances to the school building reminded me of an experience I had as a teenager. I was interested in volunteering with Deaf children on the weekends and found a place at a large, private oral school for the deaf in the town where I was living. I had acquired sign language as a child growing up and was quite fluent at the time. During my interview, it was made clear to me that I could not use signs of any kind during my job as a Saturday afternoon playground supervisor. This seemed strange to me, but I decided to give it a try. What I learned was that the playground was the great equalizer. No teachers were present, only house parents and volunteers. Immediately I noticed that everyone was signing! Where did they learn to sign? Later I learned that the deaf children who had Deaf family members were much sought-after as sign language mentors for the rest of the kids on the weekends. No matter the rules Monday through Friday, sign language prevailed on the weekends!

REACTIONS

Section II begins with three chapters that examine issues in Asian Deaf communities. One of the intriguing questions that must be considered when looking at Asian Deaf groups is the question of tonal language. In many Asian countries, people speak tonal languages. Simply stated, the meaning of a spoken word depends on the pronunciation and reception of discreet tones. Tones carry meaning. A congenitally Deaf child born into a culture that speaks a tonal language is at a profound disadvantage. Later in this book, we will discuss that situation in more depth. For the time being, as you read these chapters, it is important to be aware of the potential challenges in the life of a Deaf child whose parents and extended family speak a tonal language.

Cheng and Maroonroge expand on the notion of cultural knowing in Chapter 4, "Understanding Asian Deaf Culture: A Multicultural Perspective." They introduce the complexity and diversity of cultures within the global Asian/Pacific Islander population in the United States, particularly those with roots in Southeast and East Asia. Differences in family dynamics, including history, languages, religious beliefs, and social values combine to impact the lives of Asian/Pacific Islander children who are Deaf. Educators need to acquire global competencies in order to accurately assess and effectively educate Deaf children from these diverse populations.

In Chapter 5, Wu and Grant provide practical ways in which educators, counselors, and others can acquire global, multicultural competencies through experiential learning activities. Relationship building is key to their model for successful delivery of services to all Deaf individuals, but particularly to the diverse ethnic and racial groups within the larger Deaf community. These relationships begin and develop in the family unit. From a secure foundation in the family, Deaf children can move more confidently into broader circles in the Deaf community, bringing with them their cultural heritage, intact, as social capital. Strategies for counselors, teachers, and other "helpers" are provided, along with activities that can be adapted for use across all professional in-service and preservice development programs. These frameworks and activities encourage and support self and other awareness, reflection, and more inclusive responses to multicultural situations. Counselors, administrators, speech language pathologists, health care professionals, and others can borrow social capital from their Deaf students/clients to enrich their own cultural knowing.

Ward, in Chapter 6, shares an observational study based on her years of living and working in Japan. Certified as a bilingual–multicultural teacher of the Deaf in the United States, Ward's insights provide a lens for cross-cultural understanding of schools and programs in Japan and the United States through the eyes of a "foreigner." She admits her feelings of "not fitting" the mold of a society that values conformity. She then transitions these feelings to those of a child, born Deaf, and thus "different" and not fitting the traditional view of cultural uniformity. Her observations are based on personal relationships formed with members of the Deaf community in Japan who shared a fascinating and illuminating history of the evolution of education of the deaf over the past 100+ years. The struggles of Deaf adults in Japan remind us of similar struggles in the United States during the early to mid-20th century. They include struggles around issues such as Signed Japanese, Japanese Sign Language, interpreters, and cochlear implants. The hopes and dreams of the American and Japanese Deaf communities resonate across cultures.

In Chapter 7, Holcomb, Ostrove, and Lawrence shed light on the changing needs of interpreter training programs. As our society becomes more diverse, the preparation of interpreters to meet various linguistic needs is paramount. Recently, I had an experience that made me realize, on a personal level, that our need for multilingual interpreters is growing as fast as our physical world is shrinking. I was attending an opening of a special exhibition at a local art museum. The curator was from Spain, and she was accompanied by her Deaf daughter, Maria, who had grown up in Spain and educated orally. This young Deaf woman then moved to the United States, attended Gallaudet University, learned ASL as an adult, married a Deaf man, and uses ASL as her primary language. Now here she was, hoping to "hear" her mother's presentation. She had, up to this point, never had an ASL interpreter for her mother's lectures. The best person for that interpreting job would have been a professional trilingual (Spanish, English, ASL) interpreter, however, I was the only person who happened to be available at the moment. So, I listened to the English language interpreter who was a beat or two behind the Spanish speaker, Maria's mother. I did my best to blend the spoken languages into an intelligible ASL interpretation of the talk. It was an exhausting experience, which added to my already profound respect for trilingual and multilingual sign language interpreters. Certainly, we need more of them! In fact, it is the professional responsibility of university and college interpreter training programs to recruit and prepare this valuable support corps in our educational system. Smith (2010) presents a call to action. After reviewing recent legislation regarding K-12 educational interpreters, she states that "to date, we have largely neglected the field of educational interpreting—oftentimes marginalizing those who work in K-12 settings while failing to provide them with the support, research, education and training necessary to do their jobs effectively" (p. 185).

According to a report by the U.S. Office of Education (2009), approximately 87% of Deaf students spend a portion of their day in general education classrooms with interpreters. General education teachers have little, if any, preparation to work successfully with Deaf students and their ASL interpreters. When one adds the additional challenge of understanding the needs of multicultural Deaf students, a classroom barrier can be created (Call, 2010). To avoid a creation of potential classroom barriers, educators and others must consider how communication is facilitated and managed for Deaf students with diverse signed and spoken language needs. "Unfortunately, the general education teacher often does not receive the quantity of collaboration or consultation needed to help the student with a hearing loss function optimally in the environment" (Berndsen & Luckner, 2012, p. 113). This statement opens a floodgate of questions concerning the quality of education in the mainstream for all Deaf students and, especially, Deaf students with limited knowledge of the American system of education.

It is my opinion that interpreters must be prepared to meet the growing needs of children placed in mainstream settings and Deaf special day classes to ensure the academic success and emotional health of ethnically and racially diverse Deaf children. In Chapter 7 of this book, Holcomb and colleagues agree. They write in detail about ways in which interpreters of color can be recruited and supported to serve a diverse community. They challenge the reader to view the term "normal" through an enlarged, culturally balanced lens.

A question often asked but seldom answered is the following: "How many Deaf students of color complete advanced degrees in higher education?" The answer to this question would be an important measure of ways in which our educational system provides opportunities to ensure that Deaf students of color have opportunities to reach their maximum potential. Universities, apparently, do not track those data or, if they do, are not willing to share the information. A recent study of Deaf college students found that Deaf students obtain less information than hearing students from incidental learning. It was found that Deaf students' academic challenges are not limited to literacy but involve issues of language and cognition accessible to students who can hear and make inferences from "overhearing" incidental communication (Marschark et al., 2012).

Bourdieu and Passeron (1977) investigated the theory of cultural capital as a way in which dominant cultural groups were able to maintain power. They asserted that some communities are perceived to be culturally wealthy while others are culturally poor. Those with cultural wealth acquire specific forms of knowledge that are valued by privileged groups in society. All children enter school with skills; however, certain skills are valued in the general school context (e.g., computer literacy) whereas other skills are not (e.g., fluency in one or more sign language). Sign language fluency might be valuable to a Deaf child, but it may not carry any capital in the general school context. Spoken English fluency, however, is a form of cultural capital that is valued in mainstream academic and social contexts. The accumulated assets of Deaf people of color are not recognized in a White, middle class, English language-dominant context.

In Chapter 8, Braswell addresses some of the obstacles, both academic and personal, that can prevent students of color from attaining their goals. She explores ways in which positive social capital can be used to help Deaf students, including students of color, realize their goals for education and employment. Braswell's work reminds me of earlier investigations that examined success patterns of precollege Deaf students. In 2008, Reed, Antia, and Kreimeyer studied Deaf students in public schools and identified facilitators and detractors that contributed to academic status. Their recommendations for further research listed inclusion of student voices with regard to motivation and other factors. They suggest a study of the relationship between academic and social facilitators and detractors for Deaf students in general education classrooms. Braswell studies Deaf students at the community college level. Her initial findings suggest that success in higher education is linked in specific ways to factors of family support and precollege educational experiences of Deaf students.

Gallegos begins Chapter 9 with a question asked by a parent: What can we do better? Immediately, the reader's mind is focused on finding answers. Gallegos shares history and case studies that demonstrate the intuitions and strengths of mothers seeking support for their babies—seeking early intervention despite cultural and economic barriers. She describes the promise of universal newborn hearing screening, which may be lost to families unable to access information and professional help due to attitudinal and social obstacles. She shares the experiences of three determined mothers and their personal journeys toward resolution of their concerns regarding their babies. These stories underscore the difficulties experienced by ethnically and racially diverse parents who seek help in an unfamiliar and daunting system. Gallegos draws conclusions and makes recommendations that, if adopted, will help mediate the oppression and hegemony faced by too many families as they seek early intervention services in unfamiliar territory. These recommendations should motivate us to realize exactly "what we can do better!"

Gutierrez and Huff, Chapter 10, spotlight the comprehensive statewide services provided by the Center for Educational Consultation and Training located at the New Mexico School for the Deaf. This model program serves Deaf children in a state with many communities where the Spanish language and Hispanic culture prevail and which is home to several Native American reservations and pueblos.

The authors document how this diverse population of Deaf children and their families are served successfully, effectively, and with cultural sensitivity. The concept of Deafness as an environmental disability is introduced and discussed.

RE-VISIONS

In this section, we look beyond the traditional discussion of racial and linguistic diversity to defy stereotypes and to tell stories that, for the most part, have not been told. Included are insights into the LGBT population—a population that Dr. Michael Deninger describes as "invisible and underserved." Transgender people, those who identify with a gender other than the one assigned at birth, are long misunderstood. Presently they represent about 0.5% of the population of the United States (Steinmetz, 2014). The number of Deaf individuals in this group is unknown. In Chapter 11, Deninger uses his knowledge as a psychologist and fluent signer of ASL in a cross-cultural comparison of Deaf children with Hearing parents and gay children with straight parents. Both groups of children contend with isolation from their family and lack of early role models. They often feel misunderstood, unaccepted, and "not normal." I stated earlier that our text expands the discussion, but in this case, Deninger begins the discussion. His search of the literature found very little attention to Deaf LGBT issues. He provides strategies to improve the climate for the Deaf LGBT community and makes a strong plea for much needed research in this area. Education is vitally important, and Deninger points to the Gay Lesbian Straight Education Network (GLSEN) as a national resource to teachers and other professionals involved with supporting LGBT Deaf students and working toward a climate of acceptance and respect. Application of the GLSEN model to the education of Deaf children would be a step in the right direction.

Also new to our discussion of multicultural Deaf issues is the topic of Deafblindness. In Chapter 12, Riggio and McLetchie share their vast experience with developing programs abroad through their work with Perkins International. Deafblind children represent another population with needs that are often overlooked. The complexity of issues involved in serving congenitally Deafblind children is rarely addressed in public school special education programs. Administrators do not understand the issues involved with language acquisition or cognitive development in this population with dual sensory challenges. All too often school administrators are reticent to provide the intense, expensive, one-on-one early intervention that is needed by these children and their families. Added to that barrier is the situation of parents from ethnically and racially diverse cultures and the inaccessibility of comprehensive and comprehensible information about services for babies who are both Deaf and Blind. These children may be placed in programs for students who are Blind and not receiving tactile-signed language input or may be assigned to a Deaf special-needs class where the development of visual/tactile strategies is not addressed. In both settings, it is most likely that the cognitive strengths of these children will be overlooked or unnoticed. The subtle acts of exploration and nonverbal communication of a Deafblind child are difficult to discern, as they differ vastly from those of either a Deaf or a Blind infant or toddler. Without early, intense individual intervention, Deafblind infants and toddlers are barred from reaching their communicative and cognitive potentials.

Perkins School for the Blind and the Perkins International Program provide an entry into salient educational programs for children who are Deafblind. In Chapter 12, Riggio and McLetchie underscore the fact that "children who are Deafblind are at high risk for exclusion from education and society because of cultural and societal attitudes and the uniqueness and complexity of combined vision and hearing losses." They go on to describe some of the challenges. In their informed opinion, it is incumbent upon the educational team to expand the world of the Deafblind child to include meaningful interaction with others, independent mobility, and a strong feeling of self-worth. Perkins International has done amazing work in developing countries. A culturally appropriate communication activity for a Deafblind student in Sri Lanka is described and illustrated in this chapter. This is an excellent example of how intervention can be designed and embedded with cultural awareness and communicative intent. The Perkins International model involves the child, the family, and the village/town with the goal of making Deafblind individuals productive and fully involved members of their communities.

As classroom research evolves into the 21st century, it is difficult to find comparative studies, either qualitative or quantitative, that reveal subtle differences in the ways in which both Deaf and Hearing children learn. All children come to school with "cultural capital" that can be built upon effectively by a culturally sensitive teacher or clinician. Chapter 13 by Smith and Chapter 14 by Granda and Stoudt are based on recent doctoral dissertation research by two Deaf scholars and one Hearing scholar. Smith studied the visually accessible application of texting to increase communication skills, particularly language and literacy. Granda and Stoudt studied visually salient methods for English literacy development with a Deaf youth from Mexico. Both studies employed ethnographic methodology to make in-depth observations. Granda and Stoudt employed a single subject case study of a Deaf student, and Smith designed a case study of a Deaf second grader mainstreamed into a diverse classroom setting of Hearing students. Both chapters provide descriptions of techniques that teachers, Hearing and Deaf, can apply in classroom and clinic settings. Both chapters raise important points with regard to appropriate and **effective visual strategies** for teaching Deaf students attempting to learn English as a second language.

What is required in a just society? In Chapter 15, Folsé and Berke assert that the development of social justice is a responsibility of all school personnel. They challenge teachers and administrators to develop curricula founded on principles of social justice. The recently approved Expected Schoolwide Learning Results (Caliornia School for the Deaf, Fremont) are cited as a way to incorporate social justice into all classrooms. They describe the 20-year process that resulted in this strong, schoolwide commitment to social justice education. The concept of intersectional identities within the Deaf community is reinforced, because, as stated by Lorde (2007, p. 138), "we do not live single-issue lives." The chapter by Folsé and Berke, in effect, re-emphasizes all of the critical points regarding social justice voiced in the previous chapters of this book. All of the chapter authors, in individual ways, address the pervasive question, "What is required in a just society?"

The focus of this book has been on underrepresented ethnic and racial groups within the larger Deaf community. It must be stated, however, that the goal is for **all of us** to learn as much as possible, not only about other cultures, but about our own personal cultures as well. An objective look at our own cultural or multicultural values can promote an unbiased, open "cultural knowing" of ourselves and of others. The Harvard author and educator Howard Gardner included both Interpersonal and Intrapersonal intelligences as critical elements in his Multiple Intelligences framework (Gardner, 1983). The answer to the question "Who are you?" can be answered best when coupled with the question "Who am I?"

Although there is much to accomplish in the field of multilingual–multicultural education of individuals who are Deaf, it is important to note that, in recent years, progress has been made. Programs have been developed on the national and international scenes that demonstrate a greater awareness of the complex intersectionality of cultures that include both Deaf and Hearing groups from a variety of ethnic and racial communities. The chapters that follow are designed to provide insights into how successful, innovative, and culturally inclusive programs have been established. As John Dewey once said, "Arriving at one goal is the starting point to another."

REFERENCES

Berndsen, M., & Luckner, J. (2012). Supporting students who are deaf or hard of hearing in general education classrooms: A Washington state study. *Communication Disorders Quarterly, 33,* 111–118.

Bourdieu, P., & Passeron, J. (1977). *Reproduction in education, society and cultures.* London: Sage.

Call, M. (2010). See me through the triplicity of my world: Ethical considerations in language choices. In K. Christensen (Ed.), *Ethical considerations in educating children who are deaf or hard of hearing* (pp. 14–37). Washington, DC: Gallaudet University Press.

Gardner, H. (1983). *Frames of mind: The theory of multiple intelligences.* New York: Basic Books, Inc.

Geertz, C. (1995). *After the fact: Two countries, four decades, one anthropologist.* Cambridge, MA: Harvard University Press.

Holcomb, T. (2013). *Introduction to American deaf culture.* New York: Oxford University Press.

Humphries, T. (1977). *Communicating across cultures (deaf-hearing) and language learning.* Unpublished doctoral dissertation, Union Institute and University, Cincinnati, OH.

Lane, H., Hoffmeister, R., & Bahan, B. (1996). *A journey into the Deaf-World.* San Diego: DawnSignPress.

Lorde, A. (2007). *Sister outsider.* Berkeley, CA: Crossing Press.

Madsen, W. (1975). *You have to be deaf to understand.* Washington, DC: Gallaudet College.

Marschark, M., Sarchet, T., Convertino, C., Borgna, G., Morrison, C., & Remelt, S. (2012). Print exposure, reading habits, and reading achievement among deaf and hearing college students. *JDSDE, 17*(1), 61–74.

Padden, C., & Humphries, T. (1988). *Deaf in America: Voices from a culture.* Cambridge, MA: Harvard University Press.

Reed, S., Antia, S., & Kreimeyer, K. (2008). Academic status of Deaf and hard-of-hearing students in public schools: Student, home, and service facilitators and detractors." *JDSDE, 13,* 485–502.

Smith, M. (2010). "Opening our eyes: The complexity of competing visual demands in interpreted classrooms." In K. Christensen (Ed.), *Ethical considerations in educating children who are deaf or hard of hearing* (pp. 154–191). Washington, DC: Gallaudet University Press.

Steinmetz, K. (2014). America's transition. *Time,* June 9, 38–46.

Tabak, J. (2006). *Significant gestures: A history of American Sign Language.* Westport, CT: Greenwood Publishing Group.

U.S. Department of Education, Office of Special Education and Rehabilitation Services (2009). *28th Annual Report to Congress for the implementation of the Individuals with Disabilities Education Act, 2006* (Vol. 1), Washington, DC.

Chapter 2

From Barrio Boy to American Dream: An Interview with Dr. Robert R. Davila

ROBERT R. DAVILA, Ph. D. & OSCAR P. COHEN, Ed. D.

INTRODUCTION TO THE INTERVIEW

By Oscar P. Cohen, Ed.D.

As the car pulled into the driveway, I realized I hadn't seen him for over 3 years since his retirement as president of Gallaudet University. As president of Gallaudet, he was asked to ease campus tensions resulting from a tumultuous search to replace former President I. King Jordan. In addition, Gallaudet was in the midst of a tough Middle States Accreditation process. Davila and I, now both in retirement, had agreed to spend some time at my home in Rockland County, New York to work on a chapter for Kathee Christensen's newest book on *Multicultural Issues in the Education of the Deaf.* She had asked Bob and me to engage in a dialogue on his journey from a poor child of migrant farm workers in a southern California barrio to one of the most distinguished educators of deaf children and adults in history.

My first collaboration with Davila had been 27 years earlier, back in August 1986. I was then superintendent of New York's Lexington School for the Deaf. I was on vacation with my wife, visiting our daughter in Berkeley, California, when, to my surprise, I received a call from

Davila. He was at the time vice president of Gallaudet University and president of the Conference of Educational Administrators of Schools and Programs for the Deaf (CEASD). I of course knew of him. He was already a major figure in education of the deaf, having become the first deaf and first Latino president of the Convention of American Instructors of the Deaf, one of the oldest professional education organizations in the United States, and now as president of CEASD. I knew he was from California and had attended the California School for the Deaf in Berkeley (today the school is in Fremont)—coincidentally just about a mile from where we were visiting when the call came.

President Reagan and the U.S. Congress had just formed the Commission on the Education of the Deaf as part of the Education of the Deaf Act (Public Law 99-371). Its purpose was to create a study of the quality of educational programs for deaf people and report its findings and recommendations to Congress. Davila knew of my interest in deaf minority children ("minority" was the term used most often for non-White children in the 1980s) and asked if I would write a position paper on behalf of CEASD to be presented to the commission. The achievement gap between White deaf children and deaf children of color was significant then, too. At that time, and perhaps even now, most people perceived deafness as the primary cultural marker, excluding the significance of ethnicity and race. Most professionals, deaf and hearing, were White. Davila wanted to expand their perceptions, as did I. Out of this common interest, not only a collaboration but a friendship grew.

Born hearing in 1932 in Carlsbad, California, Davila was the fourth of six children in a family of migrant farm workers. At 8, not old enough to help harvest prunes, which meant climbing trees and shaking the fruit off, Davila's job was, with four-year old sister Rose Marie's help, to carry baby sister Mary Helen's crib to each new row of trees as his mother, father, and older siblings collected and boxed the fallen prunes. Everyone in the family was expected to put in a full day of hard work. It was in the field one hot August day while sitting by Rose Marie and Mary Helen's cribs that Davila heard his mother screaming. His father had suffered a heart attack, fallen from a nearby tree, and died. Davila's recollection of that day is as though it was yesterday.

Three years later, Davila came down with spinal meningitis. Immediately following a spinal tap in the hospital to confirm the diagnosis, he was asked by a nurse, "No te dolio mucho, verdad?" (it didn't hurt that much did it?). These were the last words he ever heard. He woke up deaf the next morning. Shortly thereafter he left the barrio, at age 11, and entered the world of the California School for the Deaf in Berkeley, 500 hundred miles away from home.

Inspired by his family's work ethic, he thrived at the California School for the Deaf, adding mastery of English and American Sign Language to his fluency in Spanish. He continued to excel at Gallaudet College (BA), Hunter College (MA), and Syracuse University (Ph.D.). He was the first deaf person of color to earn a doctorate in the United States. Davila went on to serve as the first deaf person, and first person of color, to head several major national educational organizations for the deaf, including the Conference of American Instructors of the Deaf, Conference of Educational Administrators of Schools for the Deaf, the National Technical Institute for the Deaf, the New York School for the Deaf, Gallaudet University, and a presidential appointment to the highest level position in the federal government ever held by a deaf person, assistant secretary of education in George H.W. Bush's administration.

He prides himself in knowing he will not ask anyone to do something he's not willing to do himself and that working hard is the difference between success and failure. One of his favorite stories is not about himself, but about his former boss, Al Simone, who, as president of the Rochester Institute of Technology, was observed working at his computer at 3 a.m. by a houseguest from Japan who was having trouble sleeping. The guest finally managed to go to sleep, and woke at 5 a.m. to see the president showered, dressed, breakfasted, and leaving for the office. This person, Davila believes, had it right. Now, at 84, when asked "Any regrets?" Davila replies, "None." Davila's life, his career, and his legacy provide an inspiring tale of self-discovery and resilience.

THE INTERVIEW WITH ROBERT DAVILA AND OSCAR COHEN

1. OC: As a Mexican-American growing up in Carlsbad, California and becoming deaf from spinal meningitis at 11, how aware were you of the world outside the barrio?

RD: My life, during the years before I left home to attend the California School for the Deaf (CSD), was very insular. I had very few regular interactions with the larger English-speaking communities where we had lived during the times that we were nomadic fruit and vegetable pickers. So when I went away to Berkeley, I had little, if any, expectation for what awaited me. I had only seen one deaf person before, the daughter of a friend of my mother, who was older than me and had attended the school years before me. However, I do not recall any fear of the unknown or remorse beyond the sadness and insecurity that overtook me briefly when I left the confines of my protective home. I was an alert young boy full of curiosity and eager to explore the new experiences and vistas that awaited me.

2. OC: What was the significance of your family and the barrio elders referring to Anglos as "los ricos" and "los patronos"?
RD: Looking back on my early years when I could hear, I realize that for many in the Spanish-speaking barrios where my family lived, the prevailing culture was not American but Mexican. This was probably due to the fact that few of the barrio elders, which included most parents, could speak English and they continued to identify with their home country. Holidays and celebrations, for example, observed the traditional Mexican holidays such as September 16 and Cinco de Mayo. I was born at the height of the depression, a time when many in the country were limited in choices of employment and many Mexican–Americans struggled with the English language barrier. Many had come to the United States in search of employment and the opportunity to give their children a better quality of life. Employment was probably the most precious commodity—a key to survival. Many adult workers, including my parents, worked very hard to hold on to whatever job they had. They would occasionally work beyond quitting time to better their production. This was not always for the purpose of sending a message to their employers that they were exceptional workers. This was also very much a reflection of the Hispanic character that values

loyalty and stresses hard work and doing the very best possible. I like to think that my own success in later life stemmed from this cultural manifestation.

To stress this point, I recall an incident that happened when I was about 13 or 14 years old and I was home from CSD for the summer. One Sunday, my mother was at work doing stoop labor picking vegetables as she did 6 or 7 days a week. Late that morning, my soldier brother, Gabriel, unexpectedly came home on leave only a few weeks before shipping out to the war zone in Europe. My older brother, who was waiting for his call-up to join the army, drove Gabriel and me to the farm where my mother and many other stoop laborers were working and I can still visualize Gabriel hugging my mother in the middle of a large vegetable field. I anticipated that my mother would come home with us since Gabriel's leave was only for a few days. However, she explained that the owner was expecting that the field would be completely harvested that day and she felt she needed to stay. She came home later that day to a joyous celebration, but I have always been bothered by the memory of my mother and my brother hugging in the middle of a vegetable field weeks before he left for war.

All of the employers and bosses in the fruit and crop industries were Anglos and most of them used Spanish-speaking foremen to direct workers. Because Spanish-speaking families were very dependent on English-speaking employers for survival, a reverence developed between employee and employer that was later generalized to all Anglos. I grew up thinking that in order to become successful and wealthy you had to be an Anglo. But I also believed that all parents, including my own, wanted and sought better futures for their children. Parents earnestly tried to direct their children to those opportunistic activities that could lead to success, such as staying in school, learning English, joining the army or navy during the war, getting a good-paying, long-term job, and buying a home. In short, succeeding.

3. OC: Your first encounter with Anglos was at CSD where you first met adults who were deaf, all white. Did you experience culture shock, and if so, what was that like?
   RD: To be sure, I did experience culture shock. Everyone at school had a bed of their own, ate three solid meals a day, not all Anglos were rich, some students were Hispanic like me, and soon I learned that I was as good as anyone else. And I was given a toothbrush and my first pair of slippers. At first, I thought my mother was paying for all the fine things I was getting and I was enjoying life greatly. I did pass up second helpings at the table because I knew my mother could not afford it. Once I learned that everything was free and that it was free for everyone, not just me, I literally took off. I was already used to working full days and what I had to do at school did not appear to be bone-aching work.
4. OC: It was at CSD where you encountered your first deaf adult, Leo Jacobs, who became a life-long friend. Do you remember how you felt upon first meeting him? What role, if any, did Mr. Jacobs play in your life? As a Mexican-American, in what ways were you conscious of being different from the other students?
   RD: I was at CSD during the WWII years, a time when all able-bodied males were drafted into the service and many of the school's hearing teachers went away to war. The dorms were managed by an all-deaf counselor staff assisted by a few University of California hearing graduate students who were there largely to answer the telephone and interpret occasional radio programs. Television was still the stuff of Buck Rogers.

   Dorm counselors had loco parentis responsibility and authority for the care and custody of students. Some were gruff and impatient while others were not. One who was not was Leo Jacobs. He had graduated from CSD in the 1930s and had returned as a dormitory counselor. He was a kind and compassionate person who had not yet married and always had time for the students. Because he had low service seniority, he had to work on weekend days, which could not have created a more perfect arrangement. Most school days were routine days filled with scheduled group activities and after-school sports and evening study hall. But weekends were lonely and without regular scheduled activities inasmuch as students living within driving distance of the school could go home on weekends. Students with spending allowances from home could go to the movies and football games at the nearby University of California. Students like me, who lived 500 miles from home and had no allowances, had to be creative to find activities to keep busy on weekends.

I think I learned more English from Leo Jacobs than I did from my language teachers, even though he was not a classroom teacher. He would sit us around a table and tell stories, play games, and tell jokes and challenged whoever laughed to explain why a joke was funny. That put students like me on alert. I was still learning American Sign Language (ASL) and when I saw everyone laughing, I would laugh too. But Leo Jacobs was on the lookout for pretenders like me. He would challenge me by asking, "You think it's funny?" I would answer, "Yes." Then he would ask me to explain why it was funny. What an ordeal! But what a great opportunity to learn what things really meant and not feel castigated when making mistakes. That man was my dear friend all the rest of his life. One of my proudest possessions is an autographed copy of Leo Jacobs' ground-breaking book, *A Deaf Adult Speaks Out*, which he wrote when he was appointed to sit in the Powrie V. Doctor Chair of Deaf Studies at Gallaudet University following his retirement from CSD.

When I first started at CSD, I used to think in Spanish and would say things to myself in Spanish first before resorting to English. I was surprised that although about 5% of the students at school were Hispanic, I was the only student who could speak the language fluently. I recall one day when I was in study hall with a group and one of the students told the monitor that I could speak Spanish. The teacher was not Hispanic but had learned the language in New York. She pointed to various objects around the room and I named them in Spanish. Then she started asking me to translate several ASL phrases and sentences into Spanish, which I did. I turned into a big school-wide conversation topic that lasted a few days and I was really proud inasmuch as I hardly ever drew attention to myself.

I also recall several incidents that I realized years later were discriminatory, even racist, but I did not understand their significance at the time. One day I heard that another student in my dormitory group was doing weekend gardening for one of my favorite teachers. I waited a few days before I asked the teacher if I could wash her blackboards after school. She said yes and I used that opportunity to volunteer my services to do her gardening on weekends. She looked at me and said, "Oh, I know you would do a great job and I know you need the money more, but how would I explain you to my neighbors?" I didn't know what that meant until I was much older.

Another time, the students in my dorm group were assembled one Saturday to help the dorm staff lay out mouse poison throughout the crawl spaces underneath some of the buildings on campus. The crawl spaces were only a few inches above head level and anyone venturing under the buildings had to crawl on his stomach through spider webs and other vermin nests. When the staff member in charge of the group arrived, she said, "We will let Robert do this. This is the kind of work that Mexicans do." I remember thinking, "Wow! She thinks I am better than everyone else." I was extremely proud and gratified at the praise I thought I was getting. This, too, did not make sense for a number of years.

5. OC: What challenges did your living in two cultures, Anglo culture at school and Mexican-American culture at home, present?
   RD: Naturally, as I adjusted and became fully assimilated into the CSD student population, I rapidly developed communication skills in ASL and English, formed friendships, and started to participate in all kinds of activities. I thrived in the quality of life available at the school and started questioning in my mind why my parents were poor and why we could not have the same quality of life at home. It was not long before my

perceptions about the differences between home and school took on the labels of right and wrong. At school, good performance was rewarded with praise, extra privileges, treats, etc. In my young mind, everything I learned at school was right and any departures reflected at home were wrong. For example, at the dining room at school, two older high school students sat at the ends of the table to supervise the meal and to make sure the younger students observed proper decorum and exhibited good manners. At school, we could not leave any food on our plates and bread was to be broken in half and then buttered before eating. At home my brother would leave half of his food on his plate and eat a slice of bread whole without breaking it in half. I had many problems with such departures from what I thought were the correct ways to do many common tasks. I started criticizing and telling my brothers and sisters they were doing things wrong. Since they had no idea what I was talking about, my comments often ended in yelling matches.

Another time, when I was about 13, a classmate invited me to his home for the weekend. I was excited about this because I had never visited anyone overnight in all my life. My friend's parents were deaf and they lived a long bus ride away from school. On the appointed Friday, my friend and I took the bus to his home and started walking a few blocks. I remember walking past very nice brick houses and I assumed my friend could not live in one because his parents were deaf. I figured anyone who couldn't hear was probably no better off than my parents. But I was wrong. My friend's parents came to the door and signed to my friend and me. I was flabbergasted. I had no experience with deaf adults away from school and had no idea what happened to students after they left school. That experience was very revealing to me because it helped me understand that deaf people could achieve as much, or more, than hearing people. It opened an entirely new positive expectation for my future.

I gradually learned to understand that I was functioning in two cultures and that right or wrong were not values that explained all of the differences. I do not recall ever having any lessons or experiences related to cultures or ethnicities. I learned independently as I grew up. In all the years that I was in school, at every level—elementary, high school, college, and graduate school—I was never taught by a minority teacher. In fact, I never saw one in any of the programs I attended. I actually believed for a long time that Hispanics and African-Americans could not become teachers.

But, I have to say, during the years that I was occasionally caught between two cultures and also confused trying to function with three languages, my mother, brothers, and sisters were loving and understanding and very supportive. They all knew that going away to CSD was the best thing for me, and they always treated me with love and respect.

6. OC: You were one of the few students of color at the California School for the Deaf separated from your family and your Spanish-speaking home community. Can you remember how that felt? Were you conscious of a sense of pride or honor in either location? Or were you conscious of feeling burdened—was there a sense that all eyes were on you?

   RD: Although I was leaving my accustomed life and family members at home at a tender age, it was not the traumatic experience it might have been for most 11-year-old boys. I did experience a brief period of sadness on leaving home, but I was an adventurous young boy and the exciting things that awaited me at CSD overcame any premonition of dire outcomes. The school had many other children my age who were friendly, happy, and accepting of new students like me. There were no class distinctions among the students. I had no idea who was rich or poor. We had staff persons to assist, a secure and comfortable environment to live in, and our major responsibility was to be good students and learn well. I have mentioned that I was a highly motivated young boy who arrived at the school with a strong work ethic and an inquisitive demeanor. I learned very soon in my CSD experience that rewards in life went to those who ran faster, jumped higher, performed better than others, and worked well in groups. At school the expectations were clear: do well in your studies and don't break any of the student conduct codes. I was determined to live up to those expectations.

One day, I learned that every month the top students in each class were rewarded with a downtown movie and ice cream sundaes. I asked my teacher to explain that and she said I should try to be the smartest student in class. I was a bit dubious because up until that time, I had not found learning and studying to be too difficult and assumed there was more to getting such a reward. However, that was probably the turning point of my CSD experience. I do not recall ever missing out on that monthly treat until I graduated.

I guess all I needed was the incentive.

7. OC: You've had a life-long fascination with and interest in the military. If you weren't deaf, would you have entered the military? What was that about? What do you think would have been your goal?

   RD: My interest in the military stemmed from the fact that my formative years at CSD took place during WWII and that my three older brothers volunteered for the service during that time. At school, teachers reviewed the war news in every homeroom and I loved to mention that my brothers were serving. I recall the year that the war was over in 1945 when I was in high school and we had a school play that was set in Norway during the German occupation. I wrote to my brother Gabriel, who was still serving in the occupation forces following the armistice, and asked him if he could get us German helmets and uniforms. I actually didn't expect that he would be able to do it, but he did. I was so proud of him. The play was made authentic with the real equipment.

   If I had not been deaf, I would have been of age during the Korean War and I definitely would have volunteered. And, yes, I think I would have loved to pursue a military career.

8. OC: In your early professional life, after attending a football game between two schools for the deaf, you were excluded,

along with other host school deaf teachers, from an after game party at the campus home of the hearing principal—apparently not because you were Latino but because the host decided she didn't have room for your group. What did you make of that rejection? Have you ever considered yourself the recipient of a double whammy—deaf and Latino? How does the phenomenon of dual discrimination play out? In what situations did you feel "assigned" the primary identity of deafness vs. your ethnicity?

RD: The incident that happened at the football game between the school I was teaching at and another school for the deaf where I had a number of good friends was the first occasion that I was involved in what I consider was blatant discrimination. Word had gone out prior to the game that staff from both schools were welcome to attend a social at the campus house of the host school principal. After the game, I went to the house in company with several host school deaf staff members and when we arrived we were met at the door by the principal who informed us that she didn't have enough space and refreshments for everyone and was sorry she couldn't invite us in. She elaborated also that she had not arranged for interpreters so she couldn't invite any deaf persons. I was greatly embarrassed because we could see people already inside standing in front of the picture window talking and looking at us. We practically slunk away and I felt great sympathy for my friends who had looked forward to visiting with me at the party. I do not recall any situations as blatant as this one, but I was aware of stories of discrimination that deaf staff members experienced in a number of schools for the deaf. But I also realized that I was fortunate because deaf staff members were well respected and accepted at the school where I worked.

9. OC: The Deaf President Now (DPN) movement at Gallaudet is often considered a major civil rights "win." What was won? Who won? How have deaf people of color gained from DPN?

RD: By the time that the Deaf President Now protest took place on the Gallaudet campus in 1988, I had been working at the university for 16 years and had served as a senior officer for most of those years. I was also a candidate for president in 1988, but I was the first candidate eliminated by the search committee prior to the protest even though I felt I had as good, if not better, qualifications than some of the candidates in the recommended final group. I took this as a sign of the board's intention not to appoint a deaf person. I was a vice president at Gallaudet for 11 years, and none of the other deaf and hearing candidates had a comparable experience. So the protest came and the future was changed for many deaf persons, including me.

You ask how it changed. The most dramatic consequence was that it broke the "glass ceiling" for the one job that has the most direct impact on the lives of deaf people, in general, and on deaf professionals, in particular. Since DPN, all three presidents appointed, including myself, have been deaf and Gallaudet has never been as effective and essential as it is now. Furthermore, DPN raised the aspirations of deaf people in practically every walk of life. Today, we find deaf persons involved in many areas of professional work that were considered closed to them 25 years ago. The number of deaf persons with earned doctorates leading to upper level employment areas has multiplied. The quality of life for deaf persons has been raised, and critical contributory elements can be traced back to DPN.

10. OC: DPN was the deaf world's civil rights watershed. There is a strong possibility that there will not be a viable hearing candidate for Gallaudet's presidency for a long time. As a civil rights warrior, what are your thoughts about excluding hearing persons from an authentic opportunity to be included in a future candidate pool for Gallaudet president? What if a known and respected upper level hearing college administrator or other acknowledged leaders were to apply?

RD: First off, I think it would be illegal and discriminatory to restrict the Gallaudet president position to only deaf persons. It is also reassuring to know that we have a number of outstanding deaf leaders throughout the country who could handle the job in great fashion, but the university needs to keep its options open so that it can always be in the position to hire the best available candidate. It is not inconceivable that some day the best candidate could be a hearing person. But all things being equal, if the appointed person is a qualified deaf person, it sends a very positive message to the world that DEAF PEOPLE CAN!

11. OC: Lauro Cavazos, Secretary of Education under Ronald Reagan and George H.W. Bush, was your hero long before you were considered for the position of assistant secretary. How much did Cavazos being Latino have to do with his being a hero? Did you have other Latino heroes? Deaf heroes? Others?
RD: When I was growing up, I was always looking for heroes. I developed the habit of scanning newspapers and magazines for persons with Hispanic surnames. That's how I learned about Pancho Gonzalez, the tennis player; Leo Carrillo, who had a ranch near Carlsbad; Anthony Quinn; Lee Trevino, the golf hall of famer; and others. And, of course, also Lauro Cavazos, the educator. Over the years, I learned about this amazing family who grew up on the famous King Ranch in south Texas bit by bit as news items appeared in the print media. One brother was the first Hispanic four-star general in the army. Lauro was president of Texas Tech where his brother, Robert, was an All American football star during the years that I was in college, too. You can imagine my thrill when I was interviewed by Lauro Cavazos when he was the secretary of education and I was subsequently appointed by the president of the United States on his recommendation. All of my heroes inspired me and I worshipped them all.

I had deaf heroes, too, but growing up, there were very few who achieved national recognition. Most were sports heroes, such as Ellsworth Hoy and Luther Taylor, of baseball fame. And Curtis Pride, who enjoyed the longest major league career of any deaf baseball player in history. One of my "feel good" achievements when I was president of Gallaudet was arranging for Curtis to be appointed Gallaudet's baseball coach.

12. OC: During President Reagan's tenure, you were interviewed for a high-level position within the Department of Education. You felt good about the meeting but never heard back. Eight years later, you received a similar invitation from the George H.W. Bush administration and thought to yourself "do I want to go through this again?" You did, which led to Education Secretary Lauro Cavazos, with whom you partly conversed in Spanish, asking you which of four assistant secretary openings you considered yourself qualified and were most interested in—without hesitation you responded Assistant Secretary for Special Education and Rehabilitative Services. He responded, "Yes, I agree." Where did that confidence and courage come from?

    RD: I think this was an outgrowth of the confidence I developed in myself and my abilities, which were nurtured during my happy years at CSD. I enjoyed succeeding and doing well and appreciated the praise and rewards, which often came my way. In the culture in which I was raised, the mother in a family is the central figure and is highly revered. If she asks you to jump, you don't question why, you ask how high. During WWII, with my older brothers away, I assumed many support roles for my mother, including translating Spanish to English. Picture if you will a deaf kid trying to learn English well, but also obligated to help bridge Spanish into English for his mother. Needless to say, I grew up ahead of my years because of responsibilities I had to bear. All my life I have been very able to assume responsibility and carry out my duties well.

13. OC: As Assistant Secretary for the Office of Special Education and Rehabilitation Services (OSERS) you had reached the highest federal position ever attained by a deaf person in

history, responsible for all Americans with disabilities and a multibillion dollar budget. What did your mother, brothers, and sisters think?

RD: The appointment to a high policy position in government left me feeling somewhat ambivalent. On the one hand, I was pleased and surprised that the appointment was to a subcabinet position and, on the other hand, more than a little apprehensive because I knew I was assuming a complex and demanding responsibility. I knew I had to do well. Not because I was Hispanic, but more because I was deaf. This was not a job that is learned beforehand or which a person can be trained to do rapidly. I didn't want anyone to think deaf people couldn't handle a job like that one. So I worked very hard and did well. After one year, President Bush decided to change secretaries and appointed Lamar Alexander, president of the University of Tennessee and former state governor, to replace Secretary Cavazos. Secretary Alexander arrived and said he was going to evaluate the performance of all assistant secretaries and make changes as he deemed necessary. He did his interviews and I was one of only two assistant secretaries he kept. The job was very demanding and included travel practically every weekend and responsibility for advising the administration on disability policy. I spoke to many groups representing the nation's 40 million citizens with disabilities and made decisions that affected the education and rehabilitation of millions of people. But I also made many friends and had fun now and then.

When I was appointed, my mother, not being familiar with terminology used in government, actually thought I was appointed to clerical functions in a secretary's position. She said nothing until one day I sensed her puzzlement and explained the true nature and level of the position. She was all smiles and I was glad I was able to clear that one.

14. OC: What were your major accomplishments as assistant secretary? How might they have been related to your interests in bringing attention to the needs of persons of color with disabilities?

When I started my work in the Department of Education I saw my appointment as an opportunity to clear up misconceptions about deaf persons and their educational needs. Given President Bush's popularity, I fully expected to be at my post for 8 years. All through the first 3 years nothing took place that altered this expectation and I continued to work out plans to address some of the most critical issues confronted by educators, parents, and students in the deaf education field. I had been a national leader in the struggle to clarify the meaning of inclusion as it applied to children who could not hear and, therefore, could not benefit from personal interactions with nondisabled children in public school settings. I also knew that raising this issue for open review and discussion among all groups receiving support from my office would be controversial and very likely heated because of the inability of full inclusion advocates to consider any departures from regular classroom placement for any and all children with disabilities, including deaf children. Finally, the policy guidance also posed a risk for me because a president fighting to remain in office for a second term would not tolerate any disagreements that could hurt his re-election prospects. When the economy sank below expectations and it became probable in the Spring of 1992 that President George H.W. Bush was going to face difficulty with re-election in November, I faced the dilemma of deciding how to pursue my plans to try to resolve issues facing deaf education. During the summer months of 1992, I drew together a small group of persons I highly respected to develop a policy guidance on the education of deaf children. They included Frank Bowe, whose 1988 Commission on Education of the Deaf had developed similar guidelines and principles to be observed in evaluating deaf children for the purpose of placement and identifying program services; Robert Silverstein, staff director on Senator Tom Harkin's Committee on Labor and Human Resources, who advised wisely and correctly how to tread the political waters; Rebecca Fitch, OSERS Policy Officer; Susan Murray, Director for Public Information for OSERS and former Executive Director of the National Office for Conference of Educational Administrators Serving the Deaf (CEASD) and Convention of American Instructors of the Deaf; and Frances Parrotta, my administrative assistant. This group, assisted by others, put together a final draft of the policy guidance and also assisted in identifying strategies for distribution and implementation. One person who was not actively involved in the policy guidance development activities, but who became an outstanding advocate to gain support and acceptance within the deaf community was Oscar Cohen, the same person who collaborated with me on this question-and-answer task. After my speech to the National Association of the Deaf in Denver, in which I announced my intention to address the issue of placement and program services for deaf children, Oscar marshaled the forces as much as anyone else and started a letter-writing campaign supporting my speech and announcing that I was working on a major initiative—the policy guidance.

The policy guidance focused on the dynamics of each individual deaf child's needs that needed to be taken into consideration in determining placement and identifying services in the school system. Although we had talked about such guidance for years, the government had never seriously considered developing and sending out such instructions to all the local education agencies in the nation. Individuals and groups had to be convinced that the policy guidance for deaf children would not change or impact negatively the prescribed needs and program services for all other children with disabilities. I held many meetings with people who wanted to know more and had questions to ask. The lobbying for support was time-consuming and delayed a final draft. As time was running out, one day in early October, I was called into Secretary Alexander's office to answer questions. News of the pending guidance had reached the White House through high-level access and intense lobbying on the part of full inclusion advocates and the secretary was asked if bringing out anything controversial so close to the election could or would hurt the president's re-election chances. He asked if the guidance could go out under my assistant secretary's authority to reduce any possible negative impact. Fortunately, I had developed a close and mutually trusting relationship with the secretary during the 3 years that he was my immediate supervisor and I appealed to him how important it would be to have the guidance go out under his name inasmuch as he was the nation's top educator and there was a sitting president in office. That umbrella of broad-based authority would go far in making the policy guidance official and compelling. After listening for a while, Secretary Alexander remarked, "Let's do it!"

The policy guidance went out on October 30, 1992, less than a week before the election. Twenty-some years later, it is still vitally in use. Its impact was broad and resolved a critical need. It led to new statutory language and changed virtually every Individualized Education Program (IEP) meeting for every deaf student. Later, it was used as a model for new statutory language to address the unique needs of other students with disabilities, especially those who were blind and those with behavior problems. Up until the issuance of the policy guidance, placement in the regular classroom was seen as every child's least restrictive environment. The practicality of using the policy guidance to evaluate deaf children's needs eventually promoted increased guidance in developing IEPs for children with all types of disabilities.

Another accomplishment that I believe was critical was the outcome of a conversation I had with the chairperson of the board of directors of the Florida School for the Deaf and the Blind. He had asked me if existing education laws guaranteed the existence of residential, or center, schools for the deaf and the blind in the various states. I told him that one way to investigate the issue would be for him to write to me with the policy question "Does present education law require that each state maintain residential, or center, schools for the deaf and blind?" He did write and I turned his question over to the Department of Justice through the secretary's office. Some 6 months later, the Department of Justice responded with an answer that was not exactly as we expected, but which nevertheless assured all deaf children and their parents in the country that the residential or center school option was required by law. Interpretation of this response indicates that a state does not actually have to operate such schools, but it must make their availability one of the options for children requiring them. A state without such schools would be required to buy such services from a neighboring state if it did not have such schools itself.

There were other achievements. I was especially interested in seeing deaf persons of ethnic and minority backgrounds form their own support groups. I was able to fund inaugural national conferences for both the Hispanic and the African-American communities in San Antonio and Atlanta, respectively. It was a matter of great pride that I was the keynote speaker at both of these conferences. Since those beginnings, the National Hispanic Council for the Deaf and Hard of Hearing (today it is known as the Council de Manos) and the National Black Deaf Advocates have prospered and have gained political, social, and economic strength.

Additionally, I integrated OSERS components (Office of Special Education Programs, Rehabilitation Services Administration, National Institute on Disability and Rehabilitation Research) to focus on common goals and needs, especially those related to the employment of people with disabilities. I increased parent involvement through meaningful participation in decisions about the education of their children with disabilities. I doubled the funds for grants awarded to regional community theatres of the deaf, sponsored a number of national parents of disabled children conferences, provided registration and attendance assistance to minority parents, and successfully increased the budget for my division each of the 4 years I was in office totaling about $6 billion in my final year. I traveled to speak approximately 35–40 weekends a year and made hosts of new friends and expanded communication networks with thousands.

Very importantly I was able to dismantle many barriers and misconceptions that the general disability community had developed regarding the deaf community. Through leadership and planned advocacy, I was able to mitigate the stance of many advocates for the disabled who held that deafness represented a narrow, single disability focus and was incompatible with broad-based, cross-disability top-level policy management. I recalled how more than a few advocates had taken such a strong position opposing my appointment initially on these grounds. In the end, I was able to demonstrate that I had the broad knowledge, intelligence, philosophy, insights, and ability to manage complex government programs like those in OSERS.

It was a great experience and an opportunity that was truly special, even if it was incredibly difficult.

15. OC: You faced the dual challenges of deafness and being a person of color your entire life. Where did the pluck, mettle, and audacity come from to become the first person of color and first deaf president of the Convention of American Instructors for the Deaf, first person of color and first deaf president of the Conference of Educational Administrators Serving the Deaf, the first person of color and first deaf director of the National Technical Institute for the Deaf, first person of color to become president of Gallaudet University, and first person of color and first, and only, so far, deaf person to serve as Assistant Secretary of Education?

RD: I have mentioned that I had a strong work ethic from an early age. I did not have the same childhood that many children have. I worked full days from as early as I can recall, perhaps 5 years of age. Even at home, after my father died and my mother assumed greater responsibility, all of my brothers and sisters, including me, had specific daily duties. We were a close-knit family sharing all the work. No one got off for any reason. When I went away to school, my mother would write me letters in Spanish. I didn't know how to read or write Spanish. I could only speak it. So what did I do? Throw the letter away because I couldn't read it? Write to my mother and say I couldn't help? Perish the thought! I have mentioned in an answer to another question that the mother is central to Hispanic culture and family life. Because the letters were coming from my mother, I used guile and every means at my disposal to figure out how to read and respond to them. I learned that one teacher could speak Spanish so I would copy a few words from my mother's letters and ask the teacher what they meant. After a few inquiries, I usually had enough understanding to get the gist of the letter. Then I worked on a response, although all the Spanish I wrote was written phonetically. I would say the words in my mind and then write them down as I thought they sounded. I wrote to my mother back and forth this way until I graduated.

People grow with responsibility and I was no exception. I always had to take care of myself and find solutions to issues or problems that confronted me. When I was in college, I had no spending money allowance from home so every weekend I walked around northeast Washington looking for discarded beer and soda bottles that I would take to my dorm and wash before going to the store to exchange them for the deposit money. This was not money for leisure spending. It was money I needed to buy school supplies. I did not have access to funds beyond getting only my tuition paid by California. I collected bottles regularly for 5 years, and no one ever seemed to know because I never told anyone, including my roommates. When I was 21, I was already married and living in a duplex house with the owner of both units. I recall one day he asked me how old I was and I told him. He said that was amazing because I talked like a 40-year-old man. I think that was an outgrowth of always being serious and having responsibilities from an early age.

So, in answer to your question, I have always looked out for myself, which instilled great self-confidence. That is why I developed speech in English so well. Not for myself or because of any philosophical mantra, but because for years I was my mother's link with the English-speaking world and

I was the dutiful son. Sometimes some of my deaf friends would speculate whether anyone really understood me. But that could not dissuade me from trying the best I could. I have never backed off from a challenge. I became a candidate for the office of President of the Convention of American Instructors of the Deaf over lunch during the biennial meeting of the group. I was having lunch with several friends when I found that the organization was 125 years old and had never elected a deaf president. So I said what is to keep me from being nominated from the floor during the business meeting? Apparently, there was nothing to keep me from this. So I was nominated and won. It took me a long time to figure out what had been keeping things from happening.

16. OC: You shepherded the multicultural effort in the education of deaf children in the United States by, among other things, exposing educational gaps before the Congressional Commission on the Education of the Deaf, being the impetus for the first national conferences on the needs of deaf children of color, and initiating the CEASD Standing Committee on Multicultural Deaf Children. To what extent has the achievement gap between white deaf students and deaf students of color been ameliorated? What more needs to be done?

    RD: I am not sure that the academic progress of all deaf children is being tracked uniformly and consistently throughout the country. Some state reports have excluded assessment data of all children with disabilities, including deaf children, from the general school population's data and results. Others have tested deaf children only in the areas of language arts and mathematics. But whatever the practice, we know from long experience that blind and deaf children are the highest performers on standardized tests among children with disabilities and that deaf children fare below blind children and below nondisabled children, in general. Among the general school population, children of color perform below white and Asian children. Assessment experience with deaf children also reflects the lower achievement of deaf children of color compared to white deaf children. Hispanic children are growing rapidly in number as evidenced by the 2011 California Department of Education Special Education Statewide Report that listed 3946 deaf children and 9991 hard-of-hearing children for a total of 13,937 children with hearing loss. Of this total, 7792, or 55%, deaf and hard-of-hearing children were Hispanic. Of the 3946 deaf children reported, 2213, or 56%, were Hispanic. These numbers are representative of the growth of California's Hispanic population.

Many schools point to less direct or informal indicators of the achievement of their graduates. One indicator used commonly is reporting the number of graduates who matriculate to Gallaudet University, the National Technical Institute for the Deaf (NTID) at the Rochester Institute of Technology (RIT), and California State University at Northridge (CSUN), as well as a few other postsecondary programs. While graduating from college is indeed a positive indicator of academic success, very little, if any, reporting is disseminated by postsecondary institutions regarding their retention and graduation rates. The fact is that institutions serving the deaf are confronted with the same problems that most colleges and universities report concerning students of color: leaving programs before completion, resulting in low institutional graduation rates. To be sure, more students of color are graduating and their numbers have grown steadily since I was the first minority student at Gallaudet. However, deaf students of color, in general, require more tuition assistance, remedial support, advising, and counseling to succeed in postsecondary programs. Despite this concentration of support, they are still more likely than white students to drop out before graduation.

The lower academic performance of students of color is one of our country's most serious and long-standing issues. This is not an issue related to deafness alone. It is a national social economic problem. Many students of color and their families need intervention support early in the school lives of the children in the families. Deaf students of color should be identified and assisted early in school life. Programs such as Big Brother can be very helpful by providing student contact and exposure to community life with which they are unfamiliar. When students' knowledge of their communities spans a larger group of diverse people and activities, those students are more likely to develop a broader base of interests and set realistic and positive goals for themselves, including, hopefully, doing well in academics. Families play a very influential and positive role in the education of all children, but this level of involvement is especially required with deaf children. Schools need social workers and deaf adult role models to interface with families of students of color and encourage their interest and involvement in the life's experiences of their deaf children. As difficult as this may be for many valid reasons, the outcomes vastly outweigh the sacrifices required to make it happen. I know. It worked for me and my family.

17. OC: In the 1970's through 2000, Gallaudet led the effort to compile data and conduct research regarding deaf children's educational progress, especially deaf children of color. Is Gallaudet, or any other institution, still leading the effort? How well? If not, is anyone leading this effort?

    RD: Yes, for over three decades, Gallaudet University's Research Institute tracked and maintained achievement test data of a very large sample of deaf children in a variety of program placements such as public and private schools, oral and total communication programs and day and residential schools. This task was facilitated and rendered possible because a majority of deaf children attended traditional residential or center schools for the deaf. Additionally, Gallaudet had favorable cooperation from the larger day school programs around the country. Heretofore, ability to track deaf children in these known programs facilitated the collection of annual test data. Over the past 20 years, however, the provisions of the Individuals with Disabilities Education Act and the American Disability Act, which mandate full service programs in local settings, have seriously shifted placement of deaf children to local or collaborative regional programs away from center schools. This development has made it very difficult, if not impossible to track deaf children throughout the country's estimated 14,000 school districts. It would require the U.S. Department of Education to mandate school districts around the country to submit these kinds of data annually. This could be done through the U.S. Department of Education sponsoring such a project through Gallaudet University or other higher education institution for this purpose. Otherwise, it will be difficult to collect and maintain accurate data on the assessment and achievement of deaf students in a manner that will serve their best interests.

18. OC: As a new hire at Gallaudet in 1972, you wanted to create an opportunity to bring Latino students together and asked the registrar to give you the list of all Hispanic surnamed students (e.g., Ramirez, Rodriguez, and Perez) for a picnic. Approximately one-third of about 120 students responded by asking "why was I invited—I'm not Hispanic," which surprised you. What was that about? Would you get a similar response today?
RD: I have often wondered about this experience over 40 years ago. I think it was an eye-opening revelation for me and I learned from it. I was a new faculty member at Gallaudet, the only deaf Hispanic on the faculty and eager to explore ways to reach out to the growing number of minority students at Gallaudet. So I asked the registrar if we had many Hispanic students. He responded that we had a couple of hundred and I was surprised by the number. Although somewhat dubious about his estimate, he and I agreed that one of his staff members would pick out all the Hispanic surnamed students on file, and I would use the list to set up a picnic on campus for the group. As you have said, about a dozen names turned out to be Italians, perhaps 25–30 students didn't bother to answer, another 25–30 sent me a note saying they did not consider themselves Hispanic and had no interest in what I was proposing, and still others said they were Hispanic but not from the barrio. Well, I ended up entertaining about

40–50 students and I was gratified by the effort. We talked about forming a student organization and about 20–25 actually moved forward with the idea. What impressed me about the group was that the students represented all manner of diversity that you will find in any Hispanic group. All were Americans, as I recall, because we had not yet enrolled any students from Spanish-speaking countries. Only two or three students had any knowledge of spoken and written Spanish. Quite a few reported their parents were exclusively English speaking. A few said they considered themselves white and preferred not to change that. One young man who seemed like a leader—spoke with great confidence and authority, and had a classic Hispanic surname—told me he was more French than Hispanic, but came because he loved picnics. He had the classic Hispanic profile, but his remarks did not surprise me. He asked me what country my parents were from and I kidded him that I was Irish. He looked puzzled and said, "But you don't look Irish!" And I answered back, "Neither do you look French!" He laughed and we became good friends over the next 30 years before he was stricken with cancer and died young. Eventually, he became one of our best and strongest leaders in the newly formed Hispanic association. He never again claimed to be French. Nor did I ever replay my joke about being Irish!

Today, some 40 years after this first effort to identify, befriend, and interact with Hispanic students, I think we have made some good progress. The National Hispanic Council for the Deaf and Hard of Hearing (now the Council de Manos), a national organization that I helped found with several other Hispanic and non-Hispanic leaders, is well-established and promoting activity among its various chapters around the country.

In the early days not every Hispanic deaf person would come forward to speak openly about his/her identity. There were some breakdowns among young Hispanic students regarding self-identities. Today, it is obvious that the larger majority of young Hispanics has developed a sense of pride in their accomplishments and is actively promoting their views and rights on social issues important to them. I take pride in having had the opportunity to begin exposing young Hispanics to their heritage and history many years ago. We have come a long way, but there is still much we need to do.

19. OC: Historically in the United States there has been a fissure between white deaf persons and deaf persons of color underscored by segregated schools, social clubs, and athletic teams. Is overt segregation of deaf schools, clubs, and teams a thing of the past? What about more subtle relations between and among Black, Latino, Asian, White, and gay deaf persons? What can be done to heal and build on these relations?

    RD: Many things are changing in the deaf communities around the nation. Forty years ago, approximately 85% of all school-age deaf children were educated in residential, or center, schools. These schools had vast white majorities, and many state schools in the south were segregated. I seem to remember that schools for white and black deaf students in Louisiana were not integrated until the 1970s. That was almost 20 years after *Brown vs. the Board of Education*. Even in California, where I attended the state residential school, there were few students of color—perhaps less than 2 to 3% of the student population were African-Americans and something like 5% of the students were Hispanic. Schools did not focus on diversity or even attempt to formally address ethnic and minority issues. Our nation was not there yet. Many deaf communities established de facto white-only dues, paying clubs with rented facilities for meetings to socialize and conduct the business of their organizations. Persons of color were often conspicuous by their absence. Looking back, there was serious lack of effort by the club leadership and membership to reach out to deaf persons of color and welcome them into their circle. We have come a long way, of course, but the social structures of the deaf communities have also continued to change. Clubs are no longer the main social centers where deaf people congregate; in fact, very few community clubhouses remain. Technological advances now allow deaf persons to access world knowledge and to establish independent electronic contact with friends, families, and the business community from their homes. The most common social meeting place for deaf persons is now their own homes. Many deaf persons have persons of color as friends and invite them to their homes and vice versa. But more needs to be done, although the leadership in organizations of all types and purposes in the deaf community now stresses greater social awareness and promotes and counsels more understanding, tolerance, and friendship building.

20. OC: The National Association of the Deaf, National Black Deaf Advocates, and the Council de Manos are among the leading deaf advocacy groups in the United States. How effective are they in advocating for their respective constituencies? How effective is their advocacy and their collaboration and cooperation with each other?

    RD: I think there has been very earnest and marked progress in expanding diversity within the deaf community. The organizations that you mention are very visible, and on occasions when the National Association of the Deaf, as the umbrella organization monitoring civil rights and advocacy measures, convenes a representative group to discuss matters or issues that impact across groups, African-American, Hispanic, Asian, and other ethnic and minority groups, including Gay and Lesbian representatives, participate actively. The leadership of the various regional, state, and national organizations within the deaf community is better versed on matters of representation, tolerance, acceptance, objectivity, and commitment to the democratic principles of leadership and organizational management.

21. OC: You've expressed confidence in the ability of the top third of deaf students at Gallaudet, NTID, and elsewhere to maintain a competitive edge, but given the economy, decreased demand for manual labor, and greater need for

higher level academic skills, you are less hopeful concerning the rest, many of whom are deaf students of color. What needs to change and what's the probability change will occur?

RD: I mentioned in response to an earlier question that postsecondary institutions serving deaf persons face the same retention and graduation rate concerns regarding students of color that many regular colleges and universities face. The top third of the enrolled students at Gallaudet, NTID/RIT, and CSUN are outstanding students who hold their own very well and graduate on time and go on to successful careers. Unfortunately, many other students arrive at postsecondary programs with serious gaps in their preparation to deal independently and successfully with the demands of college-level studies and the need to assume full accountability for their behaviors and outcomes. These students need remedial support, advising, and counseling and need to build friendships and relationships that foster confidence and "feel good" perspectives about themselves. Although programs do anticipate these issues and try to prepare responses or offset activities, in many cases their efforts fall short because the weight of the overall support required is too heavy for the schools to meet in every case. However, based on my experiences of many years, I fully believe that programs need to maintain a very high priority for remedial, advising, counseling, and guidance services. The presence of role model adults, including upper class students of color, is also very helpful in creating a comfortable and secure work and study environment for young people who, in many cases, are away from home for the first time.

22. OC: You've also said that what the field needs are leaders who are their own harshest critics. What do you mean and how hopeful are you that deaf children will remain, or become, sufficiently competitive to meet 21st-century demands?

RD: Yes, I think that when we accept responsibility to perform as a leader of a group, organization, or administrator of a program serving others that we are expected to work diligently and productively and hold ourselves accountable for success. We need to examine what we do, how we do it, and when we do it so that we can evaluate our own performance and make corrections or adjustments to keep us on track toward achieving the goals we are pursuing. I have always done this in situations where I was expected to lead, both as a volunteer and through my employment. If we are not our own harshest critics, others will note our mistakes, shortcomings, and oversights and we may not like what they have to say about us and the work we do. We also need to encourage those under our care or instruction to adopt similar measures when they become leaders because evaluating our own performances prepares us well to deal with unforeseen and unexpected "bumps in the road." I have always valued introspection.

23. OC: Your mother told you not to cry because going away to school was for your own good and that the family loved you. You followed her advice and restrained yourself from crying when you were afraid and encountered difficulties growing up away from home. You've said you were also good at suppressing feelings of anger that may have helped at times of frustration, discrimination, and racism. How did that advice serve you? Did you find other outlets for dealing with your responses to discrimination and racism?

    RD: Well, first of all, I think my mother should not have told me not to cry. It's alright for young boys 10 or 11 to cry when they are afraid, confused, or lonely. It is very common childhood behavior. But because my mother said not to cry, I suppressed many emotions because I did not want to defy my promise. Crying allows you to dispel pent-up emotions. I think I unconsciously expanded this suppression to cover up almost anything my mind considered negative or hurtful. Over the years, I avoided recall of hurtful experiences by erasing them from my mind. Soon after something happened that was sad or hurtful, such as deaths, accidents, or failures, unless I consciously probed my mind for recollections, I could not recall them. I recall one day, years after our marriage, my wife asking me why she had never seen me cry and whether I had any memory of ever having done so? That's when I learned how my defensive avoidance started.

24. OC: You are known as someone who doesn't ask anyone to do something that you haven't done or aren't willing to do. Why is this so important?
    RD: It has never been a matter of any real importance. Rather, it has been a reflection of my strong sense of independence. I am not the type of person who readily asks others for help or avoids as much as possible inconveniencing friends or neighbors by asking for assistance or favors. On the contrary, I am always ready to assist others and often go out of my way to be helpful. That's who I am. I left home at age 11 and came home from school only for the summer and then at age 15 never lived at home again after I went off to college. In a manner of speaking, I really grew up by myself. I took care of myself and did things for myself because I was too far away from my family to get their assistance and support. But I valued family. It is very central to the culture and values I inherited from my parents. I married 1 month after turning 21, and I have had a great family of my own that is very close and loving with each other. I have truly been blessed.
25. OC: You've had a distinguished career for close to 60 years on both national and international fronts in enhancing the lives of deaf persons and persons with other disabilities. Any regrets?
    RD: None whatsoever. I did have some disappointments and shortfalls, but I got over them and much later made up for them in some other ways. I was a candidate for the presidency of Gallaudet twice before DPN but still got appointed president years later when the university was recovering from another protest. I have been the first deaf person or the first deaf Hispanic to achieve many successes over my career. A short story about symbolism. Back in the years when Gallaudet and NTID, as federally funded postsecondary programs,

used to appear at House and Senate budget hearings to present their annual request, the Assistant Secretary for Special Education and Rehabilitative Services used to appear as the lead government witness and sit at a table flanked by witnesses from Gallaudet and NTID. During one of my last appearances at the hearings as assistant secretary, one of the senators made the remark that he had seen me sit in all the spaces provided. I sat at the table with President Merrill when I was also a witness as head of the Model Secondary School for the Deaf and Kendall Demonstration Elementary School and I sat as head of NTID when I was head of that program. And, of course, I also sat at the center space as assistant secretary. No one else has ever done so and probably no one ever will again. That remark by the observant senator truly made me feel very proud and appreciative for the wonderful opportunities that came my way.

26. OC: You've made reference to the American dream and goal of assimilation, including proficiency in English, and learning customs and mores of mainstream American culture, yet you have professed a commitment to nurturing and celebrating cultural differences of "other," especially other people's children. How do reconcile these potentially opposing ideas?
RD: I do not see both efforts at odds. In fact, they complement each other. I worked hard to get all the education I needed so I could launch a professional career. During my early years, my priorities were my family and meeting their needs, as well as accumulating the required professional credentials that would qualify me for postemployment advancement. As a matter of fact, I had already earned 42 graduate credits above my Master's degree before I even began my doctoral studies at Syracuse University. Many people observe similar sequences to advance their careers. They work hard to establish themselves first before they can turn around and help pull others up. I have tried to be the same kind of achiever. Many was the time when I was coming up in my career that I was the only minority person actively involved in organizational and

volunteer service to help others. I was accepted because others appreciated my contributions. I was a team player, not an individual with an agenda of my own. It helped me a lot that I was confident, capable, and willing to "walk the extra mile" to get things accomplished. Some call this "earning your stripes." I sure worked hard to earn mine. But, once I did, I was accepted as a contributing member willing to work hard and well to help the group succeed. I wanted to be a role model as well as set an example for other minority persons, including students, that success is achievable and open to anyone willing to work for it. But in order for any person to feel confident and be prepared to sacrifice to reach personal goals, he/she must feel good about themselves. It always starts and ends with self.

27. OC: You've made reference to when you were a child in the barrio and the elders would point to selected young men and opine about their potential future success by saying "Tu vas a salir" (loose translation: "You will get out"). Years later, Cesar Chavez adopted "Sal si puedes" (loose translation: "Get out if you can"). How did these rallying calls to succeed influence you?

    RD: Well, obviously I grew up in the days when slogans were in vogue and smart, cool-headed performers didn't need many additional incentives to succeed. You know, "When the going gets tough, the tough get going!" "An ounce of prevention is worth a pound of cure." "There is no I in Team!" You get the idea? I hung on every slogan I heard. The barrio elders were kind gentlemen who had missed opportunities to get out themselves because opportunities just weren't there. Passing judgment on young folks and predicting their success was their way of saying they cared. Of course, not everyone was able to "get out." Perhaps not everyone wanted to get out. Regardless, I left for school and my life took a big turn and I never returned to the barrio again. But I had the desire and the impetus to keep on going, and I was fortunate that the CSD "elders" were equally desirous to see all the young people in school succeed. And many of us did.

28. OC: How would you like to finish this sentence? "Bob Davila is the man who believes in working hard and purposefully creates light where there is darkness and lives by the credo 'When the world says 'Give up,' Hope whispers, 'Try it one more time.'"

    RD: Well, I like your quote. I also think you got it down correctly and I can't think of any change or addition that would make it better. I was fortunate to have great teachers, mentors, friends, family, and supporters to allow safe passage and success beyond any expectations I ever harbored. But, honestly, so many people cared, so many helped. I could not have done this alone. No way. Years ago, when we were working at a fruit farm in the San Joaquin Valley, we slept in owner-provided roofless shacks and I would lie awake in the dark and look up and count the number of meteors and comets I saw. Invariably, my thoughts would also stray to the future. Will I go to college? Probably not, it costs money. Will I have my own family? I have to find someone to marry first. And so it went. That was then and this is now. What a trip it has been! That kid looking up into the star-filled sky had no idea it would be this remarkable! Only in America!

Chapter 3

-ISMs, Identities, and Intersectionality: Implications and Integration

ROZ ROSEN, Ed.D.

This chapter focuses on -ISMs, Identities, and Intersectionality and reviews human rights movements and tenants developed by people of color, women, and Deaf people in identifying ideologies, approaches, and cross-infusions of critical theories and strategies across the broad spectrum of humanity. Complex intersections of identities will be examined, as well as human rights for Deaf people.

As a Deaf, White, Jewish, female of advanced age, I find myself continuing to define my identity or rather my *multiple identities*. The intersectionality of those identities shapes who I am: my knowledge, my perceptions, my thought processes, my reactions, my goals, and my life. I have experienced negative "-ISMs" associated with each of these human identities. I also revel in the cultural wealth I have internalized from these identities and the communities therein.

Each one of us carries a number of stories and songs inside of us. Each individual is a composite of many components—family, heritage, culture, language, education, life experiences, philosophies, ideologies, and dreams.

We embrace differences by valuing and respecting individuals. We must continue to recognize and stop racism, sexism, ableism, ageism, and many other -ISMs, such as those related to degree of pigment in the skin, weight, one's appearance, or even one's music. Some -ISMs are blatant. Others may be covert or unknown until brought forward to the consciousness. When one person is oppressed, it diminishes us all. Negative -ISMs hurt everyone. Martin Luther King stated, "Our lives begin to end the day we become silent about issues that matter. It is always the right time to do the right thing." When one person speaks out against a negative -ISM, it raises our awareness, our spirit, and our humanity.

President Obama expressed in 2012 that his view about same-sex marriage has evolved; he has come to realize that each and every one of us is a human being with thoughts, feelings, beliefs, and rights. That's the essence of it—each person is a human being.

There are equal opportunity, anti-discrimination laws and policies in education, employment, housing, communities, and government. Why? First, we are all human beings with equal and inalienable human rights, and second, involving diverse people in processes and policy formulation can help ensure more equitable and appropriate outcomes for everyone.

AUDISM AND LINGUISM

The term "audism" was coined by Tom Humphries in his 1977 dissertation "Communicating Across Cultures Deaf-Hearing and Language Learning." He defined audism as the notion that one is superior based on one's ability to hear or behave in the manner of one who hears. That term remained dormant, however, until Harlan Lane revived and expanded on the definition of audism in his 1993 book *Mask of Benevolence.* Lane defined audism as a systematic way that hearing people exert authority over Deaf people while speaking on their behalf, creating policies or documents about them, making decisions about them, directing programs or services for them, and so on. Another definition of audism, then, refers to a system of advantage based on hearing ability (Bauman, 2004; Lane, 1993a). Linguism refers to the action of discrediting, disfavoring, or attempting to extinguish a language used by a minority community, specifically in the situation of Deaf people—American Sign Language (ASL).

Dr. Lawrence Fleischer, a respected Deaf professional, described his experience with audism and linguism in "Critical Pedagogy and ASL Videobooks," a case study in which a hearing educator's values and beliefs determined educational practices and language policies in an ASL videobooks project. This project, funded around 2002 by the state of California Clearing House for Specialized Media and Technology, was designed to enhance literacy skills in Deaf students by creating signed video versions of 300 storybooks. To Fleischer's dismay, the signing was done in English word order, simply stringing signs together as if "reading aloud" or reciting without comprehending. The story concept became confused. An analogy would be to see the trees but not realize the forest, i.e., the story concept. Best practices support interpreting the story line in ASL, clarifying the story itself, which would enable the child to better comprehend the story and thus become better able to read the English version. In the ensuing correspondence between Fleischer and the state official, Fleischer offered to create Deaf-appropriate versions in American Sign Language using more visually appropriate pedagogies. Although the official overtly accepted the input, he basically summarily brushed off Fleischer's input as not meeting the project objective: "The connection between the print book, closed captions, speech and the ASL transcription must be available..." (p. 165). As a parting shot laced with paternalistic generosity, he invited Fleischer to apply for a future project grant, should one become available. Valuable pedagogical input from a Deaf professional was dismissed, leading to misguided decisions and hegemonic miseducation for Deaf children, resulting in a waste of state funds and in intensifying the deaf child's educational impoverishment (Fleischer, 2008).

Harlan Lane explained in the *Mask of Benevolence* (1993a) that because hearing people equate being deaf to being without sound, they consider being deaf as a very disabling condition. They cannot envision that being Deaf does bring in another dimension to life

(Bauman & Murray, 2009; Lane, 1993a). This disability construction or perception precludes or suppresses the realization that there is a whole other dimension to humanity, or the existence of a minority culture construction (Bauman, 2009; Ladd, 2005; Lane, 1993a).

For the past two centuries, born-deaf, sign language-using people have been placed within a succession of externally constructed models, notably the traditional "medical" or pathological model, which considers them primarily as biologically deficient beings in need of cures or fixes in order to be assimilated into society successfully (Ladd, 2005; Lane, 1984). Industry and the economy persist with the disability construction and the "fix it, minimize it, hide it, or eradicate it" mindset. Legislators pass acts and policies minimizing the minority culture with forced assimilation in the mainstream and supporting extensive research and programs such as the National Institute of Health, Deafness and Communication Disorders (NIHDCD), and Center on Disease Control to cure deafness. The NIHDCD gets more federal dollars per year than Gallaudet University and the National Technological Institute for the Deaf together. The auditory and implant industries support amplification and suppress American Sign Language, as do the oral-only option schools, in order to maintain robust enrollments and continued revenues (Eberwein, 2007; Holcomb, 2013; Lane, 1993b). Without the intrinsic knowledge and credibility of being Deaf, those hearing people serve as experts, consultants, and administrators wielding hegemonic authority over deaf people and making paternalistic decisions about policies, programs, and processes.

The term colonialism in reference to the deaf community was first used by Lane (1993b) and is manifested by social and educational policies that aim to cure or eradicate deaf people. This includes early identification with its misplaced focus on speech and aural development, mainstream education without Deaf role models and qualified professionals proficient in sign language, and oralism, which bans the use of sign language and visual aids. These actions seem to provide benefit but in fact wreak long-term damage and impoverishment (Lane, 1993b; Soloranzo, 1997). Repeated research results over the decades show that deaf students achieve far below their age-appropriate grade levels. Ladd (2013) notes that oralism, a most pervasive and oppressing system, has held global hegemonic power for the past 130 years. The pro-oralism resolution enacted by the International Congress on Education of the Deaf (ICED) in 1880 resulted in the "dark ages" for deaf people, specifically the *de facto* elimination of deaf teachers in school programs, and the loss of larger perspectives of the history, strategies, and potential of deaf students, thus oppressing the larger Deaf selfhood (Ladd, 2003, 2013). This can be considered the Deaf equivalent of the Jim Crow segregation actions, 1876–1965, in the South (Eckert & Rowley, 2013).

Educational practices such as oralism, simultaneous communication (speaking English and signing at the same time), and mainstreaming are the political and policy manifestations of phonocentric and audist metaphysical orientation and ideologies. These further entrench audist attitudes favoring changing Deaf people into hearing people (Bauman, 2004; Kusters, 2013). The educational system often tracks Deaf students into oral/cochlear implant/manual classes and often prevents these groups from interacting with each other. Some schools even have separate buses and building entrances for oral students and for signing students.

Early identification systems for babies are placed bureaucratically within the domain of the health system, which focuses on fixing the defective ear, rather than under the department of education, which focuses on cognitive development and knowledge needed to succeed in life. Hearing parents of Deaf babies are given "choices" of either oral or sign language options and are generally expected, if they choose to implant their child, to not sign with their baby (Humphries et al., 2012). Sign language usage with hearing babies is a booming business, fortified by research that, long before the baby is ready to talk, signs will boost cognition, connectivity, bonding, and communication. Expectant parents may even take sign language classes in anticipation of giving their baby a head start in life. Ironically, when the baby is identified as Deaf, the family is suddenly advised not to sign. The baby's language development is stalled, not because they are implanted, but because they are deprived of access to language. Such linguistic deprivation rarely occurs in hearing children (Humphries et al., 2012).

This deprivation leads to lack of access, diminished self-esteem, and educational impoverishment.

Hiring prejudices and preferences generally exclude Deaf people from the front lines of early identification and intervention programs. Deaf people are rarely employed as early education interventionists, therapists, or educators, especially for infants and young children or deaf children in mainstream settings. This deprivation of adult Deaf role models for Deaf babies, children, and families causes further downward spirals of miseducation.

For years, sign language was regarded as a primitive gestural system, a poor stepchild to English, by medical and educational systems. Suppression of sign language in education became rampant in the world and in the United States following the 1880 International Congress on Education of the Deaf Milan resolution to ban signs in schools. George W. Veditz, President of the National Association of the Deaf, 1904–1910, lamented "What heinous crimes have we committed that sign language should be so proscribed?" (Newman, 2006). When Stokoe's research in the 1970s affirmed that the linguistic properties of American Sign Language met all standards as a *bona fide* language, Deaf people felt validated and liberated. Deaf people view themselves as a linguistic and cultural minority—this new cultural–linguistic model empowers the deaf person and enables the deaf experience to be more properly understood and capitalized for greater success in life (Bahan, 2004; Ladd, 2005).

In 1913, George Veditz in "Preservation of Sign Language" postulated that "As long as we have deaf people on earth, we will have signs. It is my hope that we will all love and guard our beautiful sign language as the noblest gift God has given to deaf people" (Newman, 2006).

WORDS, TERMS, AND LANGUAGE

Words, terms, and language can shape, modify, or entrench mindsets. The hegemony of oralism denies the existence of the concept of a deaf child, replacing "deaf" with the terms "deafness" and "hearing-impaired." These terms focus on what the deaf child lacks rather than the child's potential strengths and qualities (Ladd, 2005). Identifying oppressing forces and renaming ourselves are ways to reclaim ourselves (Hosking, 2008). Synthesizing different discriminatory occurrences into a unifying picture of oppression and giving it a name can give us a handle on the reality of the oppression on individual and collective bases (Bauman, 2004). Audism and linguism are terms that help identify and acknowledge acts of hegemony and prejudice.

Labels such as "hearing impaired, deafness, hearing loss, and language-delayed" are negative medical terms. Paddy Ladd coined "Deafhood" as a concept to counteract medically oriented and oppressive discourses by offering a Deaf-constructed model based on Deaf people's own ontologies (i.e., Deaf ways of being in the world), emphasizing positive, beneficial experience-oriented views of Deaf people (Ladd, 2003, 2005).

Markku Jokinen, past president of the World Federation of the Deaf (WFD), has used the term "sign language users" rather than "deaf people" to integrate a much larger population who need or benefit from the use of sign language—Deaf people, family members, friends, colleagues, and service providers. "Sign Language Peoples" and "People of the Eye" are also terms used to describe the Deaf and ASL users' community.

People of color experience subtle racism and stereotyping all the time. Examples are: "You are not like them, you're different and better." "If only more of them were like you." "I don't think of you as Mexican." "You speak such good English" (Soloranzo, 1997). Deaf people experience expressions of veiled audism, such as "she is deaf *but* smart." "He is deaf *but* cute" (Galloway, 1973). Why use the word "but," which denotes a semantic contradiction, instead of "and," which denotes that both adjectives are equal and complementary? Biased perceptions affect behaviors and attitudes toward Deaf people and perpetuate hearing supremacy. "He needs a hearing secretary or wife to help him succeed." "He got a 'C,' which is good for a deaf student" (Rosen, 1983).

Language, belonging, culture, social institutions, arts, and history are the facets that create and bind a community. Naming, clarifying, and establishing identity enable decolonizing. The process of escaping the reductionist lens of labels by oppressors is liberating for the minority community (Ladd, 2013). Words and images used to portray people as disabled have a direct effect on constructed images, perceptions, and attitudes toward these people (Fleischer, 2011; Hosking, 2008). There are elements of power embedded in words, language, metaphors, and labels (Cho, Crenshaw, & McCall, 2013). Generic labels such as "hearing impaired" and "deafness" are considered oppressive by many deaf people due to connections to the hegemonic medical model (Ladd, 2013). These terms reflect deficit thinking and focus on the ear as opposed to the person. The term "deaf and/or hard of hearing" is seen as a divisive, colonialist strategy for ruling the oppressed (Ladd, 2013). During the 1970s, African-Americans proudly chanted "Black is Beautiful" and "Black Pride," although they came in all shades of skin color, from white to black; they knew it was important to be unified in their goals for equality and self-determination. Likewise, the term "Deaf" encompasses and unifies everyone with different levels of hearing. "Hearing loss" is a strange description for Deaf people, who were born Deaf and thus have never lost their hearing. A preferred term is "different hearing levels." To persist with obsolete and negative terms such as "hearing impaired, deafness, hearing loss, and deaf/hard of hearing" are classifying, pathological, and divisive actions.

"Deafhood" and "Deaf Theory" help reframe and transform perceptions from medical to humanistic and allow the cultural signifier "Deaf" to be self-defined and self-valued without relation to a "hearing other" (Smith & Bienvenu, 2007) or as a medical model.

DEAFHOOD

Deafhood is an open-ended, dynamic process of self-empowerment and liberation (Kusters, 2013; Ladd, 2005). Deafhood is a way to explore the self and the community and to identify, resist, and overcome the effects of colonialism. Deafhood highlights the validity, vitality, and value of Deaf people and their contributions to the world (Bauman, 2005; Ladd, 2005; Ladd & Lane, 2013). Deficit views are transformed into deaf-centric views. In the process of examining one's existence and ontology, the question is "why do Deaf people exist?" Are Deaf people merely a negative biological error or are Deaf people a manifestation of human diversity, created by a Supreme Being who desired a sign language-using people to experience different ways of embracing and enhancing life or as an approach to enhance global connections? The biodiversity of human experience can be analyzed, validated, and valued (Ladd, 2005).

Participants in Deafhood seminars and discourses experience a gain in their conscious Deaf selfhood, understanding the ramifications of past, present, and future actions; realizing the need for tolerance, growth, unity, and activism; and gaining a sense of liberation and acceptance of differences. The journey is a process of becoming and gaining a larger and more positive selfhood, a natural path toward full potential (Ladd, 2005). Furthermore, Ladd pointed out that individual choices (such as speech and hearing devices) should be respected as part of diversity within the community. Any activism should be toward the oppressive system (such as banning sign language and requiring auditory remediation for corporate gain) rather than toward the choices made by individuals, for themselves, per se.

MISS DEAF MARYLAND

In the early 1980s, the Maryland Association of the Deaf sponsored a Miss Deaf Maryland pageant. The contestants had to respond to an interview question on stage: "Which do you think would be better, to be mainstreamed in a public school or to attend a school for the deaf, and why?"

All contestants but one said "mainstream" and reasons for this choice included: better education, more advanced studies, better activities, real world. The sole exception was a daughter of Deaf parents; she said she loved being at the school for the deaf, being able to communicate with everyone and having full and equal access to all information and activities. Dr. David Denton, then Superintendent of the Maryland School for the Deaf, was devastated. I, too, was feeling depressed, and couldn't quite put my finger on why.

The very next morning the *Good Morning America* television news show carried a segment regarding a research study on doll preferences by Black girls. Nearly all of them chose a blonde, white doll over a black doll with black curly hair. This study, initially done by the Clarks (1947), exposed internalized racism in African-American children and concluded that self-hatred existed among minority children attending inadequate and unequal segregated schools, resulting in educational inequity and impoverishment.

A more insightful explanation crystallized a few years later, when Joyce King (1991) coined the term "dysconscious racism" in her study, published in the *Journal of Negro Education*. She defined it as the uncritical habit of mind (i.e., perceptions, attitudes, assumptions, and beliefs) that justified inequity and exploitation by accepting the existing order of things as a given (King, 1991). This led to accepting the status quo unquestioningly without recognizing and challenging systemic racial inequity.

Although much progress has been made with civil rights and equal educational opportunities, a 7-minute award-winning film documentary (2005) by Kiri Davis, *A Girl Like Me*, replicated the 1947 Clark research, with startlingly similar results.

King (2012) attributed the dire miseducation of minority students to dysconscious racism and distorted understandings within the system about inequity and cultural diversity. The deficit-thinking model results in educational policy solutions that focus on the acculturation of minority students to the values and behaviors of the dominant system (Soloranzo, 1997). The dominant system made it difficult to establish a critically transformative understanding of race and racial inequity for human freedom and perpetuated a curriculum that alienates peoples of color from seeing themselves as co-constructors of knowledge.

Vanessa Siddler Walker presented a paper at the July 2013 U.S. Department of Education Office of Special Programs Conference on the "Lost History" of African-American education.

After desegregated education became compulsory following the 1954 Supreme Court ruling on Brown v. Board of Education, African-American children in the southeastern part of the United States found themselves in "white" schools. Many of their African-American teachers from the Black schools were laid off. Consequently, it was a struggle for the transplanted African-American students to connect to their white teachers who did not have high expectations for them, who personified Eurocentric values, and who used noninclusive pedagogies and curricula. The strategies used by the former African-American teachers for effective education, instillation of citizenship qualities, direct connections, high expectations, classroom management, and community values and strategies were devalued and lost. The values and experiences of marginalized minority cultures were downplayed, criticized, or ignored (Soloranzo, 1997; Walker, 2013; Yosso, 2005). The resultant disconnect between the realities of lives of African-American children and the white educational system caused further miseducation and entrenched "dysconscious racism" within the African-American community, despite apparent civil rights advances (King, 2012; Walker, 2013).

Deaf African-American students who were suddenly transferred to newly desegregated white schools for the deaf not only experienced this same disconnect but also were confronted and befuddled by difficult relations with white-hearing teachers and "White American Sign Language." This form of communication differed significantly from the "Black American Sign Language" used in their former schools (McCaskill, Lucas, Bayley, & Hill, 2011).

This "ah-ha" understanding of dysconscious racism becomes a stepping stone to understanding the dominant forces at work during the Miss Deaf Maryland pageant interviews. Genie Gertz' dissertation expanded on Joyce King's work and labeled this internalized self-despising oppression "dysconscious audism:"

> Dysconscious audism hampers to varying degrees the Deaf individual's consciousness of Deaf identity. As a result, it undermines the deaf individual's true identity development and shifts him or her away from the Deaf center towards

> the hearing dominant majority. When the Deaf person's identity is distorted, he or she often cannot fully understand his or her own behaviors and also cannot realize, and therefore cannot resist, the hidden existence of hegemonic forces (Gertz, 2003, p. xi).

Dysconscious audism is manifested by a range of internalized oppressions, from a simple lack of self-confidence or self-belief, through identity crisis and self-hatred, to a rate of acquired mental illness double that of nondeaf populations (Ladd, 2005). To reverse this, reframing and reforming are essential. As Deaf people, cross-cultural studies of other oppressed populations help to enlighten us, enable us to identify colonialism and sociopolitical patterns, and provide us with possible strategies to reach our full potential.

CRITICAL LEGAL STUDIES AND ITS BRANCHES

Cross-cultural studies and **critical legal studies** (CLS) offer a different lens by which we can examine ourselves and arrive at some understandings and some strategies for creating positive changes.

An online legal dictionary (2013) defines CLS as "a theory that challenges and overturns accepted norms and standards in legal theory and practice." Because federal and state laws and policies may be built on ideologies, beliefs, and prejudices that legitimize the injustices of society, CLS advances a theoretical and practical project of reconstruction of the laws and, consequently, society. The underlying belief is that law is politics. Because the law is neither neutral nor value free, it perpetuates an unjust social system. Started as a discipline in 1977, some of the CLS founding members had previously participated in social activities related to the Civil Rights Movement and the Anti-Vietnam War Movement

An examination of the CLS body of postulates and its subsequent branches, based on race, gender, or disability, helps us recognize and understand the various -ISMs that exist. Parallels and disconnects become manifested in examining critical legal studies and in formulating possible strategies to achieve a more just society.

CRITICAL RACE THEORY

The **critical race theory** (CRT) began in the 1970s as an offshoot of CLS when African-American scholars and activists became involved in legal analyses of legislation, policies, principles, and ideologies to determine how class inequalities were perpetuated in the United States (Tate, 1997). There was a disconnect between the reality of class-based discrimination and racism. Liberal legal thinkers failed to identify the impact of racial ideology on society, which further subjugated people of color (Bell, 2009; Crenshaw, Gotanda, Peller, & Thomas, 1995). CRT offers a radical lens through which to make sense of, deconstruct, and challenge racial inequality and power relations in society; it examines and challenges issues around race, racial identity, and racism (Rollock & Gillborn, 2011; Soloranzo, 1997).

The five main tenets of CRT are as follow. (1) **Centrality of racism in** daily life and policies were unconsciously accepted and taken for granted as a way of life. (2) **White supremacy** governed political, economic, and cultural systems and controlled resources in society and programs. (3) **Narratives and storytelling** based on life experiences of people of color regarding racism and being racially marginalized include their historical, sociocultural, and political realities and are valuable tools to challenge racist ideology. (4) **Interest convergence** or perceived benefits to white people may lead to policy changes and advances; gains may be supported for economic or self-interest reasons of elite whites, and while seeming to advance racial equality, they may in reality affect very little improvement or long-lasting change. (5) **Intersectionality** recognizes and addresses social injustices that people of color experience, which must also be considered under the umbrella of racial inequalities (Rollock & Gillborn, 2011; Soloranzo, 1997).

The CRT tenants are applicable to the Deaf community. The literature is replete with comparable findings. (1) **Centrality of audism:** Unconscious and dysconscious audism are experienced by Deaf people who may reject sign language, special education, or support services or who may accept hegemonic practices of discrimination as their lot in life (Gertz, 2008). Bonnie Tucker (1998), a deaf lawyer, does not support affirmative action to create a more level playing field; furthermore, she argues that deaf people who reject cochlear implants should not be entitled to social services and accommodations. (2) **Hearing supremacy** dominates political, economic, and educational programs and resources (Eberwein, 2010; Fleischer, 2008; Ladd, 2005; Lane, 1993b). (3) **Sharing narratives and coping strategies** are ways of life for Deaf people (Fleischer, 2013; Padden & Humphries, 1988), as well as resistance and affirmative Deaf View/Image Art (De'VIA)(Durr, 1999; Holcomb, 2013) and media productions such as *I Love You But…*, *No Ordinary Hero*, *Switched at Birth*, and *Through Your Child's Eyes*. (4) **Interest convergence** such as mainstream education and oralism may appear beneficial but lead to a long-range lack of improvement or positive outcomes. Health and educational policies favor mainstreaming Deaf children and discourage the use of bilingual (American Sign Language and English) pedagogies to maximize what they perceive as benefits to programs, systems, and industries (Ladd, 2005; Lane, 1993b). (5) **Intersectionality** applies to the Deaf community, which is a microcosm of all races, ethnicities, and classes in the larger society (Ruiz & Holcomb, 2013; Smith & Bienvenu, 2007). Deaf people experience multiple oppressions caused by sexism, racism, ageism, heterosexism, classism, audism, ableism, and Deaf-ableism.

Solórzano (1997) applied the five tenets of CRT to educational theory, research, pedagogy, curriculum, and policy: (1) consider the intercentricity and interrelatedness of race with other forms of subordination; (2) challenge educational policies, programs, and research data in terms of objectivity and neutrality, thus revealing the dominant groups' self-interest, power, and privilege; (3) incorporate experiential knowledge, histories, and values; (4) commit to social justice and empowerment for the subordinated groups; and (5) acknowledge intersectionality and interdisciplinary approaches based on scholarship from ethnic studies, women's studies, sociology, history, law, psychology, film, theatre, and other fields. Students of cultural minority groups bring with them values from their homes and communities that should be capitalized on by the educational system for more effective and successful linkages to learning and applications to daily life.

These tenants challenge existing methods of scholarship and current pedagogies. "Schools most often oppress and marginalize while they maintain the potential to emancipate and empower" (Yosso, 2005, p. 74). -ISMs are embedded in "normative" values and "neutral" social principles and practices (Rosen, 2012). School systems are assumed to be effective, and the onus of failure is shifted to the oppressed people. Deficit thinking, a form of racism, blames minority students and families for poor academic achievement, as students enter school unprepared educationally and culturally and families seem to not value or support their child's education. Schools expect families to subsume their values to meet dominant standards. Their knowledge, language, culture, experiences, values, and stories are discounted (Ladd, 2005; Walker, 2013; Yosso, 2005).

FEMINIST LEGAL THEORY

During the late 1960s, the Women's Movement re-emerged and was strengthened, inspired by the civil rights movement and the antiwar protests. Feminists advocated for the passage of equal rights laws in education, employment, and communities, believing that such laws would liberate them from their subordinate position. The **feminist legal theory** in the United States started in the late 1970s. It postulates that law is politics. It is socially created out of categories and dichotomies (male/female) that foster inequality and do not reflect the reality of differences. Catharine MacKinnon's book, *Sexual Harassment of Working Women* (1979), postulated that formal equality cannot give women the rights women need when men do not share these needs. This dominance approach holds that current policy perpetuates women's subordination to men.

Radical feminists see patriarchy as the root of women's oppression. "The personal is political" refers to issues that are personal to a woman, such as birth control, sexuality, and marriage equality, yet are governed by policies made within a system of male domination.

The feminist legal theory identifies some causes of inequality between women and men: male dominance, adherence to traditional roles, and the undervaluation of "feminine traits," such as nurturing, empathy, and caring for others, and the overvaluation of "masculine traits," such as autonomy, aggression, and being unemotional.

Most careers historically selected by females (or limited to females) include caretaking, assisting, or helping—work that is traditionally unpaid or underpaid.

Crises can lead to change, such as the scarcity of employees during World War II, which resulted in a surge of female employees in nonfemale occupations, as personified by Rosie the Riveter. Clarence Thomas's nomination in 1991 to succeed retiring Justice Thurgood Marshall on the Supreme Court was another such crisis leading to a paradigm shift. When the all-male Senate Judiciary Committee summarily dismissed Anita Hill's accusations of sexual harassment in its confirmation of Thomas, a national debate regarding dominance, bias, injustice, and lack of female peers on critical committees was set off. This launched public awareness and policies regarding workplace sexual harassment and political activism. This contributed to the large number of women elected to Congress in 1992. The number of females and people of color who have become elected politicians and lawyers has increased significantly since then, at all levels and branches of the governance and social systems.

During the 1980s, **critical race feminism** emerged because feminist movements, while representing all women, benefitted primarily privileged white women and promoted their issues (e.g., political involvement or career-related issues) rather than those of women of different races, ethnicities, immigrants, and others. Furthermore, solutions that may work for privileged white women were of little relevance to the more urgent needs of women of color and the disadvantaged (Crenshaw, 1989). As a subordinated and minority group, women of color face insurmountable odds in dealing with public servants, administrators, policy makers, and enforcers, often creating a "us vs. them" or a male/female, white/nonwhite dichotomy.

Smith and Bienvenu (2007), in their article "Deaf Theory: What Can We Learn from Feminist Theory?," identified parallels within the Deaf community. The tenants of critical legal theories can serve as guides to further Deaf Studies, to describe and examine the experiences of Deaf people, and to analyze differences in humanity and among "subordinate" groups (i.e., gender, race, and cultural minorities) within the Deaf community. Deaf Studies, a relatively new academic discipline, also provides the framework for "Deaf Theory," which serves as a lens for analyzing aspects of the Deaf community, language and culture, to form a body of emancipatory knowledge to identify, describe, inform, and empower Deaf people (Smith & Bienvenu, 2007). The Deaf/hearing dichotomy mindset results in not understanding political realities and in perceiving the other as the enemy, such as the "angry women movement," which focused on the "evils" caused by men, rather than focusing on one's own internalized audism, classism, and racism and taking action (Smith & Bienvenu, 2007).

For decades, the leadership of Deaf social and sports organizations has been a dominantly white Deaf male domain. Experts, leaders, administrators, and spokespersons have primarily been white males. The situation is changing now with more white Deaf females, but not so much for Deaf persons of color. As with CLT, which branched out to include differences, Deaf women and people of color formed their own national organizations to advance their causes: Deaf Women United, National Black Deaf Advocates, and National Council of Hispanic Deaf and Hard of Hearing.

Smith and Bienvenu quoted bell hooks' (2000) statement that "True system reform may only come from moving away from a simplistic dichotomous oppositional stance to embrace a genuine examination of systems of domination, as well as one's own role in their maintenance and perpetuation." They tied this statement to Deaf Culture and asserted that multilayered examinations and discourses on internalized audism, as well as sexism, classism, and racism, are essential (Smith & Bienvenu, 2007).

CRITICAL DISABILITY THEORY AND ABLEISM

The dominant paradigm for understanding disability throughout most of the 20th century has been the medical model, which identifies disability as an individual medical problem and intrinsic to the person with the medical issue (Hosking, 2008; Lane, 1984; Rocco, 2002). In the 1960s and 1970s, organizations of people with disabilities, including the National Association of the Deaf, moved away from the medical model toward the social construct and took the position that the issues of disabilities were not from within themselves but were creations of society's physical and attitudinal barriers, resulting in minimal quality of access and social injustice.

The **critical disability theory** (CDT), which emerged in the 1980s, analyzes disability as a social construct and challenges ableist assumptions within society. It rejects the objectification of people with disabilities, identifies the sources of oppression within the law and programs, and promotes the potential positive role of law toward the emancipation of people with disabilities (Hosking, 2008).

The CDT incorporates the reality that disabled people are also diverse members of all other social classifications, and again, subject to varying degrees of bias and privilege, related to the disability, the degree of the disability, and the juxtaposition of race, class, and gender. For example, of all disabled federal employees, Deaf people rank last in the number employed, below the other categories of disabled federal employees.

Laws and policies, as well as litigations, have evolved from a medical into a social model for a more accessible environment and equitable opportunities in the United States. The Vocational Rehabilitation Act of 1973, Individuals with Disabilities Education Act (IDEA, 1975), Americans with Disabilities Act (ADA, 1990), and many others are federal laws prohibiting discrimination and promoting inclusion of persons with disabilities in all arenas of life, as a social good. Early identification and intervention policies attempt to decrease the consequences of the disability and the barriers imposed by the social environment to the disability, often reflecting a merger of medical and social models.

However, power resides in the dominant majority and is so ingrained that there is a lack of realization that it exists. Thomas Hehir, director of the U.S. Department of Education's Office of Special Education Programs from 1993 to 1999, put ableism in the same category as racism, sexism, and homophobia. He defined ableism as a societal prejudice against people with disabilities, ranging from overt lack of access to events or programs to more veiled expectations that disabled people should perform life tasks in the same ways as nondisabled people. "In educational practice, this would be reflected in the desire for children with very little vision to read print as opposed to Braille; having deaf children read lips as opposed to signing; or having kids with physical disabilities spend an inordinate amount of time taking physical therapy so that they might walk—even if it's just a few stumbling steps—at the expense of taking academic instruction" (Hehir, 2006).

When a policy proposal favors a movement toward mainstream services such as IDEA or a ban against sign language, oftentimes these are implemented without the cautious rigors of research prior to practice. The late Marie Jean Philip, a Deaf bilingual education pioneer, during a question and answer session of a Deaf studies conference in 1991 hosted by the Gallaudet University College of Continuing Education, elaborated as follows:

> If it is a deviation from the norm, such as ASL/English bilingual pedagogies, then intensive and exhaustive research and data is required to validate the idea or proposed policy/practice. However, if the policy proposal seems to make the Deaf child "less-deaf" such as oral/aural pedagogies or placement in mainstream schools or invasive medical surgery such as cochlear implants and funding for such, these usually meet with neither expectations for research and data nor resistance from policy makers (Philip, 1991, personal communication).

"Parents are continuously put into a situation of making choices—soup or salad—instead of understanding they can have both," eloquently stated Tony Ronco, a parent of a Deaf daughter (CSUN video, *Through Your Child's Eyes: ASL*, 2009). The key to success for Deaf children is language and literacy, not communication options. Interestingly, the U.S. Department of Education, Office of Special Education and Rehabilitative Services (OSERS) issued a directive, dated June 19, 2013, to reaffirm the importance of Braille instruction as a literacy tool for blind and visually impaired students. This statement came even though technology is increasingly being used to enable Blind students to acquire literacy skills. Why has OSERS been reluctant to issue a comparable directive regarding the importance of visual access, American Sign Language, and English literacy for all Deaf and hard-of-hearing children? When asked about this, a leader in education of deaf children rationalized, "But Braille is English and ASL is not."

Deaf people are visual beings rather than beings without hearing (Bahan, 2004). Integrating this perception into one's consciousness can liberate one from an ableist, audist position, reframe thinking, and inform appropriate strategies. Furthermore, rather than stating a dichotomy, disabled/not disabled, the continuum should include all human variations, which includes everyone, including the "temporarily able-bodied." As Liisa Kauppinen, President Emerita of the World Federation of the Deaf, stated, "A society good for disabled people is a society good for all people" (Kauppinen, 1991, personal communication).

IDENTITY AND INTERSECTIONALITY

An individual is a composite of many complex human characteristics, identities, and experiences. Those characteristics are often viewed as mutually exclusive categories in the eyes of the law. Kimberlé Crenshaw (1989) is credited with introducing the term "intersectionality" to the field in the late 1980s as a term to minimize identity politics and to acknowledge the plurality of human characteristics such as race, gender, ability, and class, which interact and influence relationships with society and political processes. The intersectionality framework includes identities and differences, connections, and conflicts. This helps expand the public lens on the dynamics of differences and sameness in the context of antidiscrimination and social movement politics in everyday life and processes (Cho et al., 2013). An understanding of intersectionality theories will do away with "single-axis thinking" and negate the obsolete mindset of "one size fits all" experienced by individuals and movements in today's social, educative, and human service fields. Intersectional approaches emphasize collaboration rather than unity (Cho et al., 2013) and include multilayered examinations and discourses on internalized oppression, ableism, sexism, classism, and racism (Smith & Bienvenu, 2007). Intersectionality analysis demonstrates varying power as related to overlapping identity categories and identifies harmful bias within "neutral" systems (Cho et al., 2013).

I was leading a number of workshops and seminars for women in the 1970s during the nascent era of the Women's Movement. During an exercise on individual introspection on identity, I asked women in the audience to envision themselves on a sinking ship with just two lifeboats—one for hearing women and one for deaf men. The question was "which lifeboat would you want to get into?" The underlying assumption was that while we were women, we also valued belonging to the Deaf community. In answer to that question, nearly all of the women picked the lifeboat with deaf men—as expected—"because communications would be easier; because we can work together to survive; because if we ended up on an island, we can create a new community." However, that question subsequently stirred a hornet's nest. One woman said, "But, my sister is hearing and I'd want to sail with her." Another said, "My best friend is hearing but knows ASL, where would she go?" We all realized at that point that we did NOT have to choose between Women/Deaf; both identities in fact belonged to us. To believe otherwise is divisive and disempowering (Ruiz & Holcomb, 2013; Smith & Bienvenu, 2007). Audre Lorde (1980) suggests that our responsibility as feminists is to come to see these connections in order to understand that the true liberation of one oppressed group cannot happen without the liberation of all oppressed people.

In the same vein, Deaf People of Color were always asked which community they felt they belonged to, which traits they felt were more integral to their lives, e.g., the Deaf community or the African-American community? The expectation in the past was that to be Deaf was the common denominator; Deaf people all experienced discrimination and a diminished quality of life. The reality of racism and classism within the Deaf community was lost on us in those days. "Black," they retorted, "because when we walk down the street, that's the first thing they see. Then when we communicate, they realize that we are Deaf, too." Being Deaf and Black was a double-whammy. Being a female made it a triple whammy. It is oppressive to ask anyone to rank their identities, each one of which is integral to the self, which is larger than a simple sum of the parts. Ruiz and Holcomb (2013) point out that ableism and classism also exist among Deaf people regarding people who may be Deaf Plus or Deaf persons with additional conditions that may be considered different or disabling.

Scott (2003) suggests that a new theory is needed: one that has a focus on pluralities and diversities instead of unities and universals. Intersectionality moves away from binary thinking toward multicultural differences, complexities, and enrichment. Moving away from an "either or" stance disintegrates the assumption that identities are in some way additive, and thus disempowering to the individual, as opposed to complexly integrated (Ruiz & Holcomb, 2013; Smith & Bienvenu, 2007). The term "diversity" has become a politically correct and safe "catch-all" term to use, as it glosses over issues facing marginalized individuals and groups; the term "intersectionality" is an actionable term acknowledging and valuing multiple identities, experiences, relationships, abilities, and needs (Ruiz & Holcomb, 2013).

The newspaper and media industries, previously lily-white and male dominated, now employ women and people of color as reporters and in other capacities in order to be relevant, authentic, and credible in their coverage of issues. They know that in addition to the "social good" of hiring diverse newscasters, the bottom line is that economic gains are realized by increasing the numbers of readers and viewers of their products.

CULTURAL CAPITAL

> Culture refers to behaviors and values that are learned, shared, and exhibited by a group of people.... Culture is also evidenced in material and nonmaterial productions of a people. Cultural capital is an accumulation of cultural knowledge, skills and abilities possessed and inherited by privileged groups in society. Cultural capital (language, education), social capital (social networks, connections) and economic capital (money, material possessions) can be acquired two ways—ones family and or formal schooling (Yosso, 2005, pp. 69–91).

Pervasive deficit thinking results in viewing Communities of Color as substandard, culturally disadvantaged, and without value. The reality is that socially marginalized communities are vital and vibrant with their own knowledge, skills, values, goals, narratives, and solutions or, in other words, **cultural capital** (King, 2013; Yosso, 2005). The six forms of capital include aspirational, navigational, social, linguistic, familial, and resistant capital (Yosso, 2005).

The experiences and narratives of People of Color yield a vast community cultural capital, which enables them to survive, resist oppression, challenge inequities, have hope, and work toward possibilities and transformations, including forming connections to schools and academia (Walker, 2013; Yosso, 2005). Through the cultural wealth lens, understandings of the multiple strengths of communities of color or marginalized people become pathways toward social justice and equality. With cultural wealth training, participants learn how arguments are framed against them, how to articulate counterarguments, and how to become empowered.

Similar cultural wealth exists in the Deaf community and in Deaf-friendly (visual, accessible, child-centered, critical numbers of deaf and language peers) educational or service programs, leading to and fortifying one's humanity, personhood, Deafhood (Fleischer, 2013). Such wealth within the Deaf community includes strategies for discovering or solidifying identity and the Deaf self, sharing stories and strategies for success, acquiring accepted behaviors and networks, building confidence, becoming a part of the "Deaf or ASL-using family," gaining emotional and social support, developing navigational skills as a consumer, citizen, and employee, interacting with Deaf and signing role models, acquiring skills in interacting with nonsigning others, expanding one's expectations and aspirations as Deaf individuals, realizing one's connections to the community and one's ability to "give back to the community" to improve lives of deaf people, and honing the ability to assert one self's personhood via a Deaf-centric world view. Thus fortified with deaf community cultural wealth, one can identify structural and attitudinal barriers, develop possible strategies to minimize social inequities, and be directly involved in developing or employing Deaf-effective solutions (Fleischer, 2013).

The Deaf community or family has high expectations for students and uses visual and deaf-appropriate strategies for success. They assert rights and challenge inequality. Understanding and internalizing these values and cultural capitals increase group consciousness and motivation, intensify community identity, and enable resistance and transformative action.

To maximize educational and social success, Anzaldúa (1990) points to the need to de-academize theory and to connect the community to the academy. Hearing families with a deaf child in all probability have never met a deaf person before. The first people they meet after their child is identified as being deaf are those with an ingrained medical model of deficit-thinking, fix-it approaches: doctors, audiologists, and early education interveners who use oral/aural pedagogies. As Andrew Solomon (2012) in his book "Far from the Tree" illustrates, a deaf child could be pretty much considered an alien within his/her own family. How then does a family find the "alien" community beyond the academy to capitalize upon their cultural wealth and to benefit from their strengths? The daunting challenge for Deaf people and humanistic professionals in the field is to bypass systemic barriers to connect with these parents so that they can become aware of successful deaf people and benefit from the power of connections, shared experiences, and Deaf-centric solutions and to transcend from medical "fix-it" models to humanistic "fit-in" approaches.

DEAF GAIN AND CULTURAL WEALTH

Deficit thinking has caused barriers and issues for the deaf community in the medical, educational, social, and legislative realms. The audiocentric, audist management of deaf people focuses on hearing loss, aural/oral remediation, clinical technology, genetic tests, and DNA re-engineering (Bauman & Murray, 2009; Ladd, 2005).

To counteract deficit thinking and actions that threaten the deaf community with misguided cures or subject them and future members to genetic engineering and genocide, it is necessary to reframe, reform, and redefine "normalcy" to create a paradigm shift in public mindsets from Hearing Loss to Deaf Gain:

> Deafness has long been viewed as a hearing loss—an absence, a void, a lack. It is virtually impossible to think of deafness without thinking of loss. Yet, deaf people do not often consider their lives to be defined by loss. Rather, there is something present in the lives of deaf people, something full and complete. We call this opposing frame Deaf Gain (Bauman & Murray, 2009, p. 3).

Deaf Gain views being Deaf as a sensory and cognitive difference with the ability to help advance the human race and unleash its potential for even greater achievements. The existence of Deaf people should be valued as God's master plan for biodiversity (Ladd, 2005). This bioethical view and valuation could occur on two planes: "…an intrinsic argument that deaf culture ought to be valued and preserved for its own sake, an extrinsic argument that deaf people should be cherished because they have something to contribute to the general society" (Bauman & Murray, 2009, p. 3). "Deaf people, as uniquely visuo-gesturo-tactile biological entities, believe they offer a different and positive perspective on what it means to be human" (Ladd, 2005, p. 13). One of the key Deaf contributions is a greater understanding of what it means to be human, of the significance biodiversity can mean.

A different modality for perceiving, communicating, and sharing helps expand on the various ways of being human and on theories regarding processes for thinking, creating, and sharing among peoples (UNESCO, 1996). The visual, kinesthetic language of signs is based on a different modality and process that convey important concepts difficult to express orally, such as the use of three-dimensional space.

Positive benefits of being Deaf, or Deaf Gain benefits, include but are not limited to: visual-based language, keen recognition of details, use of spatial relationships, community sense, collectivism, transnationalism, three-dimensional expression of stories and poems, and captions in media. Deaf designers transform space in planning furniture, buildings, and communities. Examples are wide sidewalks, open living spaces, round or oval tables that enhance sight lines and human connections during meetings, and management of light, resulting in multiple crossover benefits. Sign language enables people to communicate across great distances, through glass walls, and under water. Various research studies show gains such as enhanced peripheral skills, sharper memory of faces, greater flexibility and tolerance for ambiguity, greater spatial cognition, increased creativity and proficiency in using two languages, and making the transition to other languages. Visual linguistic elasticity made possible through the use of sign language enables Deaf people to communicate quickly with sign language users from other countries and to navigate with greater ease in other countries.

A fundamental characteristic of the human brain is called plasticity. Plasticity allows people to develop social interactions through language, be it signed or spoken (Petitto et al., 2000). Petitto's research has shown that effective cognition results through the visual pathway as well as through the aural pathway. This helps debunk the ages-old belief that only hearing and speech will lead to intelligence. Also, the recognition of sign language as a legitimate language dramatically altered how researchers and practitioners perceive the concept of language and the functions of the brain, and the realization that language includes communication but that communication does not equal language. Research has supported the use of sign language for nondeaf babies as a way to enhance cognition, human connections, and communication early in life. Ironically, when the baby is found to be Deaf, the family is advised to stop signing.

Accepting the premise of Deaf persons as members of a cultural group can lead to significant changes in the dominant (hearing) hegemony (Bauman & Murray, 2009; Ladd & Lane, 2013; Smith & Bienvenu, 2007). Moreover, an understanding of and appreciation for Deaf Gain benefits can help reduce deficit thinking and actions against a cultural and biodiverse minority group.

HUMAN RIGHTS—UNITED NATIONS (UN) AND UNITED NATIONS EDUCATIONAL, SCIENTIFIC AND CULTURAL ORGANIZATION (UNESCO) POLICY STATEMENTS

Where national laws and policies may be lacking or misguiding, a review of higher-order laws governing humanity and human rights helps illuminate and recalibrate the course for a misguided ship. This helps transform perceptions away from medical deficit thinking toward humanitarian constructs. The United Nations and its agency UNESCO have formulated a number of policy documents on human rights for people: women, children, refugees, migrant groups, persons with disabilities, racial, ethnic, and cultural minorities. These documents have been ratified by most nations. These policy documents can help inform thinking, reframe mindsets, and reform misguided practices. The World Federation of the Deaf (WFD) is awarded status by the United Nations (UN) and its agencies as the official spokesperson for the global Deaf community. The WFD position papers (www.wfdeaf.org) and the involvement of WFD representatives in UN and UNESCO meetings in policy formulation have ensured that those policy documents are relevant and support the human rights, needs, values, and goals of Deaf people everywhere.

HUMAN RIGHT OF NATIONAL LINGUISTIC MINORITIES: 1996

The UNESCO Universal Declaration on Linguistic Rights, a policy statement evolving out of the World Conference on Linguistic Rights, Barcelona, Spain, is a powerful document that defines and expands the rights of cultural minorities. Articles 3, 5, and 26 apply to language and educational rights for cultural minorities and can apply to the Deaf community. Another UNESCO declaration was formulated in The Hague in 1996. Education Rights of National (Cultural) Minorities; articles 1, 11, 12, 20 are also relevant to the Deaf community. These policy documents accord rights to national or indigenous cultural minority groups to maintain their cultures and languages and stipulate that nations must protect these rights instead of eradicating or extinguishing them. For example, Aboriginal people in Australia were forced to become assimilated into the Australian way of life and its English-based culture, language, education, clothes, and values. Aboriginal children were snatched from their families and placed in English foster homes as a way to extinguish cultural practices, knowledge, behavior, and values considered counteractive to Australian citizenship. The UNESCO declarations stipulate that cultural and linguistic minorities within a country have the right to use and learn in their own language, be taught by teachers proficient in their language, and be involved in educational systems for their children, including determining policies, curricula, and programs and being involved in the development, management, implementation, and monitoring of these programs (UNESCO, 2006). Additionally, the 1993 UN Standard Rules state that Sign Language should be considered in the education of deaf children, families, and communities. The 1994 UNESCO/Salamanca declaration includes the right to Sign Language in education.

HUMAN RIGHTS TO CULTURAL DIVERSITY: 2001

The preamble to the UNESCO Constitution affirms "that the wide diffusion of culture and the education of humanity for justice and liberty and peace are indispensable to the dignity of man and constitute a sacred duty which all the nations must fulfill...." Cultural rights are an integral part of human rights, which are universal, indivisible, and interdependent; they represent the common heritage of mankind and are, in fact, a source of exchange, innovation, and creativity. For the inclusion and participation of all citizens as a part of a civil society and peace, policy expression must include cultural pluralism and support the reality of cultural diversity as essential for humankind (UNESCO, 2001).

HUMAN RIGHTS FOR PERSONS WITH DISABILITIES: 2006

In 2006 the United Nations enacted the Convention on the Rights of Persons with Disabilities (CRPD) to promote, protect, and ensure full access and equal human rights on local, national, and international levels. CRPD explicitly states the right to Sign Language, educational quality and teachers who are proficient in sign language, professional interpreters, and technology, as well as to acquire linguistic identity, Deaf culture, and Sign Language. CRPD includes provisions for self-representation, self-determination, and full access to all arenas of life, including, but not limited to, community, education, recreation, and marketplace. CRPD is a manifestation of the mantra "Nothing About Us, Without Us." CRPD, ratified by a majority of the UN member nations and endorsed by President Obama in 2009, is still awaiting ratification by the U.S. Congress (UN, 2006).

INTERNATIONAL CONGRESS ON EDUCATION OF THE DEAF: 2010

During the 2010 ICED Congress in Vancouver, Canada, a historic milestone was created with the conference vote of support for **The New Era Accord**, which was written and introduced as a resolution to counteract and reverse the ominous 1880 ICED resolution banning sign language. The New Era Accord apologizes for the wrongful repression of Sign Language and Deaf People since 1880 and professes support for full access to language(s) and communications in the development and education of Deaf children. The full text is available on http://wfdeaf.org/news_ICED.html.

One may ask the question: Are Deaf people part of the disability community or are they members of a cultural minority? There are legal, philosophic, and systemic benefits for both views. Again, as discussed in the section on intersectionality, Deaf people have the right to claim membership to each and consequently the respect, access, protection, and benefits of the laws associated with either and both groups.

GUIDING PRINCIPLES IN CHILD DEVELOPMENT: LITERACY, BILINGUALISM, AND MULTICULTURALISM

The education of Deaf children has been a challenge since time immemorial. Jack O'Connell, California State Superintendent of Public Instruction, in his address, "Closing the Achievement Gap for the Deaf" (2007), emphasized that

> Deaf and hard of hearing children struggle to achieve academically but **not** (emphasis added) because they can't hear. There are Deaf children who do succeed. Children who have access to visual language (ASL) with families do acquire language at the same rate as hearing children and they enter school with age-appropriate language skills (http://www.cde.ca.gov/eo/in/se/agdeaf.asp).

The *Los Angeles* Times has carried several articles about the educational underperformance of children who come from Spanish-speaking homes. The Los Angeles Unified School District is under orders to revise how English learners are taught (*LA Times*, 10/11/11; http://www.latimes.com/news/local/la-me-1012-lausd-feds-20111011,0,4458591.story). African-American families made sure that their children also receive the same attention and support to become more academically ready and have joined forces with other cultural minority families in discussions and lawsuits against the educational system (*LA Times*, 5/31/12; http://www.latimes.com/news/local/la-me-schools-lawsuit-20120531,0,6752589.story).

The U.S. Department of Education (DOE) and the Office of Special Education and Rehabilitation Services have announced that they will intensify their early educational start initiative and funding to ensure that children arrive to school "Kindergarten-Ready" and graduate from high school "College and Career Ready." Moreover, both DOE and OSERS have stated that their focus has shifted to outcomes and accountability, away from counting noses or monitoring these noses. Using the Critical Legal Theories and Deafhood principles, as well as United Nations policy documents related to as human rights for cultural minorities and persons with disabilities, our challenge is to reframe and reform educational practices to make sure that this happens to ensure that educational reform is relevant and owned by the communities from which students, families, and Deaf professionals come. For Deaf babies and toddlers and their families, it is imperative that the system upholds human rights, embraces differences, and endorses best practices for the success of Deaf children toward becoming kindergarten-ready, including acquisition of languages and the multiple literacies of everyday life.

ADVOCACY GOALS FOR SUCCESS FOR ALL

When California Assembly Bill 2072 (2011) was introduced to provide parents of newly identified deaf babies with support from audiologists and four-page brochures of biased information, which mentioned American Sign Language in just two sentences, the ad hoc California

Stakeholders for American Sign Language and English (CAL-SAE) sprang into action to modify or kill the bill. CAL-SAE developed principles and met with legislators to educate them about the needs and rights of deaf babies. These principles were as follow:

- Babies have the human right to both ASL and English as languages.
- The family's first contacts should be educational and language professionals, not audiologists. The child is more than just an ear.
- The Education Department, not the Health Department, should be the lead agency—being Deaf is an educational challenge, not a medical issue.
- The family needs training and support from Deaf professionals, families with Deaf signers, and other professionals in education and community programs with deaf-centric practices.
- Accountability of the State of California is essential for successful programs for families and Deaf babies. Incorporate language benchmarks at 3- to 6-month intervals to ensure that babies are given full access to language(s). Otherwise, the child will be language-deprived. (The system labels a deaf child "language-delayed," implying that the problem originated in the child because s/he is deaf. The term "language-deprived" shifts the origin and onus of the problem onto the audist system.)
- Intervention programs must involve Deaf representatives and Deaf people of color each step of the way—nothing about us without us!

Professional ethics in the medical and educational fields, as well as human rights documents, must inform training, research, and practices and ensure the inclusion of Deaf and marginalized people. Cultural competency is an integral value when serving people with differences. Application of the indigenous terms of reference makes it explicit that community networking and cultural competency are essential to the integrity, credibility, and success of research projects about and programs serving diverse people (Harris et al., 2009). These include understanding and accepting the worth and validity of Deaf people; supporting human rights to self-determination and self-representation; recognizing the diversity, differences, and similarities within the Deaf community; and respecting the value of the community cultural capital. All efforts should be made to increase the number of Deaf professionals in projects and programs related to their community.

VALUE OF MULTICULTURALISM

A multicultural society makes us all better human beings. There are magnificent inventors, academicians, poets, farmers, homemakers, and leaders of all races, ethnicities, cultures, abilities, sexes, and ages. Their contributions enrich communities and lives for everyone. Telephones, invented to help deaf people to hear, are used the world over. Drinking straws were invented for persons with muscular challenges and are now widely used. Curb cuts and ramps are used by everyone—wheelchair users and temporarily able-bodied people skateboarding, biking, pushing strollers, and pulling wagons. Audio books for blind people are popular. Captions on TV are used in places where it is noisy, such as bars and airports. Babies who learn American Sign Language before they can talk get a head start in cognitive skills, communication, and relations with families. Deep-sea divers use ASL underwater. With ASL, people can talk through windows and across large spaces. Videophones were invented so Deaf people can see each other signing. American Sign Language is one of the most used and taught languages in the United States, and ASL proficiency leads to good careers for many people. Can one imagine the world without phones, drinking straws, curb cuts and ramps, audio equipment, captions, ASL, or videophones? These help everyone, not just deaf or disabled people.

Studies and courses in comparative cultures and cross-cultural studies as a requirement for students demonstrate a commitment to a diverse educational framework. Students need a counternarrative to the Eurocentric and audiocentric curricula and standards, sanctioned by educational systems in the United States. Diverse peoples need to be represented in curricula and materials, as well as part of educational systems.

Cross-cultural studies are vital not just for a better America but also for a better YOU in today's global community. Multicultural studies enable you to better understand yourself, your identity, your principles, and your values.

Laurent Clerc, the first teacher of deaf students in the United States, stated in 1817, "God created diversity, not to oppress the minority who are different, but to enrich the lives of all."

REFERENCES

Anzaldúa, G. (1990). *Haciendo Caras/making face, making soul: creative and critical perspectives by women of color*. San Francisco, CA: Aunt Lute Press.

Bahan, B. (2004). Deaf people as visual beings. Paper presented at Deaf Studies Today, Orem, UT.

Bauman, H.D. (2004). Audism: Exploring the metaphysics of oppression. *Journal of Deaf*

Studies and Deaf Education, 9(2), 239–246.

Bauman, D., & Murray, J. (2009). Reframing: From hearing loss to deaf gain. Deaf Studies Digital Journal, 1, Fall 2009 (http://dsdj.gallaudet.edu).

Bell, D. (2009). Who's afraid of critical race theory? In E. Taylor, D. Gillborn, & G. Ladson-Billings (Eds.), *Foundations of critical race theory in education* (pp. 37–50). New York: Routledge.

Cho, S., Crenshaw, K.W., & McCall, L. (2013). Toward a field of intersectionality studies: Theory, applications, and praxis. *Signs, 38*(4).

Clark, K.B., & Clark, M.P. (1947). Racial identification and preference among negro children. In E. L. Hartley (Ed.), *Readings in social psychology*. New York: Holt, Reinhart, and Winston.

Crenshaw, K. (1989). Demarginalizing the intersection of race and sex: A Black feminist critique of antidiscrimination doctrine, feminist theory and antiracist politics. University of Chicago Legal Forum (1989): 139. http://www.answers.com/topic/feminist-legal-theory

Crenshaw, K., Gotanda, N., Peller, G., & Thomas, K. (Eds.)(1995). *Critical race theory: The key writings that formed the movement.* New York: The New Press.

CSUN (2011). *Through your child's eyes: American Sign Language*. http://www.youtube.com/watch?v=FV69iJuXwP4.

Davis, K. (2005). *A Girl Like Me, a film documentary*. http://en.wikipedia.org/wiki/A_Girl_Like_Me_(documentary)#Synopsis

Durr, P. (1999). Deconstructing the forced assimilation of Deaf people via De'VIA resistance and affirmation art. *Visual Anthropology Review, 15*(2).

Eberwein, D. (2010). *Economic colonialism*. PowerPoint presentation in Deafhood class, September 22, 2010.

Eckert, R., & Rowley, A. (2013). Audism: A theory and practice of audiocentric privilege. *Humanity & Society, 37*(2).

Fleischer, F. (2011). The American society's constructed image of deaf people as drawn from discursive constructions of deaf people in major U.S. newspaper articles on cochlear implantation. Gallaudet University, ProQuest, UMI Dissertations Publishing.

Fleischer, F. (2013). Deaf community cultural wealth: Building successful deaf college students in a primarily hearing university. (Adapted from Deaf community cultural wealth: Building successful deaf college students in a primarily hearing university. In W. Garrow, Fleischer, J. Eugster, & D. Love (Eds.), *Stop audism conference*. Northridge, CA: Deaf Studies Department, California State University, Northridge.

Fleischer, L. (2008). Critical pedagogy and ASL videobooks. *Open your eyes: Deaf studies talking*. In D. Bauman (Ed.). Minneapolis, MN: University of Minnesota Press.

Galloway, G. (1973). *The deaf child's right to be himself*. A presentation at the 6th Forum of the Council of Organizations of the Deaf. National Association of the Deaf, *The Deaf American, 25*(9).

Gertz, G. (2003). *Dysconscious audism and critical deaf studies: Deaf Crit's analysis of unconscious internalization of hegemony within the deaf community* (Dissertation, UCLA).

Gertz, G. (2008). Dysconscious audism: A theoretical proposition. In D. Bauman (Ed.), *Open your eyes: Deaf studies talking* (pp. 219–238). Minneapolis, MN: University of Minnesota Press.

Harris, R., Holmes, H., & Mertins, D. (2009). Research ethics in sign language communities. *Sign Language Studies, 9*(2).

Hehir, T. (2006). Eliminating ableism: An interview. *Harvard Education Letter, 22*(1) (http://hepg.org/hel/article/299).

Holcomb, T. (2013). *Introduction to American deaf culture*. New York: Oxford University Press.

Hooks, b. (2000). *Feminist theory: From margin to center* (2/supend/ed.) Cambridge, MA: South End Press.

Hosking, D. (2008). *The theory of critical disability theory*. 4th Biennial Disability Studies Conference, Lancaster University, UK, September 2008 (http://www.lancaster.ac.uk/fass/events/disabilityconference_archive/2008/abstracts/hosking.htm).

Humphries, T. (1977). *Communicating across cultures (Deaf/Hearing) and language learning*. Doctoral dissertation, Union Graduate School, Cincinnati, OH.

Humphries, T., Kushalnagar, P., Mathur, G., Napoli, D., Padden, C., Rathmann, C., & Smith, S. (2012). Language acquisition for deaf children: Reducing the harms of zero tolerance to the use of alternative approaches. Harm Reduction Journal 2012, 9:16 doi:10.1186/1477-7517-9-16http://www.harmreductionjournal.com/content/9/1/16.

King, J. (1991). Dysconscious racism: Ideology, identity & the miseducation of teachers. *Journal of Negro Education, 60*(2), 133–146.

King, J., & Akua, C. (2012). Dysconscious racism and teacher education. In J. Banks (Ed.), Encyclopedia of Diversity in Education. SAGE Publications, Inc.

Kusters, A., & DeMeulder, M. (2013). Understanding Deafhood: In search of its meanings. *American Annals of the Deaf, 158*(5).

Ladd, P. (2003). *Understanding deaf culture: In search of Deafhood*. Cleavedon: Multilingual Matters.

Ladd, P. (2005). Deafhood: A concept stressing possibilities, not deficits. *Scandinavian Journal of Public Health, 33*(Suppl. 66)(http://sjp.sagepub.com/content/33/66_suppl/12.full.pdf+html).

Ladd, P., & Lane, H. (2013). Deaf ethnicity, deafhood, and their relationship. *Sign Language Studies, 13*(4).

Lane, H. (1984). *When the mind hears: A history of the deaf.* New York: Random House.

Lane, H. (1993a). *The mask of benevolence: Disabling the deaf community*. New York: Random House.

Lane, H. (1993b). Constructions of deafness. In M. Garretso (Ed.), *Deafness 1993–2013: A deaf American monograph* (Vol. 43). Silver Spring, MD: National Association of the Deaf.

Lorde, A. (1980). http://www.kickaction.ca/en/node/1499 accessed 11/5/13.

McCaskill, C., Lucas, C., Bayley, B., & Hill, J. (2011). *The hidden treasure of Black ASL: Its history and structure.* Washington, DC: Gallaudet University Press.

Newman, L. (2006). *Sands of time: NAD presidents 1880–2003*. Silver Spring, MD: National Association of the Deaf.

O'Connell, J. (2007). *Closing the achievement gap for the deaf* (http://www.cde.ca.gov/eo/in/se/agdeaf.asp)

Padden, C., & Humphries, T. (1988). *Deaf in America: Voices from a culture.* Cambridge, MA: Harvard University Press.

Petitto, L. A., Zatorre, R. J., Gauna, K., Nikelski, E. J., Dostie, D., and Evans, A. C. (2000). Speech-like cerebral activity in profoundly deaf people processing signed languages: implications for the neural basis of human language. *Proceedings of the National Academy of Sciences.* 97, 13961–13966.

Rocco, T. (2002). The invisible people: Disability, diversity and issues of power in adult education. Paper presented at the Midwest Research-to-Practice Conference in Adult, Continuing, and Community Education, Northern Illinois University, DeKalb, IL, October 9–11, 2002 (https://scholarworks.iupui.edu/bitstream/handle/1805/414/Rocco%20T%20.pdf?sequence=1, accessed 11/20/13).

Rollock, N., & Gillborn, D. (2011). *Critical race theory (CRT).* British Educational Research Association on line resource. http://www.academia.edu/1201277/Critical_Race_Theory_CRT_#

Available online at http://www.bera.ac.uk/files/2011/10/Critical-Race-Theory.pdf; accessed 11/5/13).

Rosen, R. (1983). *Hearing and deaf, each may be viewed differently... NAD Broadcaster, 5*(9), 19.

Rosen, R. (2012). *Isms and you.* Cerritos Commencement Presentation 2012 (http://www.youtube.com/watch?v=tfhwwoTMUAA).

Ruiz, E., & Holcomb, T. (2013). Why intersectionality matters. *NADmag, 13*(2).

Scott, J. (2003). Deconstructing equality versus difference. In C.R. McCann & S.K.Kim (Eds.), *Feminist theory reader: Local and global perspectives* (pp. 378–390). New York: Routledge. (Reprinted from *Feminist Studies, 14*(1), Spring 1988.)

Smith, K., & Bienvenu, M.J. (2007). Deaf theory: What can we learn from feminist theory? *Multicultural Education, 15*(1).

Solomon, A. (2012). *Far from the tree: Parents, children and the search for identity.* New York: Schribner.

Solórzano, D. (1997). Images and words that wound: Critical race theory, racial stereotyping and teacher education. *Teacher Education Quarterly, 24,* 5–19.

Tate, W.F. (1997). Critical race theory and education: History, theory and implications. *Review of Research in Education, 22*(1).

Tucker, B. (1998). Deaf culture, cochlear implants and elective disability. *Hastings Center Report, 28*(4).

Yosso, T. (2005). Whose culture has capital? A critical race theory discussion of community cultural wealth. *Race Ethnicity and Education, 8*(1), 69–91.

RESOURCE

Legal dictionary. http://legal-dictionary.thefreedfictionary.com/critical+legal+studies (accessed 11/5/13).

UNITED NATIONS AND UNESCO LINKS

Education Rights of National Minorities/Hague 1996
http://www.unesco.org/most/ln2pol6.htm

Universal Declaration on Linguistic Rights/Barcelona 1996
http://www.unesco.org/cpp/uk/declarations/linguistic.pdf

UNESCO Universal Declaration on Cultural Diversity 2001
http://www.minorityrights.org/759/international-instruments/unesco-universal-declaration-on-cultural-diversity.html

Convention on Human Rights for Persons with Disabilities (CRPD) 2006
http://www.un.org/disabilities/

Section II:

Reactions

CHAPTER 4

Understanding Asian Deaf Culture: A Multicultural Perspective

LILLY CHENG, Ph.D.
Professor, San Diego State University

SUMALAI MAROONROGE, Ph.D., CCC-A
Associate Professor, Texas A&M International University

INTRODUCTION

Our world is becoming increasingly globalized. Globalization is defined as the ability of an individual to have competence on global issues and to be aware that what we do in our everyday lives is inextricably intertwined with what goes beyond the borders of our country. There is a need to reshape the role of education with the new perspective of globalization. In order to meet the needs of our students with diverse backgrounds, including Deaf students, we must interconnect languages and cultures of the students we serve. The strategies for the 21st century are to produce Deaf educators who appreciate multiculturalism, in addition to having knowledge/skills in specific subjects/topics we teach. This chapter discusses the history, language, and cultures of the Asian Pacific Islander Americans. The focus of this chapter is mainly on Southeast and East Asia. We will examine issues related to immigration backgrounds, language, religious beliefs, and social values. In addition, we will be examining Deaf cultures through the lens of various Asian populations. The purpose of this chapter is to help educators understand the cultures and languages that Asian Pacific populations bring to the United States so that they have the global understanding and competence to work with Asian Pacific American Deaf students in the school system.

HISTORY OF ASIAN PACIFIC IMMIGRATION

Asian Pacific people have been immigrating to the United States for over two centuries. In many respects, the motivation for any Asian Pacific immigrant to the United States is to seek better economic opportunity and a chance to provide a better future for their children.

In 1960, Asian Pacific born immigrants accounted for just 5% of the foreign-born populations in the United States. Since the establishment of the U.S. Immigration and Nationality Act in 1965, the share of Asian Pacific immigrants increased to nearly 28% in 2009. The top three countries of origin of Asian Pacific immigrants are China, the Philippines, and India, as illustrated in Figure 1. California, New York, and Texas are home to nearly half of all Asian Pacific immigrants in this country. More than three-quarters of Hawaii's immigrants are from Asia.

The Pew Research Center conducted a survey of Asian Pacific American adults in 2012. There were 3511 Asian Pacific Islanders who participated in the study. This survey was based on telephone interviews with Asian Pacific Islander adults ages 18 and older living in the United States. The survey was conducted in all 50 states and was designed to include representative subsamples of the six largest Asian Pacific groups in the U.S. population: Chinese, Filipino, Indian, Japanese, Korean, and Vietnamese and other Asian subgroups. The results of the survey are shown in Figure 1. The largest U.S. Asian Pacific group was Chinese, followed by Filipino and then Indian.

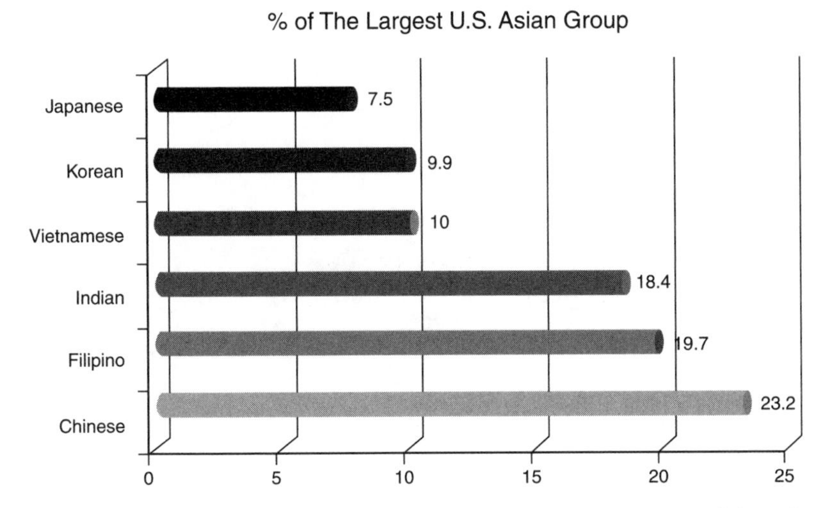

Figure 1. Six largest U.S. Asian groups. From http://www.pewsocialtrends.org/2012/06/19/the-rise-of-asian-americans/ (Hoeffel, 2012).

In most recent years, as a group, foreign-born Asian Pacific-Americans are more likely to have postsecondary education, superior English language proficiency, and higher-level occupations than the overall immigrant population. However, a closer examination of the Asian Pacific immigrant population reveals a great deal of variation by country of birth.

Asian Pacific immigrants brought with them their languages, cultures, customs, and social institutions. Over time they have made lasting contributions to their adopted country and have become an integral part of the U.S. population. The map in Figure 2 illustrates distribution of the Asian Pacific immigrant population in the United States. Stars indicate states with the most Asian Pacific immigrants, and numbers indicate the ranking of Asian populations among different states. The information is cited from the Migration Policy Institute's website. The map provides states with the largest and fastest-growing immigrant populations. The information was obtained from 1990 and 2000 Decennial Censuses and from 2010 and 2011 American Community Survey data. While the total immigrant population of the United States increased by 9.3 million between 2000 and 2011, the

Figure 2. Distribution of the Asian Pacific immigrant population in the United States.

impact of this growth varied considerably from state to state in terms of population size and characteristics.

As new opportunities to immigrate became available, the foreign-born Asian Pacific-American population, which numbered only 2.2 million (1980), grew by 2.3 million to 2.9 million (1990). From 2000 to 2010, the Asian Pacific-American immigrant population increased by an additional 2.8 million. The Asian Pacific-American immigrant population has grown rapidly over the past decade and has surpassed the number of newly arrived Hispanic immigrants since at least 2009 (Figure 3).

A century ago, most Asian Pacific-Americans were low-skilled, low-wage laborers crowded into ethnic enclaves and targets of official discrimination. Today they are the most likely of any major racial or ethnic group in America to live in mixed neighborhoods and to marry across racial lines.

Chinese were among the first group of Asian Pacific immigrants who entered the United States. Thousands of young Chinese males left their homes to work for the railroad companies and many agricultural farms during 1849–1882. Most Chinese immigrants during 1882–1965 were diplomats, merchants, and students. From 1965 to the present, Chinese immigration consisted of mixed groups of

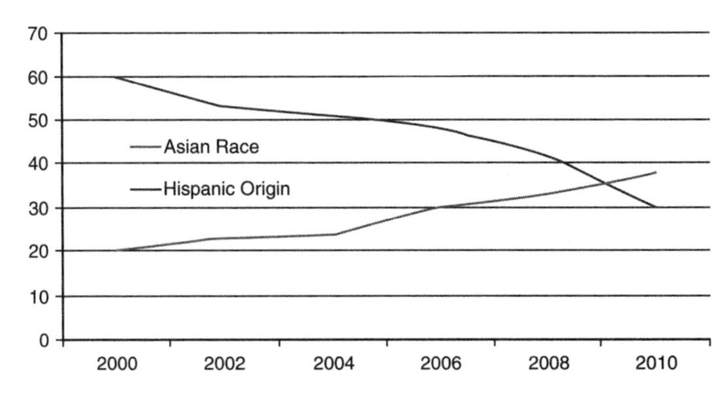

Figure 3. Percentage of immigrants by year of arrival from 2000 to 2010. Data from the PEW Research Center: Data show Asians surpass Hispanics in 2009. From http://www.pewsocialtrends.org/2012/06/19/the-rise-of-asian-americans/.

people from the highly select and well-educated class, as well as people who entered the United States to escape either political instability or repression of East and Southeast Asia. A large number of Japanese farmers arrived from 1891 to 1907. Most of these people immigrated to Hawaii. Filipinos and Koreans were the next wave of immigrants to the U.S. mainland in the 1950s (Cheng, 2000).

Japanese people began emigrating to the United States in significant numbers following political, cultural, and social changes. The main immigration was to Hawaii. Japanese immigrants were increasingly sought by industrialists to replace the Chinese. Japanese Americans have made significant contributions to agriculture in California and Hawaii. They introduced sophisticated irrigation methods that enabled the cultivation of fruits, vegeTables, and flowers on previously marginal farm lands (Niiya, 2001).

Korean emigration to the United States can be divided into three major groups. The first wave consisted of men, who contracted to work in Hawaii's sugar cane plantations during 1903–1905. The second group was made up of women who married American soldiers and children adopted into American families from 1950 to 1989. The third group was of Koreans who came under the occupational and family reunification preferences of the 1965 Immigration Act (Charr, 1996).

Although most of the early Filipinos came as laborers, there was a striking difference among the Filipino immigrants and other Asians. Most of the Chinese and Japanese immigrants stayed as a cohesive group and settled in specific areas, whereas the Filipinos were transients. They moved from city to city and from farm to farm. The Filipinos never settled into specific areas because they considered their immigration to the United States as only temporary; they saw no need to transplant their culture or build communities (Cruz, 2013).

Prior to 1975, there were very few Southeast Asian people in the United States. Due to the civil wars in Vietnam, Laos, and Cambodia, there was an influx of refugees from Southeast Asia. Many of these refugees were secondary migrants that were relocated from Thailand, the Philippines, and other countries. These refugees were sponsored by church groups or the U.S. government, and they initially lived near their host family or lived temporarily in refugee camps. Most refugees were under the care of their hosts until they were able to be independent. Many of them took advantage of the government-supported programs to attend schools or job training; then they moved on to find jobs and were able to support themselves. They had a great work ethic and were committed to making better lives for themselves and their children. At the beginning, life was hard in the United States, as many of them had very little English language skills but they were persistent, putting their focus on education. Most of them preferred to settle in California and Texas, as the weather is similar to their home countries. In addition, they formed small communities of their own. They kept their own cultures, religious beliefs, and language (Cheng, 2000).

In the beginning, most Southeast Asian refugees never dreamed of leaving their home countries. The view of their lives in the United States was one of uncertainty and loneliness. Many immigrants were separated from their families due to the war. There were three separate incidences of refugees migrating from Southeast Asia. The first group was primarily Vietnamese who came just after the Fall of Vietnam in 1975. Most people from this group belonged to the bureaucratic armed forces of the defeated government. This group of immigrants was more educated and possessed professional skills. They had higher social status with more financial resources. The second group was the "boat people" that arrived after 1975 to 1978. This group mostly escaped from war and communism. The third group was mostly family members and relatives of the first two groups who had permission from the U.S. government to enter the country. These three groups of refugees from Southeast Asia came to the United States with diverse backgrounds, experiences, and social status. From 1975 to 1990, over a million Southeast Asian refugees settled in the United States, about half of them under 18 years of age (Chuong, 1994). These Asian Americans came to the United States with dreams and hopes to excel in this new country. They were well aware that freedom came with a price tag.

There was great diversity among the Southeast Asian population. Each group had a diverse mixture of customs, education, beliefs, and values (Rumbaut, 1988). The Vietnamese, Chinese, and Hmong have similar cultural traits, including sharing extended family systems. The systems were built on the Confucian cultural model that emphasizes family relationships, duties and discipline, parental authority, and respect for the elderly. The Lao and Cambodians were more similar to the East Indian cultures in terms of religion and language. The Indian languages such as Sanskrit and Pali have influenced the Lao and Cambodian languages. Theravade Buddhism is a shared religion among Southeast Asia, although there were some Chinese influences, to a much lesser degree. Various factors must be considered when working with individuals from Asian/Pacific populations. Despite the many similarities among Asian cultures, individuals from Asian countries cannot be lumped together as one homogeneous group (Cheng, 2000). Figure 4 illustrates a world map of Asia. Table 1 shows the various regions of Asia and the associated countries

ISSUES RELATED TO IMMIGRATION

Despite the number of years that Asian Pacific groups have lived in the United States, it was not until the recent influx of immigrants and refugees that the special needs of Asian/Pacific students have surfaced. Approximately 40% of immigrants to the United States in 1990 were from Pacific Asian regions. The number of English Language

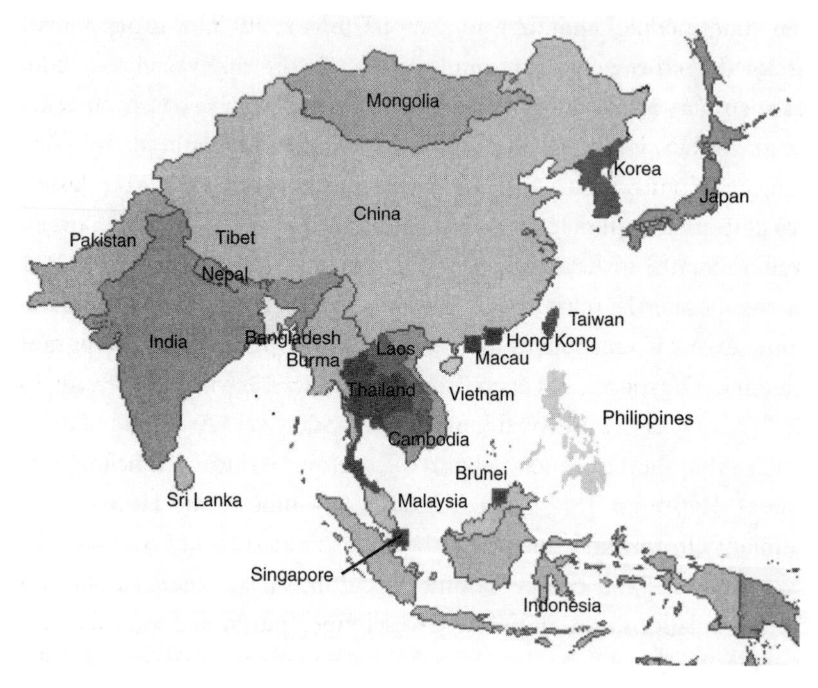

Figure 4. World map of Asia. From http://www.wpmap.org/category/asia-maps/.

Table 1. Various Regions of Asia and Associated Countries

Regions	Countries
East Asia	*China, Taiwan, Hong Kong, Macau, Japan, Korea*
South Asia	*India, Bangladesh, Pakistan, Sri Lanka*
Southeast Asia	*Myanmar, Vietnam, Thailand, Laos, Cambodia, Indonesia, Philippines, Malaysia, Singapore.*
The Pacific Islands	Hawaii, Guam, American Samoa, Tonga, Fiji, and other Micronesia Islands

*Australia and New Zwaland are among the Pacific nations
From http://unstats.un.org/unsd/methods/m49/m49regin.htm (United Nations, 2013).

Learning (ELL) students showed a steady increase. In addition to Spanish, the top languages spoken at home were Vietnamese, Hmong, Chinese, Pilipino, and Cambodian (Context, 1999). The Asian American school-age population increased more than sixfold by 1990, and 40% of the Asian Pacific-American children were first generation. The significant growth in the Asian/Pacific population in the United States went from less than 1% in 1970 to 4% in 2000. There is an expected projected growth of 400% in the next 30 years for the Asian/Pacific population (Rueda, 1993). According to the Pew Research Center (Brown, 2014), the Asian population had the fastest growing rate in the United States during the 2001 to 2013 period. It reached 19.4 million with 74% of them being immigrants. From 2001 through 2011, the number of Asian/Pacific Islander students increased from 2.5 to 2.9 million in the public school settings. Parents of immigrant students who spoke a language other than English at home are likely to be ELL. These children will need language assistance.

English Language Learning refers to any person age 5 and older who self-reported speaking English "not at all" or "not well." In 2009–2010, around 52% of foreign-born persons age 5 and older were ELL. In 2009, 80% of the entire U.S. population age 5 and older said they spoke only English at home. The remaining 20% reported speaking a variety of foreign languages. Spanish accounts for 62%, non-Asian language is 24%, and Asian language is 14% with Chinese as the leading language. Professionals in the field of education and in related fields have to provide appropriate services for these populations, and we need to prepare to deal with the cultural, social, and linguistic diversity the Asian populations present (Sue, 1986).

In a study of language skills, monolingual vs. multilingual children were evaluated with the Rossetti Infant–Toddler Language Scale (Rojas & Maroonroge, 2013).The assessment measures the language of children in six areas, including pragmatics, gesture, play, language comprehension, and language expression. The test was administered to 153 children in California. Results of this study showed a difference in the performance of children coming from language backgrounds other than a monolingual English-speaking family, as illustrated in Figure 5. The study concluded that children from Spanish and other language backgrounds were more likely to be referred for speech-language therapy. Results of this study were consistent with the American Speech Language and Hearing Association findings on language skills of children from a non-English-speaking family.

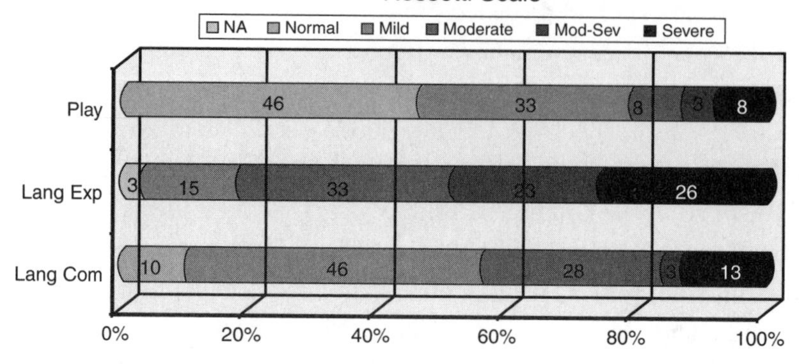

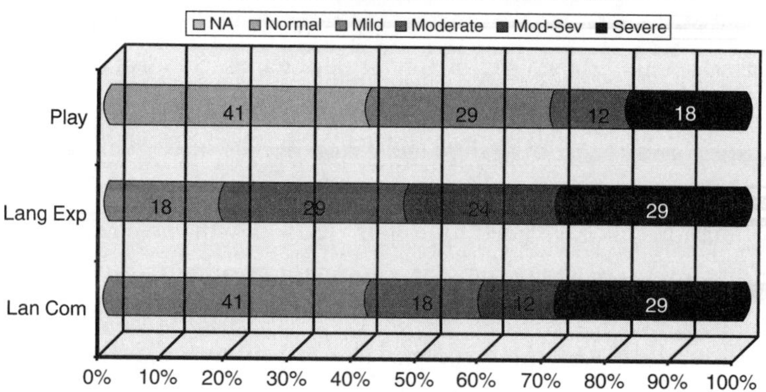

Figure 5. Comparison of play, language expression, and comprehension scores based on the Rossetti Test in children with monolingual vs. multiple languages background.

LANGUAGE BACKGROUND

There are hundreds of distinct languages and countless dialects spoken in Asia. They can be classified into five major language families, as illustrated in Table 2.

Many of the languages of Southeast Asia are tonal languages. These languages use pitch to signal a difference in meaning between words. These pitch variations are an important part of the language, just as stress

Table 2. Major Language Families within Asia

Language family	Language
Malayo-Polynesian/ Austronesian	Indonesian, Malay, Fijian and Hawaiian and Philippine
Sino-Tibetan	Sinois Mandarin and other Chinese dialects and **Tibeto-Burman Branch** are spoken in Burma Thailand and Laos Southern China, Tibet Bhutan Nepal and eastern India
Austro-Asiantic	Vietnamese, Khmer, Hmong, India and Bangladesh,
Papuan	New Guinea
Altaic	Turkey, Mongolia, Korea and Japan

From http://webspace.ship.edu/cgboer/languagefamilies.html (Boeree, 2003).

and proper word order are in the English language. In these languages, word meanings or grammatical categories such as tense are dependent on pitch level. Just as the movement of an eyebrow in American Sign Language can affect the meaning of a sign, tonal variation affects the meaning of a spoken word in languages such as Mandarin.

Asian languages differ from one another in many different aspects—they are tonal, monosyllabic, and logographic (a property of some writing systems). In Mandarin, for example, one spoken word may have four different meanings depending on the tone. When pronounced, the first tone is high level, the second is rising, the third is fall rising, and the fourth is falling (Cheng, 2000). People learning the language must gain a mastery of the tones both receptively and expressively in order to communicate effectively (Cheng, 1991). Tone perception and expression present many challenges for Deaf people. Each tone signifies a different meaning. This is illustrated in Figure 6.

One interesting study conducted by Crinion and colleagues (2009) investigated neurological differences of tonal language speakers. The study used magnetic resonance imaging to document regional structural differences in the brains of native speakers of tonal language (Chinese) and nontonal (European) languages. The subjects consisted of 31 native Chinese speakers, 7 native English speakers who had learned Chinese in adulthood, and 21 European multilingual speakers who did not speak Chinese. Results indicated that the right anterior temporal lobe and the left insula of the tonal language speakers had

Syllable	Tone	Meaning
/ba/	First tone	eight
	Second tone	To pull
	Third tone	Handle
	Fourth tone	Father

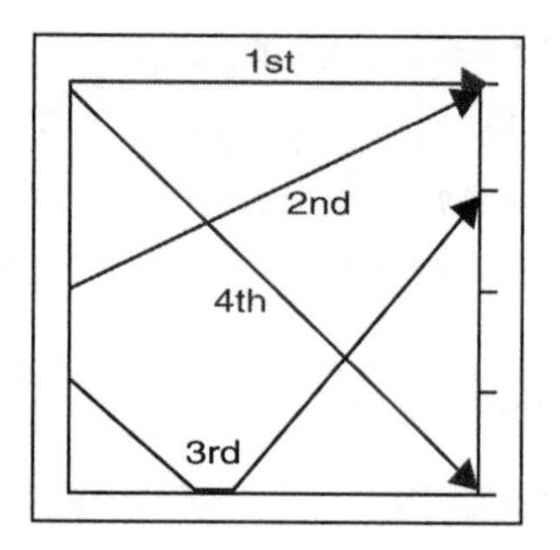

Figure 6. Variations in meaning due to variations of pitch in a tonal language.

significantly greater density in the gray and white matter compared with those who did not speak Chinese. Results suggested a neural connection between the pitch of words and their meanings (Crinion, Green, Chung, & Ali, 2009).

The Chinese language is not based on an alphabet—Chinese characters are ideographs. The Japanese written language uses a combination of Kanji (Chinese characters) and Katakana (foreign words)(Cheng, 1991). The Korean language uses an alphabet, consisting of 14 consonants and 10 basic vowels. It is a language spoken in both North and South Korea. The Khmer and Lao writing systems are based on the Indian languages of Sanskrit and Pali. Hmong and Vietnamese are alphabetical systems.

The main Asian/Pacific languages spoken in the United States are Mandarin, Cantonese, Taiwanese, Tagalog, Lao, Khmer, Hmong, Vietnamese, Hindi, and Urdu. It is essential for educators to have some background concerning these languages so that they will be able to understand why certain linguistic constructs are present or absent in students' linguistic repertoires.

RELIGIOUS BELIEFS AND PHILOSOPHY

Religion can be explained as a set of beliefs concerning the purpose of the universe and involving devotional and ritual observances. Religion consists of a moral code governing the conduct of human affairs. Major religious beliefs exist among the Asian Pacific populations.

Many of these eastern religions are becoming more and more part of the mainstream in the United States. Religion is an integral part of every Asian culture. It can impact view of life, child-rearing practices, human relations, and attitudes toward disabilities.

Hinduism

Hinduism is the predominant religion of India. Hinduism is considered the world's third largest religion after Christianity and Islam. It is also the world's oldest religion. Hinduism is a collection of distinct intellectual or philosophical points of view that embrace many traditions instead of a rigid common set of beliefs. Unlike most other religions, Hinduism has no single founder and no single scripture.

Buddhism

Buddhism remains the dominant religion of the Far East. It is an offshoot of Hinduism that began around the 5th century. Buddhism goes beyond religion and is more a philosophy of life. Buddhism focuses on personal, spiritual development and achievement of the true nature of life.

Confucianism

Confucianism is a social and ethical philosophy rather than a religion. Confucianism is built on an ancient religious foundation to establish the social values, institutions, and transcendent ideals of traditional Chinese society. It was started originally by Confucius, who was both a teacher and a philosopher in China 551-479 BCE. He taught the way of achieving an inner peace based on relationships between nature and society. Confucianism exerts a strong influence in China, Japan, Korea, and Vietnam.

Taoism

Taoism refers to a variety of ancient traditions, philosophy, and religious beliefs that are deeply rooted in Chinese culture. Taoism emphasizes compassion, moderation, and humility. Taoist practices include meditation, feng shui, and fortune telling. Taoism promotes achieving harmony with nature, pursuit of spiritual immortality, self-development, and virtuosity.

Shintoism

Shintoism is the earliest and the only native religion of Japan. Shintoism emphasizes worshipping nature, ancestors, and ancient heroes. Shintoism does not have a founder nor does it have sacred scriptures. Shintoism is a very local belief in which devotees are likely to be concerned with their local shrine. Many Japanese people will have a tiny shrine–altar in their homes to pray, as well.

Animism

In addition to the aforementioned philosophies and religions, many Asians practice "Animism," which is a common religion in Southeast Asia. Animism is a belief in spiritual beings concerned with human affairs and capable of helping or harming human interests. This religion believes that all things in nature (e.g., trees, mountains, and the sky) have souls, demons, and spirits. The head is where the chief spirit resides; touching one's head will bring bad luck to the person. People also practice "Baci," which is a common ritual in Animism. Baci is usually performed on many special occasions such as illness or death. Such practice is often regarded as a means of healing or getting rid of evil spirits. Individuals may seek advice from a priest or faith healer when family members are stricken with birth defects or illness. Ashes from burned incense, combined with herbal medicine, are used for medicinal purposes. Baci might be practiced to treat hearing loss.

Christianity

Christianity in Southeast Asia began in colonial times and continued to expand. With the exception of the Philippines where Christianity is strong, Christianity has been a minor religion in much of Southeast Asia. Christianity has had a significant impact on education and society. There was a rapid expansion of Christianity in Asia after the 1980s. Singapore, China, Hong Kong, Taiwan, Indonesia, and

Table 3. Christianity in Asia

Country of region	% of Christians based on population
Philippines	91
S. Korea	29
Vietnam	8
Myanmar, China, Taiwan	4
Japan, India	2
Thailand, Cambodia	<1

Malaysia are said to have the fastest-growing Christian communities, and the majority of new believers are upwardly mobile, urban, middle-class individuals. Asia has the second largest Pentecostal-charismatic Christian movement of any continent, with the number growing from 10 to 135 million between 1970 and 2000 (Konig & Dahles, 2009; Uhalley & Wu, 2001) (Table 3).

Cultures and Family

Asian Pacific-Americans constitute a number of national, cultural, and religious heritages, including multiple distinct subgroups, each with unique language, religion, customs, and values. Similarities exist among these cultures, but those working with Asian Pacific-Americans need to remember their different origins, ecological adaptations, history, immigration, and refugee history.

There is a hierarchical family structure in the Asian family in which males and older individuals occupy a higher status than females. Males are valued more than females because males carry on the family name. The role of the male is to provide for the family with the primary duty as good son, husband, and father. Males are authoritative and distant, display less emotion, and provide for the economic and physical needs of the family.

In general, the role of the female is to be passive and to adhere to her husband's family, be subservient to the male, perform domestic chores, and bear children. Females are more responsible for the children and serve as an intermediary between the father and the child. By tradition, Asian women were often perceived as subordinate to men and weaker or inferior. The lower expectations for women often result in lower aspirations and self-esteem. The traditional gender concepts are maintained through the socialization practice of parents and the educational system. Although many women have achieved higher education and status, the gender gap is still very strong.

Respect for ancestors and elderly is vital. There is a one-way communication system in which adults speak to children. There is collectivism in which people focus on family and children learn early in life that family is the central primary unit. The behavior of individual members is a reflection on the entire family. For discipline, shame and guilt are used to control and train children to have loyalty and honor to the family. Children must do their best to avoid shame and embarrassment to the family. Most family problems are hidden from the public and are handled within the family. Outstanding achievement will be a source of great pride for the child and the entire family.

Although many Asian Pacific-American families have lower income levels and parents with little education, current research found that Asian Pacific-Americans had a higher grade point average than White and Black Americans (Figure 7). All of the high achievement for Asian Pacific children can be attributed to higher levels of parental control and parental emphasis on achievement. The Asian

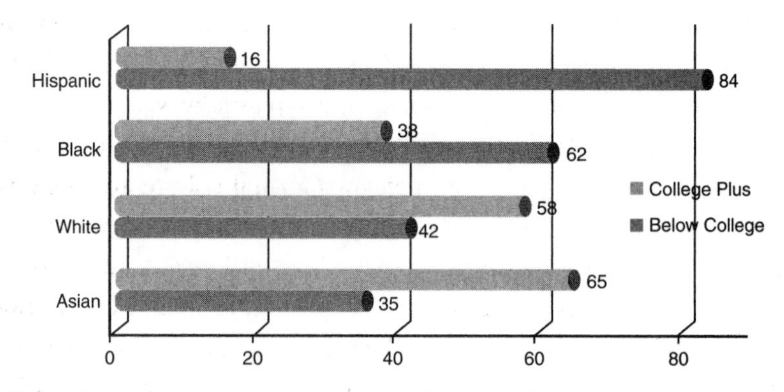

Figure 7. Education characteristics of recent immigrants by race and ethnicity. From PEW Research Center Analysis of 2010 American Community Survey.

family is more structured and focused on formal education. They believe education is important for their children's overall future success. While Asian Americans make up only 4% of the U.S. population, Asian Pacific-American students make up a much higher percentage of students in top universities around the country. The percentages are astounding: 24% at Stanford, 18% at Harvard, and 25% at both Columbia and Cornell (Abboud & Kim, 2013).

Asians are more likely to be married and to live in a multigenerational household. They are less likely to be born to an unwed mother. Among Asian Pacific Islanders, Japanese and Filipino are the most accepting of interracial and intergroup marriages. Fifty-five percent of Japanese newlyweds married non-Asians in 2008–2010 and 37% of all Asian-American women married non-Asian men (Hoeffel, 2012).

The Asian family characteristics just described are typical in most Asian families. Many other factors can alter the stereotypical characteristics, such as ethnicity and length of time in the United States. The assumption that all Asians are successful may not be true and not apply to all Asians. Not all Asians are superior students who have no problems. Some Asian students lack motivation, have learning problems, have limited English proficiency, and lack financial resources. Many parents do not understand the U.S. culture, which often leads to conflict within the family.

Different degrees of acculturation are seen in the Asian immigrants and refugees. The older population seemed to have difficulty accepting the new culture; the younger group usually was able to integrate some aspects of the new cultures into their own cultures; while the youngest group, giving up their own formal culture and identity, totally assimilated into the new culture. There are problems associated with Asian Americans living in the United States. Many of them experience conflicts between the two cultures. Children acculturate more rapidly than their parents. Conflicts may arise between parents and children if the older family members maintain traditional Asian cultural practices. When children acquire American values, they tend to perceive things in a different way.

CULTURAL BELIEFS ABOUT DISABILITIES IN GENERAL

Most Asian cultures believe that disabilities are conditions, congenital or acquired, such as blindness, cleft palate, and paralysis of the body systems. It has been a common belief to view conditions such as sensory impairment as stigmatic in some Asian cultures. Stigmas are created, in part, by the traditional attributions that link specific conditions to a punishment of sins or the possession of an evil spirit (Wathum-Ocama & Rose, 2002). In a traditional Asian family, deafness is considered to be a disability. Most Asian people choose a combination of Western and folk or herbal medicine to treat so-called disabilities. Some Asian people believe that a disability or deformity is fate; therefore, nothing can be done to treat it, so they do not seek intervention. They believe that disabilities arise from a variety of spiritual factors such as an imbalance of inner forces, bad feng shui, or the will of gods, demons, or spirits. Generally, in Asian cultures, people view a disability as the result of wrong doing by the individual's ancestors. Belief in reincarnation may lead individuals to accept physical disabilities. Some cultures view a disability as a gift from God to protect and shelter the family. Other cultures view a disability as a curse, and the individual may be ostracized from society. Attitudes toward Deaf individuals vary just as Asian cultures vary. Some define Deaf people as mute (lack of ability to learn oral language), whereas others view deafness as a curse. Deafness may be viewed as a personal embarrassment to the parents (Epstein, 1989). Attitudes are formed and influenced by religions and philosophies, including Buddhism, Confucianism, Catholicism, and Islam. For example, the mother of a Deaf child may view this as a family disgrace associated with shame and guilt (Wilson, 1996). In addition, deafness can significantly influence the ability to communicate and participate in social activities within a hearing family. This can lead to multiple negative effects influencing perception. It is only within the last 10 years that the perception and attitude toward deafness changed as the results of early intervention, medical advancement, and hearing technology. Various research studies started to find improvement in parents' attitude toward their Deaf children due to their increase in education level and professional support (Wallhagen, 2010).

Table 4. Estimate of Deaf Population and Schools for Deaf Students

Country	Total Pop (Estimate million)	Deaf (Estimate) Population	% of deaf/pop (Estimate)	# of Deaf Schools
Thailand	68,000	300,000	<1	22
Malaysia	29,000	30,000	<1	5
Myanmar	52,000	3,000,000	5	2
Philippine	89,000	3,000,000	3	17
China	1,300,000	21,000,000	2	550
Hong Kong	7,000	224,000	3	4
Japan	128,000	300,000	0	131
Taiwan	23,000	1,303,000	5	3
USA	308,746,000	2,000,000	1	Many
Canada	31,613,000	1,704,551	5	Many

DEAF POPULATION

Approximately 0.1% of the U.S. population is Deaf. According to the World Federation of the Deaf, it is estimated that there are about 70 million Deaf people in the world who use sign language as their first language or mother tongue. There is really no simple way to know the incidence of the Deaf population in Asia. According to *Ethnologue: Languages of the World* (Lewis, 2009), the estimated Deaf population is displayed in Table 4.

Based on available federal data and published research, generally 2 to 4 of every 1000 people in the United States are Deaf. More than half became deaf relatively late in life, and less than 0.01% of people in the United States became deaf before 18 years of age.

UNDERSTANDING ASIAN DEAF CULTURE FROM A MULTICULTURAL MEDICAL PERSPECTIVE

As we increase our awareness of cultural differences, we develop a pluralistic approach toward retaining our original culture and respecting cultural values of other groups. There are limited studies on the topic of how people with different ethnic backgrounds view Deaf culture. In general, people have different concepts about Deaf people.

Table 5. Participants Information and % of Knowing Deaf People

		% of Knowing Deaf People	
	# of subject	Yes	No
Hindu	20	45	55
Taiwanese SLP/Audio	50	72	28
Thai Physician	32	62	38
Thai Hearing Technician	74	88	12
Hispanic 19–34	64	28	72
Hispanic 35–54	40	37	63
Hispanic >55	21	22	78
Total	301		

In order to provide useful information on Deaf culture from a multicultural perspective, we conducted a survey related to the perception of Deaf culture in varous Asian populations. The survey was conducted in 2012 to 2014 in multiple countries in Asia. The purpose of the survey was to determine how speech-language pathologists, audiologists, audiology assistants/technicians, otolaryngologists, and pediatricians in the various Asian populations perceived Deaf culture. These professionals may be key in providing information and support to families who have a Deaf child. In addition, data from the Hispanic study on the effect of age on perception of Deaf cultures are included in this chapter for the purpose of comparison.

The survey consisted of four demographic questions and eight Deaf culture questions as shown in the Appendix at the end of the chapter. The survey was conducted with 20 American-born Hindu, 50 speech pathologists/audiologists and assistants from Taiwan, 74 audiology technicians from Thailand, and 32 pediatricians and otolarynologists. In addition, 125 Hispanics in various age groups participated. Information related to the participants is showed in the Table 5.

Procedures for the Study

Each participant was asked to complete a survey of general demographic information. Selective questions on Deaf culture were used. For each survey statement, the participant used a Likert scale to specify

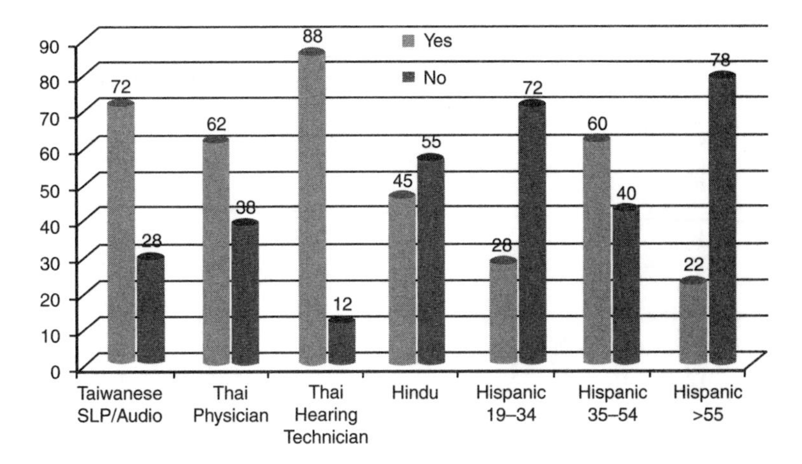

Figure 8. Percentage of participants who know a Deaf person.

the level of agreement or disagreement. Each participant was asked to respond to each survey question based on his/her understanding of Deaf culture. All particiants were adults age 18 and above. Results were analyzed and are displayed in charts.

Survey Question #1: How many participants know a Deaf person?

Results of the study (Figure 8) indicate that for the lay people group (Hindu and Hispanic), there was a less than 45% chance of knowing or being acquainted with a person who is Deaf. Even with the medical and speech language pathologists or audiologists and assistants, the rate was 62 and 72%.The hearing technicians were more likely to know a Deaf person (88%), as many of them provide hearing evaluations and hearing aid services.

Survey Question #2: Due to the limitation in communication skills, Deaf people are not as intelligent as hearing people

Often lay people believe that Deaf people lack intelligence (Figures 9 and 10) because Deaf people may have limited oral language skills. This can be related to multiple factors. Many Deaf individuals experience severe cultural deprivation due to the lack of spoken language skills.

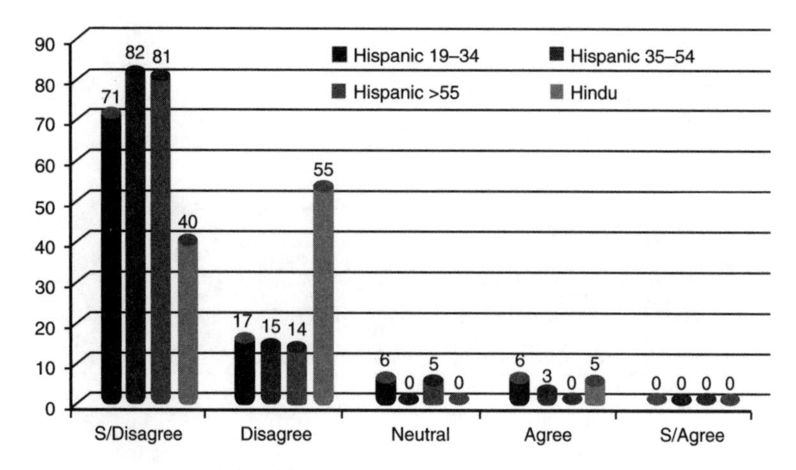

Figure 9. Comparison of American Hindu and Hispanic population on perception of "intelligence" in Deaf people.

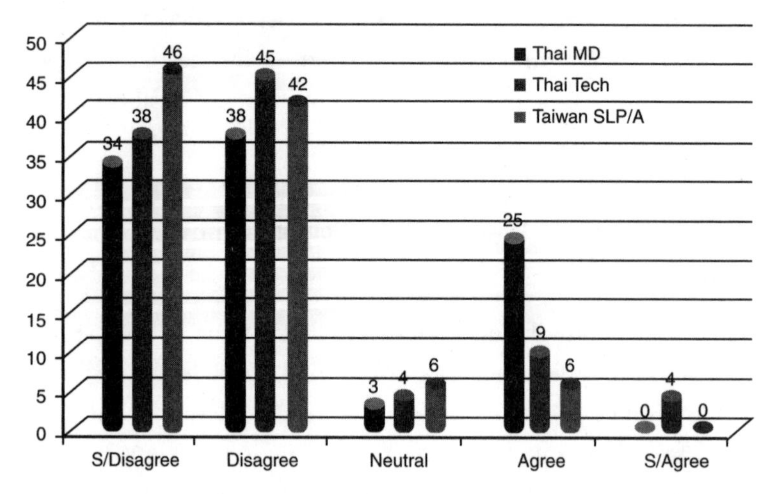

Figure 10. Comparison of medical professions, audiologists/technicians, and speech pathologists on perception of "intelligence" in Deaf people.

Some of the etiologies are also responsible for neurological disorders that result in lower intelligence. Medical conditions such as rubella, meningitis, and premature birth may be responsible for special needs among Deaf children.

Many comparative studies of the intelligence of Deaf and Hearing individuals have been published since the invention of the IQ test in the early 1900s. This kind of intensive research investigates the crucial role of hearing in assessing the development of intelligence in people. The research is important as many lay persons associate being Deaf with lack of normal intelligence. McCay Vernon was the first psychologist who documented that the research associated with Deaf students was biased. Vernon's work has had enormous impact on cognitive research with Deaf students. He examined nonverbal problem-solving abilities in Deaf children. Research that compared the nonverbal IQ of Deaf children without complicating multiple challenges to the nonverbal IQ of Hearing peers found that Deaf individuals function at approximately the same nonverbal IQ level as Hearing peers (Vernon, 2005).

Survey Question #3: Deafness is considered a handicap

Diversity exists in the perception of the condition of deafness as a handicap in both lay people and professional groups (Figures 11 and 12). The issues may be related to the definition of "handicap." The words "handicap," "impairment," and "disability" are negative medical terms that are often used interchangeably. They have very different meanings from a medical/pathological perspective. Handicap is defined as a disadvantage for a given individual that limits or prevents the fulfillment of a role. Impairment is a loss or abnormality of function, and disability is used to define any restriction or

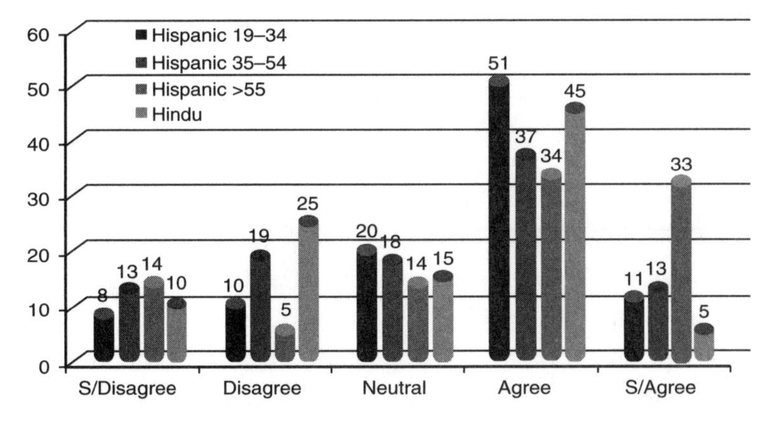

Figure 11. Perception of deafness as a handicap by lay people.

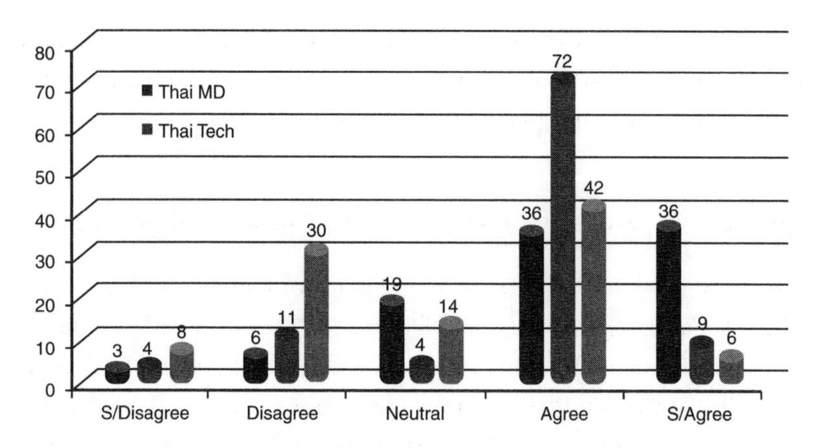

Figure 12. Perception of deafness as a handicap by healthcare professionals.

lack of ability to perform an activity. From a medical/pathological perspective, all of these limitations have been found to be related to quality of life issues (Gopinath, Schneider, McMahon, Teber, & Stephen, 2011).

Many Deaf people do not see themselves as disabled. However, deafness is considered a disability under the Disability Discrimination Act. The Act defines a disabled person as someone who has "a physical or mental impairment which has a substantial and long-term adverse effect on his ability to carry out normal day-to-day activities." Deafness is not a disability with regard to the ability to perform a job or function in a culture. Deaf people can communicate well with sign language, and some can function well with hearing aids or cochlear implants. They see deafness as a challenge but never a handicap. Some Deaf people may claim disability status in order to qualify for legal benefits under the Americans with Disabilities Act and government assistance programs. The majority of Deaf people can function well in hearing environments with the help of modern technology, interpreters, and educational programs.

We must realize that each of us views the world through the lens of our own **ethnocentricity**. Only through education and interaction with people in the Deaf community will we come to know that Deaf people may not be suffering from a pathological condition that needs medical intervention; rather, Deaf people can be proud of membership in the Deaf community. To paraphrase King Jordan, the former president of Gallaudet University, "Deaf people can do anything hearing people can do, except hear."

Survey Question #4: 90% of Deaf people have hearing parents

Asians represent one of the fastest growing cultural groups in the United States. The percentage of the Asian Deaf student population based on a 2013 survey conducted by Gallaudet Research Institute was 4% (Gallaudet, 2013), yet another survey placed the percentage of Asian Deaf adults aged 18 and over at 9.7% (CDC, 2012). Since the term "Asian Deaf" encompasses many distinct groups, such as Chinese, Korean, or Thai, to name a few, it is difficult and perhaps misleading to cite an overall percentage of the incidence of this population in the United States.

More than 90% of Deaf children are born to hearing parents who have no knowledge or experience dealing with the Deaf community (Figures 13 and 14). The birth of a Deaf child in an Asian family changes their world. Parents often experience guilt, confusion, helplessness, and depression in the initial stage, and then they may slip easily into the blame game before they seek help. Parent–child

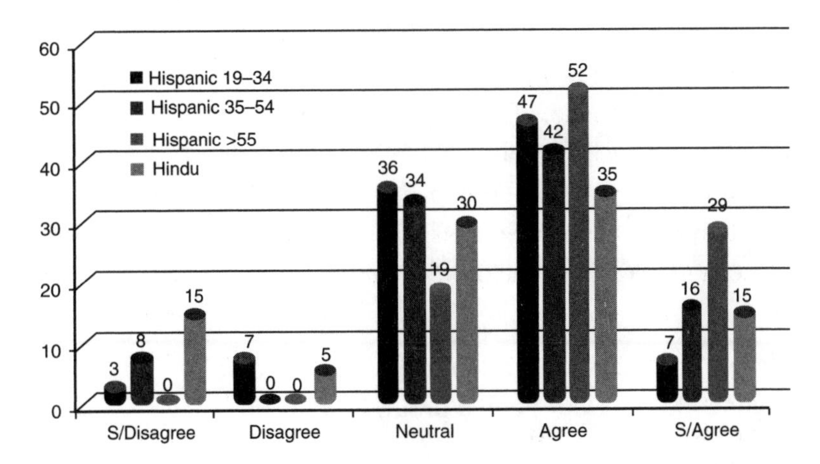

Figure 13. Perception that Deaf people have hearing parents by lay persons. Most lay people perceive 90% of deaf people have hearing parents, with less than 36% selecting neutral perception.

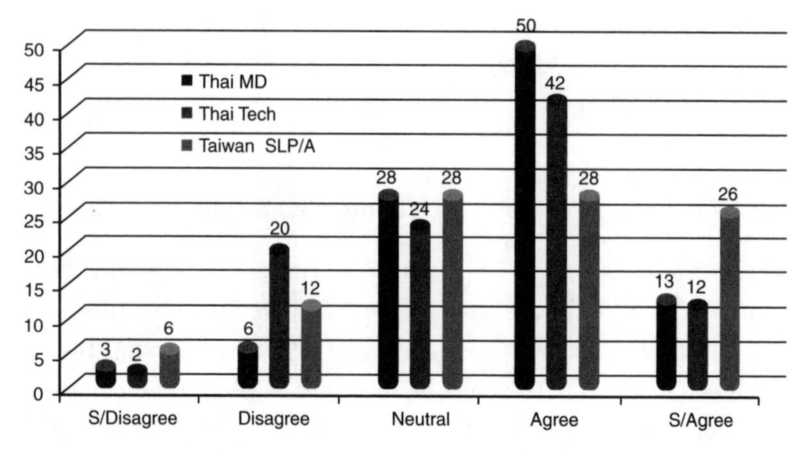

Figure 14. Perception that Deaf people have hearing parents by professional groups.

communication plays a central role in social growth, as it does in other domains of development. Hearing parents who frequently do not have a fully effective means of communicating with their Deaf child experience difficulty. These parents often view their Deaf child with uncertainty. They do not know what to anticipate in terms of goals and expectations for their child's future. They are also uncertain about their own roles on how to be effective parents with the Deaf child.

Despite the growing awareness of the overall Deaf community, there is a lack of awareness of Deaf culture and what specifically constitutes Deaf culture. Chinese people seem to view Deaf people as disabled. Parents spend money on various types of medicines to "cure" their child's deafness. Acupuncture and Chinese medicine are chosen as the main treatment. Chinese people favor spoken language over sign language. Many parents believe that sign language inhibits their child's ability to speak. (King, 2006).

Survey Question #5: Sign language is a universal language for all Deaf people around the world

Language used by Deaf Americans is referred to as American Sign Language. It is a complex language that employs hand movements with facial expression, spatial location, and body movements (Zinza, 2006).

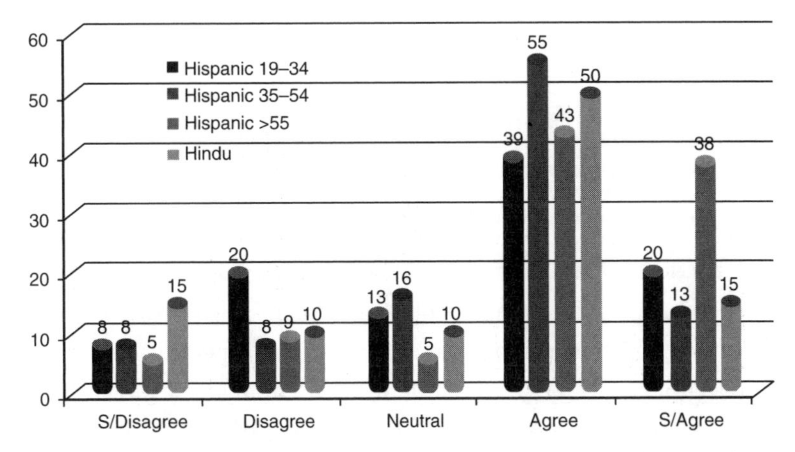

Figure 15. Perception of sign language is universal by lay people.

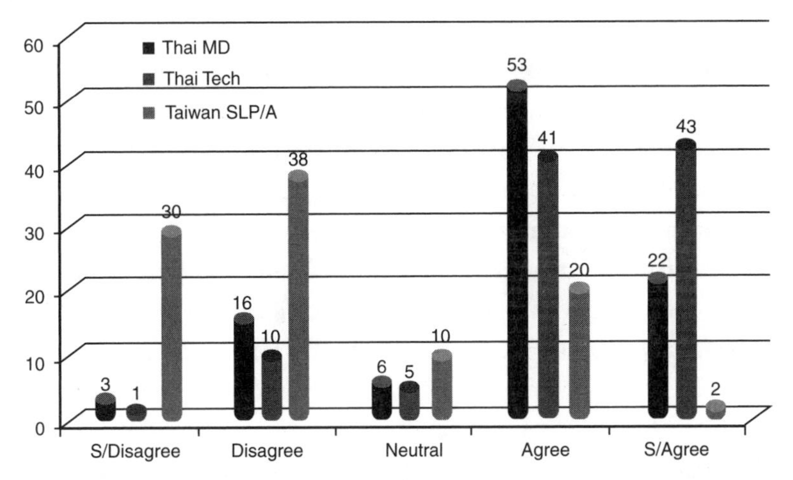

Figure 16. Perception of sign language as a universal language by professions.

Signing can be combined with fingerspelling. Signed language is not universal across the world, as each country has its own signed language. There also are regional or dialectal differences in signed languages that are similar to spoken language dialects. All sign languages have their own unique rules of syntax and semantics. Signed languages are living languages that grow and change over time.

In the current survey, with the exception of Taiwanese, most Asian subjects perceived sign language as universal. It is difficult for some hearing persons to imagine "deaf" as a "culture" or "sign language" as a real language. In fact, sign language has been documented as rich and as sophisticated as spoken languages. For most hearing people in the survey, it is a common misconception that learning sign language will interfere with oral expressive and receptive language development. Therefore, for many years, sign language was not accepted as a means to teach language to Asian Deaf children. Parents attempt to teach speech to their Deaf children. Most parents overlook the connection between hearing and speech/ language. It is difficult to develop intelligible speech perception and production without the ability to hear, especially with a tonal language such as Mandarin. Mandarin is a tonal language in which tones are crucial for determining meanings of words. With disruption in the auditory system at different regions of the cochlea, the ability to perceive tones is challenging. Several research studies have shown that hearing aids and implant devices are not effective in encoding pitch information required for tone perception; therefore, the production of intelligible speech is affected. In many instances, listeners will need to depend on context as the primary means to perceive word meaning.

Asian Americans who are born Deaf are influenced by multiple cultures and communication/language experiences. They are part of the American culture, part of the Asian culture, and part of the Deaf culture. In terms of languages, they are challenged to learn English, an Asian language, and a sign language. They are truly multicultural!

SUMMARY

It is crucial for Deaf educators to understand the family dynamics of the Deaf Asian population, as many of them have a unique, complicated, cultural background. We need to be mindful of differences among cultures and to understand the value and strength of each culture we serve. We should see the cultural differences not as a barrier, but as an opportunity to build bridges to reach out to Deaf Asian students. Our main goal is to help Deaf Asian-Americans excel and develop skills to code-switch and make progress within and among the various cultures/ languages that surround them. In order to provide quality service to Deaf Asian populations, we must examine our own beliefs, thoughts, and feelings toward the culture of people whom we serve. We need to gain knowledge and skills through professional education. We must experience the culture and be familiar with the languages of the group. The term Asian represents vast, multiple cultures and languages from East to West to Southeast Asia. It is important to recognize that Asian Americans include groups of people with mixed ethnicity and heritage. Asian populations have a complex history of immigration. Some experienced political upheavals, some emigrated voluntarily. Some may have resided in the United States for several generations, others may have arrived recently. Some Asian and American cultural concepts, values, and practices may potentially differ and even conflict. Therefore, global competence is the key to success in working with the wide variety of Deaf and hearing Asian populations.

REFERENCES

Abboud, S.K., & Kim, J. (2013). *How do Asian students get to the top of the class?* Retrieved April 14, 2013 from www.greatschool.org: http://www.greatschools.org/parenting/teaching-values/481-parenting-students-to-the-top.gs

Boeree, G. (2003). *The language families of the world.* Retrieved April 14, 2013 from http://webspace.ship.edu/cgboer/languagefamilies.html

Charr, E.E. (1996). *The golden mountain: The autobiography of a Korean immigrant, 1895–1960.* University of Illinois Press.

Cheng, L. (1991). *Assessing Asian language performance: Guidelines for evaluating limited-English-proficient.* Oceanside, CA: Academic Communication Associates.

Cheng, L.-R.L. (2000). An Asian/Pacific perspective. In K. Christensen (Ed.), *Deaf plus: A multicultural perspective* (pp. 59–92). San Diego, CA: DawnSignPress.

Chuong, C.V. (1994). *The Americans from Vietnam: A California study*. Sacramento, CA: Southeast Asia Community Resource Center.

Context (1999). *Folsom Cordova Unified School District report.* Rancho Cordova, CA: Folsom Cordova Unified School District.

Crinion, J., Green, D., Chung, R., Ali, N., Grogan, A., Price, G.R., Mechelli, A., & Price, C.J. (2009). Neuroanatomical markers of speaking Chinese. *Human Brain Mapping, 30*(12), 4108–4115.

Cruice, M. (2008). The contribution and impact of the international classification of functioning disability and health on quality of life in communication disorders. *Journal of Speech-Language Pathology, 10,* 38–49.

Cruz, D. (2013). *Filipino Americans" Asian-Nation: The Landscape of Asian America.* Retrieved 2 4, 2013, from http://www.asian-nation.org/filipino.shtml: Filipino Americans" Asian-Nation: The Landscape of Asian America. <http://www.asian-nation.org/filipino.shtml> (April 2, 2013).

Epstein, I. (1989). *Special education issues in Mainland China.* Taipei, Taiwan: International Conference on Education in Mainland China.

Gopinath, B., Schneider, J., McMahon, C. M., Teber, E., Leeder, S. R., & Mitchell, P. (2012). Severity of age-related hearing loss is associated with impaired activities of daily living. *Age Ageing, 41* (2), 195–200. Epub 2011 Nov 29

Hoeffel, E.M. (2012). *The rise of Asian Americans: Pew Research Center analysis of 2010 American Community Survey.* Retrieved April 14, 2013, from Pew Research Social & Demongraphic Trends: http://www.pewsocialtrends.org/2012/06/19/the-rise-of-asian-americans/

Institute, M.P. (2011). *Migration policy institute.* Retrieved April 14, 2013 from Migration Policy Ins. http://www.migrationinformation.org/DataHub/FB_maps/StateRankingsACS_2010_NFB_Growth_1990.pdf

King, J. (2006). When a child is born deaf. *Contemporary Pediatrics, 23*, 73.

Koning, J., & Dahles, H. (2009). Spiritual power: Ethnic Chinese managers and the rise of charismatic Christianity in Southeast Asia. *Copenhagen Journal of Asian Studies, 27,* 5–37.

Lane, H., Hoftmeister, R., & Bahan, B. (1996). *A journey into the deaf word.* San Diego, CA: DawnSignPress.

Lewis, M.P. (2009). *Ethnologue: Languages of the world* (16th ed.). Dallas TX: SIL International.

MPI tabulations of the US Census Bureau's 1990 Decennial Census and 2010 American Community Survey. (2011). Retrieved April 14, 2013, from Migration Policy Institute: http://www.migrationinformation.org/DataHub/FB_maps/StateRankingsACS_2010_NFB_Growth_1990.pdf

Niiya, B. (2001). *Encyclopedia of Japanese American history: An A-toZ reference from 1868 to the present.*

Paden, E. P. (1995). Otitis media and disordered phonologies:Some concerns and cautions. *Topic in Language Disorders, 14,* 72–83.

Pew Research Social Demongraphic trends (2012). Retrieved April 14, 2013 from Pew Social trends.Org: http://www.pewsocialtrends.org/2012/06/19/the-rise-of-asian-americans/

Rojas, J., & Maroonroge, S. (2013). *Rossetti language performance of children from multilingual backgrounds.* Laredo,TX: Texas A&M International University LBV Conference.

Rueda, R. (1993). *Meeting the needs of diverse students.* San Diego State University, CA: Presentation at the Multicultural Education Summer Institute.

Rumbaut, R., &. Ima, K. (1988). *The adaptation of Southeast Asian refugee youth: A comparative study.* Washington,DC: U.S. Department of Health and Human Services, Office of Refugee Resettlement.

Stewart,J.L., Anae, A.P., & Gipe, P.N. (1989). Pacific Islander children: Prevalence of hearing loss and middle ear disease. *Topics in Language Disorders, 9,* 76–83.

Sue, S. (1986). *Ethinic minority issues in the United States:Challenges for the educational system.* California State University, Los Angeles, CA: Beyond Language.

Uhalley, S., & Wu, X. (2001). *China and Christianity: Burdened past, hopeful future.* Armonk, NY: M.E. Sharpe.

United Nations (2013). Retrieved April 14, 2013 from United Nations: Statistics Division: http://unstats.un.org/unsd/methods/m49/m49regin.htm

Vernon, M. (2005). Fifty years of research on the intelligence of deaf and hard of hearing children: A review of literature and discussion of implications. *Journal of Deaf Studies, 10,* 225–231.

Wathum-Ocama, J.C. & Rose, S. (2002). Hmong immigrants? Views on the education of their deaf and hard hearing children. *American Annals of the Deaf, 147,* 44–53.

Wilson, M. (1996). Arabic speakers: Language and culture, here and abroad. *Topics in Language Disorders, 16,* 65–80.

World Map. (n.d.). Retrieved April 14, 2013, from Asia Map Category: http://www.wpmap.org/category/asia-maps/

Zinza, J.E. (2006). *Master ASL-level one*. Burtonsville, MD: Sign Media Inc.

APPENDIX

UNDERSTANDING DEAF CULTURE: A MULTICULTURAL PROSPECTIVE

Demographic information:

1: Please select your age group:

A: 18–23 C: 31–40 E: 50–60
B: 24–30 D: 41–50 F: More than 60

Please select your gender: A: Male B: Female

2: Please choose your education level:

A: Below High school B: High school C: College

3: Please choose your ethnicity:

A: Hispanics D: Chinese (China) G: Thai
B: Hindu E: Taiwanese (Taiwan) H: Caucasian
C: Muslim F: Vietnamese I: Others

4: Do you know anyone who is deaf?

A: Yes B: No

Please rate your perception on deaf cultures	Strongly Disagree	Disagree	Neutral	Agree	Strongly Agree
5: Due to limitation in communication skills, Deaf people are not as intelligent as normal hearing people.	1	2	3	4	5
6: Deafness is considered a handicap	1	2	3	4	5
7: Ninety% of deaf people have normal hearing parents	1	2	3	4	5
8: Signed Language is a universal language for all the deaf people around the world.	1	2	3	4	5
9: When a Deaf person does not understand what is said to him/her, it is best to repeat what was said again.	1	2	3	4	5
10: When two people who are conversing with each other using sign language and are keeping you from following your path, you should go ahead and walk through.	1	2	3	4	5
11: To get the attention of a deaf person during conversation, you should tap his/her shoulder	1	2	3	4	5
12: When communicating with a person who is using sign language, it is best to focus on the signer's face	1	2	3	4	5

Chapter 5

Experiential Learning and the Importance of Reflection

CHERYL WU
NANCY GRANT

INTRODUCTION

This chapter is a reflection on teaching multicultural competencies utilizing experiential learning activities. We believe that this training, which focused on multiculturalism, helps students, clients, and practitioners in developing compassion and in building relationships with self and others in many contexts.

Our work in providing multicultural competency training to first-year graduate students in counseling for the past 10 years evolved from our direct service experience.

WHERE WE COME FROM—A GENERATION OF DIRECT SERVICE IN SAN FRANCISCO

Our program in the San Francisco Bay Area provided counseling and social services to families with at least one deaf or hard-of-hearing family member from 1982 until 2003. The generation of youth we worked with struggled with multiple identities. Their deaf identity was understood at home through their family and ethnic community's culture in a quite different way being deaf was understood at school in the context of American education and culture. Additional intersections of identity included gender and birth order roles, sexual orientation, disabilities, language (signed and spoken) differences or delays, and more. Most of the families we worked with were low income; employment among family members was often a priority that made it difficult for parents and other family members to participate in meetings or activities promoting their deaf child's development. Many immigrant non-English-speaking parents/guardians had limited education themselves; those with more education usually were "downwardly mobile" without professional qualifications in this country. Many families struggled with English, with literacy, and with understanding (much less negotiating) the special education system.

All these factors had an impact on how these youth and their families related to each other in terms of youth development, parenting, communication, and relationship building. They had an impact on how parents and youth felt, thought, and behaved in relation to education, goals for the future, participation in social activities, independence, family responsibilities, and work.

American education (and counseling and social work, even recreation) promoted American values around independence, individual achievement, and pride (self-esteem)—values often at odds with more collectivist cultures. We had to become aware of the intragroup and intergroup tensions among families whose cultural roots were Latino/a (from Mexico, Guatemala, Nicaragua, especially), Asian (from southern/northern China, Vietnam, Cambodia, Laos, the Philippines), and African-American. In addition, our staff included deaf, hard of hearing, and hearing staff from many racial–ethnic/cultural groups with varying degrees of connection with the Deaf community, plus mostly white hearing volunteers.

Northern California is rich in allies from many communities—culturally and linguistically based programs with parent education, mental health, and other youth and family support services. We found many colleagues from culturally based service agencies genuinely and generously interested in developing relationships, partnerships with us, cross-training, and collateral work. In our experience, we found these ethnic/cultural resources were welcoming and willing to work with us on behalf of these deaf youth and their families.

In general, we found deaf community systems less welcoming of youth and families who did not fully ascribe to American values in relation to child development, adolescence and parenting practices, and/or who did not understand American Deaf culture and American Sign Language (ASL). Where the ethnic community agencies were interested in building relationships within the family, the deaf community agencies were more focused on communication skills building and accessibility for the individual youth (meaning ASL classes and ASL–English interpreters, rarely including the family's home language) and assimilation of the individual youth into the American Deaf world. Cultural difference was often understood as oppositional, audist, or anti-Deaf. There was limited intention and few resources to understand and negotiate the worldview differences and the resulting potential conflicts between the American Deaf culture and the world of the families.

Our role in providing counseling and family support services, and youth developmental activities after school and weekends, included a great deal of bridging between cultures. We have powerful heartfelt memories of performances in the San Francisco Chinese New Year Parade, intervention with Latino and Southeast Asian gangs, parent gatherings with multiple languages and interpreters, river rafting and road trips, family communication classes, and much more.

We also were fortunate to have close ties with a local adventure ropes course program serving mainly inner city youth that introduced us to experiential education and adventure-based counseling. Many of the activities developed for our master's level class began as youth development and family team-building activities, as well as training with staff, colleagues, and volunteers.

We are clear about our bias. Our values and practices related to multiculturalism promote a worldview aligned with social justice; a worldview that promotes inclusion, equity, and transparency; a world in which it is safe and healthy to trust and share AND to compete and achieve; a world in which there are multiple realities, all of which are true and valid, and sometimes in conflict.

Education and student/family support services have a powerful influence and impact on the social, emotional, and moral development of young people (and the families and communities they belong to) in addition to preparing them academically. Our goal is to prepare our counseling students to approach their work with deaf youth and adult clients with multicultural competencies.

MULTICULTURAL COUNSELING EDUCATION

For the past 10 years, we have taught a course on social and cultural diversity foundations and multicultural counseling to first-year master's level graduate students in counseling at Gallaudet University. Most of our students have been deaf, most white. They enter our course and the field of counseling with their "lived experience" as members of the deaf oppressed minority group. For about half of our students, Gallaudet is actually the first powerful Deaf cultural environment they have lived in. Except for international deaf students, many deaf students who are also people of color lack deep understanding and knowledge of their own racial/cultural group(s), although they have very real emotional and cultural identity, with strong ties to these groups. The few hearing students experience a sort of "reverse discrimination" as a minority group inside the strongly Deaf Gallaudet community. For all of our students, the environment is challenging. This diversity of identity and life experience comes together powerfully in this course. It requires students to reflect individually, dialogue with one another, and study where they are "coming from" individually and culturally. This course impacts how they perceive, understand, and interact in the world with others, and how others are likely to view and connect with them.

For many students, this course is the first opportunity to mindfully explore how they engage in the world as cultural beings. They enter this course with many ideas, concepts, and constructs that they have learned. They have opinions and know what they think and believe about what is right and wrong, good and bad. At the same time they have not looked at how, where, and from whom they have learned these things, consciously or not. They don't recognize how others, equally good people, may have very different and equally valid thoughts and beliefs about right and wrong, good and bad.

Our students are good people who want to help others, yet they often are not aware of how different "help" looks through different cultural lenses, not just individual lenses. We teach these "helpers" about culture because culture defines what is helpful. As counselors, they need to be able to recognize and hold these multiple realities in order to connect with, respect, and build relationships with their clients and colleagues. As counselors, they need to be able to work with these multiple realities with individual clients, with counseling groups, and with their school/organizational environment.

We ask students to look carefully at their own feelings, both emotional and physical, as a way of reflecting on their reactions to particular experiences. We ask them to look at themselves and reflect on what draws their attention, and how they interpret it. We ask them to try to look at themselves as others may see and understand them. We encourage them to explore potential cultural differences in what one perceives and how one interprets and gives meaning to those perceptions. We ask them to look at communication and behavior in the same way—what comes naturally to them and where that comes from—and how others might see and interpret that same communication and behavior.

There are many ways to approach providing counseling services to a multicultural clientele. We have found that experiential learning has the advantage of making linkages among cognitive, emotional, social, and moral aspects of counseling. Thus, each class session includes experiential activities geared toward this kind of learning. Each activity links directly with concepts, models, and processes that students are reading about, discussing, and studying in a traditionally academic way. Despite the emphasis on "hands-on" learning in the deaf community, we find that our deaf students especially have had very little opportunity to work with experiential learning. The Association for Experiential Education (2012) regards experiential education as "a philosophy that informs many methodologies in which educators purposefully engage with learners in direct experience and focused reflection in order to increase knowledge, develop skills, clarify values, and develop people's capacity to contribute to their communities." Participating in these activities also gives our counselors-to-be some grounding in how they might structure activities that will help their future clients. Each activity is not just an activity: it is carefully prepared and set up, then experienced, and then debriefed. Conscious learning happens during the debrief: students deconstruct what actually happened—how they felt, thought, communicated, and behaved. They learn the difference between *reporting the "facts"* (identifying step by step what actually happened) and *reflecting* on what they have just lived—considering what it tells them about themselves and others, what meaning the experience has, what it might suggest to them in terms of developing their awareness of self and others, and skills in relating to similar situations.

Three core frameworks provide a structure for students to work with their experience and to apply their academic learning.

First, Paolo Freire's (2005) praxis model provides a *process* that begins with personal, individual reflection, moves into dialogue—discussion, challenge, reflection with others—and finally into collective action for the benefit of all; recursively followed by debrief (reflection), dialogue, and further action. The "reflection" piece is the most difficult and most fruitful for students. Weekly reflective journals, structured group dialogue sessions with collective reflective journals, and collective assignments are some methods for working with praxis (Figure 1). Every assignment and every activity close with debriefing, an opportunity for reflection. Dialogue itself is a challenging aspect of our course, and we use guidelines of "listening for understanding" and "signing/speaking from the heart" as core values and skills.

We look carefully at different cultural views and practices with regard to interpersonal and intergroup communication, verbal and nonverbal communication, individualist and collectivist approaches, and adversarial versus dialogical approaches. For example, our Asian deaf students often have a subtler form of facial expression than our white deaf students. Eye contact, especially with authority figures, is much more direct in American culture than in Latino/a or Asian cultures. American Indians tend to teach, learn, and interact with more silence than more self-expressive Americans. Each of these examples is

Paulo Freire's Praxis Model for Education & Social Change

Adapted from:
Freire, P. (2005) Pedagogy of the Oppressed. New York: Continuum Publishing Co.

Transformation of Reality
Educational/Social Change

Reflection

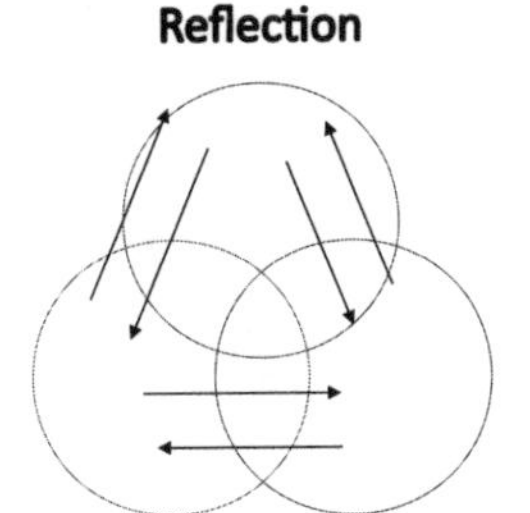

Dialogue **ACTION**

Dialogue and Reflection leads to Action for Transformation (cycle repeats)

Action without Reflection/Dialogue = meaningless activism
Reflection/Dialogue without Action = "Talk for Talk" – not going anywhere

connected with students' ethnic/cultural background. Cross-cultural interaction can be the ground for misunderstanding and conflict.

Second, Sue's (2001) tripartite model helps students sort out individual, group, and "universal" levels of experience (Figure 2). Working with this model helps them tease out the "parts" of themselves. On a personal level, they can understand themselves as unique *individuals*, unlike any other, with a history unlike anyone else. It also helps them see how they (and others) are members of racial and cultural *groups*, each of which influences their perceptions, understanding, and behavior. It gives them tools for sorting out intersections of different groups and looking at the impact that may have on the individual. Finally, it acknowledges and reinforces a sense of connectedness and a compassion for all people at the *universal* level—everyone has feelings, lives within a body, and interacts with the world.

Third, Campinha-Bacote's (2002) model for developing multicultural competency encompasses the areas of cultural awareness, knowledge, skills, and "encounter." These aspects of multicultural competency are layered and often are clarified best through the process of mindful encounter (Figure 3). Awareness is of

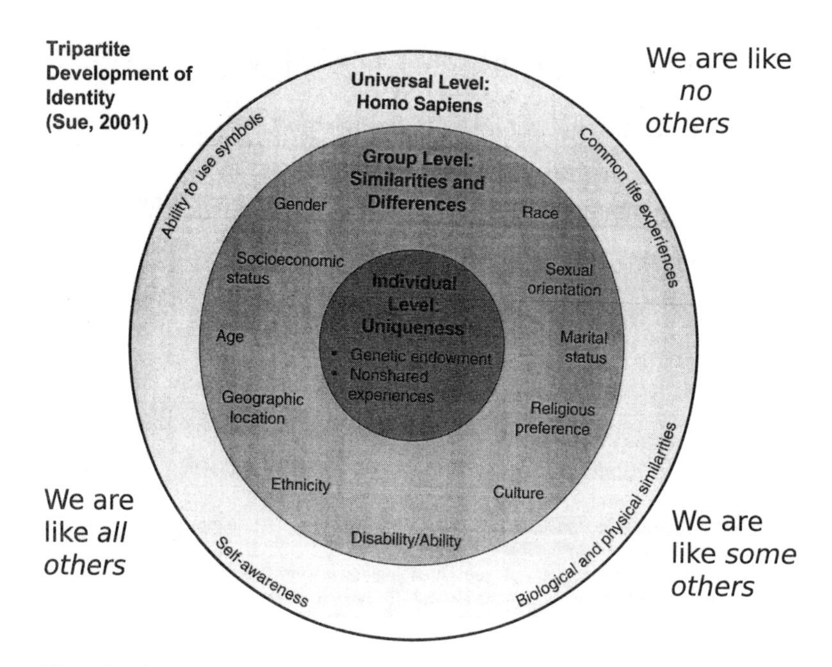

self and other, an approach that requires humility with regard to all cultures and their practices. Knowledge relates to cultures (including one's own) and their impact within the cultural group, and in relation to other cultural groups, to social power. Skills have a great deal to do with communication and interaction. Encounter has to do with actual experience, with personal experience meeting an individual or group in a cultural context. This model helps students look both inward and outward and helps them understand that there are different ways of "knowing." Encounter—whether in a classroom activity, their structured dialogue groups, or specific assignments—is the core method for helping students notice what they are (and are not) aware of and learn cross-cultural skills. Students develop knowledge through readings and specific assignments. In particular, working with cultural identity development models (Racial/Cultural Identity Development—Atkinson, Morten, & Sue, 1998; Sue & Sue, 2013; Helms White Identity Development—Helms, , 1990, 1995, 2008; Ponterotto, Utsey, & Pedersen, 2006; Deaf Identity Development—Glickman & Harvey, 1996; Leigh, 2009, 2012; Maxwell-McCaw & Zea, 2011) and applying them to themselves especially help students sort out their belonging,

LECTURETTE 4
CAMPINHA-BACOTE:
CULTURALLY COMPETENT MODEL OF CARE

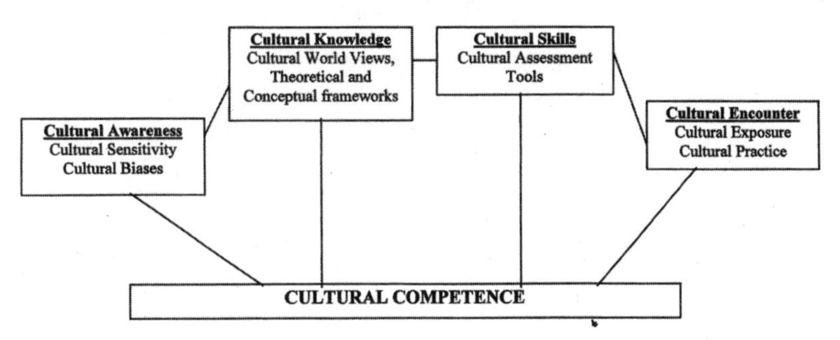

Reprinted with permission from Josepha Campinha-Bacote. (4th Edition). (2002). The process of competence in the delivery of healthcare services: A culturally competent model of care. Cincinnati, OH: Transcultural C.A.R.E. Associates.

4-34 © 2003 by NMCI Publications

their experience of different groups, and their different levels of power in different situations or contexts. Throughout the semester, students work with developing awareness, knowledge, skills, and experiencing encounters not as sequential, but rather as layered and simultaneous.

SELECTED ACTIVITIES AND ASSIGNMENTS

We would like to offer a few activities and assignments that you might adapt to your students or counselees. These activities can be used with participants at many ages and developmental levels. It is important to note that the activities should be sequenced carefully to match your group and tied to specific learning objectives. At the graduate school level, our syllabus includes very detailed rubrics for class participation and study groups, as well as specific assignments.

Quick Line-Ups

Early in the semester, students are typically confused about the difference between diversity and multiculturalism. Diversity refers to difference; schools often refer to their diverse student populations when there are students from many ethnic/cultural groups. Multiculturalism is a worldview that practices awareness, knowledge, skills, and intentional encounters in order to work toward a more equitable, inclusive, transparent society. To clarify this, and to help them start to use language about differences, we do several "quick line-ups." We ask them to line up using gestures or body language (no signed or spoken language). We start with a less emotional charge, lining up first by height, then by age, and then by skin color. Each line-up helps students look intentionally and consciously at themselves and their new classmates to identify similarities and differences without using language and to become aware of some aspects of diversity, i.e., differences. After each line-up, we debrief first their feelings, noticing how feelings become stronger and more complex as the object (height, age, skin color) has more social meaning. Debriefing requires the use of language and gives us an opportunity to look at what is typically "comfortable" or socially acceptable to talk about, how that might be different for different communities, and what is respectful language (not the same for every group or individual). Even the line itself becomes part of the discussion—typically lines appear as short to tall, youngest to oldest, and light to dark skin color. These implicit hierarchies are food for thought: students explore how it feels to be at the head or tail of a line, what it means to be in the middle, what implicit values are implied, and what feels safe and comfortable (and doesn't). At the end of the final debrief, we ask students to remember that a circle is also a line, and have them line up again in the shape of a circle. The circle helps symbolize multiculturalism: each person has an equal position, not at the front or back of a line (equity). In a circle, physically everyone can see everyone else and the process as it happens (inclusion and transparency), whereas not everyone can see interactions among others in a line. A circle generates a different feeling of connectedness than a front-to-back line. Diversity (difference) is acknowledged in the circle, but it looks different and is treated differently. Multiculturalism is a worldview and a process that values inclusion, transparency, and equity, which promote social justice.

Crossing Sides

This is one of the first activities we do. We place a long piece of masking tape on the floor. Students line up on either side of the tape, with each student facing another student. We ask them to shake hands (a common greeting in some cultures) and give the instruction to "get the other person to come to your side." In many instances, one student will grab their partner and pull them to their side of the tape. The other student will resist or not—there may be some tugging back and forth; more often, one person will just go to the other side of the tape without discussion in order to avoid conflict. Rarely, a pair will have a conversation about what the instruction means and make a collective decision about what to do.

During the debrief, students are asked to look at their feelings (emotional and physical), thoughts, behavior, and communication, and how each of these is connected to the other. Students often talk about how they feel anxious about getting the "right" response to the instruction, that it feels competitive (not collaborative), or that they act on instinct without really thinking carefully or communicating with their partner. We offer them a second chance to work with the activity, and this time the interaction has a very different kind of energy: much less competition, more eye contact, communication, more creativity in figuring out what the instruction means, and how they want to respond to it together.

Student reflections about this activity include feelings: shock that people (including themselves) immediately take sides and assume they know what their sides are, even when they have no meaning aside from their physical relationship to a piece of tape. This leads to reflection on what it means to be on one "side" or another, how that is defined, and whether one can be on more than one "side" at the same time. We extend that to what "sides" people experience in their lives. Another reflection has to do with feelings—how physical their reactions are, and how they feel about aggressively grabbing their partner, being grabbed, or witnessing this behavior; how they feel about feeling stuck, being uncertain; or the sense of stress and pressure. They are often taken aback by their own immediate nonverbal communication and lack of intentional communication—there is nothing in the instructions that preclude communication or mutual decision making. We encourage them to look at the nature of American culture, individualism, and competition to see where these reactions might come from. Diversity in the cohort generally leads to why different students chose different approaches based on their family/community cultural training. Having the opportunity to do the activity again gives them the chance to be aware of and make different choices, to communicate, to clarify the task, to be creative, and to collaborative in their problem solving. The feelings that come out of this experience tend to be more cheerful, relaxed, and interested. This activity points to the layers of multicultural competency: awareness (of self and other), knowledge (understanding of the task and its implication), skills (how to negotiate the instructions, how to communicate), and encounter (with partner and in terms of observing other pairs). This activity also points out how reflection, dialogue, and collective action can lead to a very different result than individual action. (Thanks to our friend Lauren Kucera of CoAction for introducing us to this activity.)

"I See about Me… I See about You…"

This exercise begins as an individual experience. Each student is given a mirror and asked to complete the sentence: "I see ______", making a list of what s/he "sees" in the mirror. They have several minutes for this. Usually the first few items they name are things one could see physically—brown curly hair, glasses, or a small nose. Sometimes they see that they look like a parent or sibling (which an observer would not be able to recognize). They quickly move on to descriptions of themselves that cannot be determined from just looking at them: qualities such as lonely, confident, or studious—generally things that they hope or fear others might perceive about them.

In the second part of this exercise, students are paired up and asked to name what they "see" when they look at their partner. Most students tend to use neutral terms, such as the color of eyes, color of hair, whether it is curly or not, tall or short, description of clothing, facial expression, or sometimes gender. They rarely name skin color, shape of eyes, texture of hair, or body size. Often, especially when they have run out of descriptive things to say, they begin making complimentary assessments.

The point of this exercise is to understand the difference between what can actually be observed and what is interpreted or assumed. Students explore using language about what they see: what is "okay" to talk about and what is taboo (for themselves or for the other person). They want to be respectful and polite, and also want to do the activity "right." They start to look at what it is okay to look at directly and indirectly, to notice, to mention, and what is *not* okay to notice or talk about. They reflect on how they feel about actually looking closely at someone, about being looked at; we look at how this kind of observation might be perceived and understood within and across different cultures or from different social positions (male/female, adult/child/elder, boss/worker, etc.). We also look at the discomfort students feel in being quiet when they don't know what to say, along with exploring what interpretation different cultural groups might have with regard to silence.

Despite the emphasis on eye contact and directness, considered "bluntness" in deaf culture, this activity brings up a lot of feelings for students. There's a lot of fear about offending others and taking offense at what is and is not mentioned by their partner.

Finally, we work on applying this exercise to how they counsel or "help" others. What do they first see in a client and what do they choose to pay attention to and not? We look at how not saying what is seen or not saying what is missing is actually part of seeing. How does what they observe at this surface level translate to assumptions and judgments, and how does that affect building a relationship with the client? Relationship building starts upon first meeting, beginning with this "surface" level of observation. It's important for the counselor to be aware that the client is also seeing them for the first time, making their own observations and judgments based on their own cultural lens. Counselors need to be conscious of their own perceptions and clients' perceptions of the helper. This exercise helps begin to look at the difference between visual perception and the interpretation of seeing through our cultural lens. This exercise also helps point out that our cultural interpretations increase at the point our filter starts running—when we've run out of initial objective things to "see." We tend to rely on our cultural lens to fill in blanks, add on, interpret, or make assumptions.

Multicultural Drawing

This very simple activity always brings up many feelings and judgments, which are great food for thought for our students. Four students work together, each sitting on one side of a square table, with a large piece of plain paper in the middle and a box of markers, colored pencils, and crayons to share. We ask students to share the paper, have each draw what "multicultural" means to them, and then give their drawing a title. We stress that the activity is focused on the content they present rather than their artistic expression. Students usually enjoy this "craft project," although there are always a few with anxiety about their art skills.

After they have completed their drawings, we ask students to rotate the paper at their table so that their neighbor's drawing is in front of them. We ask them to add anything they believe is missing or overlooked. They continue this rotation process until the original drawing is back in front of its original creator. Each person talks about her/his original drawing—the intention, understanding of multicultural and what it means to him/her. Then the others explain what they added and why. Finally, they dialogue about what it felt like to have others work on their drawing, and what it felt like to add to others' drawings.

This exercise always brings out a lot of competitiveness, judgment of self and others, a sense of individual ownership, and a focus on the "product" with less attention to the process. It usually raises questions about respect—what is respectful to "do to" "someone else's" drawing, even when a teacher (authority figure) directs you to do this. Hardly anyone actually talks with each other during the process; each makes his/her own decision about what to do. Sometimes there is eye contact, but rarely any dialogue. For most students, the default approach is strongly individual rather than collective. This activity helps point out that working with differing world views and life experiences can be colorful, beautiful, *and* messy/chaotic.

Finally, we apply the exercise to counseling. A multicultural approach involves real differences that may not be harmonious, bright, and cheerful. There will be conflict, ambiguity, incompletion, and confusion—the messiness of working with divergence vs. convergence, the reality of genuine differences. In this exercise, drawings are representative of individual *and* collective processes—creating an individual picture (our own perceptions of multicultural) *and* creating a collective image. This exercise illustrates the multicultural journey as an individual in relationship to others and the challenge of broadening their own cultural awareness, knowledge, and understanding. They do this through the process of individual reflection, and intentional interactions and dialogues with peers, stretching them to make room in their perspective for other possibilities. This exercise especially demonstrates creating a "third space"—mine, yours, and ours, being able to hold and honor multiple realities. Each group members' individual drawings later became part of a collective expression of multiculturalism. We point to the process of *intentionally* seeking out awareness of new social needs and influences in this "third space." Intentionally creating opportunities for a more creative, broader-based, interpersonal and intergroup interaction and engagement can lead to more authentic and compassionate relationship building.

Individual Reflective Journals (Individual)

One of the most labor-intensive assignments for the faculty is weekly individual student reflective journals. These journals help students consider more deeply their own reactions to class activities, to each other. They are one of the most helpful ways for the faculty in knowing how much students are actually taking in and how they are applying what they are learning in class. In many ways, this course is developmental as much as it is academic; individual journals give us an intensive look into the direction and depth of that development. Most of our feedback is in the form of questions as to how a student could take a thought deeper, apply it to a specific situation in everyday life or with a classmate, or put themselves in another's position. We might encourage them to ask a parent for family history. One of the most challenging things for the faculty is grading these journals. While we have very detailed rubrics, students often raise personal concerns, challenges, and conflicts to which we do our best to respond sensitively, yet in the context of this academic course.

A personal note: We have developed this course together, and usually have a similar response to what students express in their journals. However, our own cultural identities and life experiences are quite different: Often these journals give us an opportunity to feed back from different perspectives to students, most often Wu as a person of color and Grant as white and hearing.

Sharing Views Groups

"SV" groups are one of the most difficult assignments for students. The same group of four to five students meets weekly over the course of this semester and into the next semester with "Counseling Deaf People" where they look more deeply into differences within the deaf community and how to work with them. SV groups were sparked by the notion of intergroup dialogue: "... intergroup dialogue is a form of democratic practice, engagement, problem solving, and education involving face-to-face, focused, facilitated, and confidential discussions occurring over time between two or more groups of people defined by their different social identities ..." (Brimhall-Vargas, 2007; Schoem & Hurtado, 2001).

The groups are a modified form of intergroup dialogue, as SV groups occur among *individuals* rather than groups, with a purpose of helping students look at themselves and each other as members of groups. SV groups do not involve outside facilitators as is typical of intergroup dialogue. Rather the individuals in the group have the responsibility of monitoring and leading themselves.

Sharing views groups provide opportunities for students from different social and cultural identities, including (but not limited to) deaf/hearing status, to meet face to face in dialogue over a wide range of multicultural issues that carry an impact on the individual, group/organizational, and societal levels. They provide opportunities to:

- develop and practice skills in cross-cultural dialogue and "difficult conversations";
- learn to appreciate, embrace, and work with conflict/ambiguity/confusion;
- stimulate active reflection, inquiry, and challenge of assumptions and presumptions;
- examine power dynamics among and between dominant and subordinate social groups;
- build ally relationships;
- encourage one another to take action for social justice/change on individual, group, organizational, and societal levels.

Sharing views groups require developing relationships and working with each other collectively. We give specific SV assignments (such as dinner at a restaurant whose culture and cuisine are new to the group or watching a movie together from the point of view of the cultural identity development of the characters). Groups receive a handout with explicit and varied suggestions for their group process, including leadership/followership and decision making. As counselors, students may see how groups develop by experiencing and reflecting on it. Part of the SV group assignment is to write a collective journal (everyone in the group gets the same grade) each week. They have to figure out how to do that so everyone's voice is expressed equitably and accurately.

We find that SV groups are the most productive and enjoyable when students practice their multicultural competency by becoming aware of their similarities and differences, learning how to work with themselves and each other in light of those differences, having the courage to encounter each other in conflict as well as agreement, and developing group skills to ensure that everyone is included. SV groups are an opportunity to practice with each other outside the classroom, and on their own, without facilitation.

In recent years, we have seen an increase in the number of students with Usher syndrome (a genetic condition that causes progressive hearing and vision loss). There is always a mix of students who attended deaf schools versus mainstream programs, in addition to racial/ethnic diversity, sexual identity, gender, and other cultural intersections. These "many ways to be deaf" come together in SV groups. It often takes the better part of the semester for them to manage their communication mindfully: lighting, seating, pacing, and turn taking, so that everyone is included. Typically they start out being very polite, taking turns, and letting each other "pass," without a clear group process, just wanting to get along. Their concept of inclusion has to do with agreement, all being on the same page. Often there is some unexpressed conflict by midsemester, and they "agree to disagree" rather than actually addressing the differences and conflict and the judgments of each other that connect with strong feelings. They try make the process "okay" but avoid the feelings. By the end of the semester, they are listening to each others' feelings as well as thoughts more carefully, listening with compassion, and wanting to address issues of difference in a mindful way. Our feedback in their SV group collective journals often names the differences and resulting conflicts (or conflict-avoidance) and offers direct suggestions of techniques they can try out in order to develop their skills and improve their communication and relationships within their group. Sometimes they ask for faculty help/facilitation when they doubt their ability to manage conflict—we see this as a positive response to difficulty.

Cultural Encounter (Pairs)

This is often students' favorite assignment during the semester. In pairs, they decide on an "encounter" with a cultural group that is unfamiliar to them. It could be attending a Muslim mosque, participating in a Korean cultural festival, visiting a black barbershop to observe a haircut, or engaging with an LGBTQ group. Each pair is required to find a contact person who can help prepare them for the "encounter" and debrief with them afterward. (Of course, meeting with the contact person is an encounter in itself.) We provide interpreters for this assignment. Students need to prepare their cultural encounter, participate in it, debrief it, and choose some way of appreciating/"giving back" to their contact person and/or the group. They report and reflect on the cultural encounter and their "encounter" with each other as partners in this project through an in-class presentation and a paper.

Having a contact person, as well as strict guidelines, makes all the difference in this assignment. We encourage students to think of themselves as full participants—not simply observing/studying others—and not as volunteers ("doing for" someone separate from them). They begin to see the power of relationship building and are often surprised at the welcome and kindness of the contact person and his or her community. Students learn a lot about themselves and begin to reflect about where they learned their own values and social behaviors (from eye contact to dress to gender roles) because of the contrast with the community they "encounter." Often their interpreters become more "visible," and students learn something about how they can prepare interpreters and prepare their cultural contact for the use of interpreters, what role the interpreters play, and how interpreters might influence the interaction. In some instances, they begin thinking about multiple language interpretation when the cultural group's language is different than English.

When we look at the multicultural competency framework (awareness, knowledge, skills, and encounter), this deliberate and structured cultural encounter gives students an experience of appreciation, a joy in diversity. It helps them see that relationship building is possible and beneficial—that they can be and find allies in many places. As counselors, it gives them a hint of how they might increase their own awareness, knowledge, skills, and contacts in order to work with deaf people who are from families or communities different from their own.

This course continually challenges us to look at our own expectations. This comes up with the cultural encounters. Typically, we hope that through their cultural encounter, students will gain deeper understanding of the depth and impact of culture on relationship building. Each year, we are again surprised at how excited they seem to get simply from exposure to a new culture and highly contained conversation. It tells us that they have not had this kind of experience before, that intentional cultural encounters are very new to them. Even when students have traveled to other countries or done service projects, they have not engaged directly and have not reflected on what the difference they experienced means.

Simulations In addition to the activities we have created ourselves, we make use of commercially available simulations. Some of them are startlingly effective and have a literature about their use.

Ecotonos. We highly recommend Ecotonos (Nipporica Associates, 1997) as a way for students to experience how quickly groups can develop a culture, even an artificial one, and how members become bonded to their group. In this simulation activity, students are divided into three groups and are given three cards, each with a set of social behaviors that match their culture. Their cards might describe the degree of physical proximity that is comfortable (close, touching or distant, without physical contact), different kinds of eye contact (or lack thereof), communication (turn taking versus talking at the same time), or other aspects of cultural engagement. Their task in forming their group is to define the behaviors on their group's cards. They work with individual differences within their group and learn how to support and encourage each other while they do this. Continuing to use their group behaviors, they develop a "creation myth" for their group—where they come from, why they behave the way they do, what their people are like, and what they value. Finally they are given a collective task: to build a bridge that expresses their culture. (Each of the three groups is given exactly the same materials for bridge building.) Once they are well into their building project, and by this time their cultural behaviors are well established, we introduce a migration. Members from each of the three groups leave and join other groups in such a way that there is now one group that has a majority of people who started out together and a small minority of newcomers, one group that has an equal number from two different groups, and one that has representatives from all three groups. (So each group now has a different sort of diverse mix.) They are encouraged to work together to complete the bridge-building project, which will be of benefit for everyone. They continue to practice the cultural behaviors they learned in their original groups. Because of the cultural behavior cards they were given, differences are bound to arise in how different groups express appreciation, closeness, agreement/disagreement, etc. Once the bridges are complete or well on their way, we regroup together, and each original cultural group shares their "creation myth" and the meaning of their cultural behaviors.

Once students have gained an understanding of each others' "cultures" and the reason for their behaviors, they can see how and why misunderstandings and conflicts developed, and they reflect closely on how they each and collectively reacted emotionally, physically, and behaviorally to their new group. They reflect on how quickly they adopted their cultural behaviors and allegiance to their cultural group and how they missed them and struggled to work with the differences in the new groups.

Finally, students apply their learning to real-life experiences. Simulations are especially powerful ways of developing and practicing multicultural competencies, as students bring nothing but themselves to the activity. It's always surprising how quickly "them" and "us" develop. They get to review the actual thoughts and feelings that come up for them in the face of a multicultural challenge, to see what choices they actually make, and to learn what biases they have that help or hinder the collective situation. Debriefing and reflection are especially important. Simulations can be intense for participants, and "de-roling" or letting go of the roles they have just played is critical. This is also excellent practice for counselors to learn something about what triggers difficult emotions for them, to develop skills in managing themselves while they participate in a group activity.

We use Ecotonos as an introductory diversity simulation to set the pace, the context for the course. The process of the activity reflects the journey of learning basic diversity and multicultural terminology and constructs. It helps students see the development of their awareness, knowledge, and skills (especially in cross-cultural communication) through the process of encounter. It suggests the possibility of creating a third space, introduces the potential for relationship building, and promotes ally relationships.

Films

We often use films as a way to work with multicultural issues. When students can step back and take the point of view of different characters, it makes a difference to their understanding of the situation, which they can then apply to their lives and work.

My Brown Eyes. At the end of the semester, we utilize a short film with only a sentence or two of dialogue (captioned, of course) about a young Korean boy's first day at a new school. We have students watch the film and have them notice their reactions and judgments about all the characters. Then they work in small groups, with each group representing a character or group of characters: the young Korean boy, his non-English-speaking parents who work long hours, the understaffed school principal and teacher (a new teacher), other students in the class (all white), and three boys on the playground who try to play with the new boy and all end up in a fight. Instead of analyzing what happened conceptually, which is what they expect, we ask our students to describe what happened and what they felt *from the point of view of their character(s)*.

As we debrief this activity, students always express the difference between analyzing, "assessing," the judgments they made when they first watched the film and how they have much more understanding and compassion and a better sense of the whole system when they represent even one character's point of view.

Finally, we have students develop an intervention plan for this school that addresses the needs and strengths of all the characters, with a goal of inclusion and equity for all involved.

Deaf–Hearing

Adapting experiential activities to a mixed deaf/hearing group, and including other accessibility factors such as students with Usher syndrome or other disabilities, can be a challenge. Preparing enough space, ensuring sight lines, adapting written materials to be visually friendly, and utilizing interpreters creatively are important to consider. Ensuring there is enough time to complete each part of an activity *and* to debrief and de-role is critical.

In the past few years, there has been much more written about intragroup exploration within the deaf world and about intersections of difference within the deaf world (Leigh, 2012).

One of the most intense cultural differences for our students is the deaf–hearing divide that is highlighted in the higher education cultural enclave of Gallaudet. We study deaf identity development, and ask our deaf students to look at themselves through that lens. We also call attention to hearing people's identity development. We have adapted Janet Helms' (2008) model of anti-racist white identity development, which happens in the context of white privilege, to anti-audist hearing identity development, which happens in the context of hearing privilege. We encourage students to apply this developmental model to hearing students at Gallaudet and to hearing families of deaf children. We encourage active exploration and dialogue around this issue: counselors work with hearing and deaf colleagues and with children and adults from deaf and hearing families. They need to be prepared to facilitate discussion that will help bridge the differences between deaf and hearing cultures.

IMPACT

This course, interweaving academic and experiential learning, leads to significant changes in student development. For those who begin with a limited consciousness of their dominant cultural identity (e.g., white, hearing, male, heterosexual), the development shows in their ability to see and understand themselves as cultural beings, to have awareness and pride in their own culture, and to see how that can be a benefit in their commitment to social change. They begin to be aware of themselves as members of a cultural group, where previously they saw themselves simply as "individuals." It helps them understand that others are likely to see them as members of the dominant group as well, not simply as an individual—deaf will see them as hearing, people of color will see them as white, women will see them as men, and LGBTQ will see them as straight—and that means something in terms of building relationships.

Students from target groups (e.g., people of color, deaf, female, LGBTQ, and others) often find a sense of relief in looking at their cultural identity development—applying the models to themselves helps them sort out their relationships, where their reactions to white, hearing, male, or straight people comes from through their own life experience. It often raises questions for them about their ethnic heritage and encourages their engagement with family members to learn about this. It also helps them see that people from dominant groups go through a cultural identity developmental process as well, that they really are unintentionally unconscious, unaware of the power their group has in relation to others.

Once they begin to really grasp on a personal level what it means to be a "cultural being" with multiple and layered identities on individual, group, and universal levels, students then move deeper in their understanding of the more complex construct of "intersectionality." Instead of trying to choose a single identity "Deaf first," "Asian first" in a hierarchical way, they begin to see how their own (and others) identities intersect in different situations and settings. These intersections can influence how they perceive and are perceived by others, and how those perceptions impact their connection. Different types of discrimination and disadvantage—as well as privilege and advantage—occur as a consequence of the combination of identities. For example, in a Deaf-centered agency, being White and Deaf can confer advantages that a Black Deaf person working in the same agency might not have. In the same setting, a White Hearing person may also have less advantage compared to the White Deaf individual based on his/her "hearing" status, even though that hearing status likely confers an advantage in the larger world. Looking at the same individuals in a predominantly "hearing" agency that hosts a deaf program within it, the same White Deaf person may now experience less advantage compared to his/her White "hearing" counterpart; and a person of color (deaf or hearing), this individual may continue to experience disadvantage compared to both White Deaf and hearing co-workers. Of course, this depends on the agency—in an intentionally culturally competent agency, all individuals are allies to one another, to each other, and to those who are not represented by individual staff members. One's social identities, depending on the setting, and whether an identity is considered an "oppressed" or "privileged" identity will intersect with each other in ways that can be mutually augmenting or diminishing. The intersection can mitigate or undermine a person's status and thereby significantly impact relationship building between and among individuals and groups (Clark & Brimhall-Vargas, 2006).

Hearing (and hard of hearing) students learn to "own" their hearing privilege and approach their deaf classmates with more humility and less of a reaction to perceived "reverse audism." Often our students with Usher syndrome become more aware of not being included by fully sighted students as they are not (yet) culturally competent with regard to deaf–blind peers. Over the course of the semester, deaf–blind students tend to "own" their identity, feel empowered to advocate for themselves, and work with their sighted peers as allies who are developing their cultural competencies through their encounters with deaf–blind peers.

Students also increase their awareness of their own feelings and reactions, both emotional feelings and physical behavior, evident in body language, facial expression, and proxemics. They begin to identify their own triggers. Deaf students may be triggered by hearing people asking ignorant questions or making ignorant remarks about deaf people—they begin to recognize this as ignorance, as a lack of awareness, knowledge, encounters with deaf people, or a lack of skills. And they begin to be able to see how they may have that same kind of ignorance with regard to culture and cultural identity; the cultural encounter assignment in particular encourages this awareness. Being more aware of their own feelings, triggers, behavior, and body language—bringing these things to consciousness—gives students more choice in how they think about and respond to difference. We find it helps them become curious rather than dismissive or threatened, interested in difference rather that put off, appreciative of differences, and curious about what it means and how to bridge differences.

Self-awareness is the key, the first step. It allows them to pause, question, and recognize that they don't know everything, that there are further knowledge and skills to be sought. Reflection, dialogue, and collective action encourage students to "encounter" each other mindfully, to develop awareness of their similarities and differences, and to develop skills in challenging similarities and handling differences. Ultimately, as students understand about their own and others' cultural identities, they become more curious and flexible, are more interested in seeking cultural information and resources, and can take culturally based assumptions or behaviors less personally. All of these leave these future counselors more able to stay present and engaged in the moment and in the situation.

Student final journals at the end of the semester consistently point to individual development and to a deeper understanding of and commitment to social justice as counselors and as individuals.

CLOSING

Our work together has challenged us to explore our own identities. We come from quite different backgrounds and life experiences. Wu is Chinese-American, hard of hearing, and the youngest in a highly educated professional family with international ties, in which everyone was hearing. Her spiritual identity and practice as a fifth-generation Christian inform her work and relationships significantly. Her professional training is in psychology. Grant is white, hearing, and the oldest child with three younger brothers. Her father was very hard of hearing; neither parent completed college. She was raised Episcopalian in suburban Connecticut and has practiced Tibetan Buddhism for the past 10 years. Her professional training is in social work. Over the 25 years we have known each other, our cultural differences have been a source of interest and exploration, occasional conflict, and joy. We have chosen these central frameworks of praxis, the tripartite model, and multicultural competency and of considering the "whole person" in terms of ongoing development (cognitive, physical, emotional, social, moral/spiritual) as core concepts and practices that have enriched our work and our lives. We do our best to "walk our talk."

We find that each new cohort of students enters this class with both trepidation and excitement, having heard from previous cohorts that this class will both drive them crazy and provide a basis for deep personal growth. We wish this were not the first time they encountered experiential learning processes that promote reflection and dialogue, which can help lead to multicultural competency. We encourage other educators and counselors, no matter the age of your students or clients, to engage in this kind of experiential learning. Deaf students especially need not only to have opportunities to experience multicultural situations, individuals, and interactions, they need reflection, dialogue, and the opportunity to participate in social action on behalf of others as well as themselves. The world needs deaf students, colleagues, and friends to be an active, vital "voice." Practicing the mindfulness, compassion, humility of increasing awareness, and building the cultural knowledge and feeling, thinking, and behavioral skills that come with multicultural competency will lead to more productive reflection, dialogue, and action both within the deaf community and in the larger society.

REFERENCES

Anand, R. (2004). *Cultural competency in health care: A guide for trainers* (3rd ed.). National Multicultural Institute, Washington, DC: NMCI Publications.

Association for Experiential Education "What is Experiential Education?", Association for Experiential Education, Retrieved 8/7/2012

Atkinson, D.R., Morten, G., & Sue, D.W. (1998). *Counseling American minorities: A cross cultural perspective* (5th ed.). Dubuque, IA: Wm. C. Brown Publishers.

Brimhall-Vargas, M. (2007) Words of Engagement (WE): An Intergroup Dialogue Program presentation at the Department of Counseling, Gallaudet University, Washington, DC.

Campinha-Bacote, J. (2002). *The process of competence in the delivery of healthcare services: A culturally competent model of care* (4th ed.). Cincinnati, OH: Transactional C.A.R.E. Associates.

Clark, C., & Brimhall-Vargas, M. (2006). *Walking our diversity talk.* A one week Diversity Education Training Workshop sponsored by the Diversity Committee of Professional Education Programs Committee, Gallaudet University, Washington, DC.

Freire, P. (2005). *Pedagogy of the oppressed.* New York: The Continuum International Publishing Group Inc.

Glickman, N.S., & Harvey, M.A. (1996). *Culturally affirmative psychotherapy with deaf persons.* New York: Routledge.

Helms, J.E. (1990). *Black and White racial identity: Theory, research, and practice.* New York: Greenwood Press.

Helms, J.E. (1995). An update of Helms's White and people of color racial identity models. In J.G. Ponterotto, J.M. Casas, L.A. Suzuki, & C.M. Alexander (Eds.). *Handbook of multicultural counseling* (pp. 181–191). Thousand Oaks, CA: Sage.

Helms, J.E. (2008). *A race is a nice thing to have: A guide to being a white person or understanding the white persons in your life* (2nd ed.). Hanover, MA: Microtraining Associates.

Koh, J.J. (1994). *My Brown Eyes* (film). San Francisco, CA: National Asian American Telecommunications Association.

Leigh, I. (2009). *A lens on deaf identities: Perspectives on deafness*. New York: Oxford University Press.

Leigh, I. (Ed.)(2010). *Psychotherapy with deaf clients from diverse groups.* Washington, DC: Gallaudet University Press.

Leigh, I. (2012). Not just deaf: Multiple intersections. In R. Nettles & R. Balter (Eds.), *Multiple minority identities: Applications for practice, research, and training.* New York: Spring Publishing Company.

Maxwell-McCaw, D., & Zea, M.C. (2011). The Deaf acculturation scale (DAS): Development and validation of a 58 item measure. *Journal of Deaf Studies and Deaf Education, 16,* 325.

Nipporica Associates (1997). *Ecotonos: A multicultural problem-solving simulation.* Yarmouth, ME: Intercultural Press.

Ponterotto, J.G., Utsey, S.O., & Pedersen, P.B. (2006). *Preventing prejudice: Guide for counselors, educators, and parents*. Thousand Oaks, CA: Sage Publications, Inc.

Schoem, D., & Hurtado, S. (Eds.)(2001). *Intergroup dialogue: Deliberative democracy in school, college, community and workplace*. Ann Arbor, MI: University of Michigan Press.

Sue, D.W. (2001). Multidimensional facets of cultural competence. *Counseling Psychologist, 29,* 790–821.

Sue, D.W., & Sue, D. (2013) *Counseling the culturally diverse: Theory and practice* (6th ed.). Hoboken, NJ: Wiley.

NOTE: There are many more activities than we have been able to share here. If you are looking for an activity for your group (students, families, clients, professional team, etc.), please contact us, and we will help you find, adapt, or create something to meet your goals (Cheryl.Wu@gallaudet.edu, ncgrant.work@gmail.com).

ADDITIONAL RESOURCES

Experiential Education Resources
Association for Experiential Education: www.aee.org/resources
Project Adventure: www.pa.org
Teambuilders 8: www.Teambuilders8.org (deaf focus)

Multicultural Education and Diversity Training & Consultation Resources
Center of Excellence for Cultural Competence: nyspi.org/culturalcompetence
International National Multicultural Institute—Formerly known as the "National Multicultural Institute," iMCI is a private, nonprofit organization, iMCI will maintain NMCI's focus on diversity and inclusion in the not-for-profit, healthcare, education, government, and small business sectors.
Institute for the Study and Promotion of Race and Culture: http://www.bc.edu/schools/lsoe/isprc/
Multicultural Education Internet Resource Guide—Jan.ucc.nau.edu. This guide to over 50 websites was created to assist multicultural educators in locating educational resources on the Internet.
Multicultural Pavilion—EdChange: www.edchange.org
National Center For Cultural Competence: www.nccc.georgetown.edu
National Education Associates (NEA)—Resources for Addressing Multicultural and Diversity
National Institute for Multicultural Competence: www.coedu.usf.edu/zalaquett/nimc/nimc2/sp.htm
Social Justice Training Institute (SJTI): www.sjti.org

CHAPTER 6

Education of the Deaf in Japan: An Observation

JENNIFER WARD
San Diego County Office of Education

Japan is a largely homogeneous society, with the Japanese race making up 98.5% of the total population (Nomaki, 2011). As a foreigner living in Japan for almost 8 years, one thing I found is that it can be challenging to be "different" in a society that favors conformity and uniformity. It is often looked down upon to be different, to state one's opinion, or to not conform to the norms of society. Being different can feel like a handicap in and of itself at times. I have experienced first-hand the discrimination and isolation of being different and not fitting in.

Due to this pressure to conform and not stand out, being deaf can have a negative stigma for deaf individuals and their families. One deaf teacher at a prefectural school for the deaf told me that, in a country where the divorce rate is fairly low [according to Health Ministry statistics, the divorce rate was approximately 27% in 2012. However, this rate has doubled since 1990 and continues to rise (Ministry of Health, Labor and Welfare)], an unusually large number of students at the school came from single mother homes. She believes that one cause for this is the belief that the child's "disability" (in this case deafness) is a result of a wrong doing or sin in the mother's past, which may lead to divorce. While not everyone I spoke to believe this to be true, she feels that it is not an uncommon belief held among Japanese people (N. Akiyama, personal communication, February 12, 2103).

My time in Japan was not spent teaching Deaf students but teaching at a private school in Gunma prefecture. Gunma is a rural part of Japan located about 115 km north of Tokyo. I did, however, spend time with several members of the Deaf community and teachers from two different prefectural schools for the deaf and visited a prefectural school for the deaf, as well as a private school for the Deaf in Tokyo.

HISTORY

Before 1979, deaf people in Japan were considered incompetent, due to mental and/or physical diminished capacity. In order to perform any legal acts in regards to property (i.e., apply for a housing loan), they were required to obtain permission (Japanese Federation of the Deaf, 2013). Deaf individuals didn't obtain the right to drive until 1973, and then only with the use of hearing aids. It wasn't until as recently as 2006 that individuals considered profoundly deaf were given the right to drive, without the use of hearing aids. However, they must display a special mark on their car (on both the front and the back of the car), as well as attach a wide mirror when driving. Failure to do so results in a fine of up to 20,000 yen (Topics on Deaf Japan, 2013).(This is true for beginning and elderly drivers as well. There are different marks to distinguish the category of the driver.) Prior to World War II, education for deaf individuals was not mandatory. On the contrary, most deaf children were kept home to work and help out with the household and labor in the fields. They often had little to no interaction with other deaf individuals. The first school for the deaf opened in Kyoto in 1878 (originally called the Kyoto Blind–Mute Institute). This school came to be established during a time when the Japanese government was trying to create a more modern society. Gradually more prefectures followed suit and established schools for the deaf. However, as attendance was still not mandatory and students had to pay for the bulk of their expenses, many parents did not see the benefit of educating their deaf children. Their view was that education was a waste of time and money and that their children were more valuable as a source of labor (Nakamura, 2006).

It wasn't until 1948 that school attendance was mandatory for deaf children. Compulsory education in Japan does not necessarily mean that all children must attend school. Rather, it signifies that the government has to provide everyone with an education. Whether they take it or not is up to them (Nakamura, 2006). This "compulsory education" is up to the end of middle school, after which students choose whether they will continue onto high school or not. It is also based on social promotion—meaning that students are advanced to the next grade automatically, regardless of attendance or performance. Because of that, some parents with special needs children still opt to keep their children at home versus attending school.

There have been many advances in the education and rights of deaf individuals living in Japan since the early 1980s. However, through the interviews and interactions I had with deaf individuals, as well as hearing teachers of the deaf, their shared opinion is that there is still a long road to be paved. Prior to the 1970s, deaf individuals did not have many career options. They were limited to occupations such as sewing, carpentry, and the printing industry (Japanese Federation of the Deaf, 2013). They received lower pay and didn't enjoy the same job stability as their hearing co-workers. As recent as 2001, the Japanese government amended the discriminatory laws against deaf individuals. On the Japanese Federation of the Deaf's website, there is a message from a deaf pharmacist stating that even though she had passed the license exam to become a pharmacist, she wasn't rewarded the license due to her deafness. When the disqualifying clauses for the deaf were taken out of the laws in 2001, she then received her pharmacist license.

One teacher I met shared with me her experience in trying to pass the teaching exam in her hometown prefecture of Osaka. The exam includes an interview portion, which requires speaking and listening. She was not allowed to have an interpreter present, and after much struggle the Board of Education agreed to waive the interview portion of the test. However, without the interview portion, the teaching license could not be granted and she "failed" the interview. Therefore she could not become a teacher in Osaka prefecture and decided to move to the

Kanagawa prefecture, where she again took the teaching exam. The exam in Kanagawa does not include a listening portion and therefore was able to pass and is now a teacher at the Kanagawa School for the Deaf (N. Akiyama, personal communication, February 12, 2013).

EDUCATION

There are approximately 102 deaf schools located throughout Japan (the numbers I found ranged from 102 to 106), with the majority of them teaching via the oral method. Enrollment in schools for the deaf across Japan is dropping, resulting in small class sizes. At both schools I visited, class sizes ranged from two to seven students. While most state schools for the deaf have dorms, few students live in them. Students who live too far to commute to the school typically attend their local public school. It wasn't until 2006 that a special education system was approved (it went into effect in April 2007). Schools for the blind, deaf, and disabled changed their names to "special-needs schools." This law outlined the special education system in regards to the support provided to all children with disabilities, including deaf children.

While many schools for the deaf adhere to the oral method of education, signing is becoming more acceptable in schools (Kakuta, 2010). However, there is a distinction between Japanese Sign Language (JSL) and signed Japanese. Due to the fact that most teachers in schools for the deaf are hearing and lack proper training and JSL skills, they tend to sign and speak simultaneously. At Gunma School for the Deaf, signing is not allowed in the preschool program, and elementary teachers seldom use sign support when teaching. At the middle and high school levels, students are given more freedom to use sign, but the lessons are still taught orally (with some signed support). One reason for the push for oral education is that Japanese is the only language recognized in Japanese schools by the Ministry of Education, therefore approved curricula using sign language doesn't exist. Sign language is "permitted" at the middle and high school levels, but only as a support to spoken Japanese. As Karen Nakamura states (U-Turns, 2000), research has shown that schools for the deaf are vital for Deaf communities, identities, and sign languages. This is true in Japan as well, but the rapid decrease of students attending schools for the Deaf due to mainstreaming is having a large impact on the future of the Deaf community. One group, D PRO, who seeks to expand the use and awareness of JSL, as well as bilingual bicultural education for deaf children, is feeling a growing sense of urgency in regards to the decreasing number of students enrolled in schools for the deaf across Japan. With more and more students being integrated into public schools, it is becoming more difficult to pass JSL and Deaf culture onto younger generations (D-Pro website, 2013).

One of the major obstacles in the field of Deaf education in Japan is the lack of teacher training programs and teachers experienced in teaching students who are Deaf and Hard of Hearing. According to several teachers I spoke with, special education courses at the university level are lumped together to include deaf, blind, and disabled. Teachers who enter the field of Special Education receive one or two courses related to deafness and deaf education, and are then deemed qualified to teach students who fit into any of the three categories. Teachers of the deaf who learn sign language do so of their own volition but are not required to do so. (I am hesitant to call it JSL, as it may be more similar to signed Japanese.)

The Japanese education system, in both regular and special education settings, follows the practice of transferring teachers to new schools and positions every few years. While this practice can have some positive results, such as giving teachers the chance to work in a variety of environments, class sizes, and teaching styles, the downside when it comes to special education is huge. Teachers with no training or education in special education can be placed at a school for the deaf, blind, or in any other special education setting. Two of the teachers I spoke with from the Gunma School for the Deaf shared their personal experiences. Both are trained as English teachers—one teaching at the high school level and the other junior high school. Only one has any training in special education, but not specifically in teaching deaf students. The other had only worked in public schools prior to her current placement, and again had no experience teaching deaf students. Both know basic sign language due to the fact that they had attended local sign language groups and learned on their own, as well as on the job. Both teachers teach English through spoken and written English, with some support in signed Japanese. According to them, teachers at their school receive hands-on training the first year. They shared with me that they, along with their colleagues, at times feel hopeless because they lack the proper training and tools to teach their students effectively.

Nakamura delineates three main generations and the impact that their time of birth may have had on their education (U-Turns, 2000).

The first group is the pre-War generation, individuals born in the 1900–1930s. At this time, education was not yet compulsory for deaf individuals (as I mentioned earlier, many children were kept home to work on the farm or help out with household chores versus being sent to school). This resulted in many adults from this generation with little to no formal education and a high rate of illiteracy (Japan's literacy rate according to the CIA World Factbook is 99%). Because they did not have the chance to meet and interact with other deaf peers, they tend to use local or home signs. Due to isolation in their younger years, they lack a cohesive language, and as a result, communication is a major issue for individuals of this generation. They struggle to communicate with doctors and other health care workers, which leads to poor health care and health problems, and thus a shorter life span. Many women of this generation were forcibly sterilized, and men and women alike were often forced to marry a hearing spouse against their will.

The next group is identified as the war and postwar baby boom, born in the 1940–1950s. During this time frame there was an increase of children with hearing loss due to the development of new antibiotics and immunizations. This is the time when compulsory education began for deaf children; therefore, there was a large increase of students who attended schools for the deaf. Verbal skills were valued over signing skills, thus the push for the oral education of deaf students. High school graduates at this time were often limited to teaching woodwork, beautician skills, sewing, and so on.

The third group is called the "new generation" and includes individuals born in the 1960–1980s. The 1970s saw a shift toward mainstreaming, which resulted in a decrease in enrollment in schools for the deaf across the country. In 1975, the total population at schools for the deaf was 13,897 students, in 1995 it was 7537. Students who remained at these schools tended to be students with multiple disabilities, learning disabilities, or those who struggled academically and were not at the top of their class. Individuals in this generation tended to learn sign language after high school and often identify themselves as hard of hearing versus deaf. Most entered the job market upon graduating from high school versus attending college due to a lack of interpreters. (Tsukuba University of Technology, a university for deaf and hard-of-hearing students, doesn't provide instruction in sign language, nor provide interpreters. Classes are taught through spoken Japanese.) Another factor contributing to the low number of students who continued on to college is the rigorous entrance exams (this is true for high school as well). At Gunma School for the Deaf, high school students can choose among three different tracts: IT, barber, and the "regular" course. At the time I visited the school, 50% of the students were in the IT course and the other 50% in the regular course. The regular is further broken down into special education and regular education. Of the students in the regular education course, approximately 50% go on to college. There were 25 students in total in the high school, which means that 12 or 13 were in the regular course. According to the teachers, more than 50% of these students have special needs, which leaves approximately 6 students in the regular course. If 50% of those students go on to college, only approximately 3 students will continue their education after high school.

The three groups just outlined claim to have difficulty in understanding members of the other groups due to language differences and educational backgrounds. Nakamura summarizes the three groups as follows (U-Turns, 2000):

- Pre-War deaf individuals use a mix of JSL and home signs. They follow the grammar of JSL but do not include fingerspelling and tend to not voice.
- Postwar deaf individuals communicate using JSL signs but mix JSL and Japanese grammar systems. They tend to voice and sign simultaneously.

- New-generation deaf individuals can be broken down further into the following subgroups:
  - Individuals who identify as Hard of Hearing and who use JSL and new signs with Japanese grammar structure. They tend to not voice or use fingerspelling.
  - D groups are individuals who consider themselves Deaf, both physically and culturally. Their method of communication is through JSL and new signs, following the new JSL grammar and no voicing.

Note: The D groups are often seen as radical and exclusionary, or too "American."

The individuals I spoke with all shared similar experiences as mentioned previously: all attended public schools without access to interpreters, all learned sign language later in life, and all felt a disconnection with the Deaf community growing up. Two of the women are part of the "new-generation" group, and as adults are very active in the Deaf community and in the movement to recognize JSL as a language. The third woman is part of the baby boom generation. She held a career as a hairdresser prior to retiring.

There are two private schools for the deaf located in Tokyo: Japan Oral School for the Deaf and Meisei Gakuen.

The Japan Oral School for the Deaf was established in 1920 by an American couple serving as missionaries in Japan (Nippon Rowa Gakko, 2013). When their daughter lost her hearing due to illness, the mother returned to the United States so that their daughter could attend an oral school for the deaf in Chicago. Seeing that she had great success, they then decided to open a school for the deaf in Tokyo. Other schools for Japan followed suit and adopted the oral method of education.

Meisei Gakuen was established in April 2008 and is the first (and to date only) bilingual/bicultural school for the deaf in Japan (the school year in Japan runs from April through the following March). I had a chance to visit this school in June 2013 and spoke with some of the administrators, as well as observed preschool and elementary classes. Approximately 60 students study at Meisei, from preschool to junior high school. I was interested to learn that hearing parents were the driving force behind the establishment of this school. Being unsatisfied with the education their children were receiving at other schools, they, along with some educators and members of the Deaf community, established Meisei Gakuen.

In 1999, "Tatsunoko Gakuen" was established in Tokyo, providing classes for deaf children. The classes were held on Saturdays and introduced deaf children and their parents to the idea of bilingual bicultural education. The current principal of Meisei Gakuen, Yoko Kaya, is a Deaf woman who is in her first year as principal. A former teacher at a school for the deaf in Tokyo, she was part of a group who started Tatsunoko Gakuen. Ms. Kaya said that several of the parents whose children attended those classes expressed interest in bilingual bicultural education for their children and were a driving force in the start of Meisei (Y. Kaya, personal communication, June 17, 2013).

Another school for the deaf in the Nara prefecture is also becoming a pioneer in reforming education for deaf children in Japan. They have taken on a different approach to education—by placing emphasis on having fun while learning and working together (and in the process building group skills) versus forcing speech reading and oral skills (Nakamura, 147) The school has seen positive results. An increasing number of students are staying at the school and not transferring to mainstream settings. The academic scores are better, and speech training is done later. Other deaf schools throughout Japan are looking toward Nara Prefectural School for the Deaf as a model, but hesitantly. Another first is that the school hired the first and only deaf kindergarten teacher in Japan. The teaching exam for kindergarten requires singing and playing the piano, which have prevented deaf individuals from passing successfully.

The Tsukuba University of Technology is a technical college for deaf and visually impaired students located in Tsukuba city, Ibaraki prefecture. It opened its doors in 1990 and graduated its first students in 1993. In 2005 the name was changed to the National University Corporation Tsukuba University of Technology and was upgraded from a college to a university. There are two campuses: Kasuga and Amakubo. The Kasuga campus is for visually impaired students, and all majors are in the field of health science. The Amakubo campus is for deaf and hard-of-hearing students. This campus is divided into two departments: the Faculty of Industrial Technology for the Hearing Impaired and the Research and Support Center on Higher Education for the Hearing and Visually Impaired. Majors available to students in the Faculty of Industrial Technology for the Hearing Impaired division are Information Science, System Engineering, and Synthetic Design (National Tsukuba Corporation Tsukuba University of Technology, 2013).

COCHLEAR IMPLANTS

Cochlear implants (CIs) were first introduced in Japan around 1990. Initially, they were limited to postlingual adults (over the age of 18). In 1998, new regulations were added to include children older than 2 years of age (Honjo, 2001). It is now estimated that 55% of implant recipients are under the age of 18 (the minimum age set by the Japanese ENT Academy is 18 months). This shows an increase in the past 10 years. Cochlear implants, including diagnosis, implantation, mapping, and aftercare, are covered by Japanese national health care insurance. The profession of audiology is virtually nonexistent in Japan. The main responsibility for treating and working with individuals with cochlear implants falls on ENT doctors and speech pathologists. Speech pathologists take on the role of the audiologist in that they perform duties related to audiometry, as well as do technology fittings. Of the school-aged children who are fitted with a CI, approximately 67% are placed in mainstream educational settings. From 2008 to 2011 there was an increase in students with CIs at special needs schools (i.e., schools for the deaf).

SIGN LANGUAGE

Japanese sign language takes on two forms—JSL and manually coded Japanese. While sign language seems to be gaining more acceptance in deaf schools across Japan, it is signed Japanese, not JSL, that is being used. There are various reasons for this, some of which I will explain here.

As mentioned earlier, it is not usually accepted in Japanese society to be different or stand apart from the norm. An important part of Japanese culture is the language, and Japanese people are expected to share this linguistic aspect, which includes children and individuals with hearing loss. Learning the Japanese language—both spoken and written—is vital to their identity as Japanese citizens (Honna & Kato, 2003).

The majority of teachers for the deaf are hearing and speak and sign at the same time while teaching. According to Kakuta (2010), teachers feel they have to teach sign language, not use sign language as the language of instruction. Teachers also lack training in sign language and deaf education. That, combined with the rotation system in which teachers change schools every few years, makes it difficult for teachers of the deaf to obtain the necessary skills in order to teach their students effectively.

There has been an increase in interest in sign language among the hearing population in recent years as well. Many cities and town have what are known as "sign language circles" in which hearing and deaf members of the community gather (usually on a weekly basis) to learn sign language and to socialize. These circles have become quite popular throughout Japan and are the means in which many teachers of the deaf acquire their sign language skills.

In addition, the Japan Broadcasting Corporation (known as NHK), Japan's only public broadcasting system, started a TV program in 1977 for the deaf and hard-of-hearing population of Japan (Honna & Kato, 2003). Called "For Hearing-Impaired Persons," the weekly program presents current events in sign language. NHK also presents a weekly program to teach Japanese Sign Language (started in 1990). The purpose of this 30-minute program is twofold: hearing individuals can learn sign language (or at least the basics) and deaf persons can learn new signs and expressions, as well as study the structure of their language further. Concurrently, NHK began airing a news program presented in JSL and accompanied by spoken Japanese.

Sign language interpreting services began in 1973 (Japanese Federation of the Deaf, 2013). However, it wasn't until 1989 that the Minister of Health and Welfare, at the request of deaf groups, established a certification program for sign language interpreters. This program includes the Sign Language Certification Examination. Several of the individuals whom I spoke to shared the frustration that, although the interpreting system is changing and improving, there is still a lack of qualified interpreters, and one may not always be available when needed.

Despite the advances made, as recent as 1986 a Deaf political candidate was denied the right to have his speech interpreted. This in turn started a campaign that spread nationwide to allow election campaign speeches to be interpreted (Japanese Federation of the Deaf, 2013).

The Deaf individuals I spoke with all shared a common sentiment in regards to sign language interpreters: despite training programs and a fairly new certification exam, there is a lack of qualified interpreters across the country. One individual I spoke with told me that often interpreters are chosen from the community sign language groups, either by deaf individuals or by the city office in charge of sending out interpreters. Hearing individuals are chosen (at times) based on their skills in JSL, rather than by passing an exam or certification program (M. Takahashi, personal communication, March 2, 2013).

The Japanese Association of Sign Language Interpreters (JASLI) was established in May 1991. This organization is made up of individuals who have passed the national interpreting exam and are certified interpreters. According to the article on their website, about half of the members work as full-time interpreters, while the remaining are either part-time or volunteer interpreters. One problem the JASLI faces is the lack of successful candidates. There are less than 100 interpreters each year who become certified interpreters, with the majority of them living in and around large cities. Another problem is that of the interpreters who are currently working, only about half of them are certified. Sign language interpreters in Japan are paid low wages. In 1997 JASLI established a code of ethics for sign language interpreters and in 2002, along with the National Association for Sign Language Interpretation, the National Training Institution of Sign Language (Japanese Sign Language, 2013). JSL is not standard, leading to confusion and misunderstanding. This causes a problem for interpreters as they learn one set of signs in their sign language courses, other signs via the Sign Language News, and still different signs in dictionaries and from deaf individuals.

In 1991, an organization called D PRO was established to promote respect for Japanese Sign Language and bilingual education for deaf individuals. D PRO was established as result of the 11th World Deaf Congress held in Tokyo in July 1991. The World Federation of the Deaf had announced their policies regarding respecting the sign language of each country and the importance of bilingual education for the deaf. However, members of the Deaf community in the host country of Japan felt that they were not recognized as having their own language and culture (D-PRO, 1999)

As found on their website, D PRO's vision statement is as follows:

> We believe that Deaf people are a linguistic minority group that uses Japanese Sign Language, a language that is different from Japanese. We seek to realize a society that respects Deaf culture and JSL and treats them with equal status as Japanese language and culture, a society in which Deaf people can live as Deaf in a Deaf-like manner.

In Osaka, there is an organization made up of Deaf individuals by the name of Deaf Shock. The name stems from the shock individuals who were mainstreamed feel upon meeting other deaf adults, learning sign language, and realizing that they are part of a cultural/linguistic minority and not disabled.

I had the opportunity to speak one on one to three deaf women ranging in age from 34 to 62 years of age (the two younger women have good knowledge of ASL, having studied at Gallaudet University; therefore I was able to communicate directly with them. For the third interview, a friend with some knowledge of Japanese sign language assisted me by interpreting). Despite the large gap in age, they shared very similar educational backgrounds and life experiences. All three attended public schools for the majority of their educational years. All three women experienced the frustration and isolation of being deaf in a hearing school, without an interpreter and therefore without access to the same information and education as their hearing peers. All three women were forbidden to sign at home, learned sign language at a later age, and married hearing men. One woman shared with me her experience as it relates to services available to deaf individuals. Doorbell and smoke alarm lights are provided by the government but, in this case, because a hearing person lived in the house as well (her husband) the government would not provide these accommodations. To get around this she changed the way her household is registered with the government so that she became the head of the household. She was then granted these devices. (In Japan, each household must register at the city office. Typically the male is listed as the head of the household and the woman is listed under him, along with any other dependents.)

CONCLUSION

While there have been many advances in the rights and education of deaf individuals, it is the consensus of the people I met and spoke with that there is still a long road to be paved. Even in 2013, I heard deaf individuals referred to as deaf–mute by their friends and acquaintances, although not commonly. Deaf individuals still struggle with their identity and place in society. They continue to face discrimination and the fight for the same opportunities and rights as their hearing peers. In a society where women are still paid less than men and still fight to gain equality, the fight for the Deaf community is not over. But the gains made in the past few decades are noteworthy and show promise for the future.

REFERENCES

D PRO Homepage (1999). Retrieved May 12, 2013, from http://www.d-pro.net

Deaf Japanese History: 2006–2009 (n.d.). *Topics on Deaf Japan*. Retrieved July 29, 2013, from http://deafjapan.blogspot.com

Honjo, I. (2001). Cochlear implant: Update. *Japan Medical Association Journal, 44*(5), 205.

Honna, N., & Kato, M. (2003). Establishing sign language in deaf education in Japan: A sociolinguistic approach. *International Communication Studies, XII-3*, 37–50.

Japanese Federation of the Deaf | JFD's English Website (n.d.). Retrieved June 23, 2013, from http://jfd.or.jp/en

JASLI (n.d.). *Japanese Association of Sign Language Interpreters homepage*. Retrieved June 18, 2013, from www.jasli.jp/about01e.html

Kakuta, M. (2010). Sign language variation and implications for deaf education in Japan. *Educational Studies, 52*, 191–198.

Ministry of Health, Labor and Welfare (n.d.). Retrieved May 5, 2013, from http://www.mhlw.go.jp/english/

Nakamura, K. (2000). U-Turns, "Deaf shock," and the hard-of-hearing: Japanese deaf identities at the borderlands. In L. Monaghan, K. Nakamura, & G. Turners (Eds.). Hamburg: Springer-Verlag.

Nakamura, K. (2006). *Deaf in Japan: Signing and the politics of identity.* New York: Cornell University.

National Tsukuba Corporation Tsukuba University of Technology (n.d.). *National Tsukuba Corporation Tsukuba University of Technology*. Retrieved June 8, 2013, from http://www.tsukuba-tech.ac.jp/english.index.html

Nippon Rowa Gakko (n.d.). *Japan Oral School for the Deaf homepage*. Retrieved June 18, 2013, from http://www.nrg.ac.jp/english

Nomaki, H. (2011, March 29). Is Japan a Homogeneous Country? *American Daily Herald*. Retrieved April 25, 2013, from americandailyherald.com

Oliver, J. (2013). New Expectations: Pediatric cochlear implantation in Japan. *Cochlear Implants International, 14*(1), S13–S17.

The World Factbook (n.d.). *The World Factbook*. Retrieved July 28, 2013, from https://www.cia.gov/library/publications/the-world-factbook/fields/2103.html

CHAPTER 7

Preparing Future American Sign Language/English Interpreters of Color: Lessons Learned from an Interpreter Preparation Program

THOMAS K. HOLCOMB, Ph.D.
Professor, Deaf Studies Ohlone College

AUNDREA LOVE, NIC
Interpreter Ohlone College

CHRISTINE NAKAHARA, MA, NIC
Interpreter, De Anza College

JOAN M. OSTROVE, Ph.D.
Professor, Psychology Macalester College

INTRODUCTION

The Deaf community is as diverse as the hearing population of the United States. Accordingly, there is a need for the interpreting community to reflect the changing face of America. Findings from a survey conducted among interpreters of color who graduated from an interpreter preparation program in Northern California revealed that not only is there a need for a concerted effort to recruit people of color to the interpreting field, but also to support them through interpreter preparation programs. The support can come in many different forms, including the provision of mentors and diversified stimuli such as language models, teaching tools, and reading materials. With this kind of support, the feeling of "otherness" experiences by interpreting students of color will become less of an issue. This is critical as students of color reported feeling the burden of "representing" an entire community when sharing their personal experiences and thoughts as individuals of color. Finally, a look at white privilege and how it contributes to a false sense of "normalcy" is recommended for all students as well as faculty members.

PREPARING FUTURE INTERPRETERS OF COLOR: ARE WE DOING ENOUGH?

There has been a repeated call to diversify the community of American Sign Language (ASL)/English interpreters (e.g., Jones, 1986; McKee & Davis, 2010; National Multicultural Interpreter Project Curriculum, 2000). This is due to the fact that the vast majority of certified interpreters are white. Ohlone College has a long history of preparing interpreters for the diverse community of the San Francisco Bay Area; 24% of graduates from the program are nonwhite. The current study was conducted to examine the experiences of students of color who went through Ohlone's rigorous 2-year interpreter preparation program.

The program adopts a cohort model in which students take all courses together for 2 years with the goal of promoting a safe environment for learning, taking risks, and collaborating. To this end, students spend those 2 years working closely together developing their linguistic, interpreting, and interpersonal skills, as well as their intercultural and world knowledge. The class size is limited to 10 to maximize the learning experience. Because of the small class size and intensive learning environment, students are prompted to explore cultural issues throughout the 2-year experience, on both academic and personal levels.

The goal of the study described in this chapter was to better understand these experiences by documenting the thoughts and feelings of the alumni. After a brief review of relevant literature, findings from this study are reported. At the end, we discuss the implications of the findings and make recommendations for interpreter education programs throughout the nation.

LITERATURE REVIEW

As is true in the United States in general, the U.S. Deaf population is becoming increasingly racially and ethnically diverse (see, e.g., Anderson & Miller, 2004/2005). This growing diverse population (both Deaf and hearing) typically is served by predominantly white (and female) interpreters. For example, the Registry of Interpreters of the Deaf (RID) conducted a survey (2011) and of the 9604 respondents who reported their race, 88% identified as white; of the 10,611 who reported their gender, 87% identified as female[1] (RID, 2011). There are (at least) two ways to address this challenge: (1) recruit, train, and support more interpreters of color and (2) increase the multicultural competence of all interpreters (especially, but not exclusively, white interpreters).

The concept of "culture" and the importance of understanding cultural differences are highly familiar to interpreters, whose work is inherently cross-cultural. The recognition of a distinct Deaf Culture is a cornerstone of education in Deaf Studies, ASL, and interpreter preparation curricula. Not only are hearing students taught that Deaf people have a unique, visually based culture replete with language, shared history and customs, stories and poetry, politeness strategies, and so on, but they learn that they, too, come from a "hearing culture" with its own set of assumptions, ways of being, history, language, customs, etc. (e.g., Holcomb, 2013; Lane, Hoffmeister, & Bahan, 1996). Culturally based concepts are an integral part of understanding relationships between Deaf and Hearing people and between signed and spoken languages. Interpreter trainers have incorporated concepts from intercultural training to describe and teach about the work that

ASL–English interpreters are engaged in (e.g., Mindess, Holcomb, Langholtz, & Poyner, 2006). As McKee and Davis (2010) note, however,

> … the discourse of the sign language interpreting profession has tended to characterize consumers and languages in a binary distinction as Deaf or hearing, at times perhaps implying that these social categories are homogenous, mutually exclusive, and all-encompassing primary identities. While the Deaf-hearing contrast is obviously central in defining the context of our work, *this dualism potentially dulls our perception of the multiplicity and fluidity of identities, allegiances, and language resources that Deaf and hearing participants (and interpreters) bring to interpreted interactions* (p. vii; italics added).

Issues of diversity and intersectionality within the Deaf community are increasingly recognized and attended to in Deaf Studies as well as in interpreter education programs (e.g., Bauman, 2008; Mindess et al., 2006; National Multicultural Interpreter Project). In addition to an acute self-consciousness with respect to within-group diversity based on language usage and audiological status, the Deaf community realizes that it is "not immune to ideologies of oppression" (Bauman, 2008, p. 11) and recognizes the ways that multiple identities (and sources of discrimination) based on race, gender, and sexual orientation operate within the Deaf community (see, e.g., Bienvenu, 2008; Brueggemann & Burch, 2006; Dunn, 2008; Kelly, 2008; McCaskill, Lucas, Bayley, & Hill, 2011). Indeed, much critical work in Deaf Culture and Deaf Studies that has helped establish a social/cultural (as opposed to medical) model of deaf people and Deaf Culture draws important parallels and distinctions with racial/ethnic minority groups and between, for example, racism and audism (e.g., Davis, 2008; Dunn, 2008).

Increasing attention to racial and ethnic diversity in the Deaf community suggests the critical need for parallel attention to these issues within the interpreting community. The National Multicultural Interpreter Project has been at the forefront of efforts to diversify and increase multicultural competence in the interpreting profession in the United States. Their mission is "to improve the quantity and quality of interpreting services provided to individuals who are D/deaf, hard of hearing, and deaf–blind from culturally diverse communities by providing educational opportunities, recruiting culturally diverse interpreters, and enhancing cultural sensitivity with the profession" (curriculum overview; p. ix). In addition, professional interpreter organizations such as the National Association of Black Interpreters (NAOBI) and Mano à Mano (the organization of trilingual—Spanish/English/ASL—interpreters) provide important advocacy and mentoring opportunities for Black and Latino/a interpreters.

Despite increased awareness of issues of cultural identities and ethnic diversity in interpreter training texts and programs, very little scholarly work has addressed the experiences of interpreters of color (although *VIEWS*, the quarterly publication of the Registry of Interpreters for the Deaf, has regular columns devoted to the work of NAOBI and Mano à Mano and has published articles about the importance of diversity and cultural competence in the interpreting profession). There are two important exceptions to this gap in the literature and although they were published more than 25 years apart, they share critical themes.

The first is Jones' (1986) paper from the 1985 Convention of the Registry of Interpreters for the Deaf, which detailed critical issues related to Black interpreters and Black Deaf people. Jones noted that discussions of "Deaf" and "hearing" communities usually refer to white communities and may not address issues of critical importance to, for example, Black Deaf and hearing people in interpreting contexts. For instance, Black Deaf individuals often prefer Black interpreters, "sometimes even when such interpreters are judged to have less skill by (commonly elite) white interpreter criteria" (Jones, 1986, p. 61). Black interpreters believe that the interpreting profession is not concerned enough about people of color, that it does not encourage Black interpreters, and that classroom training is "not geared to adequate preparation of Black prospective interpreters to interpret for Black Deaf individuals" (p. 62). They also feel that they are judged unfavorably for being monolingual in non-Standard (Black) English. Jones' work also points to other expressions of racism in interpreting situations. For example, white Deaf people's conception of interpreters is that they are white and that white interpreters' conception of Deaf people is that they are white; white hearing interpreters express discomfort or fear about working in situations with Black consumers, and both white interpreters and white Deaf people are much less likely to have experience interacting with Black people than Black people (Deaf or hearing) are to have with white people.

The second is a more recently published study of Black sign language interpreters in the United Kingdom (Obasi, 2013). Although all of her interviewees reported positive experiences as interpreters, results of extensive in-depth interviews revealed that the participants also have many struggles. Their challenges included balancing visibility as Black people with an expectation of invisibility as interpreters, low expectations of sign language competency, and a high level of scrutiny of their work. In addition, the interviewees reported a lack of representation of Black people and Black culture in their training in both sign language and interpreting, subtle and blatant racism not only from white interpreters and Deaf people but also in the content of the material they were interpreting, and resistance to their raising issues of race and racism in the profession.

The themes in these two published articles resonate with the experiences of individual interpreters of color. For example, Smith (2012) notes that her experiences as a Black woman growing up on the south side of Chicago offer both advantages and disadvantages as an interpreter. She is an effective advocate, she can adapt to a wide variety of environments, and she understands struggle. At times, however, she has felt isolated and like she does not "fit in" with white interpreters and has preferred assignments that would allow her to work with other interpreters of color. Other interpreters of color note the strong connections between their own ethnic communities and the Deaf community (for an example of parallels between Native American culture and Deaf culture, see Handy, 2010).

There are two consistent—if not always explicit—themes in the work from the perspective of interpreters of color reviewed earlier: (1) the challenges of being a "minority" in a substantially white field (and in a context in which one is also a member of the hearing majority) and (2) the need for an examination of whiteness and white privilege.

Experiences of isolation, separation, and racism among people of color in the primarily white interpreting field are not unique to this profession. Research on the experiences of students of color at predominantly white institutions of higher education, for example, demonstrates that they face blatant and subtle discrimination and racism, exclusion, and isolation, with pressure to "represent their race" while simultaneously being expected to defy stereotypes about people from their ethnic groups (see, e.g., Aries, 2008; Feagin, Vera, & Imani, 1996; Steele, 1997).

Whiteness and white privilege have received increasing attention in critical race and other identity studies fields, especially since the publication of McIntosh's (1988/2007) now classic essay on unpacking the invisible knapsack of white privilege in which she enumerates a long list of unearned—and easily unnoticed—advantages she receives daily as a result of being white. Subsequent work on the topic emphasizes that a critical feature of whiteness and white privilege is that it is hard for white people to recognize or acknowledge—it is "normal," illusory, invisible; it is characterized by racial dominance and an ability to avoid having to notice or think about any issues of race; it is grounded in a myth of sameness and individualism (see, e.g., hooks, 2008; Tochluk, 2008). As Kivel (2007) notes about white people,

> ... we are the mainstream culture—we are in the culture of power. Wherever we look we see ourselves, our language, our values, our images, and our history. We are given little sense of the importance of cultural competency and an overinflated sense of the importance and centrality of our culture.... We have been trained to think that other cultures are less literate, less civilized, less efficient, less practical, less worldly, and not sanctioned by God (pp. 1–2).

The concepts associated with "privilege" are not unfamiliar to sign language interpreters. Within the interpreting profession, however, issues of privilege almost always refer to being hearing (itself a critically important form of privilege) and hardly ever to being white. How might it matter that interpreter training happens in the context of whiteness and white privilege (even as it seeks to unpack and make visible the realities and consequences of hearing culture and hearing privilege)?

What follows are findings of alumni of color who went through the Interpreter Preparation Program (IPP) at Ohlone College. Two research questions guided this study:

1. Did students of color report that their experiences of going through the Interpreter Preparation Program were substantially different than those of their classmates?
2. What strategies for making it through the program were especially beneficial for students of color?

METHOD

Participants

All alumni of color from the Ohlone IPP from 1997 to 2012 were invited to participate in this study. A total of eight Black alumni, nine Asian alumni, and two Hispanic/Latin@ alumni (who identified primarily as Hispanic) were identified. Students of color represent 24% of the total number of students who graduated from Ohlone in the past 15 years. A 100% return rate was achieved for the questionnaire.

Instrument

A 10-item questionnaire (see Appendix) was developed to learn about alumni of color's experiences as students in an interpreter preparation program. The questionnaire was slightly modified for each ethnic group to address their unique experiences more directly.

Procedure

Contact information for alumni of color was obtained from the department's database on graduates. An email was sent to all alumni of color who graduated from the program within the past 10 years, inviting them to complete the questionnaire online. The questionnaires were returned and responses were compiled for each group. Upon completion of the data collection, themes that emerged in each group were identified by the first, second, and third authors (a white Deaf professor, a Black interpreter, and an Asian-American interpreter). In turn, these themes were compared across groups to seek similarities and differences among them.

Findings

While many unique personal narratives from participants were documented, many expressed similar thoughts and feelings to one another, both within each ethnic group and across the three ethnic groups. Most respondents had favorable experiences of going through the program and are proud to be associated with the college. However, almost all of them shared some challenging experiences and made recommendations that could make the program more culturally sensitive to students of color. These will be the focus of the following section.

Themes Across all Ethnic Groups

The four most recurrent themes among the alumni groups regardless of ethnicity were (1) comparable experiences of going through the program, (2) the need for ethnic diversity in teaching models and materials, (3) discomfort about being expected to represent their communities, and (4) the need for classmates and professors to be more aware of their white privilege. These themes are discussed further here.

Comparable experiences. In response to the question regarding whether or not their experiences of going through the program were comparable to their classmates, almost all respondents (except for two Black alumni and one Latina alumnus) replied yes. More specifically, the alumni felt that the work they had to do, the treatment they received from their professors, and the challenges they had were shared by everyone in the program. As one Black and an Asian alumni explained:

> I think my experience in the IPP was comparable to my classmates on many levels, yes. I definitely know that I had a different perspective on many things because of my ethnicity and general life experience. Nothing [was] too significant that I can think of, however.

> I think the only way my IPP experience was not comparable to my non-Asian classmates was that when I interned with Deaf mentors and interpreters, more likely than not I would intern with mentors who are not from my culture or ethnic background.

However, two Black alumni and one Latina alumnus felt strongly that their experiences were not comparable. For example:

> As a Black student, I felt as a minority in such a small setting, going through the cohort I was like a "mystery" to my classmates, and was consequently ignored. Curriculum-wise, I don't think there was any difference in the education I received, but socially it was difficult to overcome the feeling of "otherness" that I felt starting the very first day of the program.

A Latina alumnus commented:

> I most definitely had additional challenge to overcome in order to become an interpreter of the deaf. Although I grew up in an environment where English was constantly used, it was a challenge to interpret from my third language to my second language. I thought it was going to be easier but the use of slangs and other regional expressions of the English language were a challenge to understand and interpret.

As mentioned earlier, almost all respondents felt that they were treated the same as their white classmates as they progressed through the program. Perhaps that is a problem in and of itself, where the unique needs of various ethnic groups were not given much consideration.

The need for ethnic diversity in teaching models and materials and reducing feelings of "otherness." Although the overall student population at the college, as well as the entire Bay Area population, is diverse and is not dominated by one ethnic group, the interpreter preparation program was experienced as white-centric. Most professors in the program are white. Most language models shown on videos are white. Most reading materials are prepared by white people. Most students in the program are white. Most mentors are white. This quote from a Black respondent exemplifies this perspective, which was shared by many in the survey:

> [If I were to make recommendations for change] I would look for more minority Deaf (visitors and videotaped texts) and interpreters who can share their experiences with the class throughout the entire two years. The differences in their everyday life, their signing style, and their attitudes about certain topics in the field are some things that are gravely missing from the current IPP structure.

Because people of color represent an extremely small percentage of interpreting students, they often have to contend with feeling like an outsider, an "other," while attending a program that is populated primarily by the majority culture. They, therefore, are vulnerable to inappropriate comments and/or behavior (often born of ignorance of their culture, not of malice) or, as was mentioned in the survey responses, a feeling that they inadvertently became a representative for their entire race. This pressure, coupled with the rigors of an intense program, can make for additional stress on students of color. Several respondents mentioned the importance of mentors who share the same ethnic background, with whom they could begin the valuable work from day one of expressing feelings of isolation and "otherness" with the goal of reducing their frustration. The mentor can become a "safe haven" with whom students can discuss positive solutions to these feelings and events as they may occur. Furthermore, the mentor can serve as a role model and source of inspiration to the fledgling interpreter. As two alumni explain:

> It would be great to have mentors of color, especially other interpreters. I was lucky to be able to work with X and X during my Deaf mentorship, with whom I still keep in contact. I would have very much liked to work with Asian interpreters during my interpreting mentorship. And again, the more diversity we see in the people who teach us, in the videos we watch, in our classmates, etc., the better we all will be.
>
> ...connecting students of color with mentors of color would be awesome... but only if that student is interested.

> Either through faculty or through events … or bringing in more guest speakers, and of course, the internships. I didn't really connect with interpreters of color or Asian interpreters (except a few individually from [another cohort]) until well after the program. Imagine connecting to those communities while still a student! Then having those mentors in your life when you're ready to start working. Very empowering.

Furthermore, several respondents felt that the readings and discussions about the experiences of people of color, both deaf people and interpreters, need to reflect their contemporary lives as opposed to the lives of the past. For example, many reading materials and DVDs are outdated, making the information contained in them obsolete.

Finally, survey respondents emphasized the importance of more widely recruiting students of color to populate IPP cohorts. Many of the alumni mentioned a dearth of awareness in their communities about ASL interpreting as a vocation. One Black alumnus recounted her experience trying to learn more about the field of interpreting, "When I wanted to become an interpreter, … I had no frame of reference and no one to ask. I had to blindly research everything about deafness/ASL myself...". Another Black respondent commented,

> I had not even heard about this profession until I went to [a local community college] and was in my third semester of signing classes, and I don't think professional interpreting is a well-known field among several parts of the black community. Many people I encounter and tell what I do have no idea what I'm talking about but are very intrigued.

A Latina respondent described how she had no idea about trilingual interpreting opportunities until she started the program. "I enter the program without knowing that trilingual opportunities will approach me. I always had a separation between English/ASL and English/Spanish. I never imagined [I] could become Spanish/ASL, ASL/Spanish, or all together."

The respondents cautioned that it is critical to be culturally sensitive when targeting specific groups for recruitment purposes. For example, one respondent explained her perspective on recruitment as follows: "I am not sure that there is a specific technique or approach for people of color. I think as long as it's done respectfully, it matches all students of color." Another respondent stated, "I'm not sure about culturally sensitive approaches because the degree of sensitivity that each person feels is so individualized."

Although many respondents did not have specific approaches to recruiting members of their communities to the interpreting profession, several suggestions were offered. For example:

> I would recommend that more awareness efforts be made at the local high schools. Leaders from the Deaf community could target clubs in high schools with large Hispanic enrollment and arrange for small group presentations to discuss the needs of the local Hispanic Deaf community and what the steps are to become an interpreter.
>
> It might be great to have Deaf Hispanic/Latinos and Hispanic/Latino Interpreters to inspire and attract future interpreters. Have a website in Spanish to really target and attract people from the community.
>
> Make sure that the need for black interpreters is known throughout these groups. Make sure a clear path is laid out for those that would like to pursue this profession. For example, make it clear that an IPP is an option after finishing the ASL program. Offer progressive ASL classes at Ohlone for students to be able to gain and hone their skill as well as set IPP goals.
>
> There are a lot of Black people that might be intrigued with the idea of becoming an ASL interpreter, but they are simply unaware that the field even exists. I often run into Black people who are just not exposed to ASL or the interpreting field at all but are enthusiastic about hearing more upon learning of it. So if IPPs would like an increase in the enrollment of people of color, they need to expand the places they seek out these students.
>
> In Asian culture, sign language interpreting is not widely considered a profession. I know for a fact that my

> Asian classmates and I have been asked by our family/relatives when we are going to be done with our "sign language thing" and find a real job. Many Asian students easily succumb to their family's expectation and decision of what their future career should be. I think it is important to convey to Asian students/candidates of the program that sign language interpreting indeed is a respectable profession and one can make a living from it.
>
> I encourage you to emphasize the importance of diversity in the interpreting profession. An Asian Deaf person would feel a greater connection and be more comfortable with an interpreter with the same cultural background. The program should inform all students that there is a great need for more interpreters of color.

In this sense, ethnic communities are an untapped source for expanding the pool for future interpreters. Going to where it is more likely that people of color will be and providing more exposure to Deaf people and interpreting in these communities will increase the likelihood of attracting more people of color to the profession. As the numbers of interpreters of color and the exposure to a variety of teaching models and materials increase, the feeling of otherness among interpreting students of color will diminish.

Discomfort about being expected to represent their communities. Respondents also expressed strong feelings about being expected to represent their ethnic communities as they progress through the program. They preferred to be free of this burden and wanted their thoughts, feelings, and opinions expressed in class to be viewed as their own and only their own. Adding to the burden, students of color were frequently seen as experts on topics related to diversity. In fact, some of them said that beyond having a physical appearance of being nonwhite, they had very little expertise about "diversity." For instance, Hispanic students do not always speak Spanish. Many of the Asian students were born in California and have never traveled out of the state. Furthermore, there are subcultures within each group that influence the experiences and perspectives of each individual. Such subcultures might include generational status, immigration status, age, gender and LGBTQI identity, and socioeconomic status, all of which lend to diversity within these ethnic groups. This makes it practically impossible to make generalizations about individual groups, and it is inappropriate to burden students of color with this responsibility. A number of Asian respondents share their sentiments on this topic as follows:

> I often felt that in class discussions about ethnicity I was looked to for answers as a representative of an entire group of people and not as speaking solely for myself.
>
> I'm speaking more as an American who knows only English and ASL and less as an "Asian"... I always wish there was a way to avoid "tokenism" but I'm not sure how...I would hope that the "one" is never asked to represent the entire diversity of all non-whites in the world. There are times I worry that the only reason I'm asked to do something or be a part of something is because I'm not white... Recognizing those who speak multiple languages would be amazing and connecting them with other multilingual interpreters. And, very important although difficult to encompass, to recognize that "Asian" means multiple languages and multiple cultures, not just one.

In contrast, one Asian respondent wished she had done more in educating her classmates on the cultural nuances and different cultural characteristics that are important to her community so that they could be better prepared to serve this population.

> ... I don't think I educated my classmates enough about the different cultural characteristics that I was taught throughout my life. I feel that I could have done more or could have taken more initiative in educating my classmates. I know that my classmates will make some cultural errors but that is part of the interpreting profession and you can't be an expert in every nationality. This is a lifelong learning experience and can't be learned in a 2-year program.

The added burden of being responsible for representing an entire community can be difficult and contributes to the feeling of otherness. This burden is often not shared by the majority, which makes it even more necessary for students and faculty members alike to understand their white privilege.

White privilege. Respondents reported that little focus was put on the history, the community, or the experiences of contemporary Black, Asian, and Hispanic Deaf people, who often have quite a different life experience from their white Deaf peers. For an interpreter working in an area where the chances of having more diverse clientele are high, a lack of relevant ethnic/cultural knowledge can become an issue for the interpreter's success at effective cultural mediation. Students who are unprepared for these settings may find themselves at a loss when trying to facilitate communication without the proper cultural nuances. This lack of attention to nonwhite communities underscores the importance of examining white privilege throughout the interpreter preparation program.

Although the privileges of the majority, such as being white, hearing, Christian, and heterosexual, were discussed frequently throughout the program, some respondents commented that both faculty and students are not always fully cognizant of all the privileges they have as white people. Because of this, the program is basically seen as being white-centric with little consideration of the unique needs and challenges faced by people of color on a daily basis. These challenges include being the only student of color, having all white teachers and mentors, dealing with mostly white stimuli, or participating in field work assignments in predominantly white communities. All these have an aggregated effect not only on students of color, but on white students, as these experiences contribute to the sense that white is "normal." As one Black and one Hispanic alumni explained,

> I didn't feel there was any focus on cultural competence in my experience with the IPP. Since the cohorts are so small I don't think it would be impossible to adapt to people of color in the courses. I don't think it was a conscious oversight, I think it's more related to ignorance of that type of need.

> During the time I was a student of the IPP, there were no topics that involved or included Hispanic heritage or references, nor were there Hispanic mentors, hearing or deaf, to partner with.

In addition, respondents felt that interpreting students are not exposed adequately to the vast number of events that are attended by minority Deaf people and/or are interpreted by interpreters of color. The result is a deficit in the knowledge of the types of settings that exist where cultural sensitivity and intercultural skill are necessary. As these alumni explained when asked what they would do if they were to redesign the program,

> I would design a curriculum that gives an overview of Deaf populations of color, and encourage students to attend Deaf events specific to these populations. When I was in the IPP, although I knew about Bay Area Asian Deaf Association by word of mouth, it would have been nice if the different organizations and the populations were taught to me formally in a class. I would also set up a panel of Asian interpreters, or invite them to class as guest lecturers, to share their experiences in the field. Same can also be done with Asian Deaf people.
>
> I would also have included at least 1 Deaf event organized by people of color to gain a better perspective of what's happening in our field with other minority groups, or I would have liked to find speakers from these different backgrounds to come in and talk about what it means to work in these communities.
>
> I would assign more "ethnic exposure" assignments; I think many of your white students could benefit from being more culturally aware as well as seeing the different accents that Deaf minorities have.

Being mindful that the lives of many students do not resemble those of professors would help the curriculum be less white-centric and more responsive to the realities of many different communities. Through regular exposure to a multicultural curriculum, white students are more aware of experiences that might differ drastically from their own. With increased awareness on the part of white students, students of color would not feel as marginalized.

Issues Specific to Ethnic Groups

In addition to these three themes that were common to all three ethnic groups, there were issues that were unique to specific populations.

Asian alumni. To begin with, Asian students identified several challenges that they felt were unique to their population. These include cultural differences between deaf people and many Asian families associated with communication norms. For example, showing facial expressions while conversing is frowned upon among many Asian families while it is an important grammatical aspect of ASL. Similarly, being soft-spoken is a trait that is difficult to break for many Asian students. Respondents reported that professors are not always sympathetic to this kind of challenge, one where Asian students need to balance the cultural expectations of their own homes and the necessity of developing critical interpreting skills in class.

> Growing up in an all-Asian household, I was surrounded by very quiet and soft-spoken people. I struggled with voicing out loud, trying to raise the volume of my voice in order for everyone to hear me. I know that this is required in our profession but I felt that none of my classmates had a problem with this, which bothered me throughout the program.
>
> The only challenge I could think of would be in regards to our facial expression. Asian people, in general, are not as expressive as Caucasians, including Deaf Asian people. I was often told I was not expressive enough. I always wondered is it because the grammatical intent isn't being shown on my face or was it just not enough in comparison to my Caucasian classmates?

Furthermore, Asian respondents felt that Americans in general and many Ohlone professors and students are not aware of the differing experiences among Asian-Americans (e.g., when families immigrated and how long they have lived in the United States). Fortunately, because of the plentitude of fellow Asian students studying at the college and a large Asian population in the Bay Area, Asian alumni reported that despite the issues discussed earlier here, they did not feel isolated while going through the program. Asian students reported that they felt their best support system was found in their classmates, teachers, and staff, as well as in the diverse student body at Ohlone College and the Bay Area. They were often encouraged and comforted "to be around an Asian Deaf population on campus" and said that "the support, camaraderie, and respect shared and freely given were unparalleled" by each cohort. The following two quotations describe this sentiment clearly:

> My IPP experience was very positive in general because of the diversity of the Deaf population on campus, as well as within my own cohort. This made it easy for me to learn more about Asian Deaf culture, and more comfortable to attend Asian Deaf events. I imagine the situation would be quite different for an interpreting student who is the only Asian person in his/her class. In that case, the program probably should do a little more in connecting said student with the Asian Deaf and interpreting population, if he/she wishes.
>
> [It was great] to be around an Asian Deaf population on campus. I was lucky that Ohlone has such a large population of international students. In addition, many of my classmates were Asian, either ethnically, or both ethnically and culturally. The diversity really helped me feel comfortable as I went through the program.

Hispanic/Latin@ alumni. Just like the Asian alumni, the experiences of Hispanic alumni varied a great deal, depending on their family backgrounds. One was born in the United States and did not speak Spanish at all. Another alumnus moved to the United States as an adult and struggled due to her limitations with English. Contrast the experiences of two Hispanic alumni when asked if their experiences were comparable to their classmates:

> No, I felt my challenges were similar to my classmates. Even though I am a first generation Mexican American …

> my primary language was always English. I didn't face the challenges other Hispanic people had whose primary language was Spanish.
>
> It always bothered me that I always felt behind in my performance and voicing exercises. I needed more support in these areas to feel equally skilled compared to my classmates. I was fortunate during my last semester in the program my instructors allowed me to do some voicing from ASL to Spanish. It provided me with a sense of what I could do after graduation.

Black alumni. In contrast, Black alumni expressed a strong feeling of otherness while going through the program. Because Black people represent an extremely small percentage of ASL interpreters in general and the college population at Ohlone specifically, they often have to contend with feeling like an outsider, an "other," while going through the program. For this reason, the provision of Black mentors from day one is strongly recommended. As one respondent describes the situation,

> I often felt that in class discussions about ethnicity I was looked to for answers as a representative of an entire group of people and not as speaking solely for myself.... They, unintentionally I feel, left me out of group activities and conversations. I did not feel like part of the group fairly often and this is a place where a support system is very important

DISCUSSION/CONCLUSION

This study illuminates the need for the interpreting field to take a hard look at itself with respect to how interpreting students of color are recruited, supported, and nurtured. It is likely that the findings of this study can be extrapolated to the majority of interpreter preparation programs, especially since very few people of color are currently being recruited and prepared to enter the profession.

It is noteworthy that the majority of the respondents in this study initially reported that they had an experience comparable to that of their white classmates while going through the interpreter preparation program. However, as our questions became more specific and the respondents' answers went deeper, we noted that students of color and white students differ in important ways with respect to their IPP experiences. This disparity between the initial, more superficial, and subsequent comments offered in the survey should encourage those who run interpreting preparation programs to actively seek feedback from all of their alumni. Only then can the learning environment be truly optimal for all, including students of color. The findings from this study indicate four major areas of consideration. They include (1) the feeling of otherness, (2) the need for diversified teaching approaches, (3) the burden of representing an entire ethnic group, and (4) the impact of white privilege. These issues will be examined further here, and implications for the field will be discussed.

The Feeling of Otherness

More often than not, students of color found themselves being the only one from their ethnic group in their cohort. Consequently, they often experienced a feeling of otherness while going through the program. Some factors contributing to this feeling were similar across all three groups while others were unique to specific ethnic groups.

For example, in many Asian cultures it is not typically appropriate to use overly expressive facial expressions, loud voices, or large gestures. While this challenge is often discussed within the Asian interpreting community, it is rarely addressed in the interpreter preparation program. As a result, Asian students often struggle with conflicting expectations throughout their program. This contributes to a feeling of otherness among Asian students, as their non-Asian peers do not have the same challenge.

Another challenge deals with the linguistic competency that is required of interpreting students. Hispanic/Latin@ and Asian students for whom English is not their first language often struggle in trying to work with second and third (or even fourth) languages in their assignments. This contributes to a feeling of otherness, as their peers, whose native language is English, do not have similar struggles.

However, when given the opportunity to work with their native language, they often find it easy to excel. Unfortunately, professors are unable to evaluate their work across these other languages, as they do not possess skills in languages other than ASL and English.

For Black students, this feeling of otherness often emerges because the college itself does not have as many Black students, both Deaf and hearing, in its student body as it does Asian and Hispanic/Latin@ students. This, by itself, makes it even more isolating for Black students as they have limited peer support outside the program compared to Asian, Hispanic/Latin@, and white students.

To reduce the sense of otherness and to increase everyone's cultural competence across multiple domains, an aggressive recruitment effort to attract individuals of color to interpreter preparation programs needs to take place. Almost all respondents in this survey reported that they did not realize when they were growing up that interpreting could be a viable career option. Often, it was not until they took a sign language course in college that they discovered this field of study. An additional challenge is the misconceptions associated with the profession. Interpreting is often viewed as charity work that will someday lead to a more respectable profession such as nursing, teaching, or counseling. Correcting this general misunderstanding and the specific misconceptions within particular ethnic communities will be an important component of recruiting and supporting a more diverse pool of interpreting students. With an increased number of students of color in interpreter preparation programs, the feeling of otherness should be diminished. This feeling also could be reduced by a stronger presence of people of color among the teaching personnel and educational stimuli.

The Need for Diversified Teaching Approaches

Given that the majority of working interpreters and college training personnel are white and the fact that most educational stimuli are also primarily white, it is imperative that we increase the visibility and involvement of people of color in the preparation of future interpreters. There are several different ways to accomplish this.

For example, interpreter preparation programs must develop a strategic plan to recruit students of color. We must make an extra effort to locate educational stimuli that reflects the demographics of the deaf community more closely. A commitment to attend relevant conferences, such as the triennial Deaf People of Color conference and the biannual National Black Deaf Advocates conference, must be made. Program design, recruitment, and instruction must be done in collaboration with various segments of the Deaf community. A participation in events that are well attended by diverse segments of the Deaf community must be required of interpreting students and faculty alike. People of color must be recruited to teach courses within the program. Mentors of color must be readily available to students of color, as well as to white students. Only then can future interpreters be properly prepared to work with a diverse population of Deaf consumers, interpreting colleagues, and hearing people at large.

The Burden of Representing Their Ethnic Groups

A common refrain from the alumni who participated in this research is the sentiment that in voicing their opinions and experiences, they are perceived by people outside their culture as speaking for all people who share the same cultural background. Consequently, people of color are sometimes cautious about sharing their viewpoints in mixed groups. Several respondents mentioned this point and noted how uncomfortable they were when they felt they were being seen as representatives of their entire race.

The alumni that participated in the survey are, for the most part, vastly different from each other. The sample represents people who are second-, third-, and more-generation Americans, but also those who immigrated to the United States relatively recently. The Asian alumni have heritages that span various countries within Asia. These countries have their own traditions, values, and languages. Bearing that in mind, how can anyone apply one person's opinion to such a varied group of people? Likewise, the Black alumni represented here come from various backgrounds as well and as a result cannot speak for the entire African diaspora. The same can be said for the Hispanic/Latin@ population.

It is recommended that instructors and students in interpreter preparation programs regard their students as separate individuals with widely varying backgrounds, knowledge bases, and experiences. In the same manner that it is generally understood for the majority culture that one person does not speak for all the people who belong to that race, interpreting students of color (and people of color in general) would prefer to be seen as individuals and valued for the skills and experiences they bring to the field, even as they are simultaneously recognized as having a cultural, ethnic, and racial heritage that is not white and therefore not the dominant culture in the United States.

The Impact of White Privilege

The findings of this study reinforce the information gleaned from the literature that interpreter preparation programs continue to be white-centric. This continues to occur despite the shift in demographics in many parts of the country. Although diversity, privilege in general, and cultural sensitivity play an increasingly prominent role in the curriculum of many interpreter preparation programs, including the one at Ohlone College, faculty members need to be mindful of their own white privilege and examine how that has influenced their recruitment strategies, curriculum design, and expectations for student outcomes directly or indirectly. To this end, faculty members need to commit themselves to aggressive solicitation of feedback from students of color, alumni of color, interpreters of color, and consumers regarding program design, curricular offerings, and teaching approaches. This, in turn, will help enhance the overall experience for all students and reduce the potential of maintaining the status quo of a white-centric learning environment throughout interpreter preparation programs. Ultimately, this will help attract people of color to the field of interpreting and make the profession more reflective of and responsive to the demographics of the Deaf community in particular and the United States in general.

REFERENCES

Anderson, G.B., & Miller, K.R. (2004/2005). Appreciating diversity through stories about the lives of Deaf people of color. *American Annals of the Deaf, 149,* 375–383.

Aries, E. (2008). *Race and class matters at an elite college.* Philadelphia, PA: Temple University Press.

Bauman, H-D.L. (Ed.)(2008). *Open your eyes: Deaf studies talking.* Minneapolis, MN: University of Minnesota Press.

Bienvenu, M.J. (2008). Queer as Deaf: Intersections. In H-D. L. Bauman (Ed.), *Open your eyes: Deaf studies talking* (pp. 264–273). Minneapolis, MN: University of Minnesota Press.

Brueggemann, B.J., & Burch, S. (Eds.)(2006). *Women and deafness: Double visions.* Washington, DC: Gallaudet University Press.

Davis, L. (2008). Postdeafness. In H-D. L. Bauman (Ed.), *Open your eyes: Deaf studies talking* (pp. 314–325). Minneapolis, MN: University of Minnesota Press.

Dunn, L. (2008). The burden of racism and audism. In H-D. L. Bauman (Ed.), *Open your eyes: Deaf studies talking* (pp. 235–250). Minneapolis, MN: University of Minnesota Press.

Feagin, J.R., Vera, H., & Imani, N. (1996). *The agony of education: Black students at white colleges and universities.* NY: Routledge.

Handy, K. (Summer, 2010). A bi-cultural journey: The story of Samantha Hatfield. *VIEWS,* 14.

Holcomb, T. (2013). *Introduction to American Deaf culture.* NY: Oxford University Press.

Hooks, B. (2008). Representations of whiteness in the Black imagination. In P. S. Rothenberg (Ed.), White privilege: Essential readings on the other side of racism (pp. 19–23). NY: Worth Publishers.

Jones, P. A. (1986). Issues involving Black interpreters and Black Deaf. *Interpreting: The art of cross cultural mediation, Proceedings of the Ninth National Convention of the Registry of Interpreters for the Deaf* (pp. 61–68). Silver Spring, MD: RID Publications.

Kelly, A.B. (2008). Where is Deaf herstory? In H-D. L. Bauman (Ed.), *Open your eyes: Deaf studies talking* (pp. 251–263). Minneapolis, MN: University of Minnesota Press.

Kivel, P. (2007). Multicultural competence. Retrieved July 18, 2012, from http://pkivel.com/index.php?option=com_flexicontent&view=items&cid=23:article&id=67:multicultural-competence-&Itemid=15

Lane, H., Hoffmeister, R., & Bahan, B. (1996). *A journey into the Deaf-World.* San Diego, CA: DawnSignPress.

McCaskill, C., Lucas, C., Bayley, R., & Hill, J. (2011). *The hidden treasure of Black ASL*. Washington, DC: Gallaudet University Press.

McIntosh, P. (1988/2007). White privilege: Unpacking the invisible knapsack. In P. Rothenberg (Ed.), *Race, class, and gender in the United States* (7th ed., pp. 177–182). New York: Worth Publishers.

McKee, R.L., & Davis, J. (2010). *Interpreting in multilingual, multicultural contexts*. Washington, DC: Gallaudet University Press.

Mindess, A., Holcomb, T., Langholtz, D., & Poyer, P. (2006). Reading between the signs: Intercultural communication for sign language interpreters (2nd ed.). Boston, MA: Intercultural Press.

National Multicultural Interpreter Project Curriculum. Retrieved July 16, 2012 from http://www.epcc.edu/NMIP/Pages/Curriculum.aspx

Obasi, C. (2013). Race and ethnicity in sign language interpreter education, training, and practice. *Race, Ethnicity and Education, 16*, 103–120.

Registry of Interpreters for the Deaf (2011). Annual report to the members. Retrieved January 3, 2013, from http://www.rid.org/userfiles/File/pdfs/About_RID/RIDFY2011AnnualReport.pdf

Smith, S. (2012). Overcoming challenges as a sign language interpreter of color. Retrieved July 16, 2012, from http://www.streetleverage.com/2012/07/overcoming-challenges-as-a-sign-language-interpreter-of-color/

Steele, C.M. (1997). A threat in the air: How stereotypes shape intellectual identity and performance. *American Psychologist, 52*, 613–629.

Tochluk, S. (2008). *Witnessing whiteness: First steps toward an antiracist practice and culture*. Lanham, MD: Rowman & Littlefield Education.

APPENDIX

PREPARING ASL/ENGLISH INTERPRETERS FOR A DIVERSE COMMUNITY: ARE WE DOING ENOUGH?

Interview Questions

1. As a person of color, do you believe that your experiences of going through the IPP were comparable to your classmates? Or did you feel you had additional challenges that were unique to you and probably to other Asian [Black/Latino/a] students?
2. If you were to redesign the program, what would you incorporate in the new program that would be especially important to Asian [Black/Latino/a] students?

3. Do you feel your classmates are adequately prepared to work in the ethnically, racially, and culturally diverse community in general and to the Asian [Black/Latino/a] community?
4. What bothered you the most about your experiences going through the program, which may not be true for your classmates?
5. What was most helpful for you as a person of color as you went through the program?
6. Should there be special attention for students of color such as having a mentor, making sure they are given a warm welcome, and such?
7. How should people of color be recruited to the program? Are there culturally sensitive approaches that we may include for Asian [Black/Latino/a] students?
8. "We must learn to observe, empathize, and appreciate other people's ways of doing things to become culturally competent" (Kivel, 2007, p. 2). Did we do enough to do this for you and your classmates in the program?
9. There is a strong emphasis on understanding Deaf culture and recognizing that there is a hearing culture. Did the cultural concept transfer successfully to the experiences of people of color, both deaf and hearing alike? What more do interpreting students need to know, do, and understand?
10. Any other comments?

Chapter 8

Strategies for Success in Higher Education: A Focus on Deaf Students

PATRICIA BRASWELL, Ed.D.

INTRODUCTION

This study was designed to provide insight regarding how Deaf individuals attain personal and academic success within postsecondary educational institutions. As a result, this study addressed the following questions:

1. What are some of the strategies and support mechanisms used by Deaf individuals that lead to academic success?
2. By what means is success measured in institutions of higher education?
3. What improvements are suggested to ensure more successful outcomes?

Research has shown that Deaf individuals, specifically those with congenital hearing loss, comprise less than 5% of the California community college student population (Choy, Horn, Chun, & Nuriet, 2000). Within that group are students of color. Therefore, we must also examine issues and practices related to diversity, access, and student equity. It is important to understand factors that relate specifically to personal and/or academic success for all Deaf individuals in order to ensure that institutions of higher education are providing the support needed to assist them in meeting their personal, professional, and academic goals.

A critical factor to examine with regard to the personal and/or academic success of individuals who are Deaf is the idea of **social capital**. Condeluci, Ledbetter, Ortman, Fromknecht, and DeFries (2008) defined social capital theory as an array of support offered by friends, family, and acquaintances that is available to all individuals, including those with and without disabilities. It has been suggested that access to social capital may be limited for people with disabilities and therefore may contribute to their inability to develop networks and friendships (Condeluci et al., 2008). The direct relationship of social capital to the academic success of Deaf community college students was studied.

Today, approximately 66% of all community college students will not complete a degree in the 8 years after completing high school. Reasons for nondegree completion point specifically to incoming students being underprepared for college-level math and English (Rosenbaum, Redline, & Stephan, 2007). Furthermore, Choy and colleagues (2000) suggest that a large population of these students will also not have passed the California High School Exit Exam. California community college students are finding themselves underprepared for college-level coursework and too often are caught in a cycle of remediation classes. At the same time, costs for services provided to this population of students, including sign language interpreting and real-time captioning, continue to rise.

During the spring of 1998, the California State Chancellor's Office collaborated with the Workload Task Force by developing a system to track the delivery of services for students with disabilities. Deaf students were included in this group. Community college staff were trained to use the system, monitor the data collection, and analyze data. The goal of the system was to calculate the relative cost of providing services to students using data collected on all services delivered during the spring, summer, and fall semesters of 1999. Data analysis determined that the average cost per term of serving a Deaf student far exceeded the cost of serving a student in any other category ($1356 versus $73–$221 for the others). This was largely because of the high level and high cost of interpreting services required (Choy et al., 2000). Complicating matters even more is the fact that assessments documented the reduced English skill level of Deaf students, as compared with other groups of first-year students, as they transitioned from high school into postsecondary institutions.

O'Connell (2007) reported that the California Department of Education (CDE) found that only 8% of Deaf students scored proficient or advanced on the California Standards Test for English-language arts. In math, only 10% of Deaf students scored proficient or advanced. As a result, Deaf students entering postsecondary institutions were unprepared to meet the academic rigor encountered in higher education settings. O'Connell (2007) noted that the CDE further suggested that a hearing loss in and of itself does not predetermine a Deaf student's academic success. Rather it is the lack of early access to comprehensible language in the environment during infancy. Consequently, the CDE highlighted the benefits of early exposure to comprehensible language for children who are Deaf as it relates not only to successful language acquisition but also to literacy development.

MacSweeney, Waters, Brammer, Woll, and Goswami (2007) found that a Deaf learner's process for successful language acquisition is correlated directly to their preliminary introduction to signed or spoken languages. Phonological awareness also differs for Deaf children as compared to their hearing counterparts. Phonology for spoken languages is based on auditory/articulatory elements; however, for signed languages, which are visual, these elements are hand shapes, movements, and locations along with facial expression (MacSweeney et al., 2007).

Regarding students with disabilities, in general, findings from a southern California institution of higher education, which we will call Bayside Community College, indicated that during the fall 2007 semester, 17,301 students were enrolled. Of those students, 825 (4.8%) were identified as having a disability. With regard to class completion, students with disabilities completed 61.3% of their courses in contrast to a 67.5% completion rate of courses taken by their nondisabled counterparts (Braswell-Burris, 2010). In spring 2007, 579 degrees and 275 certificates were awarded. Of those awards, 36 (6.2%) of students with disabilities completed degrees and 9 (6.9%) students received a certificate (Braswell-Burris, 2010).

Regarding goal attainment for students who are Deaf, it should be noted that from spring 2000 through spring 2005, there were 72 Deaf students who attended Bayside Community College in southern California. Of those 72 students, 2 students who did not identify a goal of degree completion earned a degree successfully. Of the 26 Deaf students **who declared a goal of earning a degree,** zero actually earned a degree. Findings from existing literature regarding the lack of success in academic achievement for Deaf individuals led to the development of this study.

This study asked the following question: How do Deaf individuals attain personal and/or academic success? The study examined how Deaf community college students utilized effective strategies to assist them with meeting their personal and academic life goals. A qualitative-grounded theory approach was selected and used to investigate learning outcomes for Deaf individuals who obtained gainful employment, completed a workforce training program, or completed a degree in higher education.

One-on-one interviews with Deaf individuals were conducted as part of the research process. Based on the research findings, recommendations were made for program development and service delivery. These recommendations are intended to support the personal and academic success of Deaf students in postsecondary educational settings.

Charmaz (2006) indicated that grounded theory involves making comparisons from data to construct abstractions and then connecting those abstractions back to data that have been collected. The information gathered in this study was obtained from semistructured standard interviews that were conducted with seven Deaf individuals who met their own personal or academic goals. Participants were selected due to their previous experiences in a workforce training program, postsecondary institution, and/or their ability to become gainfully employed.

Participants in this study included seven individuals who identified themselves as Deaf and who met the criteria of being successful in meeting either an academic or a personal, professional goal. From a pool of 35 individuals, 15 prelingual Deaf individuals were identified as potential participants for the study. Additional criteria for participation in the study included a unilateral/bilateral severe-to-profound hearing loss or a unilateral/bilateral moderate hearing loss and a primary communication modality that involved American Sign Language (ASL) or a signed system with or without the use of spoken English. For the intent and purposes of this study, this investigator worked collaboratively with postsecondary and higher education faculty and staff to develop a list of 32 potential candidates. A pool of 15 potential participants who met the criteria was identified. An additional review of the criteria was conducted to determine how many participants would actually qualify for recruitment in the study. Criteria for participation in the study were narrowed down to three categories: (a) a Deaf individual who had obtained a degree from a 2- or 4-year educational institution, (b) a Deaf individual who was currently employed and working a minimum of 15 hours per week, and (c) a Deaf individual who had completed a vocational/workforce training program. The recruitment process resulted in a total of 7 actual participants in the study.

Test questions were designed for the interview protocol to be used in the study. A pilot study was conducted in order to provide the investigator with feedback regarding the interview questions that were developed for the study. Specific information sought from the pilot study related to whether the questions were clear and concise. Deaf individuals who met the criteria for participation in the study, but were not among the 7 subjects selected for the study, were recruited for the pilot study. Pilot study participants were given an overview of the study by the researcher and allowed time to ask any questions regarding the study prior to completing the interview. A sample interview protocol was given to each pilot study participant with instructions to provide feedback to the researcher regarding the clarity of the interview questions. Participants completed the interview within a 35-minute time frame.

Results from the pilot study indicated that the interview protocol questions were comprehensible and appropriate for the study. It was also determined that the interview protocol had an adequate number of questions to gain the information required and that no changes should be made to the language used in the questions.

Additional pilot study results yielded information regarding the use of an interpreter, that is, Deaf participants were given a choice as to whether or not they wanted to utilize interpreting services during their interviews. Feedback from the pilot study participants indicated that the use of interpreters during the interviews was appropriate. Furthermore, pilot study results were used to make changes to the interview protocol to ensure objectivity, integrity, and confidentiality.

Based on results from the pilot study, an open-ended interview protocol consisting of 16 questions was developed for the format of the formal study. Questions consisted of background information, family history, language acquisition, educational history, and postsecondary academic and personal experiences, as well as workplace experiences. The interview protocol asked participants to provide information regarding any support services used in both workplace and postsecondary settings. The protocol was based on published literature reviewed by the investigator, incorporating the conceptual framework of social capital. Subsequently, the interview protocol became the foundation for conversations during interviews between the participants and the researcher.

Subjects were interviewed over a 1.5-month period. Interviews were structured into 1-hour interviews with consideration given to the language differences between the Deaf subjects and the investigator. Based on pilot study results, participants were given a choice of whether or not they wished to utilize an interpreter as a facilitator of communication during the interviews. It should be noted that based on pilot study results, when an interview was conducted without the use of an interpreter, a video camera and digital recorder were used to ensure reliability of the conversations. For those participants who chose to utilize the services of an interpreter, the researcher met with the interpreters prior to each interview to discuss any issues related to the study that required clarification.

This study involved an in-depth analysis of data, which included interview transcripts and researcher notes taken after the interview. Merriam (1998) indicated that data collection and analysis are simultaneous activities in qualitative research. She further suggested that analysis begins with the first interview, the first observation, the first document read. Coded written summaries were created after each interview.

The next step in the data analysis process was the development of a thorough transcription of audio voice recordings, which were completed by a professional transcriber. The transcription was evaluated to compare the video and audio recordings for triangulation and accuracy. The video recordings were reviewed to check for accuracy of the information relayed during the interviews. The transcription was coded line by line. Charmaz (2006) revealed that line-by-line coding works particularly well with detailed data about fundamental problems or processes whether these data consist of interviews, observations, documents, or ethnographies and autobiographies. Focused coding was used to compact codes and develop themes and categories. Relationships between categories were further identified to determine how the codes related to each other and could be formulated into possible theories.

This method allowed the investigator to explore data for implicit actions and meanings, to compare data to data, and to identify any gaps in data (Charmaz, 2006). Seven Deaf individuals participated in this study. The strategies and support mechanisms that led to their personal or academic success were examined. All of the participants in the study had attained personal or academic success as defined by the study criteria. Five of the participants had earned Masters Degrees, one participant was completing a Masters Degree, and one participant was in the process of completing a Bachelor's Degree. In addition to attaining academic goals, all of the participants in the study had also attained personal success as defined by their employment goals. Four of the participants were employed in higher education, two in the K-12 educational system, and one in law enforcement. Participants in the study represented different backgrounds and had varied life experiences. However, the participants shared commonalities by way of communication choices/options, primary and secondary educational settings, and the pursuit of career paths. Study participants consisted of four females and three males who ranged in age from 27 to 60 years. Representation of ethnicity among participants included five Caucasian, one African-American, and one Latino subject.

Five of the participants utilized American Sign Language as their primary modality of communication, one participant used both ASL and spoken English for communication, and one participant used only spoken English and depended on the visual modality of speech reading as the preferred method of communication.

Social capital has been defined by Condeluci and colleagues (2008) as support offered from an array of family, friends, and acquaintances. Social capital and social networking are necessary to build relationships, resources, and communities. Several categories emerged in the interviews with study participants. A description of these emergent categories is as follows.

1. **Cultural identity** plays a significant role in building social capital, as it provides a connection to culture, language, beliefs, and community.
2. **Role models** provide a concrete foundation for the participants to meet and interact with both Deaf and hearing individuals within various environments, therefore expanding social capital for the participants.
3. **Supportive parents** are vital to the development of social capital for the participants in this study. They provided the participants with a strong support base and a sense of belonging within the family structure.
4. **Family support** is beneficial in the social and emotional development of the participants and assists with strengthening their access to social capital by providing the participants with extended family connections, shared values, and traditions.
5. **Code switching** is another important factor that assists the participants with access to social capital. The ability to move

easily from one language to another allows the participants to engage in communication exchanges with individuals from various backgrounds, thereby creating a social network for the participants.

6. **Direct communication** is the most significant factor that led to the development of social capital for the participants. This communication modality had a positive impact on the participants' ability to communicate their thoughts, feelings, and desires effectively without the need of facilitated communication in academic and social settings. When the participants used direct communication, they were able to broaden their social capital by connecting with people and the community directly, which by definition is the underlying principal encompassing the social capital theory.

Access to social capital may be beneficial to Deaf persons due to the fact that they are usually treated as a homogeneous group when, in reality, the population is dramatically variant (Bullis & Davis, 1995). The Deaf community is as diverse as other communities. Hearing professionals must be cognizant of this fact when delivering services to Deaf individuals. Cultural understanding and sensitivity have been a bridge to the appreciation of differences that exist among hearing and Deaf individuals while parallels are shared as they relate to having the same goals and dreams (Benedict & Sass-Lehrer, 2007).

The analysis process for the seven interview transcripts resulted in 70 codes, which were collapsed into 23 categories. Further analysis resulted in 12 distinct themes that emerged from the data. Of the 12 themes, 10 factors **significantly** influenced the personal and academic success of the Deaf participants in the study.

The themes that were prevalent as a result of the study reported here were used as a guideline to suggest implications for practice and program recommendations. Additionally, the findings of this study were used in determining strategies to assist Deaf individuals with reaching personal or academic goals in educational institutions.

As stated previously, 12 themes emerged; however, 10 themes most specifically represent factors and/or mechanisms that led

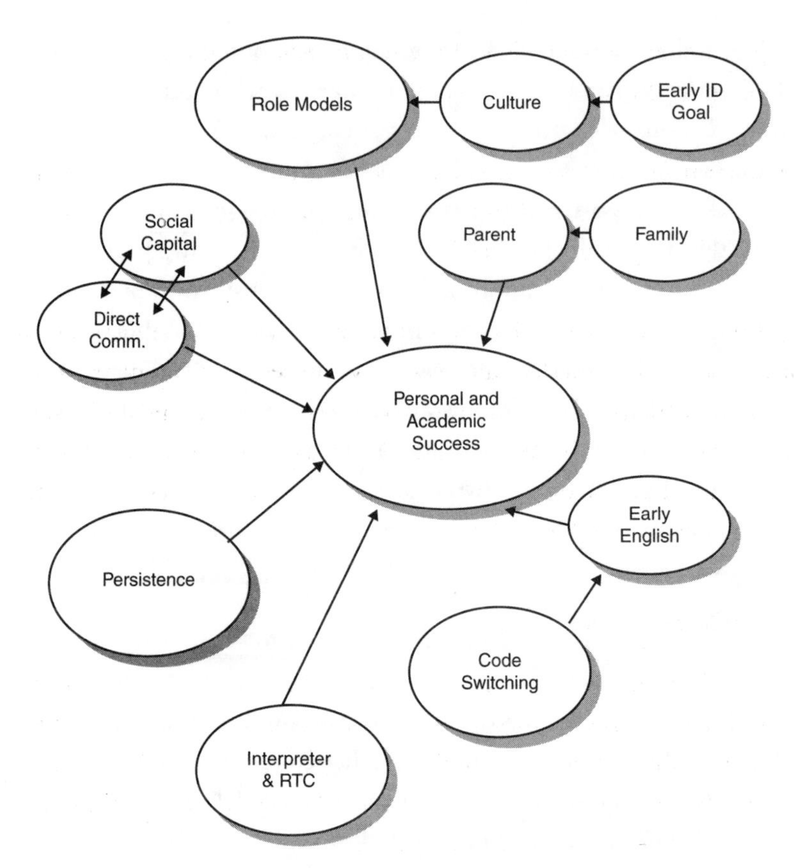

Figure 1. Factors influencing personal and academic success in Deaf or hard-of-hearing individuals. RTC, real-time captioning.

to personal or academic success by the study participants. These 10 themes were role models, cultural identity, parental involvement, family support, early identification of a personal or academic goal, early exposure to English print and language, code switching, interpreting and real-time captioning services, persistence, direct communication, and social capital (Figure 1).

Two additional themes—frustration with communication and feelings of isolation and exclusion—emerged during the data analysis process; however, they did not contribute significantly to personal or academic success for the study participants. Another study in the future might address ways in which successful students cope with frustration and isolation.

The following is a review of the first question that was proposed as the focus of this study.

Question 1: What were some of the strategies and support mechanisms used by Deaf individuals that lead to academic or personal success?

Research findings indicated that the strategies and support mechanisms used by Deaf individuals to achieve success were strong personal support, academic support, communication strategies, and social support. These factors were significant in assisting the study participants with achieving personal and academic goals in their personal and professional lives.

Strong Personal Support

A prevailing factor that led to academic and personal success for Deaf individuals in this study was a strong personal support system, including support by parents, core family members, and extended family and friends. Included in personal support was the presence of role models.

Parental involvement was significant in shaping the lives and decisions that the participants made regarding postsecondary educational choices, language preferences, values, and self-identification. Parental involvement encompassed parental advocacy, and parental commitment to education. During childhood, the parents were integral in ensuring that the participants had an enriched educational experience. The parental choices for education provided preparation for the participants to attain academic success in higher education.

Collaborative efforts between some parents and teachers during early childhood assisted the participants with developing a sound foundation for learning. This is consistent with the research by Watson and Swanick (2008) who reported that any disconnects between parents and teachers should be resolved in order to provide consistency in literacy approaches. In addition, parental involvement helped shape the participants' core value system as it related to positive personal development.

Deaf individuals who attained personal or academic success had tremendous support from their families. Family support included immediate and extended family members and provided the participants with a strong sense of self, stability, and independence. Participants benefited from engaging with their families by developing positive self-esteem and self-confidence. Family support was not limited to the nuclear family; it also included friends, mentors, and role models.

Role Models

All of the study participants had a role model at some period in their lives. Some of the participants found role models early on and others during young adulthood. These role models were influential in helping shape the Deaf persons' ideas related to life experiences. Whether the participants were introduced to role models as children, young adults, or later in life, role models played an integral part in the participants' personal and/or academic success.

Extended Support

The ability to draw strength from family and friends in order to maintain their own motivation and persistence was an important factor. The subjects' ability to persist despite life interferences was a considerable factor in accomplishing their goals. A few of the participants described periods in their lives when they dealt with feelings of loneliness, isolation, and depression. However, their desire to persist academically and professionally was remarkable. The participants were able to draw on their strengths and high self-expectations to pursue degree completion and/or enter the workforce.

Academic Support

Academic supports included an early exposure to English literacy in educational environments, the support offered by interpreters and real-time captioning services within classroom settings, and the ability to identify a personal or academic goal before leaving high school.

Early exposure to English literacy was a dominant factor in assisting the participants with personal and academic success. All seven participants were exposed to an oral or mainstream education during early childhood where American Sign Language was not used in the classroom. In addition, all seven of the participants were exposed to spoken English and English print at home. This study supported the theory that early literacy intervention helped create a pathway to the development of English reading and writing skills. English literacy skills, then, led to academic success in primary, secondary, and postsecondary education. This supported Lang (2002) hypothesis that early intervention and academic preparation in elementary and secondary programs have an undeniable direct bearing on the academic success of Deaf students in higher education.

Communication Strategies

Communication strategies that led to the personal and academic success of the participants included the ability to **code switch** between communication modalities. Code switching was described in this study as the ability for a Deaf individual to switch his/her communication modality in order to communicate with other people successfully. The participants reported that they developed code-switching skills during early childhood that stayed with them throughout their lifetime. This skill allowed the participants to engage actively in a multitude of environments and increased their social networking capacity.

Social Support

Social supports that contributed to the success of the participants included the identification of cultural identity. This was a significant factor that influenced the personal and academic success of the Deaf individuals who participated in the study. This concept was consistent among all study participants and related specifically to the participant's acceptance and understanding of their language, culture, identity, and community.

Each of the study participants defined their cultural identity by their language preferences, communication modalities, and social settings. The majority of the participants had struggled with their cultural identity at some point in their lives. It was evident from the study findings that when the participants chose a communication modality for themselves, they accepted their cultural identities almost simultaneously.

Based on the study findings regarding the factors that influence the personal and academic success of Deaf individuals, the following implications for practice in institutions of higher learning can be made.

IMPLICATIONS FOR PRACTICE

1. **Role models** are a significant factor in the personal and academic success of Deaf individuals. Positive role models, especially those who share the student's culture(s), serve as visible examples of academic achievement and personal success. Role models assist Deaf individuals with the development of strategies for communication, life skills, and of social capital. Role models are essential to the personal and academic success of Deaf individuals.
2. **Cultural identity** is a major influence in the attainment of success by Deaf individuals. An acceptance and understanding of the values, beliefs, and traditions that encompass cultural identity are significant to Deaf individuals pursuing higher education or who decide to enter the workforce.
3. Deaf individuals who **identify a personal or academic goal early on in their development** have a higher chance of obtaining goal achievement.
4. **Positive parental involvement** was a fundamental component to the personal and academic success of Deaf individuals as they recalled their K-12 experiences.
5. **Extended family support** was another beneficial factor that assisted Deaf individuals with reaching personal and academic success. Therefore, a positive family unit that supports early access to communication will enable the Deaf individual to feel connected, safe, and an integral part of the family.
6. While interpreting and real-time captioning services assist Deaf individuals with accessing communication in academic arenas

and workplace settings, it is imperative that these **support services** are matched to the preferred language modality of the individual.

7. Public and private sector programs delivering services to Deaf individuals must provide **direct communication** in order to promote access to social capital. This population benefits exponentially from experiences that utilize a direct communication model. This is essential to the development and access of social capital. In addition, early exposure and development of English literacy are critical to the academic success of Deaf individuals in postsecondary education and for those who seek to enter the workforce.

RECOMMENDATIONS

1. Educational programs at the primary, secondary, and postsecondary levels should design and implement programs that have a role model component embedded within the core curriculum. These programs should seek to recruit and hire role models who represent diversity in language, culture, and ethnicity. In addition, role models should include family members, educators, professionals, and members of the Deaf community.
2. Community-based programs, primary, secondary, and postsecondary educational settings should strive to develop and implement practices that assist Deaf individuals with examining their cultural identities.
3. Educational learning environments should assist Deaf individuals with an early introduction to a variety of academic or personal goals. Early childhood educational programs should strive to incorporate goal-setting practices as part of their curriculum-based instruction in order to increase Deaf children's awareness of potential goals. Secondary and postsecondary educational institutions should develop and implement programs that further target strategies for the identification of personal or academic goals.

4. Early in the education of their child, parents of Deaf children should have a commitment to ensuring that their child is placed in the most appropriate educational environment to meet his/her needs. Parents should work toward being advocates for their children in the development of their educational and personal experiences. During the early development of Deaf children, parents should work toward collaborative partnerships with teachers, counselors, and other educational support staff to ensure direct involvement in their child's educational placements. Parental involvement, parental advocacy, and a parental commitment to education unequivocally assist children who are Deaf to reach their personal and academic goals. Educational settings should strive to develop student orientations and academic advising workshops that promote collaboration with the college community.
5. Families must include Deaf children in social events, family outings, and extracurricular activities in an effort to promote health and wellness. Family support should include, but not be limited to, the immediate family, extended family members, family friends, and the community at large, thus assisting with the development of social capital and social networking experiences. Postsecondary educational settings should develop and implement programs for Deaf individuals that assist the families with learning about first-year experiences for college students. These programs should seek to promote independence, as well as inclusion of families, and should be ongoing throughout the college experience.
6. Interpreting training and real-time captioning programs must produce interpreters and real-time captionists proficient with a high skill level in order to ensure that all service delivery systems are of the utmost quality. Support service providers at the postsecondary level who deliver quality interpreting and real-time captioning services maximize the opportunities for Deaf individuals to attain personal and academic success. Institutions of higher education should develop and implement ongoing evaluations of interpreters and real-time captionists. These evaluations should provide ongoing feedback regarding the performance levels of support service providers within

Disabled Students Programs and Services. The effectiveness of facilitated communication is a vital factor that directly influences goal attainment for Deaf individuals.

7. Programs should seek to develop and implement methods of instruction that incorporate *direct communication* as an alternative to facilitated communication. Deaf individuals learn best when communication is accessible without the need for a third party. Institutions of higher education must employ direct communication whenever possible when educating individuals who are Deaf.

CONCLUSION

As colleges continue to have discussions regarding access and success for all students in higher education, they must consider that Deaf students face unique challenges in the attainment of personal and academic success. Deaf individuals enter our college campuses and workforce training programs in an effort to gain independence through completion of their goals. This study has identified specific strategies and support mechanisms that lead to personal and academic success. It is imperative that educators and community-based service providers develop and implement linguistically and culturally appropriate programs to assist the Deaf population with attaining personal, academic, and employment success. The recommendations based on this study can serve as an effective tool to impact positive changes in the lives of Deaf individuals who aspire to reach their dreams!

REFERENCES

Benedict, B., & Sass-Lehrer, M. (2007). Deaf and hearing partnerships: Ethical and communication considerations. *American Annals of the Deaf, 152*(3), 275–282.

Braswell-Burris, P. (2010). *Factors affecting the educational and personal success of deaf or hard of hearing individuals.* San Diego State University, San Diego, CA: Unpublished doctoral dissertation.

Bullis, M., & Davis, C. (1995). Transition achievement among young adults with deafness: What variables relate to success? *Rehabilitation Counseling Bulletin, 39*(2), 130–150.

Charmaz, K. (2006). *Constructing grounded theory: A practical guide through qualitative analysis.* London: SAGE.

Choy, S.P., Horn, L.J., Chun, S., & Nouri, F. (2000). *Services to students with disabilities: A study of workload and costs.* (Report prepared for the Allocations Task Force and Chancellor's Office, California Community Colleges.) Berkeley, CA: MPR Associates.

Condeluci, A., Ledbetter, M.G., Ortman, D., Fromknecht, J., & DeFries, M. (2008). Social capital: A view from the field. *Journal of Vocational Rehabilitation, 29*(3), 133–139.

Lang, H. (2002). Higher education for deaf students: Research priorities in the new millennium. *Journal of Deaf Studies and Deaf Education, 7*(4), 267–280.

MacSweeney, M., Waters, D., Brammer, M., Woll, B., & Goswami, U. (2007). Phonological processing in deaf signers and the impact of age of first language acquisition. *NeuroImage, 40*(3), 1369–1379.

Merriam, S.B. (1998). *Qualitative research and case study applications in education.* San Francisco: Jossey-Bass.

O'Connell, J. (2007, February). *Achievement gap for the deaf.* Speech presented at Sacramento, California as part of the annual State of Education Address. Retrieved September 15, 2007 from http://www.cde.gov/eo/in/se/agdeaf.asp

Rosenbaum, J., Redline, J., & Stephan, J. (2007). Community college: The unfinished revolution. *Issues in Science and Technology, 23*(4), 49–56.

Stanford Achievement Test 9th Edition Form S: Norms booklet for deaf and hard of hearing students (1996). Washington, DC: Gallaudet University Press.

Watson, L., & Swanick, R. (2008). Parents' and teachers' views on deaf children's literacy at home: Do they agree? *Deafness and Education International, 10*(1), 22–39.

Chapter 9

What Can We Do Better?

Hispanics Navigating Newborn Hearing Screening to Early Intervention

ROSEMARY GALLEGOS
Superintendent, New Mexico School for the Deaf

> "So I just told them is there anything that we can do better you know to make sure where we can help her" –Antonia

INTRODUCTION

Antonia gave birth to a baby girl in a hospital 40 miles across the state border from her home in New Mexico. The baby looked healthy and received all her routine screenings. Right in Antonia's room, the technician checked the baby's hearing and explained to Antonia what the test was for. She remembered that "They took me step by step what they were doing, what was happening." Antonia's baby referred on the hearing screening, meaning that more tests were necessary to determine if there was a hearing issue that needed to be addressed.

As early as 1963, visionary leaders (Marion Downs Infant Hearing Website) strove to raise awareness of the critical need for newborn hearing screening. Before the advent of universal newborn hearing screening in 1993, young children who were deaf or hard of hearing were not identified until parents became concerned that their child was not talking. Detection did not occur until the average age of two and a half, too late to impact early language learning. The notion of a critical period for early communication stimulation has been corroborated by landmark studies showing the efficacy of early intervention for deaf children as soon as possible but not later than 6 months (Calderon, 1998; Yoshinaga-Itano, 2003).

The story of Antonia and her baby bear evidence that the long road traveled by these visionaries has met with fruition. Although Antonia left the hospital feeling anxious about the tests, she had early information from the hospital that fueled her own determination to do what was necessary to help her baby. Unfortunately, not all families and babies receive the necessary support that Antonia did.

Almost half of infants who receive a hearing screening that indicates more testing is necessary do not receive follow-ups. This is because the journey through the medical and early intervention system can be complicated. Given the complexity of the process, and the need to begin early intervention services by the age of 6 months, all families, especially minority families, are at risk for getting lost in the system. Although Hispanics are the largest minority in the United States, there is no research and scant literature on the characteristics of hearing screening, diagnosis, and intervention programs that support this growing population effectively.

What characteristics are linked to the successful arrival into early education services for a baby who is deaf or hard of hearing in a Hispanic family where the home language is Spanish? Taking a strength rather than a deficit perspective, this study gathered information from three mothers who live in New Mexico and who navigated through the professional milieu successfully to verify that their child was deaf or hard of hearing. By the age of 6 months, each of the babies was enrolled in an early intervention program. Before meeting the three successful mothers, it is important to understand the history, importance, intended structure, and challenges of newborn hearing screening.

BACKGROUND

Early Hearing Detection and Intervention (EHDI)

The inception and application of universal Newborn Hearing Screening, followed by the identification of hearing loss within the first 3 months and enrollment in early intervention by 6 months of life, is a major advance in the projection of positive outcomes for children who are deaf or hard of hearing (Joint Committee on Infant Hearing, 2000, 2007; Moeller, 2011; White & Forsman, 2010). These outcomes include age-appropriate language skills and social emotional development. Early intervention can result in enhanced vocabulary and reasoning skills (Meinzen-Derr & Wiley, 2011; Moeller, 2000; Yoshinaga-Itano, 2002, 2011).

The terms "early intervention" and "early education" are used interchangeably. When describing the established EHDI process, the term "early intervention" is used for congruence with that literature. The term "early education" is a more positive term signifying strengths, whole child, and a developmental perspective and is used in all other references in this chapter.

Given the groundbreaking research that links outcomes with time of entry into early intervention services, numerous national and local policies have evolved. The Joint Committee on Infant Hearing (2007), along with public health agencies such as the National Institutes of Health and Center for Disease Control (CDC), recommends a **1–3–6 timeline** whereby children are screened for hearing by 1 month, diagnosed with a hearing loss by 4 months, and enrolled into specialized early intervention services by 6 months. Forty-one states and one territory have grants through the CDC or the Maternal Child Health Bureau to establish EHDI systems to support families in meeting this goal (National Center for Hearing Assessment and Management, 2012). Federal legislation has been promulgated (Early Hearing Detection and Intervention Act of 2010; Section 399M of the Public Health Service Act), and 43 states have laws related to newborn hearing screening (NCHAM, 2012). New Mexico passed Senate Bill 101 in 2001, requiring hearing sensitivity testing for all newborn infants.

Universal newborn hearing screening (UNHS) holds promise as the first step in allowing a solid developmental foundation for children who are deaf or hard of hearing.

Concerted efforts have produced common goals and systems at the national and local levels to support the efficacy of this practice. However, too many families and children are not navigating the complicated process from hearing screening at the hospital, through the diagnostic process, and finally to early educational services. Progress in moving through the system can be hampered by a variety of factors. One significant factor is that many primary care physicians do not often encounter children with a hearing loss and, therefore, lack knowledge about the referral process. Another factor is the situation of families who are unable to locate and/or access an audiologist in their community for a diagnostic evaluation.

Families need clear information. They report that inadequate information leaves them feeling overwhelmed and unsure of their next steps (Larsen & Munoz, 2012; Matthijs et al., 2012). They describe having conflicting emotions between grief and feeling positive about the implications that early identification portends (Young & Tattersall, 2007). Within a few months, families encounter a myriad of specialists, including medical staff, social service workers, early interventionists, and educators. This need to intersect with strangers is prompted by a test—not by the families' own observations and misgivings about their child's development (Luterman, 2001). In addition, most parents have never encountered a person who is deaf or hard of hearing except perhaps elderly people, which can precipitate anxiety about their child's future. On learning that the result of their child's hearing screening indicates that more testing is necessary, parents are thrust into an unanticipated maze of emotions, appointments, and questions.

The Joint Committee on Infant Hearing (JCIH) lists the essential team of professionals that are likely involved with a family as they navigate the EHDI process. These are "pediatricians or primary care physicians, audiologists, otolaryngologists, speech-language pathologists, educators of children who are hard of hearing or deaf, and other early intervention professionals delivering EHDI services" (JCIH, 2007). Table 1 shows an example of the networks of professionals that

Table 1. Professionals Involved in the EHDI System

Screening	Audiology evaluation and diagnosis	Early intervention
Nurse	Audiologist	Audiologist
Screening technician	Primary care provider (PCP)	Health insurance agent for hearing aids
Doctor (obstetrician)	Otolaryngologist	Deaf mentor
State EHDI coordinator	Geneticist	Early educator
Discharge coordinator	Other medical specialists	Service coordinator
PCP		Speech language pathologist
Consult for procedures for rescreen at hospital or different location		Specialists (such as occupational therapist, vision specialist)
		Parent advocate
		Cochlear implant screening team
		Bilingual (ASL/ English) program
		Spoken language program

families in New Mexico encounter as they move through the EHDI system. As can be seen, families are compelled to engage with multiple medical, social service, and educational agencies that are probably unfamiliar. In addition, some of the persons they encounter may not necessarily be family friendly or responsive to diversity.

Children who fail a screen but do not receive an audiological evaluation to determine a diagnosis or do not enter early intervention are described in the literature as **"loss to follow-up (LFU)."** The CDC reported in 2009 that 97.4% of infants were screened for hearing at birth. Forty five percent (45.1%) of those infants that did not pass screening were lost in the system and never received a diagnosis. Of those children who did receive a diagnosis of a hearing loss, only

66.2% were enrolled in early intervention by the recommended age of 6 months (CDC website). The accuracy of the data, however, is problematic. States and territories need improved data management systems that can track children diagnosed with a hearing loss and also determine when and if early intervention services for children had positive outcomes (White, 2010; Yoshinaga-Itano, 2011).

In New Mexico, the average age of referral to early intervention is 11 months (Corwin, 2011) with a wide spread of efficacy of the EHDI system demonstrated by children referred to early intervention as young as 1 month old and as late as 6 years old. Only 22% of eligible Hispanic children whose home language is Spanish were receiving early intervention services before age 1. Given the documented positive advantages of newborn hearing screening, the rate of loss to follow up for a diagnosis and early intervention is unacceptable. Continued efforts are needed to identify strategies that will make the EHDI system accessible to all families.

Risk Factors

Sociodemographic factors for risk include nonwhite race, minimal health insurance, young maternal age, more than two children at home, substance abuse, and late onset of prenatal care. All of these factors are predictive of LFU after a newborn hearing screen (Folsom et al., 2000). Liu and colleagues (2008) reported similar findings with children born to women "who were racial or ethnic minorities, had public insurance, or smoked during pregnancy." Their babies were found to be at higher risk of LFU for audiological evaluation. It is interesting to note that in the study by Liu and colleagues (2008), lack of enrollment in early intervention was related to the health of the child, whether there was a hearing loss in one or both ears, the degree of hearing loss, and birth weight rather than sociodemographic factors. This may indicate that families require a more relationship-based approach from an early interventionist in addition to the medical professionals. The assistance of an informed early interventionist would help families move from hearing screening to an audiological evaluation in a timely manner. Typically, early intervention specialists who are trained to engage in family outcomes and priorities are not assigned or involved until a child has been identified with a hearing loss. Instead families rely on medical professionals to guide them and convince them of the importance of seeking out additional evaluations for their child.

Recognizing the success that the New Mexico School for the Deaf (NMSD) local early intervention providers have had in engaging families, a recent change has been made. The New Mexico EHDI program now teams with NMSD to place early interventionists with families to facilitate the movement from hearing screen to diagnosis. In regions of the state that are rural and have high minority populations, this approach seems to be alleviating the LFU experienced by Hispanic and Native American families.

Hispanic Children

According to the U.S. Census Bureau (2012), Latino/Hispanics are the most populous and fastest growing minority group in the country. "Between 1989 and 2009, the percentage of public school students who were White decreased from 68 to 55 percent, and the percentage of those who were Hispanic doubled from 11 to 22 percent. By 2009, Hispanic enrollment had exceeded 11 million students (IES National Center Education Statistics, 2011)." When compared to other states, New Mexico has the highest percentage of Hispanics at 46.7%. According to the Gallaudet Research Institute (2011), 30.4% of all Deaf students are Hispanic or Latino with a high of 47.1% in the western United States. Hispanic children comprise 48% of the children currently enrolled in New Mexico's early intervention program for Deaf and hard-of-hearing children.

Educational trends document the challenges Hispanic/Latino children face. In 2005, only 50% of Latino students graduated from high school (Gandara & Contreras, 2009). In 2011, only 21% of Latinos had acquired an associate's degree or higher compared to Asians at 57%, Whites at 44%, and Blacks at 30% (Santiago & Soliz, 2012). In New Mexico, results of the 2011 National Assessment of Education Progress show a 26% math and 20% reading achievement gap between White and Hispanic students. Graduation rates in New Mexico in 2010–2011 were at 75.6% for Whites and 64.1% for Hispanic students (New Mexico First, 2012). A review of the literature on academic achievement of Deaf and hard-of-hearing children by Karchmer and Mitchell (2003) indicated that these students experience the "same relative performance difference" as hearing children, with racial and ethnic minority groups scoring lower than the white majority.

Schools have not been successful in meeting the needs of Latino students because educational environments do not capitalize on the students' learning characteristics for achievement such as their home language. In addition, schools are not equipped to deal with powerful social and economic realities such as poverty and racism and are resistant to change (Gandara & Contreras, 2009). The field of Deaf education has yielded few efforts to design curriculum or special programs for Latino students who experience the same attitudinal and societal barriers encountered by students in general education (Delgado, 2000, 2001). It is prudent for early intervention and medical providers in the EHDI process to consider how recommended practices for early intervention, and for infants and toddlers who are Deaf and hard of hearing, intersect with the educational, social, and economic realities of all Latinos.

Family Centered Practice for Children Who Are Deaf or Hard of Hearing

Dunst and colleagues (Dunst & Trivette, 2009; Dunst Trivette, & Deal, 1988) describe a family-systems model that focuses on the interaction between a family's concerns and priorities, family member abilities and interests, a family's support and resources, and the capacity-building/help-giving practices of the interventionist. These concepts are mirrored in Part C of the Individuals with Disabilities Education Act (IDEA) that requires:

> a family-directed assessment of the resources, priorities, and concerns of the family and the identification of the supports and services necessary to enhance the family's capacity to meet the developmental needs of the infant or toddler; and

> a written individualized family service plan developed by a multidisciplinary team, including the parents, as required by subsection (e), including a description of the appropriate transition services for the infant or toddler (IDEA, 2004).

Early interventionists who work with Deaf children and their families also implement a framework that is family centered and consider family priorities, resources, and cultural perspectives (Sass-Lehrer, 2012). The Gallaudet 2010 annual survey reports that 77% of Deaf children are born to families that are not Deaf. As a result, the field has recognized the importance of consistent availability of Deaf or hard-of-hearing role models to promote child and parent development of language and communication and enhance the child's self esteem and self awareness through interaction with the Deaf community (Abrams & Gallegos, 2011; Sass-Lehrer, 2012; Watkins, Pitman, & Walden, 1998).

Early Education for Hispanic Children Who Are Deaf

Information, although limited, on specific strategies and recommendations in working with the Deaf Latino populations during the EHDI process in early intervention and in educational settings is available through (1) CDC-recommended practice documents, presentations, and parent materials and (2) literature reviews, narratives, and status reports (Christensen & Delgado, 2000; Delgado, 2001).

Early Hearing Detection and Intervention programs are instructed to be culturally responsive in major policy documents (JCIH, 2000, 2007). In addition, the U.S. Department of Health and Human Services Office of Minority Health mandates that all recipients of federal funds provide language access services; this agency also provides guidelines for culturally competent care (OMH website). There is little evidence that more than a few states institute these directives, and there is only slight exploration of the reaction of or feedback from Hispanic families to EHDI policy, protocol. and recommended practice for early intervention. Programs work with Latino families without research to guide practice or prompt policy reforms at program, school, or state levels.

What strategies do EHDI programs use to differentiate services to Hispanic families? Recognizing the "apparent prevalence of loss to follow up among culturally and linguistically diverse populations," the CDC–EHDI Diversity Committee conducted a survey to identify challenges state EHDI programs have in reaching diverse families in the EHDI process and to postulate on strategies for improvement (CDC Presentation, 2012). They found about 25% of the 43 states surveyed use demographic information to reach out to racial/ethnic groups. The following strategies, intended to increase follow-up and provide timely and accurate information to diverse groups, were reported by states:

- Over 50% of respondents make available educational materials in English, Spanish, and other languages, e.g., PSAs, resource guides, videos, brochures/fact sheets, and letters to parents.
- A small percentage pretest educational materials with target audiences.
- Types of staff used to reach out to families included bilingual staff, parents of children with hearing loss that speak Spanish, certified interpreters, and outside agencies. Some states also use telephonic interpretation. While this represents varied approaches, only two states reported using certified Spanish interpreters and only eight reported using bilingual Spanish/English staff.
- Forty-six percent provide staff with training in culturally and linguistically appropriate service delivery.
- Fewer than 10% of birthing facilities and audiology clinics use certified interpreters, bilingual staff, or telephonic interpretation to provide EHDI information to non-English-speaking parents. Twenty percent of early intervention programs use certified interpreters, 12% use bilingual staff, and about 5% use telephonic interpretation.

Some limited resources are available for early educators working with Hispanic families. The SKI*HI Institute (SKI*HI Institute website) produces materials translated into Spanish for providers, as they implement family-centered early intervention programming for children who are Deaf or hard of hearing. Both SKI*HI and the CDC also have materials translated into Spanish that are culturally relevant, such as stories of other Hispanic families who have Deaf children. In addition, the CDC developed a flyer to help guide EHDI programs in reaching out to ethnically diverse populations. Unfortunately the document has been removed from the CDC website, as it was published in 2007 and has not been updated for reposting.

Provision of materials in Spanish and the use of Spanish-speaking providers are probably the predominant strategies used to support Hispanic families; however, from results of the CDC survey, even those strategies are used minimally. While access to information in the family's language appears critical, it is unclear whether this single approach will have an impact on families' ability to meet the EHDI timelines. It is more probable that the milieu of variables that impact LFU for Hispanic families needs to be approached within a family's systems of priorities and supports such as that described by Dunst and Trivette (2009).

In an early intervention system such as the EHDI process, the values and mores of a family systems approach should guide every step, including hearing screening and diagnosis. In order to provide better services and increase the number of children who move from a hospital screen to early intervention successfully, we need to understand the parental and cultural perspective and discover common, as well as differentiated, services that can support the rapidly growing Hispanic population. Parent involvement has become integral in policy development of Part C of IDEA and in the EHDI process (DesGeorges, 2003), but there is no literature that indicates that information has been culled from Hispanic families. There is a dearth of research regarding this population.

A starting point is a broad examination of the experiences of Hispanic families as they navigate the EHDI process. This will lead to identifying the characteristics of the medical and early intervention system that are present for families who are accessing services by the recommended child age of 6 months. What are the characteristics of families who interact with the system successfully?

In order to explore the experiences of the Hispanic family in the EHDI process, a qualitative method was used, specifically a phenomenological approach. A phenomenological study allows the researcher to ascertain the meaning and commonality of the "lived experiences" (Creswell, 2007) of Hispanic families as they interact with each stage of the EHDI process of hearing screening, diagnosis, and enrollment in early intervention. Following is a narrative of the journey of the three mothers whose babies were screened for hearing loss and found to be Deaf (to protect the identity of the families, pseudonyms are used for their names). The narrative provides us with insights into their "lived experiences." This chapter is based on a study conducted through the University of New Mexico, approved through UNM IRB, May 14, 2013.

THREE MOTHERS

Interviews were conducted with three mothers whose children were below the age of 2 years and who were enrolled in early intervention by the child's age of 6 months. One child had entered early intervention services by 1 month of age and two children were receiving services by 6 months of age. The mothers each live in a different city in New Mexico, representing northern, southern, and eastern parts of the state in both populated and rural areas. All three mothers are bilingual, identifying Spanish as their home language. They were able to conduct interactions necessary to obtain social services and early education services for their children in English, if Spanish was not available.

During the interviews, the mothers shared their experiences in navigating the newborn hearing screening system at the hospital and with the audiologist for identification and early intervention. They also shared their emotional reactions on learning that their child was Deaf or hard of hearing, and they offered advice for parents going through a similar experience.

Antonia

Antonia and I talked by phone. At the time of the interview, her baby was 5 months old. She was just beginning to receive early intervention services, having been visited recently by the intake coordinator in the area. She was very willing to talk to me and share her story. Antonia lives in southern New Mexico and her baby was born in a hospital in Texas, about a 40-minute drive from her home. In order to obtain a rescreen, she had to return to the hospital two times before meeting with an audiologist in her hometown to go through a final identification process. Antonia's case differs from the other two families in that her baby was not born in New Mexico, so the NM EHDI tracking system through its Department of Health did not support her in getting to an audiologist or early education interventionist. Instead, Antonia reached early education through a strong, informal network in the community. The early educator happened to be in the audiologist's office working with another family and was told about Antonia.

Antonia describes initially feeling bad and scared, "I was kinda scared to listen to that you know because she is my baby and I felt real bad." Five months later this is the advice she would give to other parents: "I would give them to not be scared and do what is possible to help your children. And that it's something normal and it's nothing to be scared about—just to go with your heart."

Bettina

Bettina allowed me to come to her home during the time she had reserved for the regular visit with her early educator. Bettina is very busy. She works three jobs and recently overcame a number of challenges to getting her trailer moved to its present location. Bettina manages all daily and financial functions of the home, as well as the care of the children. Bettina's baby was 18 months old at the time of our visit. Bettina and her baby entered early education services when her baby was 6 months old. Her baby was born in a hospital in the town where she lives. In her community, follow-up screening is at a private physician's office. She was able to visit the physician multiple times only after she had managed to apply for and get Medicaid. From there she was referred to an audiologist in Albuquerque, a 60-mile drive, where she received a final confirmation that her daughter's hearing loss was moderate to severe.

Bettina remembers intense feelings of sadness and anger at finding out her baby was Deaf, calling her grandmother often to cry and talk about how she felt. She did enjoy her interaction with the Deaf adults she has met; however, it was not easy to manage all the necessary appointments around her busy schedule. Her advice to other families is to "keep eye on their baby and see if something wrong—keep on it, take them to the doctor. It is helpful for them for the parents to know, to see what happened to your kids and what you can do about this age. When they get older it is more difficult to understand your kids. It is a lot different when you start early. You learn a lot."

Carla

Carla lives in the outskirts of a small community in eastern New Mexico. Carla has access to a working phone sporadically but always calls her early educator to let her know how to reach her until she has a new phone number. Carla and her husband are very quiet and reserved. Her husband works outside the home, and Carla takes care of the house and all child issues. Once when Carla's husband lost his job, Carla had to look for work. As a result, early education services for her baby stopped for about a month. I talked to Carla by phone for this interview but a year earlier had visited with her in her home. When I walked in with her early educator, she was holding her baby and looking worried. At that time, her baby was only 6 months old and she was concerned because he had stopped breathing the week before and had to have medical intervention.

Carla's baby is medically fragile. Because of this, her early educator thinks she was identified quickly by doctors and the NM EHDI program as needing services immediately. As a result, the system mustered to get early medical and educational services to her baby very quickly. Carla's baby was born about 20 miles from her home. Although he had many medical issues, the hospital did screen his hearing and informed Carla that she needed to follow up by calling an audiologist. She went to an audiologist in the same community as the hospital and immediately there was referred to early education services from the NM EHDI system. Carla and her baby were enrolled in early education by the time he was 1 month old. Carla remembers being worried and wanting to know more about her son's hearing so that she could determine what he needed. She appreciates all the help she has gotten and sees her baby doing better. Her advice to parents is "I would tell them it would be good for them to follow up with all the appointments for the baby because that would be something good for their baby to have… like if he needs a hearing aid and didn't have a hearing aid, it wouldn't be the same without a hearing aid so that the baby can have more contact with the parent."

WHAT CAN WE DO BETTER?

"What characteristics are linked to the successful arrival into early education for a baby who is Deaf or hard of hearing in a Hispanic family where the home language is Spanish?" In order to answer this question, significant statements were extracted from three verbatim transcripts of interviews with the families and four verbatim transcripts of interviews with the early interventionists. From these significant statements emerged the following themes.

Parents as Advocates, Skill Sets

The skill sets of the mothers, as revealed by interviews, are characterized by grit, determination, and a sense of responsibility to care for their child. The parent as the advocate theme, more than any other, permeated the content of the responses. This theme can be categorized further into four subthemes. The three mothers were the primary decision makers and service navigators for their child within their family structures. All three exemplified the following subthemes:

- Self-determination
- Bilingual Spanish–English skills
- Ability to follow through on referrals for services Consistent use of services offered
- Consistent use of services offered

Self-determination. All three mothers took on the tasks of making multiple appointments with doctors and specialists and problem solving social service requirements needed to get through the identification system. Two of the three mothers are responsible for ensuring that fundamental needs of the family are met, such as earning income, providing housing, and paying for utilities.

> I think it is a family that has been really able to hang with the number of appointments that it takes early on especially I think at that point she was a single mom and she is working, then you have transportation, you have negotiating time off from your job. She was really able to do that. (Early Educator)

All three mothers, with varying levels of assertiveness, effectively requested next steps from the professionals. They all managed the logistics necessary to make and meet the multiple appointments prescribed for completing the screening process, receiving a confirmation of the hearing loss, and entering early intervention:

> And she didn't pass the test. I got discharged like that but they told me I have to make an appointment to ear, throat, and nose to get a test. So I got the test again and she didn't pass the test. I went back for like three times maybe. (Bettina)

Bilingual Spanish/English skills. All three mothers are bilingual in Spanish and English. The mothers in the interviews did not mention language as a factor in any of their responses. The early interventionists, however, commented that though the mothers may prefer Spanish, they are able to participate in phone calls, appointments, and visits from professionals in English, thus keep the system moving for their child:

> ...also because mom is bilingual that also helped because even though she prefers Spanish whenever a therapist showed up she needed to make a phone call for a doctor or going to (the audiologist) she could deal with English. (Early Educator)

Persistence and follow through. Mothers and early interventionists stressed repeatedly the importance of following through with recommendations, referrals, and appointments. Although these families did not always have the fundamental means of time or money, the mothers figured out how to muster resources in order to make the appointments and keep them. In addition, they were not intimidated by pursuing hard to make appointments or interacting with the multiple medical and educational providers they encountered:

> When she was born they made her a newborn hearing test and she failed it so they said well come back and we will do another and she failed that one again and went again and she failed again so she failed three newborn hearing tests.... Yes, all three of them were at the hospital and then I went to a specialist here in (my town) and he was the one who made her the hearing test." (Antonia)

Use of offered services. All mothers in this study were open to accepting services for their child, saw services as beneficial and positive, and were grateful for the help they were getting for their baby. They were agreeable to recommendations made at each stage in the process of ongoing early intervention services. One parent, because of time constraints, has had to limit the number of service providers who make home visits from the early intervention program but is actively planning for her child's enrollment in preschool:

> Because I at least you know have somebody helping me out with him in his development. And because I know I have help when I need something I will just let them know and they will help me. (Carla)
>
> I think she was afraid, I think, but the minute I told her I had information about her baby and some concerns about his hearing and she said oh yes. (Early Educator)

Two of the three mothers were very forthcoming about their feelings of sadness at the time their child failed the screening test and were identified as being Deaf or hard of hearing. All three parents were anxious to get the testing done to ascertain if their child had a hearing loss. One parent expressed her desire early on to know about the results in order to understand what her baby was going to need. Two mothers also talked about meeting people who assured or showed them that everything was going to be okay. The stages of the grieving process (Kubler-Ross, 2009) were evident in the interview content from all parents at different levels. Feelings of sadness, worry, and anger followed by acceptance were shared. Even though the stages of grieving are not finite, will reoccur, and often take time to manifest, the experience described by two of the families depicted a fairly clear and rapid progression through the stages, ending with expression of normality related to being Deaf or hard of hearing:

> They killed me that day. Yeah because they give me the answer that day and then I said I feel so bad because nobody in my family is deaf or lost hearing. Nobody. It was a real big surprise. It changed my world. (Bettina)
>
> The one that I liked was (Deaf Role Model) because she was fun. I had fun that day. She was signing because she is completely deaf. She was telling history about one time she went to McDonald's and how she got the service. She is like a normal person. (Bettina)

All the families interviewed were successful in achieving the milestone of receiving early intervention services by the time their baby was 6 months old. However, barriers and challenges surfaced in the interviews. In contrast to the experiences of the three families in this study, early interventionists described examples of other families where these same challenges became barriers to reaching early intervention services. For two of the families in this study, these obstacles were linked to lack of financial resources. The mothers reported challenges with childcare, having a working phone, paying bills, transportation, and time constraints concomitant to their family structure as the mother, the primary childcare provider, also worked outside the home:

> When mom wasn't there that was hard but once dad got a job and mom was home then it was back on track. I think that was the difficult time when dad lost his job and they couldn't afford not to work. (Early Educator)

All of the mothers were clear that the tests at the hospital were a screening, not a final diagnosis, and that it was important to follow up with additional tests. The information they received at the hospital was the catalyst to follow the recommendations to confirm or disprove the presence of a hearing loss:

> At the hospital when he was born they gave me his information on when he was born they did the test at the hospital. They gave me his thing that they did there that he didn't pass so I had to follow up with the doctor with his ears. (Carla)

Although the referral protocol for additional testing varied by region in the state, each hospital had some type of linkage to outpatient 2nd screen, the family's physician, and an audiologist. After they left the hospital, the NM EHDI system served as a safety net for two of the families whose children were born in NM hospitals. Early interventionists were contacted by the NM Department of Health Children's Medical services with the names of these families. The early intervention program was aware early in the process—in some cases before the final diagnostic evaluation was completed:

> He was born December 14. They did NBHS on the 14 and 16 they rescreened him and there was a phone call (from NM EHDI system) for a follow-up contact. They were the 16, 21st, 27st then another phone call January 6, 13, 19, and the 20th. All those phone calls were trying to help mom to get more testing on him... So on January 10th there was also a referral to us. So that was wonderful. That is not usual. That was great. So we got in the picture right away. (Early Educator)

Effective strategies by the hospitals included conducting the screening, informing the families that a screening had been done, and providing information to the families about next steps. The hospital or a physician then reported results to the state's tracking (EHDI) system. The next steps varied in complexity, sometimes requiring multiple visits by the family back to the hospital or to another center and multiple phone calls to make appointments. These families, who had characteristics that enabled them to navigate the system effectively, were able to work through the complexity.

For the two children who were born in NM hospitals, a referral to early intervention was made by the state EHDI system. It is not clear whether the audiologists made a formal referral to early intervention in any of the cases. It appears that the state EHDI system is referring to early intervention at the same time a referral is made to follow up for diagnostic testing. This serves as an important safety net to families in linkage to public resources, early intervention, and follow-up screening or diagnosis. The safety net for the family not born in New Mexico, and therefore not in the NM EHDI system, was the network between the local early interventionist and the audiologist who sees the early interventionist often in his office with other families. This is a tenuous, informal system, but it worked in the case of one family in this study.

Barriers

When asked about things that stood in the way of getting services, two families responded that everything was fine. One mother talked about how long it took to get appointments:

> I really don't think I have had a hard time. I've had everything I needed. All his paperwork I have it in a binder. So that made it easy for me cause when they ask me for something I have it there. I can let them know what is going on with him but everything has been o.k. (Carla)

Early interventionists also encounter potential barriers in contacting families. They described the system's reliance on phones, multiple appointments, second-screen protocol that requires families to have a Medicaid card, and the lack of a dependable, formal referral protocol from the hospital to the audiologist to early intervention:

> I know a lot of our Spanish speaking families don't have a cell phone or have a number but they are not always connected. Phones aren't the secure way to depend on because it doesn't always happen that way. (Early Educator)

> (Private physician) is the point of 2nd screen for newborn hearing screen... Because one of the tricky things is that (private physician) won't see families for 2nd screen until they have a Medicaid card in hand. (Early Educator)

Helpful Early Intervention Program Strategies

Early intervention programs exhibited a range of helpful strategies. Key among these was the use of interpreters, identification of Spanish-speaking providers, timeliness, and effectiveness in establishing rapport and trust with families:

> I called with an interpreter and set up a time.... I think being responsive quickly and for the family having access in their first language. She actually is very fluent in English but still technical and new information she liked having it in Spanish and we had those resources available. (Early Educator)

In New Mexico, the hospital or doctors will report child-specific information to the NM EHDI system if the family is viewed as high risk. The EHDI system (Children's Medical Services) in turn will contact the family and the NMSD Early Intervention program. NMSD Early Intervention will contact and visit the family and assist them while they are making appointments to get a diagnostic evaluation and facilitate a seamless entrance into early intervention. This safety net was evident for two families where the children were born in New Mexico. When the early interventionist received the information, she contacted the family within a day and immediately started to connect the family with other resources pertinent to their needs:

> Always the first thing, you know is making the phone call right away. She was not with early intervention. We got them before (other local Early Intervention Program) got involved... I'm thinking we should have a team working because of medical issues and she said "yes" so I helped her make a phone call right away to the service coordinator to get the plan, to get the IFSP going and the O.T. and all the other services going as well. (Early Educator)

Early educators established rapid rapport with families who were all willing to receive home visits. Families reported consistently that they feel comfortable with their early interventionists, they call them for information, and they feel that they care. Families also clearly expressed a sense of relief after meeting Deaf adults:

> Me and my boyfriend were very happy because it was a different experience for us. We've never met anybody like that. They (deaf adults) made it seem so easy; you know what I mean? They told us there was nothing different except they have a different way to communicate. We were really happy about that. (Antonia)

WHAT CAN WE DO BETTER? CONCLUSIONS AND RECOMMENDATIONS

Limitations of the Study

Hispanic mothers who identified their home language as Spanish, but who also could speak English, were interviewed in this study. Families who are Hispanic and both parents speak English are still considered to be in the high-risk category for "loss to follow up." It is difficult from this study to separate cultural influences from language barriers, and therefore caution is given when generalizing trends to monolingual English-speaking Hispanic families or monolingual Spanish-speaking Hispanic families. Also, the researcher conducted the interviews with parents in English, which may not be the mother's first, preferred, or strongest language. This may, to some extent, have inhibited the mothers from expanding their narratives and may have resulted in an omission of important information.

Predominant Characteristics of the Subjects in This Study

There is marked interdependence between the players (hospital, audiologist, early intervention) in the EHDI system and the parents of Deaf children. Hospitals, especially, carry a critical role in initiating the system, giving parents clear information, and triggering safety nets for families by ensuring a connection with the parents' physician or the state's EHDI tracking system. Parent tenacity or "grit" is critical and is actualized by the ability to handle new and emotional information, motivation to confirm the hearing loss by following through on referral information from the hospital, mustering resources to make and keep multiple appointments, and being open to using services that are offered. Parents who welcome the support of professionals benefit from positive interaction. The highly visible presence of early interventionists in the EHDI referral process and the extensive network with local resources support the family further in completing the intervention process.

Table 2 weighs predominant characteristics or strategies of each theme for its influence in propelling the system forward. Items are listed as highly critical if the answer is affirmative to the question "Had this action or characteristic not been present, is there a strong likelihood that the child would not have entered early intervention by 6 months of age?" Items are listed as "critical" if the answer is not a clear "yes" or "no" but data show horizontality, appearing in data for at least two of the families. A third column lists recommendations and implications for the EHDI system related to each characteristic found in the study.

SUMMARY

It is generally accepted that underrepresented ethnic groups, such as Hispanics, face issues such as oppression and hegemony. At least two of the three families in this study faced cultural, linguistic, socioeconomic, and educational differences from the professionals with whom they were compelled to associate. Their circumstance of having a child fail (refer on) a hearing screening pushed them into navigating a plethora of social support and medical systems, while dealing with financial challenges. The purpose of the study was to find out what "worked" for these families so as to influence the system and increase the number of children reaching early intervention by 6 months of age. Each of the families was asked what advice they would give to other families. In this way, families in this study joined in a shared interest and voice to improve the hearing screening system for other families and their babies.

Table 2. Predominant Characteristics or Strategies of Each Theme

Predominant characteristics	Importance	Recommendation/implication
Parent skill set—Self-determination	Highly critical	Facilitate family-to-family linkage to influence a "can do" attitude. Identify parents who have been successful in accessing resources for their baby to serve as liaison and support to other families.
Parent skill set—Bilingual Spanish–English skills	Critical	Provide materials in Spanish and professionals who speak Spanish to ensure that information is clearly understood.
Parent skill set—Persistence and follow through	Highly critical	Establish universal safety nets that track the progress of children referred for follow-up after a hearing screening. Employ early interventionists to support the transition from hospital hearing screen to identification.
Parent skill set—Using offered services	Highly critical	Examine skill sets of medical and early intervention specialists needed in establishing trust and rapport with families.
Progression through the grieving process	Highly critical	Introduce Deaf adults to families early in conjunction with entrance into early intervention.
Working phone	Highly critical	Investigate consistent ownership of working phones and provide phones to families for 6 months or until the identification process (audiological) is completed.
Clear communication with parents from hospital staff about screening, results, and next steps	Highly critical	Ensure that hospital staff is trained to provide clear communication to families about the purpose of a hearing screening, critical importance of making an appointment with an audiologist, and anticipate with the family what will happen next.

(continued)

Table 2. Predominant Characteristics or Strategies of Each Theme *(continued)*

Predominant characteristics	Importance	Recommendation/implication
Referral from the hospital or location of second screen to NM EHDI tracking system	Highly critical	Ensure that infants who refer on a hearing screening are automatically placed in the state's centralized tracking system and that families receive a personal phone call or visit to support their transition to an appointment with an audiologist.
Referral from NM EHDI tracking system during the screening process (before identification) to early intervention	Highly critical	Develop capacity in early intervention programs to support families in the identification and diagnostic process. Apply this process for all families, not just those deemed "high risk" to loss to follow-up.
Linkage of early intervention program with local audiologists for families not born in the state	Highly critical	Ensure that early intervention providers have strong linkages to local audiology practices. This will facilitate a referral to early intervention when a family whose child was born in a state other than their current residence and is not in the state's EHDI register.
Use of interpreters or Spanish-speaking providers for intake into early intervention	Critical	Build capacity to provide information to families directly in Spanish or through qualified Spanish interpretation at all stages of the EHDI process.
Early interventionist best practice: Quick follow-up, ability to establish trust and rapport, local resource network, specialized knowledge	Highly critical	Ensure that the state has adequate numbers of early interventionists who live regionally and are quick to respond to a referral, have the ability to establish trust and rapport with families, know local resources, and have specialized knowledge of infants who are Deaf.

The parent characteristics revealed in this study and categorized as "grit" may also be present in non-Hispanic families. Similarly, recommendations garnered from this study can be supportive of any family, regardless of ethnicity. However, in this small subset, these mothers, who would be considered "at risk" because of socioeconomic and social capital factors, displayed a characteristic that could be described as determination or fearlessness. This personality trait appears to be the most important catalyst on the parent's part for moving through the system. A further study is indicated to determine the source of "grit" in these families. It is advisable that providers within systems such as EHDI check their assumptions about families who are from underrepresented and low socioeconomic groups and their ability to muster resources for their children. Lack of social capital and financial resources did not block these parents from getting services for their child. They were open to information and displayed fearlessness in navigating the system. They were very forthcoming in their sense of sadness and anxiety about the prospects of their child being Deaf or hard of hearing, but that experience seems to have propelled them forward rather than preventing their follow-up.

On the part of the EHDI system, it is clear that families must be given understandable and complete information at the hospital. It is also clear that the hospital is the key precipitator of the process. Their submission of child-specific information to the state's EHDI system and a primary care physician for follow-up and support to families in understanding the next step in the process is a critical safety net.

Safety nets must also include a partnership between the local early intervention program and the family through final identification to ensure seamless entrance into early intervention. Early intervention programs must have qualified providers who understand family centered practices, are situated locally to provide quick contact with families, have the skills to establish trust and rapport, know how to partner with and locate applicable local resources, and have specialized knowledge in development of the child who is Deaf or hard of hearing. Programs should also have resources such as materials in Spanish and qualified Spanish language interpreters, as well as providers who speak

Spanish and are Hispanic. This study also illuminated the importance of Deaf individuals meeting with the family as they enter early intervention. This can help the family conceptualize the future of their child as positive and hopeful and motivate the family to persist with the long-term commitment to early education.

REFERENCES

Abrams, S., & Gallegos, R. (2011). Deaf role models making a critical difference in New Mexico. *Odyssey, 12*.

Calderon, R., & Naidu, S. (1998). Further support for the benefits of early identification and intervention for children with hearing loss. *Volta Review, 100*(5), 53–84.

Center for Disease Control (CDC). What's your baby's hearing screening result? Retrieved September 12, 2012 from http://www.cdc.gov/ncbddd/hearingloss/freematerials.html

Center for Disease Control (CDC)–EHDI Diversity Committee (2012). Delivering EHDI Services to Diverse Populations. EHDI Conference Presentation.

Center for Disease Control (CDC). Summary of 2009 National CDC EHDI Data. Retrieved October 2, 2012 from http://www.cdc.gov/ncbddd/hearingloss/2009-Data/2009_EHDI_HSFS_Summary_508_OK.pdf

Center for Disease Control (CDC)(2007). Bringing Early Hearing Detection and Intervention (EHDI) to minority populations, http://www.cdc.gov/ncbddd/ehdi

Christensen, K., & Delgado, G. (Eds.)(2000). *Deaf plus: A multicultural perspective*. San Diego, CA: DawnSignPress.

Corwin, J. (2011). Effective partnering of state agencies to achieve early hearing detection and intervention benchmarks. *Odyssey, 12*.

Creswell, J.W. (2007). *Qualitative inquiry & research design.* Thousand Oaks, CA: Sage.

Delgado, G. (2000). How are we doing? In K. Christensen & G. Delgado (Eds.), *Deaf plus: A multicultural perspective* (pp. 29–39). San Diego, CA: DawnSignPress.

Delgado, G. (2001). *Hispanic/Latino deaf students in our schools*. Knoxville, TN: Postsecondary Education Consortium

DesGeorges, J. (2003). Family perceptions of early hearing, detection and intervention systems: Listening to and learning form families. *Mental Retardation Developmental Disability Research Review*, 9, 89–93.

Dunst, C.J., Trivette, C.M., & Deal, A. (1988). *Enabling and empowering families: Principles and guidelines for practice*. Cambridge, MA: Brookline Books.

Dunst, C.J., & Trivette, C. M. (2009). Capacity-building family systems intervention practices. *Journal of Family Social Work, 12,* 119–143.

Early Hearing Detection and Intervention Act of 2010 (HR. 1246, S. 3199)

Folsom, R., Widen, J., Vohr, B., Cone-Wesson, B., Gorga, M., Sininger, Y., & Norton, S. (2000). Identification of neonatal hearing impairment: Recruitment and follow-up. *Ear and Hearing, 21*(5), 462–470.

Gallaudet Research Institute (2011). *Regional and National Summary Report of Data from the 2009–2010 Annual Survey of Deaf and Hard of Hearing Children and Youth*. Washington, DC: GRI, Gallaudet University.

Gandara, P., & Contreras, F. (2009). *The Latino education crisis.* Cambridge, MA: Harvard University Press.

Individuals with Disabilities Education Improvement Act of 2004, 20 U.S.C. § 1400 et seq. (2004).

IES National Center for Education Statistics, U.S. Department of Education (2011). *The Condition of Education 2011,* 1–5, 28.

Joint Committee on Infant Hearing (JCIH)(2000). Year 2000 position statement: Principles and guidelines for early hearing detection and intervention programs. *Pediatrics, 106*(4).

Joint Committee on Infant Hearing (JCIH)(2007). Year 2007 position statement: Principles and guidelines for early hearing detection and intervention programs. *Pediatrics, 120*;898 DOI: 10.1542/peds.2007–2333

Karchmer, M.A., & Mitchell, R.E. (2003). Demographic and achievement characteristics of deaf and hard of hearing students. In M. Marschark & P. E. Spencer (Eds.), *Oxford handbook of deaf studies, language, and education* (pp. 21–37). New York: Oxford University Press.

Kubler-Ross, E. (2009). *On death and dying what the dying have to teach doctors, nurses, clergy and their own families*. Abingdon, Oxon: Routledge.

Larsen, R., Munoz, K., DesGeorges, J., Nelson, L., & Kennedy, S. (2012). Early hearing detection and intervention: Parent experiences with the diagnostic hearing assessment. *American Journal of Audiology, 21,* 91–99.

Liu, C., Farrell, J., MacNeil, J., Stone, S., & Barfield, W. (2008). Evaluating loss to follow-up in newborn hearing screening in Massachusetts. *Pediatrics, 121*(2), e355–e343.

Luterman, D. (2001). Closing remarks. In E. Kurtzer-White & D. Luterman (Eds.), *Early childhood deafness* (pp. 149–155). Baltimore, MD: York Press.

Marion Downs Hearing Center. About Marion Downs. Retrieved August 7, 2013 from http://www.mariondowns.com/about-marion-downs.

Matthijs, L., Loots, G., Mouvet, K., Van Herreweghe, M., Hardonk, S., Van Hove, G., Van Puyvelde, M., & Leigh, G. (2012). First information parents receive after UNHS detection of their baby's hearing loss. *Journal of Deaf Studies and Deaf Education,* doi: 10.1093/deafed/ens020.

Meinzen-Derr, J., Wiley, S., & Choo, D. (2011). Impact of early intervention on expressive and receptive language development among young children with permanent hearing loss. *American Annals of the Deaf, 155*(5), 580–591.

Moeller, M.P. (2000). Early intervention and language development in children who are deaf and hard of hearing. *Pediatrics, 106(3),* e43.

Moeller, M. (2011). Language development: New insights and persistent puzzles. *Seminars in Hearing, 32*(2), 172–181. doi: 10.1055/s-003101277239.

National Institutes of Health. It's important to have your baby's hearing screened. Retrieved September 14, 2012 from http://www.nidcd.nih.gov/health/hearing/pages/screened.aspx

National Institutes of Health. Early identification of hearing impairment in infants and young children. Retrieved October 5, 2012 from http://consensus.nih.gov/1993/1993hearinginfantschildren092html.htm

National Center for Hearing Assessment and Management – NCHAM (2012). Retrieved October 10, 2012 from http://www.infanthearing.org/

New Mexico First (2012). New Mexico Progress Report 2012 Edition.

Santiago, D., & Soliz, M. (2012). *Latino College Completion in 50 States, Executive Summary*. Washington, DC: Excelencia in Education. Retrieved July 22, 2012 from Edexcelencia.org/eaf/50states

Sass-Lehrer, M. (2012). Early intervention for children birth to 3: Families, communities and communication. In *The NCHAM book, a resource guide for early hearing detection and intervention* (pp. 10-1–10-15). Utah State University: NCHAM, National Center for Hearing Assessment and Management. Retrieved October 9, 2012 from http://www.infanthearing.org/ehdi-ebook/2012_ebook/Chapter10.pdf

Section 399M of the Public Health Service Act (42 U.S.C. 280g-1)

SKI*HI Institute, Utah State University. Retrieved October 4, 2012 from http://www.skihi.org/

Trivette, C.M., Dunst, C.J., & Hamby, D.W. (2010). Influences of family-systems intervention practices on parent-child interactions and child development. *Topics in Early Childhood Special Education, 30,* 3–19.

U.S. Census Bureau (2012). Most children younger than age 1 are minorities, Census Bureau Reports. U.S. Census Bureau Newsroom. Retrieved September 14, 2012 from http://www.census.gov/newsroom/releases/archives/population/cb12–90.html

U.S. Department of Health and Human Services Office of Minority Health. National Standards on Culturally and Linguistically Appropriate Services

(CLAS). Retrieved October 10, 2012 from http://minorityhealth.hhs.gov/templates/browse.aspx?lvl=2&lvlID=15

U.S. Department of Health and Human Services, Health Resources and Services Administration. Maternal and Child Health Bureau. Retrieved October 3, 2012 from http://www.hrsa.gov/about/organization/bureaus/mchb/

U.S. Preventive Services Task Force - USPSTF (2008). Universal hearing screening for hearing loss in newborns. Retrieved October 3, 2012.

Watkins, S., Pittman, P., & Walden, B. (1998). The deaf mentor experimental project for young children who are deaf and their families. *American Annals of the Deaf, 143*(1), 29–34.

White, R., Forsman, I., Eichwald, J., & Muñoz, K. (2010). The evolution of early hearing detection and intervention programs in the United States. *Perinatology*, *34*(2), 170–179.

Yoshinaga-Itano, C., Coulter, D., & Thomson, V. (2001). Regular articles: Developmental outcomes of children with hearing loss born in Colorado hospitals with and without universal newborn hearing screening programs. *Seminars in Neonatology*, *6*(6), 521–529. doi: 10.1053/siny.2001.0075

Yoshinaga-Itano, C. (2003). From screening to early identification and intervention: Discovering predictors to successful outcomes for children with significant hearing loss. *Journal of Deaf Studies and Deaf Education, 8*(1).

Yoshinaga-Itano, C. (2011). Achieving optimal outcomes from EHDI. *ASHA Leader*, *16*(11), 14–17.

Yoshinaga-Itano, C. (2011). Risk and resiliency of infants/toddlers who are deaf: Assessment and intervention issues. In D.H. Zand and K.J. Pierce (Eds.), *Resilience in deaf children: Adaptation through emerging adulthood* (pp. 87–111). New York: Springer Science + Business Media. doi: 10.1007/978-1-4419-7796-0_4

Young, A., & Tattersall, H. (2007). Universal newborn hearing screening and early identification of deafness: Parents' responses to knowing early and their expectations of child communication development. *Journal of Deaf Studies and Deaf Education*, doi:10.1093/deafed/enl033.

Chapter 10

A Multilayered Approach to Statewide Support Services

PRISCILLA SHANNON GUTIÉRREZ
CINDY HUFF
New Mexico School for the Deaf
Center for Educational Consultation and Training

NEW MEXICO SCHOOL FOR THE DEAF AS A STATEWIDE SERVICE AGENCY

The New Mexico School for the Deaf (NMSD) has provided statewide support to school districts and families for several decades. In the 1960s, NMSD established several satellite preschool programs across the state. Statewide early intervention for deaf and hard-of-hearing (D/HH) children until age 6 began in the early 1980s when NMSD was awarded funding through a competitive legislative appropriation process. Later that same decade, NMSD established an Educational Resource Center to serve the state in a similar way that Gallaudet University is a national resource.

From that early start, NMSD outreach programs have evolved and expanded with increasing support from the administration and service appeals from around the state. Deaf children and youth throughout New Mexico, and the school programs that serve them, continue to need the expertise and support of NMSD, whether they have just been identified, attend one of NMSD's preschools, or attend public school programs. The New Mexico School for the Deaf was the first public school in New Mexico and also has the distinction of being the only land grant school for the deaf in the country.

In addition to the main school campus in Santa Fe, statewide outreach work happens through four mechanisms.

1. Early Intervention and Involvement Division—the arm of the agency that provides home-based support for families of deaf children 0–6 and the education of other early intervention professionals through workshops, trainings, and working relationships.
2. Satellite preschool programs—NMSD programs housed in locations that have critical mass warranting the establishment of early childhood programming.
3. The Center for Educational Consultation and Training—The center is the arm of the agency that provides consultation to public schools around the state, educational team training, Individualized Education Program (IEP) attendance, student evaluations, family workshops, American Sign Language (ASL) instruction, and summer intensives in Santa Fe.
4. Statewide systems change—through relationships with the Department of Health and the Public Education Department, NMSD is seen as the primary resource related to the education of deaf and hard-of-hearing students, resulting in involvement and influence in state level discussion and decision making

Like many other states, most of the D/HH children in the state are served by their local education agency (LEA). Currently, 323,066 students are enrolled in 863 schools throughout New Mexico. The majority of these students (52%) are Hispanic. Caucasians make up the second largest group of students (32%), with Native Americans comprising the third largest group (11%). Out of the total student population in New Mexico, less than 1% is identified as deaf or hard of hearing. This is slightly less than the typical average of 1%, begging the question of whether there is an underidentification of students in the state.

Ethnic diversity is prevalent throughout New Mexico. Many Latinos can trace their roots within the state back several centuries to the 1600s when colonists from Mexico first entered the area. The state was part of Mexico until 1846 and remained a territory until 1912, when it officially became a state. Spanish is the native language of many families, and Hispanic culture is a strong influence throughout the state. This is evidenced by weekly newspaper features and television broadcasts in Spanish, as well as a large number of dual language programs.

The state is also home to several Native American reservations and pueblos, including the eastern section of the Navajo Nation—geographically the largest reservation in the country. The extreme isolation and lack of services found on the reservation are in sharp contrast to the average urban American experience. Three-quarters of all people in the United States who live without electricity reside on the Navajo reservation. It is conservatively estimated that 37% of the 48,000 households within the reservation lack electricity. Sixty-five percent who reside on the reservation live at or below the poverty level, with an annual per capita income of $6124. Forty-eight percent of the homes do not have running water or indoor plumbing, and 80% have no central heat (Carey, 2011).

The center's database has a total of 245 students whose educational teams receive consultation and support from the department. Sixty-one percent of these students attend school in rural counties. Within the urban areas, there are only nine school districts that provide a center-based deaf or hard-of-hearing program with a trained teacher of the deaf. The vast majority of students in both urban and rural settings attend general education programs, while several of the Native American students attend Bureau of Indian Education (BIE) schools, in places such as Acoma, Pueblo Pintado, and Zuni.

The state of New Mexico presents several unique challenges for the center's educational consultants responsible for support to schools and families with deaf or hard-of-hearing children. While the state's larger cities, such as Albuquerque, Las Cruces, and Farmington, have populations between 45,000 and 550,000, most of the state's residents live in rural areas where services such as adequate health care, food shopping, or available gas stations can require driving considerable distances. According to data from the Economic Research Service Rural–Urban Commuting Areas, 27 of the 33 counties within the state are considered rural (U.S. Department of Agriculture, Economic Research Service, 2013). While tourism, oil, and gas industries are part of the state's economy, agriculture continues to be the main source of income for residents of the state. This includes dairy, cattle, and sheep ranching.

New Mexico's poverty rate of 20.8% is the second highest in the United States—well above the national average of 15.2%. One-fifth of the state's population has incomes that fall below $18,500. Many of these households are single parents with multiple children (Renaud, 2012). Thirty-seven percent of children live with families where one or both parents do not have year-round, full-time employment (Coley & Baker, 2013). And the third annual Feeding America Report ranks New Mexico, at 30.2%, as the state with the highest number of children in the country that go hungry (New Mexico Annual Social and Economic Indicators, 2012)(Figure 1).

Recent research indicates that income has now surpassed race and ethnicity as the great divide when it comes to school outcomes. Income-related achievement gaps have continued to grow as the gap

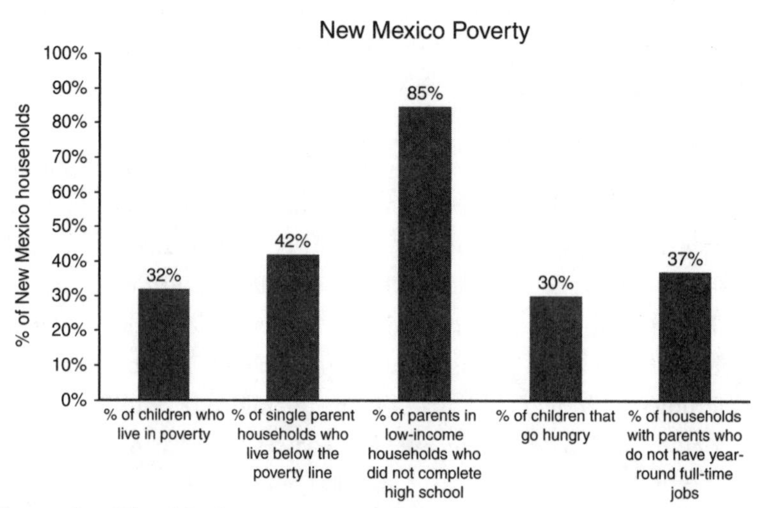

Figure 1. New Mexico poverty statistics.

between the richest and the poorest American families has surged over the past decade. Currently, the achievement gap between the poor and the nonpoor is twice as large as the achievement gap between black and white students (Coley & Baker, 2013). The staggering levels of poverty, low-income single-parent families, hunger or food insecurity, and lack of parent education in New Mexico amplify the challenges to access that deaf and hard-of-hearing children face in schools.

With the description of NMSD as a school and statewide agency, and with state dynamics as a backdrop, this chapter focuses on how a multilayered approach of services and staff contributes to outcomes for D/HH children. The Center at the New Mexico School for the Deaf is guided not only by the mission, vision, and beliefs of NMSD, but also by four internal principles: (1) the belief that the "disability" of deaf and hard-of-hearing children is a direct result of their environment, not of their hearing loss; (2) the knowledge that relationships with NMSD, schools, and families provide the basis for the center's philosophy and critical resources to support the work; (3) the awareness that building multiple layers of service opportunities allows for the unique needs and preferences of NMSD's target audiences; and (4) the utilization of staff self-reflection and consumer feedback allows programs to continually evolve, expand, and maintain excellence.

DEAFNESS AS AN ENVIRONMENTAL DISABILITY

"Fifteen-year old Christal lives in a small community on the eastern edges of the Navajo Reservation with her parents and siblings. Her community consists of an elementary school, housing, and a water tower. The family must drive 25 miles to the nearest market, gas station, or health clinic. The nearest hospital is an additional 100 miles away. Christal is the only deaf person in her family and community. Sign language is her primary language for communication and for learning. She has limited skills in written English. None of Christal's family members have learned to sign, with the exception of a few home-based signs or gestures. Recently her ongoing struggles and frustration with communication breakdowns at home, as well as school, have resulted in aggressive behavior not previously seen. Several years ago her

parents purchased hearing aids. They continue to hold fast to the belief that someday their daughter will learn to talk, although she hardly ever uses her hearing aids.

Christal has attended Bureau of Indian Education programs for most of her schooling, including a residential program in a neighboring community. The nearest center-based deaf education program is approximately 100 miles away. She currently attends high school at a public school program.

The BIE was able to provide an itinerant deaf education teacher and signing aide during Christal's primary years in school. For 2 years, the itinerant teacher provided support on a biweekly basis, working closely with her and the signing aide assigned to Christal's classroom. One of the center's educational consultants also provided support and resources on a monthly basis. During this period, Christal had the most access of her entire educational career. However, once the itinerant teacher resigned, the signing aide opted for a change and was reassigned to a different classroom.

From fourth grade through her current sophomore year, Christal has attended school without an interpreter or signing aide. The intensive curricular emphasis on phonics and decoding during her elementary and middle school programs and the lack of meaningful peer and adult interaction at school and within her rural community have been major contributors to Christal's markedly delayed language, academic, and social skills."

The recognition that the "disability" of deaf and hard-of-hearing children is a direct result of their environment, not of their hearing loss, is a steadfast belief among our team. This belief shapes the content of materials and training, depicting the environmental features that nurture typical development for deaf and hard-of-hearing children in their families and their school programs.

Deafness is not inherently disabling; rather, environments lacking stimulation and meaningful interaction are causes of the delays often seen in deaf children. The **environmental disabling** of many students, despite the best of intentions by parents and school staff, is profoundly apparent to the department staff when visiting school programs around the state. The high percentage of families who live in poverty or are low income, even those in the larger cities, reduces the deaf child's ability to overcome environmental challenges. In a number of households, more than one language is spoken, further complicating a child's ability to successfully navigate language, and communication in general, within the family and the community at large.

The cultural diversity within the state factors into the deaf child's experiences at home and at school. Many Native American families harbor a historically generated sense of wariness toward Caucasian service providers. Sufficient trust can take years to develop with families, and in some instances doesn't ever quite happen. Eye contact, especially between male tribal members and females, is considered disrespectful, and a male tribal member may refuse to speak directly to a female nontribal member. Contact with Native families can be a challenge for non-Natives who hold different cultural perspectives. Tribal members living on the reservation, as well as the outskirts of towns such as Gallup or Grants, do not have physical addresses, residing on un-named rural roads. Families that do have cell phones can be difficult to contact, as coverage in these areas is often spotty. Prepaid service minutes often get used up by midmonth and additional minutes cannot be purchased until the family receives additional funds.

A sociocultural perspective (Vygotsky, 1978) suggests that learning and development cannot be separated from the context in which they take place. All learning is rooted in meaningful social interaction that is influenced by community, culture, and the society at large. Language, as the vehicle or tool that allows learning to occur in humans, plays a critical role in the development of cognition and communicative competence.

Whether spoken or signed, language functions as a means to process information, construct meaning, form memberships in communities, develop cultural identities, and participate in human interaction. For many deaf children, however, the normal mechanism by which humans form social relations, communicate, and learn is disrupted, resulting in linguistic and cognitive deficiency (Garton, 1992). The cognitive tools and linguistic skills required for academic success in the school setting often are delayed in deaf children because language deprivation diminishes access to meaningful interaction and learning.

A cultural deficit viewpoint (Sue & Padilla, 1986) attributes the academic failure of any language minority student to cultural deficits that are considered inherent either in the group itself or in its culture. This viewpoint subscribes to the false belief that language minority groups and non-English native language users are incapable of meeting social and academic challenges within the larger majority culture. When an educational curriculum negates a cultural group's ways of knowing and using language, a type of cognitive dissonance occurs within the student that impedes learning (Shannon Gutierrez, 2002). The experiences of linguistically diverse students, especially those raised in poverty, tend to be quite different from the experiences of more economically and socially advantaged students. These differences become evident when they go to school and struggle to adapt to school culture and the curricula used within school programs (Nieto, 2002). For deaf children for whom sign language is their primary and/or most accessible means of communication, a cultural deficit viewpoint considers the use of spoken language as superior and an overarching goal of deaf education.

Consultation to parents from the medical community at times espouses an either/or stance in terms of spoken or sign language use in the belief that spoken language is the ideal to which deaf children must aspire in order to attain academic success. However, recent studies in neuroscience contradict this stance—they have confirmed that the capacity of the human brain can learn both visual and spoken languages. Increasing evidence documents that regardless of the child's hearing status, early bilingual exposure to both a visual and a spoken language can change the neural circuitry in the brain in advantageous ways (Mitchiner, Berlin Nussbaum, & Scott, 2012).

The heavy emphasis on phonics embedded in mandated curricula often found in public schools has translated into pedagogical practices in many deaf classrooms that emphasize simultaneous speaking and signing. The deaf student's inability to access phonemes and spoken language further isolates them from the curriculum and often contributes to their delays in literacy development.

Many individual children in the more isolated areas of the state are the lone deaf child within a 100-mile radius. For deaf students, regardless of the mode of communication, the lack of peer and adult interaction within the school setting, as well as the home setting, amplifies the deaf child's sense of isolation and diminishes his/her sense of membership in his/her community and classroom. This in turn, often leads to socioemotional difficulties that manifest themselves in extreme passivity on the one hand and physical outbursts on the other.

The staff in a majority of rural schools has had limited experience or training in working with D/HH students, compounding the child's lack of access to communication and learning. Surprisingly, this is also true in the more populated areas of the state because of the limited number of trained teachers of the deaf within the state. New Mexico does not require teachers who work with deaf students to have deaf-specific certification or training. Rather, general special education training is considered sufficient by the public education department for licensure to work with deaf or hard-of-hearing students. Around the state, districts often struggle to recruit qualified personnel such as educational audiologists, speech and language pathologists, or certified interpreters. New Mexico passed legislation for interpreter licensure in 2009, enacting a specific set of criteria for full licensure, while providing a 5-year window for current interpreters to meet the criteria for licensure. Districts now have to draw up contingency plans, as the window is about to close for many of the provisionally licensed K-12 interpreters working in schools.

The statewide lack of deaf education expertise can lead to gross misunderstanding of the needs of students, even those who utilize amplification or have a unilateral loss. Regular education teachers often find themselves struggling to understand sound fields or FM systems and often are unable to troubleshoot when the amplification system does not work properly. Without appropriate guidance from an educational audiologist, schools may purchase equipment that will not sync correctly with the student's hearing aid or cochlear implant.

In many locations it is not uncommon for deaf students who rely on visual language and visual learning to have virtually no access to an interpreter or a licensed teacher of the deaf for most, if not all, of their schooling. Additionally, the lack of resources, such as Internet access, libraries, or local deaf role models, within these communities severely limits a family's ability to learn sign language or to understand the implications of their child's deafness. Limited resources further complicate the development of successful academic and socioemotional outcomes of deaf or hard-of-hearing students.

Yet another challenge to improving outcomes for D/HH students is that many special education directors have no background in special education, let alone deaf education. Budget constraints have forced some districts, as well as BIE schools, to assign building principals as the special education director. Often these building-level administrators receive little, if any, training in special education law or best practice. Additionally, some programs that lack sufficient related service staff are moving toward long-distance services wherein students receive speech and language support, as well as counseling, via remote video. For students who rely on sign language, the need for an interpreter or a signing aide can compromise the efficacy of such remote-based approaches.

However, the lack of deaf education expertise within so many of the districts around the state is one of the factors that contribute to the expanding demand for NMSD services. Since 2010, the center's seven educational consultants who provide support to school districts have attended an annual average of 103 IEP meetings and 47 Communication Considerations pre-IEP dialogues, have averaged 400 on-site consultation/school visits, and provided an average of 46 workshops or trainings to school programs. Workshops included topics such as working with deaf or hard-of-hearing students, interpreted education, postsecondary transition, literacy, and amplification, as well as a number of student-specific workshops at the school building level. As part of the department's support to school districts, NMSD has also conducted an annual average of 21 diagnostic evaluations, which provide educational teams with invaluable, in-depth information on the student across a variety of domains that can lead to improved instructional program design.

Another factor that has contributed to the increasing demand for the department's services is recognition of NMSD as the major in-state resource for consultation and support services by a variety of state agencies such as the New Mexico Public Education Department (NMPED), the New Mexico Commission for Deaf and Hard of Hearing Persons, and the New Mexico Division of Vocational Rehabilitation. Evidence of this recognition includes development by department members of NMPED technical assistance documents, presentations at special education directors' meetings, planned trainings around the state for Division of Vocational Rehabilitation offices, development of the Communication Considerations IEP Addendum, and a recent Public Education Department webinar on the addendum for special education directors and IEP team members.

RELATIONSHIPS ARE KEY TO FORWARD MOVEMENT

Relationships drive all things. In order to make things happen, the center's staff must form, nurture, and grow mutually beneficial relationships with a large audience that includes NMSD colleagues within and outside of the department, school district staff (administrators, classroom teachers, special educators, K-12 interpreters, SLPs, transition specialists, IEP coordinators, etc.), families, and state agencies such as NMPED. It is the slow and steady development of these relationships that lay the foundation that allows the work of the center to take place.

A direct linkage with New Mexico School for the Deaf and its expertise provides a critical resource to support the center's work. By design, the majority of the department's staff is based on the main campus in Santa Fe. Despite the extensive travel requirements, the home base of Santa Fe makes the team a part of the NMSD community and the collective work of the agency. Additionally, the center's team has a heightened understanding of NMSD school programming, classroom staff, and how those programs and people can serve as a resource to support public school programs and Center for Educational Consultation and Training (CECT) events on this campus. NMSD school staff members participate in our work as occasional visiting trainers to schools around the state, as consultants/advisors to the center's team related to content/training development, and as staff during CECT events such as the ASL Immersion Program, ASL classes, and Family to Family Weekend. Additionally, the department works closely with NMSD's Early Intervention and Involvement staff to support the transition of 3 year olds into school programs around the state. Once children have entered school, the center's team begins supporting their educational teams to provide optimal programming.

In working with school district staff, much energy is given to forming strong working relationships with all staff serving the D/HH student. Each district, each school, and each classroom have different dynamics. Observing those dynamics and the internal culture of each environment helps the center's educational consultant navigate the environment in order to have more impact and influence. Recognizing the pressures felt by educators guides consultants in where and how to offer support. School consultation focuses how to change outcomes for individual D/HH students while shaping long-term programmatic change at the district level.

Families are the key to their child's success. The center has historically formed relationships with families through participation in the IEP process. Through this engagement, parents are exposed to educational consultants' contributions that help shape their understanding of the components of a quality educational program, their child's specific language and communication needs, and the social–emotional impacts their child may be facing. CECT also offers parent-specific workshops regionally, an annual family to family event, and ASL instruction through classes, a summer immersion program, and home-based instruction through NMSD's AmeriCorps Sign Language Teacher Program.

The center's educational consultants and AmeriCorps sign language teachers know that change happens through relationships. Strong relationships sustain through challenging times and difficult conversations. They grow through joint effort and investment.

A MULTILAYERED APPROACH...

"Four-year old Marco, part of a large family, was born in ranching country. Both of his parents are exclusively Spanish speaking. The nearest town has a population of just under 3000 individuals, with an average per capita income of $16,692. Marco received bilateral cochlear implants at an early age, but the considerable distance to the nearest mapping center resulted in many missed appointments. Having no deaf education teacher or other specifically trained staff at school also impacted his ability to benefit from the implants. Marco's parents were not sure whether or not

to use sign language. Their uncertainty was influenced by the implant doctor, who warned the family that signing would have a negative impact on spoken language and auditory skills development.

Marco received bimonthly Deaf Mentor and Parent Advisor consultation from NMSD's Early Intervention and Involvement Department from the time he was 1 year old. Upon Marco's entry in school, the educational consultant provided monthly supports to the educational team in the form of classroom observations/recommendations, sign language resources, training, and participation in IEP meetings. The aide assigned to Marco learned some sign language largely through the weekly lessons provided by a native sign language teacher from NMSD's AmeriCorps Sign Language program. Despite the investment, communication with Marco continued to be a challenge for the staff, peers, and the community as a whole. The team had a strong desire to make a difference, but the limited training and language skill slowed Marco's academic progress dramatically. The aide, who speaks some Spanish, took on the role of interpreter during IEP meetings with the parents. Unfortunately, the lack of fluid communication during these meetings often resulted in misunderstandings. Marco's parents were tentative to ask questions and initiate conversations, often leaving IEP and other meetings frustrated because of the communication barriers. The family, recognizing the need to begin learning sign language, took advantage of attendance at ASL Immersion Week and, soon after, moved to Santa Fe in order for Marco to attend NMSD. He is now in a program that provides a stimulating signing environment, deaf peers, and the chance to maximize the benefits of his implants. Being in Santa Fe allows the family to be exposed to the deaf community, increasing their communication with Marco."

There are many locations in New Mexico that present similar challenges to Marco's situation. Recognizing the inability to create an optimal and comprehensive learning environment for D/HH students in many locations, the center's goal is to maximize the potential of a deaf child living in a resource-limited location. One would assume these challenges apply primarily to profoundly deaf children, when, in fact, many hard-of-hearing students, thought to be fine, are floundering academically, socially, or both. The communication mode of the student has little to do with whether or not they are able to thrive in these rural locations. It is only through a multilayered program approach—for school staff, hearing peers, family members, and the child himself—that shifts can be made.

Hispanic families culturally view educators with a deep sense of respect for their expertise, which often translates into hesitation to participate or offer an opinion, and in extreme cases, a "whatever you say" approach to their child's education. Districts may not provide sufficient translation support during IEP meetings or when sending home important school information, which not only can seem intimidating to Hispanic parents, but also leaves them in the dark in terms of understanding quality programming, making informed decisions, and participating as IEP team members effectively.

Given the wide-ranging cultural and resource diversity in the state, the center must provide a menu of programming options that allows audience members to engage in a variety of ways that work effectively for them. A "one size fits all" approach to training and information dissemination just would not work. This multilayered approach requires creative and, sometimes, nontraditional programming. A significant amount of department work takes place outside of the 8:00 a.m.–5:00 p.m. timeframe and in unexpected venues. As an example, trainings and critical mass opportunities for families often occur on weekends or during evenings in locations such as public libraries or local pizza restaurants.

The NMSD's educational consultants are trained deaf educators with a collective wealth of classroom experience. The department also houses an AmeriCorps sign language teacher program. This consists of native ASL users who live in remote areas teaching ASL in the homes of families and in the schools deaf children attend. Both educational consultants and AmeriCorps members are keenly aware of what they can and cannot offer. They function within their roles as deaf educator and sign language teacher. If other expertise is needed, the team refers to other professionals, sometimes accessing the support of members of NMSD school staff.

The educational team provides no-cost consultation and training, by invitation of the LEA, at the student level, the classroom level, the school level, and/or the district level. This support takes the form of student observations, IEP attendance, workshops, content-rich institutes, district administrator meetings, program strategic planning, and student evaluations held in Santa Fe. These offerings are designed to be a professional exchange, with the consultants and the school staff working collaboratively to make favorable change for the students. The consultant works with the classroom or school staff to create and implement a plan that will support their environment uniquely.

In addition, large-scale learning events happen through the department. Each summer, NMSD's Santa Fe campus hosts a Family to Family Weekend event, two ASL Immersion Programs, and a 4-day K-12 Interpreter Intensive. ASL classes are held each fall and spring in Santa Fe and Albuquerque, and AmeriCorps ASL teachers provide a wide variety of sign language events, classes, and tutoring all over the state.

All initiatives, large or small, interact to create comprehensive and impactful programming for our audiences. The flexibility of the programming supports the engagement of those we strive to impact most.

THE EVOLVING ROLE OF SELF-REFLECTION AND CONSUMER FEEDBACK

One of the strengths of the department is the varied ways that self-reflection and mentoring are incorporated into the work of the department consultants. Input from school districts and parents also play a strong role in improving the operations of the department, expanding and/or fine-tuning services, and developing new initiatives or projects.

As part of reflective practice, on a yearly basis each consultant develops a professional development plan. Personal and professional goals are developed in consultation with their supervisor and are based in the real, lived experiences of each individual working in schools and with families. These goals typically address educational support to schools, strategic planning, support to department initiatives, and individual personal growth. Monthly check-in meetings with supervisors offer consultants an opportunity to troubleshoot issues that require support or guidance, as well as celebrate successes. These meetings also provide consultants an opportunity to decompress from school visits that have proven emotionally difficult or stressful.

On-site mentoring from the coordinator of educational support to schools offers consultants additional support and guidance. Consultants select a district or school program to which the coordinator will accompany them. These partnered visits provide an extra pair of eyes during observations or meetings with staff that provide valuable insights—not only for the individual consultant but also in terms of capturing the state's "big picture" for both short-term and long-term planning.

Ongoing dialogue during monthly department meetings helps establish and maintain professional boundaries with districts and families. Frequent group philosophical exploration promotes a cohesive and consistent message that is disseminated by the team around the state. Educational consultants recognize when we cannot or should not be providing guidance or consultation in an area where we lack expertise, e.g., audiology services or mental health counseling. A strong sense of camaraderie and a commitment to the philosophical underpinnings of the department and NMSD mean there is no need to save face with one another. Consultants recognize that no one person has all the answers—individual and collective strengths contribute to the center's ability to affect outcomes around the state.

PARTING THOUGHTS

The multilayered approach espoused by the New Mexico School for the Deaf, Center on Educational Consultation and Training highlights the fact that there is no one magic, silver bullet when it comes to addressing the needs of deaf and hard-of-hearing children. In addition to relationship building, the key to any effective intervention or consultation lies in providing a range of services that are sensitive to culture and demographics, and that are tailored to the communities served, whether located in rural or suburban areas. The context or milieu in which the deaf or hard-of-hearing child is raised and schooled cannot be separated from the child.

A multidisciplinary team approach that recognizes individual and collective strengths, as well as limitations, can enable any outreach program for the deaf to provide higher levels of quality consultation and support services to families and schools. Collaboration, mentoring, and reflective practice among team members should characterize the work and reflect both short-term and long-term planning.

The concept of deafness as an environmental disability should give pause to educational teams working with D/HH and be an impetus for analyzing whether school programming inhibits or encourages access to the curriculum and development of the whole child. Educational teams that find themselves unable or limited in their ability to meet the needs of deaf or hard-of-hearing students should look to their state schools for the deaf as centers of expertise and potential support.

Deafness as an environmental disability should also be an impetus for school staff to analyze the socioemotional well-being of D/HH, as reflected by ongoing meaningful interactions and relationships with peers and adults. Educational teams need to recognize whether students are full-fledged members of their classroom or school community and then determine necessary supports in order to avoid token membership brought on by limited communication and interaction.

Without full access, deaf and hard-of-hearing students will continue to struggle in school programs and their human potential will not be maximized, despite the best efforts of any educational team. However, when multilayered, collaborative efforts between educational staff and statewide outreach programs such as The Center for Educational Consultation and Training at NMSD are put into place, strides can be made toward raising awareness and implementing quality programming for deaf and hard-of-hearing students.

REFERENCES

Bray, S.W. (2005). A case of giving. *Navajo Institute for Social Justice*. Retrieved from http://www.nisj.org/articles.html

Carey, H., Jr. (2011). Bringing lights to Navajo homes. *Navajo People, Culture, and History.* Retrieved from http://navajopeople.org/blog/bringing-lights-to-navajo-homes/

Coley, R.J., & Baker, B. (2013). *Poverty and education. Finding the way forward.* Princeton, NJ: Educational Testing Service Center for Research on Human Capital and Education.

Deaf Students Education Services Policy Guidance, 57 (1992). Federal Register 49275.

Garton, A.F. (1992). *Social interaction and the development of language and cognition.* Hillsdale, NJ: Lawrence Erlbaum Associates.

Mitchiner, J., Berlin Nussbaum, D., & Scott, S. (2012). *The implications of bimodal bilingual approaches for children with cochlear implants*. Research Brief #6. VL2 Research Group. Washington, DC: Gallaudet University.

New Mexico Annual Social and Economic Indicators 2012. Retrieved from http://www.bizjournals.com/albuquerque/blog/morning-edition/2013/06/new-mexico- has-countrys-hungriest.html

Nieto, S. (2002). *Language, culture, and teaching*. Mahwah, NJ: Lawrence Erlbaum.

Renaud, J. (2012). New Mexico cities with most, least low-income families. *Albuquerque Business First.* Retrieved from http://www.bizjournals.com/albuquerque/news/2012/07/02/new-mexico-cities-withmost- least.html?page=all&appSession=598118849559604&RecordID=&PageID=2&PrevPageID=1&cpipage=1&CPISortType=&CPIorderBy

Shannon Gutierrez, P. (2002). In search of bedrock: Organizing for success with diverse needs children in the classroom. *Journal of Latinos and Education 1*(1), 49–64.

Sue, S., & Padilla, A. (1986). Ethnic minority issues in the United States: Challenges for the educational system. In *Beyond language: Social and cultural factors in school language minority students* (pp. 25–72). Los Angeles, CA: Evaluation, Dissemination, and Assessment Center, California State University at Los Angeles.

U.S. Department of Agriculture Economic Research Service (2013). New Mexico counties data sets. Retrieved from http://www.ers.usda.gov/data-products/county-level-data-sets/population.aspx?reportPath=/State_Fact_Sheets/PopulationReport&fips_st=35

Vygotsky, L.S. (1978). *Thought and language.* Cambridge, MA: MIT Press.

Section III:

Revisions

CHAPTER 11

Lesbian, Gay, Bisexual, and Transgender Deaf Students: Invisible and Underserved

MICHAEL DENNINGER, Ph.D., LPC, NBCCH, CT-NLP & EMI™
Phoenix Counseling & Hypnotherapy

INTRODUCTION

Lesbian, gay, bisexual, and transgender (LGBT) students and deaf or hard-of-hearing students share one salient demographic. Both groups, by and large, are raised by parents who are different from them. More than 90% of deaf and hard-of-hearing children are reared by parents who have normal hearing (Gallaudet University Research Institute, 2010). It is believed that an even higher percentage of LGBT youth are raised by heterosexual parents, even though no research was found to support this contention. Being reared by parents who are hearing (for deaf youth) or heterosexual (for LGBT youth) can cause cultural ambiguity in a child, particularly if families respond negatively with shame or disapproval because of the child's differentness.

As a result of these parent/child discrepancies, the majority of deaf and LGBT children have to search for an identity and a community of people in their own image. The going can be rough for both. Many never connect meaningfully with their respective cultures. Deaf children are less likely to be exposed to American Sign Language (ASL), Deaf Culture, and Deaf role models and are misunderstood by hearing parents. LGBT children quickly learn that same sex attractions and gender-variant behaviors are unacceptable and that they will suffer consequences if they persist in expressing their natural inclinations. In addition to harassment and assaults at school, these kids are sometimes expelled from their homes by disavowing parents. Both groups experience isolation in the family, at school, and in the community. Consider the plight, then, of children who are both LGBT and deaf or hard of hearing.

Historically, the medical profession and educators have viewed each of these groups through a pathological lens, with interventions focused on deficits, disease, and abnormalities— problems that could only be addressed by approaches designed to return the child to *normalcy.* Examples would be conversion therapy for LGBT students and a preference for oral education in the case of deaf children.

Gallaudet President Edward C. Merrill condemned the overzealous emphasis on oral methods in a poignant address he gave at the International Congress on Education of the Deaf in Tokyo (Merrill, 1975). In his revolutionary remarks he chastised educators for "prostituting" the education of "thousands and thousands" of deaf children in the name of speech and speechreading. He also asserted the right of deaf children to be taught in their native language, directly challenging 100 years of oppressive, oral pedagogy. Propelled by a fervent identity movement among Deaf Americans, the use of ASL for instruction and inclusion of Deaf Culture concepts in school curricula had gained acceptance by the turn of the century. The pathological model, as applied to deaf children, lost favor.

Positive portrayals of the LGBT community in school curricula and the provision of services to these students remain very much the exception more so than the rule. As will be seen in research presented in this chapter, LGBT students experience higher levels of harassment and physical assaults than any other minority group in elementary, secondary, and college settings. However, the future is brighter now that legislative, judicial, and policy-level victories are being won on behalf of the LGBT community.

LGBT BACKGROUND INFORMATION

On a warm June evening in 1969 a riot exploded outside the Stonewall Inn, a gay bar in New York's Greenwich Village. Metropolitan police officers had roughed up the inn's customers during a raid, and the bar's patrons fought back for the first time. The upheaval continued for 3 nights and spawned the first "Pride" celebrations in commemoration of the "Stonewall Riots" a year later. These historic events, which launched the gay and lesbian civil rights struggle, were part of what was known in earlier years as the Gay Liberation Movement.

Much has changed in the four and one-half decades since then. In 1973 being gay or lesbian was "depathologized" by the American Psychiatric Association when the organization removed homosexuality from its diagnostic and statistical manual. In the 1990s the Gay Lesbian Straight Education Network (GLSEN), an organization fostering gay–straight student clubs in our nation's schools, grew into an influential national force. In academia the Center for Lesbian and Gay Studies was established in 1991 at the City University of New York, promoting scholarly research into sexual minorities and stimulating the establishment of other university centers. In the 2000s, state sodomy laws, which had been used to prosecute gay men, were overturned by the Supreme Court (*Lawrence v. Kansas*, 2003). In addition, rapid progress toward marriage equality was assured when the nation's highest court found key sections of the Defense of Marriage Act unconstitutional (*Windsor v. United States*, 2013) and overturned California's Proposition 8 (*Hollingsworth v. Perry*, 2013). These are only a few of the many advances won since that mayhem in Greenwich Village.

LGBT TERMINOLOGY

The labels preferred by the LGBT community to describe its members have also changed. In the early days of the movement, the umbrella term "gay" was embraced by the majority of homosexual, bisexual, and gender-variant individuals as representative of the entire community. Preferred terminology is now more precise, having evolved slowly over the years via writings and the oral discourse of LGBT opinion leaders. The exploration of acceptable labels is common in the early stages of an identity movement. Oppressed groups tend to be cautious and strategic about their branding. They want to be in control of the messaging, having learned that language exerts great influence over the shaping of perceptions.

LBGT descriptors developed in much the same fashion that the deaf community acted to determine its own labels, by extinguishing uncomplimentary terms such as "deaf mute" and "hearing impaired." In the end, the terms "deaf and hard of hearing" were adopted by the community to describe its members and the capitalized word "Deaf" was selected to represent all that is Deaf Culture. (It should be noted that wherever the single term "deaf" appears in this chapter, it is meant to connote both deaf and hard-of-hearing students.)

The all-inclusive term "gay" has now been replaced by variations of the basic acronym "LGBT," representing *lesbian, gay, bisexual, and transgender.* Some publications and organizations still place the "G" before the "L"—"GLBT" (see http://glreview.org), evidence of a mild but enduring competition between men and women for the first spot. However, LGBT is used most prevalently at the present time. Other acronyms include LGBTQ, with the "Q" representing *questioning*, LGBTQQ, with the second "Q" representing *queer*, and LGBTQQA, with the "A" representing *androgynous.* Occasionally, an "I" is included, representing *intersex.* Interested readers are encouraged to explore current usage in greater depth using other sources. Although not definitive or exhaustive, the National Lesbian and Gay Journalist's Association has produced a stylebook supplement on terminology designed to guide media portrayals of LGBT people (NGLJA, 2012). This chapter uses LGBT because that seems to be the common convention. However, the author recognizes that this acronym does not fully represent the fluid spectrum of identities and gender variance in the community.

Before exploring the status of LGBT deaf students, a more nuanced review of associated terminology is warranted. Defining terms and clarifying their interrelatedness are not easy tasks, but one source provided a well-researched exposition of language germane to the LGBT community. Cawthon and Guthrie (2011) describe *sexuality* as having three components: *sexual orientation*, *sexual behavior*, and *sexual identity*.

1. ***Sexual orientation*** is determined in relation to the partners to whom a person is drawn both sexually and emotionally. *Homosexuals* are attracted to individuals of the same sex, *heterosexuals* are attracted to the opposite sex, and *bisexuals* are attracted, at least to some degree, to both sexes. An individual's *sexual orientation* is considered fixed. In a *New York Times* opinion piece addressed to scientists in Uganda, American geneticist Dean Hamer (2014) referred to sexual orientation as "immutable." He added that no scientific evidence exists that homosexual or heterosexual orientations are learned behaviors. Sexual attractions may not be fully understood during young adulthood, and need clarification, but they are stable over the lifetime. Individuals may deny or suppress *homosexual* or *bisexual* attractions. However, *sexual behaviors* help illuminate the underlying *orientation.*
2. ***Sexual behavior*** describes the sexual acts in which an individual engages and with whom. Regardless of one's *sexual orientation*, individuals at times may engage in *sexual behaviors* that run contrary to their *orientation*, for a variety of reasons. For example, a *homosexual* man might choose *heterosexual* women as sexual partners in order to avoid the cultural and institutional stigmas associated with homosexuality.
3. ***Sexual identity***, the most complex of the components, was described by Ryan and Futterman (1998) as having four elements: *sexual orientation identity*, *gender identity*, *sex roles identity*, and *physical identity*.
    a. *Sexual orientation identity* refers to labels that LGBT individuals have created to describe themselves (*gay*, *lesbian*, or *bisexual*). Although similar to *sexual orientation* categories (*homosexual*, *heterosexual*, and *bisexual*), these identities are limited to sexual minorities, incorporate gender, and make no reference to heterosexuality. Although the two concepts do overlap, often causing confusion, it is important to understand how they differ.

b. *Gender identity* refers to an individual's emotional and psychological sense of self with regard to gender and whether one self-identifies as a man, woman, or *transgender* (i.e., a person whose identity does not conform to the gender assigned at birth). *Transsexual* is a related term that describes a *transgender* person who aspires to alter, or has actually altered, their body through medical means to "fit" their *gender identity* more closely.
c. The third element, *sex roles identity*, signifies biologically determined outcomes that would normally result from one's sex assignment (e.g., pregnancy for women and facial hair for men).
d. *Physical identity*, the fourth and final element, is composed of societal expectations that are associated with the genders (e.g., attire or mannerisms).

REVIEW OF LITERATURE

A review of professional literature revealed no academic texts, journal articles, presentations, or professional writings regarding the elementary, secondary, or postsecondary education of LGBT deaf students. A few references were found that dealt with other aspects of the LGBT deaf community, but none were about educational issues. One article from more than 25 years ago appeared in *American Annals of the Deaf.* In "Considerations on Deafness and Homosexuality," Phaneuf (1987) concluded that the absence of research on deaf homosexuals was strong evidence of the need to study this population. Unfortunately, her recommendation went unheeded., After conducting his own review of numerous academic databases, Abernethy (2013) determined 26 years later that the research advocated by Phaneuf was never undertaken. One other source was a doctoral dissertation by Klinger (2007) that investigated the psychosocial development of gay, lesbian, and bisexual individuals. She also reported a dearth of professional literature on the deaf gay and lesbian population.

In contrast, a literature review conducted by Rankin, Weber, Blumenthal, and Frazer (2010) of all LGBT higher education content found an "explosion" of 6000 new references between 2003 and 2010. Whereas research into LGBT deaf issues in education never got underway, the study of LGBT nondeaf topics at the postsecondary level has mushroomed. This lack of research attention seems remarkable. It could suggest a simple lack of interest, a prevailing discomfort with the topic among educators, or even a bias against studying LGBT issues among academics in deafness.

A small number of LGBT deaf-related websites were found on the Internet (e.g., http://planetdeafqueer.com), but all dealt with social or cultural aspects of this group. Websites that market print and nonprint educational products relating to deafness or Deaf Culture, such as DawnSignPress (http://dawnsignpress.com), Gallaudet Press (http://gupress@gallaudet.edu), Clerc Center at Gallaudet (http://clerccenter2.gallaudet.edu/products/?a=all), and ASL Rose (http://aslrose.com), offered no materials on LGBT deaf topics.

Since the onset of YouTube a number of years ago, LGBT deaf individuals and their allies have been posting ASL video narratives about topics of interest. A YouTube search using the terms "deaf, gay, lesbian, and transgender" found no videos concerning subjects relevant to the education of LGBT deaf students among the first 30 pages of postings.

In a response to an email query sent to the Conference of Educational Administrators in Schools and Programs for the Deaf (CEASD), Ronald Stern, the organization's president, confirmed that he was also unaware of any journal articles or presentations given at professional meetings about LGBT deaf students. He added, however, that CEASD was planning a renewed focus on diversity and that the effort would include the needs of LGBT students. Following that communication, emails were received from four school heads confirming the establishment of student organizations specifically in support of LGBT students. This could be an emerging trend among special schools. Clubs were reported in existence at American School for the Deaf, California School for the Deaf at Fremont, Indiana School for the Deaf, and

Washington State School for the Deaf. Only these schools were reporting, so there may be others.

The majority (75%) of our nation's school-age deaf and hard-of-hearing children are educated in general (public) education settings. The other 25% are educated in center or special schools (Gallaudet University Research Institute, 2011). Very few special schools have working relationships with local school districts. Even where affiliations do exist, it is unlikely that deaf students could access LGBT services provided by public schools. LGBT deaf students attending public schools may access services offered to LGBT-hearing students, but no data are available to confirm this. Similarly, only anecdotal data exist regarding LGBT student services in special schools for the deaf.

Perhaps the biggest hindrance to assessing the status of LGBT (deaf or hearing) students is the fact that no national estimates exist as to their numbers in elementary, secondary, or postsecondary education programs in the United States. This is due to the fact that schools do not collect this information and because young students may be uncertain of their sexual orientation. Furthermore, many students who do identify as LGBT remain closeted, as living openly can trigger discrimination, harassment, and physical assaults.

At the same time, the percentage of lesbian, gay, or bisexual adults in the entire population is not clear either, with study estimates ranging from 4 to 12% (Thoresen, 1998). Controversy persists about the most accurate methods of collecting this information. Gates (2011) cited several reasons for the range in estimates, including differences in "LGB" definitions used, divergent survey methods employed, and changes in survey questions over time. Gates (2011) also argued that the percentages tend to be underestimated, if they are based solely on how respondents self-identify (as is often the case). Although Gates (2011) found that only 3.5% of the population in his study self-identified as gay, lesbian, or bisexual, 8.2% reported they had engaged in same-sex behaviors and 11% acknowledged same-sex attractions.

If behaviors and attractions are also accepted as evidence of gay identity, the percentage moves much closer to the widely reported 10% figure found in the Kinsey Studies from the middle of the last century.

Grollman (2012), of the Kinsey Institute, confirmed that the reason the estimates have come down over the years is, precisely, because they are often based solely on how individuals self-identity. He also found that the majority of individuals who have engaged in same-gender sex nevertheless identify as heterosexual, not bisexual, muddying the waters even more.

ELEMENTARY AND SECONDARY EDUCATION—THE GLSEN SCHOOL CLIMATE STUDY

Although the incidence of LGBT students is not known, one organization has reported key findings concerning the experiences of LGBT middle and high school students in our nation's schools. Since 1997 GLSEN has studied negative school climate indicators (harassment and assaults), as well as the benefits to school climate from interventions such as LGBT clubs, anti-bullying policies, supportive staff, and LGBT-inclusive curricula (GLSEN, 2011).

The organization's 2011 National Climate Survey included responses from 8584 students between the ages of 13 and 20. Data were collected from all 50 states and represented 3224 unique school districts. Sixty-eight percent of the sample was white, about half was female, well over half identified as gay or lesbian (61%), and another 27% identified as bisexual. Respondents were in 6th to 12th grade, with the largest numbers in grades 10 and 11.

Harassment and Physical Assaults

Table 1 shows the extent to which LGBT respondents in the survey reported harassment and assaults in the school environment. Findings indicated that about 85% of the students heard the word "gay" used negatively. Sixty-one percent heard negative gender expression remarks and 71% heard words such as "dyke" or "faggot" frequently or often. Fifty-seven percent heard homophobic remarks from teachers or staff, and the same percentage heard negative gender expression remarks from school personnel. A full 82% were either called names or threatened due to their sexual orientation in the past year. Sixty-four

Table 1. Percentage of LGBT Middle and High School Students Reporting Harassment or Physical Assaults in School

LGBTQ students reported . . .	
1. Hearing the word gay used negatively	85%
2. Hearing negative gender expression remarks	61%
3. Hearing "dyke" or "faggot" frequently or often	71%
4. Hearing homophobic remarks from school staff	57%
5. Hearing negative gender expression remarks from school staff	57%
6. Being called names or threatened due to sexual orientation in the past year	82%
7. Being harassed verbally due to gender expression	64%
8. Being cyber bullied via text or Face Book	55%
9. Being pushed or shoved due to sexual orientation in the last year	38%
10. Being pushed or shoved due to gender expression in the last year	27%
11. Being punched, kicked, or injured with a weapon due to sexual orientation in the last year	18%
12. Being punched, kicked, or injured with a weapon due to gender expression in the last year	12%

percent were harassed verbally in the past year because of their gender expression. Cyber bullying was reported by over 55% of LGBT students in the form of text messages or Face Book posts.

With regard to physical assaults, over 38% of the respondents reported being pushed or shoved in the past year due to their sexual orientation; 27% because of gender expression. Over 18% were assaulted physically (punched, kicked, or injured with a weapon) due to their sexual orientation in the past year; over 12% due to their gender expression.

Perhaps the most surprising finding of this study was that LGBT high school students were two to four times more likely to be harassed verbally than students based on religion, race, ethnicity, or disability. Further, LGBT students were 3 to 15 times more likely to be victimized (i.e., physically harassed or assaulted) than based on race, ethnicity, or disability.

Harmful Effects on Students

The study also confirmed how unsafe school environments are linked to harmful effects among students. LGBT youth were significantly more likely to skip classes or miss entire days of school. LGBT students in schools with higher levels of victimization were less likely to express plans to pursue higher education. They also demonstrated higher levels of depression and lower levels of self-esteem, indicating the psychological consequences of victimization. Apart from this study there is ample anecdotal evidence of this problem in the nation's media portrayals of youth suicides following victimization at school.

The generally high rate of harassment in schools was exacerbated by student beliefs that school personnel were unlikely to do anything when LGBT students reported incidents. Over 60% of students who had been harassed or assaulted did not report the incidents, most often because they believed no action would be taken or the situation would get worse for them. Thirty-seven percent of the students who did report incidents responded that no action was taken, reinforcing their beliefs.

Strategies for Improving Climate

The GLSEN study also revealed how school climates can be improved for LGBT students. First, the establishment of Gay–Straight Alliances (GSAs) or similar clubs can make a difference. Students with GSAs in their schools were less likely to hear homophobic remarks, to experience higher levels of victimization (23% vs. 39%), or to feel unsafe (55% vs. 71%). Yet, less than half of the respondents (46%) reported having a GSA or similar club in their school.

Similarly, positive representations of the history of LGBT people in a school's curriculum (an inclusive curriculum) had an effect on school climate. Students heard fewer homophobic and negative gender expression remarks. They felt less unsafe (43% vs. 68%) and missed less school (18% vs. 35%) than students in schools without inclusive curricula. They also reported classmates as being somewhat or very accepting of LGBT people (68% vs. 33%). Unfortunately, only 17% of the students responding said they attended schools with an inclusive curriculum.

Another factor that can improve the climate for LGBT students is the presence of supportive personnel in schools. Fewer students in schools with more than six supportive teachers or staff reported feeling unsafe (53% vs. 76%). In addition, students in schools with supportive staff had higher grade point averages (3.2 vs. 2.9), missed school less in the past month (22% vs. 51%), and were only about a third as likely to report they had no plans to attend college (5% vs. 15%).

The most powerful factor in reducing anti-gay bullying and harassment was the specific naming of student characteristics such as sexual orientation, gender identity, or gender expression in comprehensive school policies or laws, rather than citing vague or nonspecific terms. Students in schools with comprehensive policies reported hearing homophobic remarks less frequently when compared to students in schools without comprehensive policies (60% vs. 73%). A very small percentage of the students reported that their school actually had a comprehensive policy (about 7%), and only 15 states and the District of Columbia have such policies.

Although the study reports that there has been a slight decrease nationally in the level of bullying and harassment of LGBT students since the studies were initiated, results clearly show that the incidence remains alarmingly high. The level of harassment of transgender students has remained unchanged. And although it is evident that student GSAs, inclusive curricula, supportive staff, and comprehensive policies and laws can foster improvements in climate, these factors are found in a very small percentage of our nation's schools.

If the frequency of bullying and harassment of LGBT deaf students mirrors that of the respondents in this study, then deaf students are also negatively impacted by victimization at school. They may be targeted even more in public schools because of the dual stigmas resulting from disability and LGBT status. How these students fare in special schools cannot be established because data were not collected from these students. If special schools were to participate in the GLSEN School Climate Study, data could be analyzed to shed light on the status of LGBT deaf students in center schools.

POSTSECONDARY STUDENTS—CAMPUS PRIDE

At the postsecondary level, the experiences of LGBT students are strikingly similar to their middle and high school counterparts with regard to harassment and assaults. In contrast, much more is known about their LGBT status. Higher education students have developed a better sense of their sexual orientation and gender status, having moved through puberty and likely had more sexual experiences than younger LGBT students. According to the Guttmacher Institute (2013), more than 70% of all American adolescents have had sex by the age of 19. The findings of a study of adolescents indicated that gay, lesbian, and bisexual students were significantly more likely than heterosexual students to have had intercourse (Massachusetts Department of Education, 2006). Another difference is that more LGBT college students have come out than younger students.

In any case, the two groups are very similar in the extent to which they experience threats to their integrity from verbal harassment, intimidation, and physical assaults in the educational environment.

"The State of Higher Education"—Demographics

Founded in 2001, Campus Pride is a national organization dedicated to creating safer and more inclusive LGBT-friendly college and university campuses through leadership development, support programs, and services. One of the organization's most useful efforts has been the publication of a college-level campus climate survey. Similar to GLSEN's K-12 survey, Campus Pride's 2011 publication called "The State of Higher Education" is the most comprehensive compilation of opinions about LGBT experiences on American college campuses. The study collected information from 5149 students, faculty, staff, and administrators, representing every state and every type of higher education institution in the nation (Rankin et al., 2010).

Of the respondents, 38% identified as men, 48% as women, 5% as transgender, and 8% as "other." Thirty-three percent identified as gay, 20% as lesbian, 12% as bisexual, 16% as queer, 16% as heterosexual, and 2% as asexual. Almost one-half of the respondents were undergraduates (46%), and graduate students accounted for 17% of the group. Faculty comprised 10% of the population, staff 21%, and administrators 7%. Twenty-six percent of the respondents identified as people of color. The specific racial breakdown reported was as follows: 77% white, 8% multiracial, 5% Latino/Hispanic, 5% Asian, 4% African-American, 1% American Indian, and 1%Middle Eastern. Nine percent of the respondents reported being disabled. Within that group, psychological disabilities were reported by 57%, physical disabilities by 33%, and learning disabilities by 32%.

Seventy-five percent of the total group reported being "out" to friends about their sexual identity. Undergraduates were the least likely to be "out" to immediate family members at 46% when compared to graduate students and employees at 70%. A full 90% of faculty, staff, and administrators were "out" to professional colleagues.

Citing data from this study and previous LGBT climate studies (Dolan, 1998; Noack, 2004; Rankin, 2003), the Campus Pride authors affirm how, similar to the GLSEN findings from middle and high schools, LGBT students at the college level are more likely to have encountered injurious experiences than any other marginalized group.

The size and complexity of this study preclude a succinct summary for this chapter. In its executive summary, research results are clustered under a number of "challenges." A few of the challenges are presented here along with associated research findings to illustrate several relevant campus climate factors described in the study.

Identity and Harassment

First, the study reported that self-identified lesbian, gay, bisexual, and queer (LGBQ) respondents experienced significantly more harassment and discrimination than their heterosexual allies. They were twice as likely to experience harassment (23% vs. 12%) and to report derogatory remarks (61% vs. 29%). They were also seven times as likely to report the harassment was based on their sexual identity (83% vs. 12%).

Second, the respondents who identified as transgender (i.e., transmasculine, transfeminine, or gender nonconforming) reported experiencing harassment and discrimination at higher levels than those who identified using the gender binary (man or woman). Over 30% of transgender respondents reported experiencing harassment compared to approximately 20% of respondents who identified as men or women. Further, most transmasculine (87%) and transfeminine (82%) respondents reported that gender expression was the basis for their harassment when compared to respondents who identified as men (20%) and women (24%).

Another "challenge" supported by study data was that respondents who report multiple "minoritized" identities (e.g., person of color and lesbian) also report experiencing multiple forms of oppression. As an example, respondents of color were 10 times more likely to report racial profiling than their white counterparts (20% vs. 2%) and to cite race as the reason for harassment. However, the study confirms that sexual identity is the principal risk factor for harassment for both respondents of color and white students.

Identity and Perception of Climate

With regard to overall views of campus climate, the study found that LGBQ students (all categories) were significantly less likely to feel comfortable with campus climate than their heterosexual allies. Transgender students reported significantly more negative perceptions of climate than those who identified with the gender binary. And, as one might predict, the "intersection" of multiple cultural and social identities resulted in significantly more negative perceptions of school climate.

Identity and Harmful Effects

Similar to the GLSEN study, strong evidence shows that students in the Campus Pride study experienced harmful effects as a result of sexual identity bias. LGBT students were most likely to consider leaving school, to fear for their safety, and to avoid discussion of their sexual identity due to threats and fear of consequences. They were also the most likely to disagree with their institution's responses to LGBT policies, procedures, programs, and curricula.

Best Practices

The Campus Pride study also recommended several best practices that higher education institutions were encouraged to adopt. Inclusive policies, integration of LGBTQQ issues and concerns into curricular and cocurricular education, appropriate responses to anti-LGBTQQ incidents and bias, "brave spaces" for student dialogues on campus, and comprehensive counseling and healthcare were among the strategies suggested.

POSTSECONDARY INSTITUTIONS FOR THE DEAF

To examine the current status of LGBT programs and services for deaf students at the postsecondary level, a list of questions was sent to Gallaudet University, The National Center on Deafness (NCOD) at California State University at Northridge (CSUN), and National Technical Institute for the Deaf (NTID) at Rochester Institute of Technology (RIT). All three programs responded. Information was sought about whether the programs offered credit-bearing courses concerning LGBT culture or topics, whether there was an on-campus LGBT deaf student organization, whether there was a LGBT faculty/staff organization, and whether there were full-time staff devoted to serving LGBT deaf students. The programs were also asked what support services they provide to LGBT deaf students, whether the institution participated in the Campus Pride survey, and whether information about LGBT bias-related incidents was collected and analyzed.

Before summarizing the responses, it would be helpful to first understand how these college programs differ. Both NTID and NCOD are "integrated" programs, meaning they are part of larger "parent" institutions for hearing students. Both of these programs offer extensive support services in the form of interpreters, note takers, and captioning services for deaf students taking classes with hearing students. Each also offers credit-bearing courses solely for deaf students taught by faculty who use "direct communication" in American Sign Language. At NCOD these courses are limited to introductory English and mathematic topics taught through the CSUN academic departments by ASL using faculty. At NTID these offerings are more extensive. Majors can be taken in several technical fields taught within NTID, leading to associate degrees that prepare students directly for work. Students can also earn associate degrees that articulate with bachelor programs by taking integrated classes with hearing students. Certainly, the differences between NTID and NCOD are more complex than presented, but most evident is the extent to which they offer separate classes for deaf students.

Gallaudet is not an integrated program, although it has a small number of hearing students who matriculate at the undergraduate level and a sizable number enrolled in its graduate programs. The language of instruction at Gallaudet is ASL, so the use of interpreters in classrooms and in the provision of support services is generally limited to those situations where faculty or staff members are still developing ASL proficiency. The differences in these three institutions will also impact the manner in which instruction and support services are delivered to LGBT deaf students.

A summary of responses to questions sent to the three institutions is organized here by topic for clarity and comparisons.

1. ***Full-time staff for LGBTQ students:*** Gallaudet and CSUN/NCOD reported having full-time positions dedicated to serving LGBT students. The position at CSUN serves deaf and hearing students at the university. The title of that position is Coordinator of the Pride Center and LGBTQ Initiatives. Gallaudet had established a new, full-time position called Coordinator of the LGBTQA Resource Center reporting to the Director of Multicultural Student Services. At the time Gallaudet returned its responses, the position had not yet been filled. At NTID, an instructor in the Women and Gender Studies Department is also the Coordinator of RIT's GLBT Center that serves both deaf and hearing students. Both RIT/NTID and CSUN/NCOD report that services are made accessible to LGBT deaf students via the use of interpreters. At RIT/NTID students who can sign are hired to work as assistants in the campus GLBT Center.

2. ***Credit bearing courses:*** The institutions were asked if credit bearing courses devoted primarily to the study of LGBT people were offered and whether they were open to all. Another question asked whether courses were offered that included significant information about LGBT people as a part of a larger topic (e.g., multiculturalism or oppression). RIT reported offering three courses: Introduction to LGBT Studies, Queering Gender, and Queer Looks (film course) open to all students. NTID listed two credit bearing courses: Multiculturalism and Deaf Culture, offered only to deaf students, with imbedded LGBT content.

Gallaudet did not report offering any courses devoted primarily to the study of LGBT people and their culture. They did, however, report four credit bearing courses open to all students with imbedded LGBT information. They were Dynamics of Oppression, Disability Studies, Multicultural Deaf Lives, and GSR 150, a pre-major required course on gender and sexuality.

CSUN reported offering a minor in Queer Studies open to all students and requiring a total of 18 credits: three required courses and three electives. Among the 10 courses listed on the university website were Perspectives in Queer Studies, Gay Male Writers, Lesbian Writers, and Queer Studies Senior Capstone. In addition, CSUN reported that LGBT topics are covered in courses in human sexuality. NCOD does not offer any separate courses for deaf students about LGBT issues nor any courses with LGBT-imbedded topics.

3. ***Faculty/staff and student organizations:*** None of the three institutions reported having a LGBT faculty/staff organization, although Gallaudet reported the existence of a LGBTQQI faculty/staff list serve. RIT/NTID respondents reported they meet through committee work and informally at other times, but they are considering establishing a more formal organization. Both NTID and Gallaudet reported having active LGBT deaf student groups—the Rainbow Society at Gallaudet and SPECTRUM at NTID. At RIT/NTID interpreters

also allow participation by deaf students in the five campus-wide (integrated) LGBT organizations. CSUN/NCOD does not have a separate LGBT student group but encourages its deaf students to participate in the various LGBT student organizations on campus for which interpreters are provided.

4. ***Campus Pride participation:*** RIT/NTID indicated that it had participated in the Campus Pride survey in 2012, and they plan to continue participating. The Campus Pride website features a "LGBT-Friendly Campus Climate Index" that includes RIT in its listing. Out of a possible five "stars," RIT was awarded an overall 3.5. It was rated highest for LBGT Student Life (5) and lowest for LGBT Campus Safety and LGBT Academic Life (2 each). RIT should be commended for participating in the survey proactively. Gallaudet indicated that the university plans to participate, but the impediment has been language accessibility when surveying deaf students. One wonders how and to what extent NTID students participated in the RIT survey, and how language issues were addressed. CSUN indicated that it planned to participate in the survey in spring 2014.
5. ***Cocurricular programs and support services:*** All three institutions reported offering a variety of cocurricular programs for students. Among those reported were "Safe Zone" training for faculty, workshops on LGBT issues for all students, "Pink" graduation ceremonies for LGBT grads, mentorship programs that pair students with faculty/staff who are LGBT themselves, LGBT Celebration Weeks, and safe sex training, among others. All three institutions offer counseling in ASL to LGBT students for identity or relationship issues.

At Gallaudet the LGBTQA Resource Center is intended to serve as a cocurricular program in addition to its other student support functions when it becomes fully operational. At the time of Gallaudet's response, the resource center was an unfunded mandate, but this did not seem to prevent temporary personnel from providing services and support to LGBT students.

At RIT/NTID student/staff dinners are sponsored for students who are "ALLY" or LGBT to encourage mentorship and support. NTID also reported sponsoring attendance for two to four students at the Rainbow Alliance for the Deaf Conference held every 2 years. The Rainbow Alliance is the national organization in support of LGBT deaf individuals that has chapters across the country and in Canada.

The Pride Center at CSUN/NCOD reported offering no specific services designed for LGBT deaf students, but they do provide interpreters for all of their larger scale programs. The CSUN Counseling Services Department offers eight free counseling sessions for all hearing and deaf students. One of the counselors is fluent in ASL and part of the LGBT community.

Gallaudet and RIT/NTID alternately host a unique, nonprofit, annual leadership conference for LGBT college-age deaf students called ColorFEST. Held each year at Gallaudet or RIT/NTID, the conference's purpose is to enrich the lives of LGBT college youth.

6. ***Numbers of LGBT students and bias-related incidents:*** None of the three institutions reported collecting information about the number of LGBT deaf students in attendance. The response from RIT indicated they were "not allowed to" collect LGBT status information, but they do maintain data about who attends their programs and who uses the GLBT center. Although not specifically reported by Gallaudet and CSUN/NCOD, it is assumed that they also collect program attendance information for reporting purposes.

The practice of not doing anything that might "out" LGBT students is common in educational institutions. This is a complicated issue due to the prevailing belief that one's sexual identity is private information that should not be disclosed by others. At the same time, knowing the numbers of any type of student helps justify services. Perhaps a time will come when institutions will be free to routinely request information about LGBT status along with other demographic data. It will have to be a time when the consequences for coming out are much less severe.

None of the three institutions reported collecting and analyzing information about bias-related incidents involving LGBT deaf students. The coordinator of the GLBT center at RIT indicated he works closely with the institute's counseling center and public safety department to examine each case. This may also be the practice at Gallaudet and CSUN/NCOD, but that information was not provided. It would seem that a practice of collecting information about LGBT deaf incidents would not only have the potential to reduce the overall number of incidents, it might also inform each institution about the need for student programming.

SUMMARY, IMPLICATIONS, AND RECOMMENDATIONS

The three postsecondary institutions have demonstrated a visible commitment to addressing the needs of college-level LGBT deaf students. However, very little is happening at the middle and high school levels. One could argue that the reasons for this shortfall relate to age differences, the coming out process, and pressure from parents or religious organizations not to serve LGBT students. The glaring fact is that no one is writing or talking broadly in the profession about LGBT deaf students at any level. For all intents and purposes, they are invisible.

Most assuredly, making matters worse is the fact that LGBT deaf students represent the intersection of two (at a minimum) oppressed identities—deafness and LGBT status. Multiple research studies have confirmed that (hearing) LGBT students at all levels are victimized much more than would be the case based on race, religion, ethnicity, or disability alone. When you combine LGBT status with deafness, wouldn't that make it worse? We don't know. And these studies also verify the consequences of this mistreatment—lower self-esteem, depression, negative perceptions of school climate, lower GPAs, and school absences, among others. Is there any reason to assume this would not also be true for LGBT deaf students at all levels? Yet, professionals in deafness know next to nothing about this population. Questions are waiting to be answered. Are the incidence rates the same as in the hearing population? Do they stay in school? Are they also more at risk for self-harm, substance abuse, disease, or dropping out? Currently, judgments about the status of LGBT deaf students have to be inferred from studies of hearing LGBT students. It is time for that to change.

Educational leaders in deafness could begin by openly acknowledging the presence of LGBT deaf students, their challenges, and their contributions. Students do not have to be "outed" for that to happen. Referencing LGBT students in the same way one talks generally about sports teams, scholars, or other marginalized groups (e.g., students of color) will send a message of acceptance. Silence foments insecurities. Recognition builds self-esteem.

Acceptance should be followed by a commitment to address the needs of LGBT students with strategic initiatives. These could include evaluation studies or demographic research (e.g., in cooperation with Campus Pride or GLSEN), policy guidance (from CEASD, Gallaudet, or NTID), and model program development and implementation (at the school, state, or national level). Schools and programs at the middle and high school level could begin by adopting the effective "best practices" from the GLSEN study.

With no information at all in the professional literature about the education of LGBT deaf students, the time for building a body of knowledge has come. The very worst that could happen is this: Someone will review the literature in another 25 years and conclude that there is still a paucity of research related to LGBT deaf students.

REFERENCES

Abernethy, M. (2013).Waiting to be heard: On being deaf and gay. *Pop Matters.* Retrieved February 12, 2014 from http://popmatters.com/archive/contributor/132/

ASL Rose. Retrieved March 4, 2014 from http://www.aslrose.com/aslroseintro.php

Cawthon, T., & Guthrie, V. (2011). In M. Cuyjet, M. Howard-Hamilton, & D. Cooper (Eds.), *Lesbian, gay, bisexual and transgender college students* (pp. 291–326). Sterling, VA: Stylus Publishing.

Clerc Center at Gallaudet University. Retrieved March 4, 2014 from http://clerccenter2.gallaudet.edu/products/?a=free

DawnSignPress. Retrieved March 4, 2014 from http://www.dawnsign.com/

Dolan, J. (1998). Gay and lesbian professors: Out on campus. *Academe, 84*(5), 40–45.

Gallaudet University (2010). *Annual survey of deaf and hard of hearing children and youth.* Gallaudet Research Institute. Retrieved March 3, 2014 from http://research.gallaudet.edu/Demographics/2010_National_Summary.pdf.

Gallaudet University Press. Retrieved March 4, 2014 from http://gupress.gallaudet.edu/

Gates, G. (2011). *How many people are lesbian, gay, bisexual and transgender?* The Williams Institute: UCLA School of Law. Retrieved February 22, 2014 from http://williamsinstitute.law.ucla.edu/research/census-lgbt-demographics-studies/how-many-people-are-lesbian-gay-bisexual-and-transgender/

Gay and Lesbian Review: A Bi-monthly Magazine of History, Culture and Politics. Retrieved March 3, 2014 from http://www.glreview.org/.

Grollman, E. (2012). Who are lesbian, gay, bisexual and transgender Americans? *Kinsey Confidential: Sexual health information from the Kinsey Institute.* Retrieved February 22, 2014 from http://kinseyconfidential.org/lgbtamericans/

Guttmacher Institute. Facts on American teens' sexual and reproductive health. *In Brief: Fact Sheet.* Retrieved February 23, 2014 from http://www.guttmacher.org/pubs/FB-ATSRH.html#5a

Hamer, D. (2014). An open letter on homosexuality to my fellow scientists in Uganda. *On the ground.* Retrieved February 23, 2014 from http://kristof.blogs.nytimes.com/2014/02/20/an-open-letter-on-homosexuality-to-my-fellow-ugandan-scientists/*Hollingsworth v. Perry*, 570 U.S. 12–144 (2013)

Klinger, A. (2007). *The social development of an invisible minority: The deaf gay and lesbian population.* University of Hartford: Unpublished doctoral dissertation.

Kosciw, J., Greytak, E., Bartkiewicz, M., Boesen, M., & Palmer, N. (2011). *The 2011 National School Climate Survey: The experiences of lesbian, gay, bisexual, and transgender youth in our nation's schools.* Austin, TX: Gay, Lesbian & Straight Education Network.

Lawrence v. Texas, 539 U.S. 558 (2003)

Massachusetts Department of Education (2006). *2005 Youth Risk Behavior Survey.* Massachusetts Department of Education website. Retrieved February 2, 2014 from http://www.doe.mass.edu/cnp/hprograms/yrbs/05/default.html.

Merrill, E. (1975). *New measures of credibility: Universal rights and progress in education of the deaf.* Paper presented at the International Congress on Education of the Deaf. Tokyo, Japan, August 20–25, 1975. Contained in the archives of the Gallaudet University Library.

Noack, K. (2004). *An assessment of the campus climate for gay, lesbian, bisexual, transgender persons as perceived by the faculty, staff and administration at Texas A&M University*. Texas A&M University: Unpublished Doctoral Dissertation.

National Lesbian and Gay Journalist's Association (2012). *Stylebook supplement on lesbian gay bisexual and transgender terminology*. Retrieved March 3, 2014 from http://nlgja.org/files/NLGJAStylebook0712.pdf

Phaneuf, J. (March, 1987). Considerations on deafness and homosexuality. *American Annals of the Deaf, 132*(1), 52–55.

Planet Deaf Queer. Retrieved March 4, 2014 from http://www.planetdeafqueer.com/

Rankin, S. (2003). *Campus climate for gay, lesbian, bisexual and transgender people: A national perspective.* Washington, DC: National Gay and Lesbian Task Force Policy Institute.

Rankin, S., Weber, G., Blumenthal, W., & Fraser, S. (2010). *2010 state of higher education for lesbian, gay, bisexual and transgender people.* Charlotte, NC: Campus Pride.

Ryan, C., & Futterman, D. (1998). *Lesbian and gay youth.* New York: Columbia University Press.

Thoresen, J. (1998). "Do we have to call it that?!" Planning, implementing, and teaching an LGBT course. In R.L. Sando (Ed.), *Working with lesbian, gay, bisexual and transgender college students: A handbook for faculty and administrators* (pp. 255–263). Westport, CT: Greenwood.

Windsor v. The United States, 570 U.S. 12-307 (2013)

CHAPTER 12

Services for Learners who are Deafblind: An International and Multicultural Perspective

BARBARA A.B. McLETCHIE, Ph.D
MARIANNE RIGGIO, M.Ed.

INTRODUCTION

Children who are Deafblind are at high risk for exclusion from education and society because of cultural and societal attitudes and the uniqueness and complexity of combined vision and hearing losses. This is particularly true in low- and middle-income countries, where resources are scarce.

This chapter explores issues and strategies for working within developing countries to create sustainable systems that lead to quality early intervention, education, and transitions to adult life for children and young adults who are Deafblind and their families. It is based on the professional experiences of the authors' work in developing countries.

Every country has unique cultural, demographic, social–political, and economic factors to consider. In low- and middle-income countries, there are many barriers to providing education for children who are Deafblind. Too often, they do not have access to education because of poverty, negative societal attitudes, little or no support to families, transportation challenges, lack of trained teachers, and inadequate learning materials. It is important to keep these issues in mind when developing partnerships within countries to support the development of services for learners who are Deafblind and their families. In some cultures, the care of the child who is Deafblind is the responsibility of the grandparents—usually the grandmother. In other countries, because of poverty, children who are Deafblind may be left alone while parents go to work. In other cultures, a child who is congenitally Deafblind is viewed as a curse—imagine the impact on the child.

UNDERSTANDING THE NEEDS OF LEARNERS WHO ARE DEAFBLIND

Individuals who are Deafblind have both a hearing and a vision impairment that is severe enough to affect communication, mobility, and access to information and the environment. People who are Deafblind may also have additional challenges that are physical or cognitive. Only a small proportion of people who are Deafblind are completely Deaf and completely Blind. As a result, service planning and delivery require appropriate responses or strategies (http://www.deafblindinternational.org/PDF/Guidelines).

The Deafblind population is very heterogeneous, from children who have vision and hearing losses and can go on to very independent lives to those with significant additional disabilities, who will require a great deal of lifelong support. This isolating disability creates challenges for educators to build their students' abilities in communication, concept development, and social competence.

Students who are Deafblind, like all students, are individuals and have strengths and needs that are very specific to their identity. Each will require an individually tailored educational experience. There are children who are born Deafblind and others who become Deafblind later on. For example, some children are born Deaf and acquire vision loss later, while others are born with vision loss and become Deaf later. Again, this exemplifies the diversity of the population. There are, however, some common challenges for all people who are Deafblind that should be considered by those who provide educational services:

Typically, people who are Deafblind experience isolation from other people and the environment. The major challenge that educators face in diminishing this isolation is to build their students' abilities in communication and social competence. Communication provides access to the curriculum and all learning, including developing social relationships and meaningful friendships.

A meaningful and quality education for a learner who is Deafblind must involve families, paraprofessionals, and professionals working together to support the child's educational growth and social development.

Children who are born Deafblind have difficulty learning concepts and skills that other children learn very naturally in their homes. Children learn naturally by watching, hearing, and exploring. For example, children learn about cooking by watching parents cook, and they help as they are able. They also learn about self-care skills by imitating what they have seen others do during their daily routines. Most children are not taught language or to speak, but learn language naturally because they are constantly immersed in a multitude of conversations.

Children, in general, come to school with a wealth of concepts, skills, and communication abilities that provide the foundation for accessing an academic curriculum. Children who are Deafblind do not have access to these natural learning opportunities.

The presence of Deafblindness has a dramatic impact on a child's social and communication connections and on all aspects of personal development. A meaningful and high-quality education for a learner who is Deafblind must involve families and service providers working together to support the child's social development and educational growth. Unless partnerships are forged with families from the earliest age possible, children who are Deafblind are at a very high risk for failure in school and isolation from others. Educators must respect that families know the most about their children, and families are critical partners in the educational process. Families also need support to create opportunities that will promote their child's development and inclusion in the flow of daily life at home, in school, and in the community.

UNIQUE INSTRUCTIONAL NEEDS

Vision and hearing are often called the distance senses, meaning that it is through these senses that we are connected to the world beyond our personal body space. Children who are Deafblind cannot see the world or may see in very distorted ways. Likewise, they are deprived of opportunities for natural language acquisition because they are Deaf. These combined and complex sensory losses greatly challenge their ability to access people, to form meaningful reciprocal relationships and concepts about the world around them. Therefore, for the person who is Deafblind, the world is very small. Developing the child's communication abilities with others, fused with natural real life experiences, allows the student's world to become bigger and bigger.

In order to address the complex challenges of Deafblindness, there are common educational practices that are effective for learners who are Deafblind.

- Establishing a trusting teacher–student relationship is fundamental.
- Following and using the child's likes and interests as the springboard for learning.
- Utilizing a conversational approach to the development of meaningful communication (e.g., joint attention, shared topic, turn-taking, balance of turns, a safe and comfortable environment)
- Using the child's natural forms of communication while modeling the next highest level (e.g., child may touch the cup to request more to drink and teacher responds using a simple sign for "drink")
- Providing continual access to communication and literacy throughout the day
- Providing routines to develop anticipation and memory, and to minimize anxiety and confusion
- Teaching through naturally occurring activities of daily life
- Providing a clear beginning, middle, and end to activities
- Providing choices
- Embedding communication in all activities

- Sharing in activities with another person
- Connecting activities with one another throughout the day

Schools in developing countries have fewer professional resources and materials than are available in developed countries (e.g., computers, high-tech augmentative communication devices, learning kits, teachers and paraprofessionals). Often times, however, a high dependency on materials can become a barrier both to the building of a strong teacher–student relationship and relationships with peers and to the development of meaningful concepts about the world—a great challenge to people who are Deafblind. A lack of material resources can encourage teachers to be creative and use real-life natural learning materials and routines that result in meaningful and functional curricula.

This activity from Sri Lanka shows ways to encourage students at a variety of levels engaging in the preparation of a coconut snack (Figure 1). Many skills can be taught through this activity, such as motor skills, sequencing, basic concepts (big/little, soft/hard), hygiene, and social and communication skills.

1. Discuss coconuts.
   a. Have the students identify them, through questions such as "What is this?", "Where does it come from?", "What do we use it for?" (Figure 2).

Figure 1.

Figure 2.

   b. Talk about the features of coconuts, asking questions such as "Are they hard or soft?" Students can compare the size, weight, shape, and texture of different coconuts.
   c. Count how many coconuts there are.
2. Gather or purchase coconuts. Ideally the students should be involved in getting coconuts for this cooking activity.
3. Discuss the plans for the cooking activity.
   a. Talk about what food item will be prepared.
   b. Identify which pieces of equipment will be needed.
   c. Talk about any special preparations, such as the need to clean off the tables first and wash hands.
4. Have the students participate in all steps of the process, at whatever level of participation they are able (Figure 3).
   a. Invite the students to help to clean off the tables and wash their hands to prepare for the activity.

b. Ask the students to gather the materials and ingredients for the activity (bowls, grater, plates, etc.). It is helpful if these are kept in a predictable location and labeled with print/Braille/textures/objects/pictures so that students can find them more easily.

5. Encourage the students to be as independent as possible.

Ask the students to use both hands and provide support using **hand under hand** (rather than hand over hand). This will allow them to be more in control and to feel what the adults are doing (Figure 4).

Figure 3.

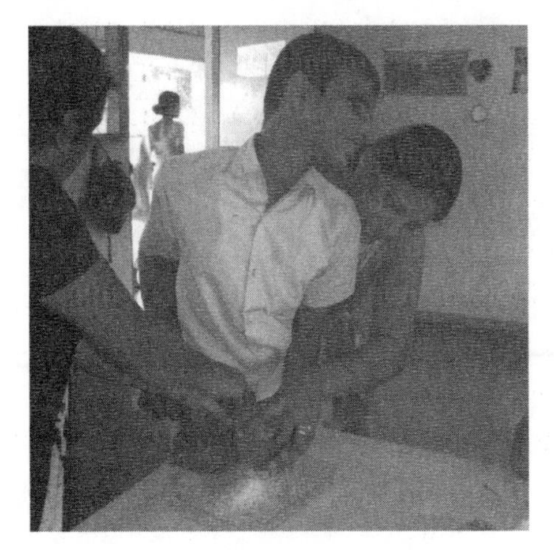

Figure 4.

6. Have the students take turns. Students can sit in a circle around a table so that each one is involved throughout the activity. This helps reinforce social and communication skills (Figure 5).
7. Eat the snack that the class has prepared! It's nice to give students the immediate reinforcement of eating what they have prepared (Figure 6). If there is extra food, it can be shared with other classes, sent to the student's house or residential hall, or sold.
8. Talk and write about the activity after it has been completed.

Figure 5.

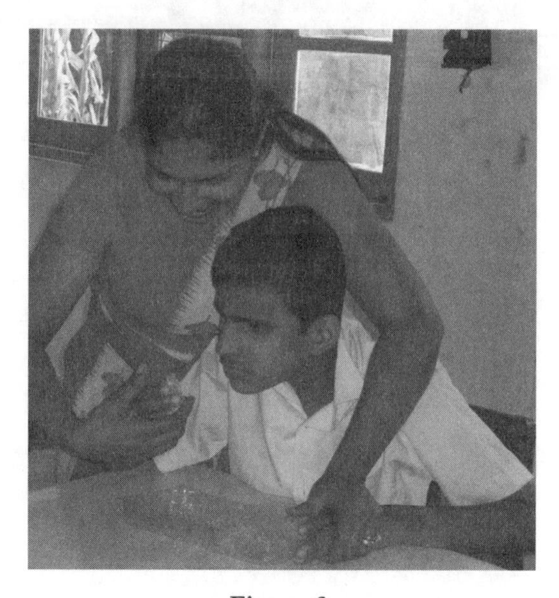

Figure 6.

This activity lends itself well to a language experience story, where the class tells about what happens, writing down whatever they are able to write or dictating to the teacher or another adult who writes it down. The story can then be illustrated with tactile illustrations, including small shreds of coconut or the shells or other related items mentioned in the story. Excerpt from Perkins International Transition Asia website (http://www.transitionplanningasia.org).

EVOLUTION OF SERVICES

Many countries go through common processes in their evolution of quality educational services: creating awareness, developing model programs, and building linkages among programs, universities/teacher training colleges, and ministries of education.

Throughout the world, the education of learners who are Deafblind is a relatively new and specialized field. The population of children who are Deafblind is highly diverse. The causes of Deafblindness vary from country to country based on factors such as immunization programs, gender equality, nutrition, health care, or survival of children with low birth weight.

Around the world, the vast majority of children who are born or have acquired Deafblindness do not have access to education or, if they do, it is by teachers who have little training to be able to adequately meet the unique educational needs of children with this complex disability.

In some countries, the field of education of children who are Deafblind was grounded in the development of early model programs. In these programs, the knowledge and skills necessary to work with children with disabilities were cultivated and continue to evolve and expand. Many of these pioneering programs became the training grounds for new teachers entering the field. Model programs also became resources for other professionals and family members that provided training, support, and information. Many became centers that promote advocacy for equal access to quality education for all children.

In some developing countries, the challenge is the creation of model educational programs that can also become the foundation for the establishment of much broader based services. Programs and services best evolve through partnerships of skilled educators and families who work in collaboration with governments to affect systems change. The goal of any individual or organization that wishes to support the development of services must enter into the endeavour with the vision that countries will be able to ultimately **sustain and continue to evolve services** with minimal or no outside support.

In some developing countries, there are well-established international nongovernment organizations (INGOs) that work toward the development of high-quality special education programs. In the course of the past few decades there have been a handful of INGOs (e.g., Perkins International, CBM International, and Sense International) that have worked to support the development of Deafblind educational services.

While the development of model educational programs is critical, it is necessary to work toward the establishment of a comprehensive and sustainable system of services. Collaboration with ministries of education, teacher training programs, parent organizations, and disabled persons organizations is essential to the development of quality services from birth to adulthood.

Each country has a different starting point and various paths to achieving quality education for children who are Deafblind. For example, in India, in the early 1970s two women began a program for students who were Deaf and Deafblind in one of their homes. They worked primarily with their religious community to raise funds to establish a small school. The founders also sought out the training and needed support to improve and expand their work with children who were Deaf and Deafblind. This support came from Gallaudet University, Perkins School for the Blind, and Sense, UK. From this beginning, India now has multiple schools serving children who are Deafblind; a system to provide in-service training for families and professionals throughout all regions of the country; two government recognized teacher training programs working with individuals who are Deafblind; and nationally recognized teacher competencies in visual impairments and multiple disabilities, including Deafblindness.

In Kenya, aside from one school that was established specifically for students who are Deafblind, there were and are many special units for students who are Deafblind at schools for the Deaf. These were established through **collaborative partnerships** among three INGOs (FSDB/SHIA, Perkins International, and CBM). Many tribal and cultural challenges influenced the development of these programs and leaderships within these programs.

In the Ukraine, a unit for students who are Deafblind was established at the school for students who are blind in the western part of the country. The director of this school approached both CBM and Perkins International for support. It was decided that Perkins would take the lead in providing in-service training and consultation to develop the knowledge and skills of their teaching staff. In all of these cases, the collaboration among the agencies that provided professional support was essential to cohesive planning and support.

In both India and Kenya, services for students who are Deafblind were linked with programs for Deaf students. This is unusual, as most programs for students who are Deafblind were established at schools for the blind in the United States and other countries throughout the world. Given the tremendous **communication** challenges facing learners who are Deafblind, it would seem logical that schools for the Deaf can provide better opportunities for natural communication to occur.

In other countries, initial broad-based training can be offered on country-wide or regional levels to provide awareness about children who are Deafblind. This can be a catalyst for the development of services. For example, in Asia, in the early 1990s, a regional training series was offered for teachers from six countries that had begun to serve students with visual impairment and multiple disabilities or Deafblindness but had little or no training and support. This training was designed to build teacher competencies and to create the beginnings of a regional network of committed professionals who could share the practices and challenges of working with students who are Deafblind. From these training efforts emerged a cadre of professionals and program administrators who became dedicated to developing high-quality services for Deafblind children and youth within their organizations.

Many schools began classes for learners who are Deafblind or visually impaired with multiple disabilities. Training efforts became more school based with consistent support from skilled educational consultants who established true and sustained partnerships in training, support, and collaboration. Teachers and administrators often became empowered to develop their own model programs that reflected their own values and traditions.

Teacher Training

Worldwide, there is a tremendous shortage of trained personnel in the education of Deafblind students. Higher education has a crucial role in developing awareness, changing attitudes, and building the knowledge and skills of **all** future teachers.

In addition to educational practices for learners who are Deafblind that have already been discussed, teachers who are trained in Deaf Education should be trained in **tactile sign language** and accommodations for students with reduced visual fields. Persons communicating with a learner who is Deafblind must consider the distance from the person who is Deafblind and the vertical and horizontal frame in which signs should be expressed. For example, students with Usher syndrome often require a greater distance and a smaller frame. Teachers should also learn other tactile adaptations, such as tactile fingerspelling, raised print, or printing with block letters into the palm. Most important, teacher training in education of Deaf students must include training in functional vision assessment for basic screening for vision loss. Often, students who are Deaf will not admit that they have difficulty seeing or are losing their vision. Likewise, teachers of students with visual impairment should receive cross-training in issues related to the education of Deaf students.

Teachers in general education classrooms need specialized support and training to include all children effectively. They must begin by changing attitudes toward students with special needs. As the needs of children within the educational system change, teachers and others who provide care and education need opportunities for ongoing training and support to stay current with best practice in the field.

Training Staff Outside of Their Home Countries

The idea of bringing teachers outside of their own countries for advanced studies in education of Deafblind students is one that is often debated because of the often dramatic cultural differences. It is, however, a strategy that can be very successful.

One of the big incentives for study abroad is if the program is linked to a school program where there is maximum opportunity to be immersed in classrooms where teachers in training can have hands-on experience working with experienced teachers. The Perkins International, Educational Leadership program is an example of this. Teachers who have experience in their home countries working with students who are Deafblind can study in this program for a period of 6 to 9 months. The program combines practical lectures with experiences in classrooms working with master teachers, as well as in the dormitories. It is the blend of theory and practice that strengthens competencies and confidence to become agents of change when they return to their home countries.

Involving Parents and Family Members

Unless partnerships are forged with families from the earliest age possible, Deafblind children are at very high risk for failure in school.

In many developing countries, children who are deafblind are kept at home and hidden from the community. Community-based rehabilitation (CBR) was started as a model of serving adults in their home communities. Over time, CBR has become a model for reaching people of all ages. Through these programs, CBR workers travel to rural areas to identify children and adults with special needs, including children who are Deafblind. Often, village elders, religious organizations, and others of the community will assist in this effort. CBR has become a valuable system for identification, services, and follow-up. It has also become the catalyst for the acceptance of people with special needs and the belief that these people can learn. In some cases it has resulted in the establishment of special programs within the community.

The CBR model is conducive to providing training in communication for all family members, as well as members of the village, which results in the child becoming a fully involved member of his/her community. CBR workers have also worked with families to develop income-generating projects for the person who is Deafblind. For example, these projects include growing mushrooms, harvesting rice, massage, weaving, and sale of handcrafted items. By becoming a financially contributing member of the family, the Deafblind person has improved self-esteem and has increased opportunities to build personal connections.

In countries that have comprehensive special education laws, family members have been the primary advocates for systems change. By creating strong partnerships with families, we not only build stronger educational programs, but we also create advocates for positive systems change.

Building Systems of Services

The creation of model programs, development of professional capacities, and empowerment of families laid the foundation for the creation of public policies that will assure that all children who are Deafblind are identified and entitled to receive quality educational services from infancy through young adulthood.

It is important to understand the special education laws and systems that exist in a country, as well as to analyze the implementation of services and the need for new services. For example, some major questions to answer may include the following.

- Is special education mandatory?
- Do schools use an Individual Educational Planning process?
- Is there provision in special education laws or regulations for specifying different categories for students in need of special education?
- Is there a definition of Deafblindness that is endorsed by the Ministry of Education?
- What types of teacher training courses or programs are currently in place?
- What systems are in place for identifying Deafblind children from birth to adulthood? Is there a linkage between identification and service provision?

- What services exist for Deafblind or other low incidence special education populations?

Analysis of the answers to these questions will give direction to the types of partnerships that should be forged, as well as set priorities for strategic planning for a process of collaborative work with existing resources in an individual country.

Any organization providing assistance within developing countries must be respectful and responsive to the individuals and systems that have common goals. Common goals are the cornerstones for meaningful and productive partnerships that will result in systems change. A valuable role for agencies from outside a country is to help facilitate collaboration among families, educators, administrators, consumers, and government officials that promote problem solving and positive actions.

For example, in one country, although there was a well-established school program for students who are Deafblind, the lack of training programs for teachers of these students was a problem and a priority. There was a specialized teacher training program in the education of children who are Deaf, so with the support from specialists in the education of Deafblind students, the teacher training program coursework was expanded to include competencies in working with Deafblind students. Later, the program developed two new courses specific to the education of Deafblind students and students with additional special needs for all aspiring teachers at the college.

The development of high-quality services for the diverse population of students who are Deafblind and their families requires sensitive, thoughtful, and collaborative planning. Careful study of the existing system for special education, as well as services for students who are Deafblind, will help guide the quality growth of services. Without model schools linked with teacher training, colleges will not be successful in preparing teachers to work with this highly diverse group of learners.

Learners who are Deafblind are a heterogeneous group. There are common instructional approaches that must adapt to the needs of each learner with communication and social interaction as ultimate goals.

Partnerships among family members, educators, administrators, and government agencies are critical to the success of any program and to the growth of a quality system of serving people who are Deafblind.

In both emerging and developed countries, all teachers need pre-service training and continuing education in teaching children with special needs, including children who are Deaf, children who are Blind, and children who are Deafblind, and the impact that additional disabilities may have on these populations. **This is a worldwide need.**

REFERENCES

Advancing education for all children who are blind or visually impaired with multiple disabilities (2011). Watertown, MA: Perkins School for the Blind.

Deafblind International—Service Guidelines http://www.deafblindinternational.org/PDF/Guidelines

Miles, B., & Riggio, M. (Eds.)(1999). *Remarkable conversations: A guide to developing meaningful communication with children and young adults who are deafblind.* Watertown, MA: Perkins School for the Blind.

Perkins International Transition Planning Asia: www.transitionplanningasia.org/perkins-international

Riggio, M., & McLetchie, B.A. (Eds.)(2008). *Deafblindness: Educational Service Guidelines.* Watertown, MA: Perkins School for the Blind.

UNICEF Report: The State of the World's Children 2013 http://www.unicef.org/sowc2013/

Chapter 13

Let's Text at School: Visual Connections across Cultures

COLLEEN L. SMITH
Doctoral Candidate Claremont Graduate University and San Diego State University Joint Doctoral Program

> "It is, in part, this critical commitment to act in behalf of freedom and social justice that also serves as a model for their students to discover their own personal power, social transformative potential, and spirit of hope."
>
> –Antonia Darder

In the age of social transformation, visual knowledge, a form of cultural capital, is connected with information exchanges in our social and academic networks. Classroom teachers can implement balanced discourse where students are engaged in academic discourse alternatively between (1) signed or spoken and (2) written languages with the goal of enhancing each student's articulation skills. This study began with a second-grade Deaf student mainstreamed utilizing American Sign Language (ASL)–English interpreters in two culturally diverse English-speaking classrooms. All students participated in print discourse for at least an hour daily facilitated by two hearing classroom teachers, one African-American and one Anglo-American, each with an eye for visual details. The classroom teachers and the Deaf

Table 1. Multimodal Discourse Model

Verbal discourse	Verbal–text discourse	Text discourse
33%	33%	33%

researcher shared the significance of engaging in visual-learning activities promoting peer connections across cultures. Nine specific examples of visual-based activities are also shared in this chapter.

INTRODUCTION

Visualize students entering an onsite classroom while communicating verbally (signed or spoken) and then sitting down at their computers and engaging in academic discussions via a written language with classmates. If the best way to acquire a language is to use it, are we, for instance, texting via a printed language sufficiently at school? If the goal is to sign/speak and write with fluency, shall we balance between verbal and written academic discourse in classrooms acquiring specific content knowledge and key concepts?

Better yet, educators could implement an optional balance among three literacy approaches (Table 1), which consist of (1) verbal discourse, (2) verbal–text discourse, and (3) text discourse.

This chapter focuses on opportunities to engage in synchronous text discourse via printed English among students and two classroom teachers utilizing the wide diversity of low- and high-tech tools available to us. Use of pen/paper, instant messaging, and chat rooms are examples of real-time synchronous communication tools. There is, after all, a paradigm shift where information exchange is easily accessible not only verbally but via text.

We are multi-texting and expanding our communities of practice where we can conveniently communicate locally, nationally, or internationally (Greenhow & Gleason, 2012). Technology has continued to significantly transform the art of learning. In fact, texting has become culturally relevant and is a motivating learning tool (Greenhow & Gleason, 2012). Furthermore, Ochoa (2003) asks, "Are we hindering or promoting status equalization within our school communities?" Thus, it is time to transform from spending more time communicating verbally to balancing between verbal and written academic discourse in traditional classrooms, giving students increased opportunities to network utilizing specialized key concepts.

In addition to examining synchronous written discourse opportunities, this chapter also discusses the academic benefits specifically for (1) students of color, (2) students who are deaf or hard of hearing, and (3) students of diverse learning strategies. Academic benefits include opportunities to communicate directly via a printed language, becoming active participants engaging in motivating and culturally relevant activities.

SOCIAL DISCOURSE SPACE

Historically, the challenge with the social discourse experience of writing to communicate emerges when some individuals are not comfortable with it as a means of exchanging information. It could be argued for another form of collective social capital (Bowels & Gintis, 1976; Coleman, 1990; Putnam, 1993; Spring, 2001). Some, if not many, individuals would limit their writings or type for merely functional purposes. It is a rarity to encounter another individual willing to text–talk beyond barely essential or superficial issues, be it in regards to the color of a particular wine or an in-depth discussion of an automotive glitch. However, times are now changing, and people are developing a positive attitude and a level of comfort in terms of writing or typing for communication purposes.

Some of us, as ASL and English text speakers, know that others need familiarity with actual experiences to develop comfort with the use of text to talk with ease. Because we are actually an underrepresented population and quite small in number, efforts to spread awareness of this discourse pedagogy would require massive amounts of time and logistics. It is fortunate, however, that the use of real-time text–talking has gone mainstream. The media now reports and forecasts extremely rapid growth in the volume of text messaging and online chat conversations. In addition, Grinter and Eldridge (2001) state that text messaging has changed how teenagers use smart phones to communicate and coordinate. Yuan (2003) reports increased preferences of online chatting as opposed to face-to-face interactions.

A case can be made that some of us continue to struggle or resist the processes of writing. Can the argument be made that our nation's dominant language is that of a spoken form? In addition to attitudes and ideologies of language, one could argue that one of the rationales of our existing condition is that our discourse writing experiences are limited, especially in classrooms, and not adequately utilized in an interactive and instantaneous fashion. To exchange information spontaneously in a text form between peers and educators is a tool—perhaps the most critical one. It cannot be emphasized enough that timing is an essential factor where real-time (or synchronous) text–talkers are given opportunities to respond immediately to one another and enhance language and learning development (Yuan, 2003).

Visual text is defined as including pictures, visual signs, sign language, and written language (Boal, 1985). Currently, information exchange is significantly impacted again where we continue to increasingly attend to visual input through the use of wireless multimedia interfaces such as smart phones. News networks have increased the use of visual text in their reporting (i.e., CNN's-captioned news ticker). The future should bring us the trend of increased open captioning. Public announcements should include visual text. Arrival/departure data boards at major airports across the nation could utilize open captions of airport announcements, for instance.

On December 31, 2005, the *New York Times* headlined an article, "Text Messaging Push for Use as Disaster Warning Systems," as recommended by specific experts, bolstering the importance of real-time text. The writer, John Schwartz (2004), reported that the use of a wireless short message service in 2004 could have jumpstarted governments' warning networks theoretically, saving thousands of lives by alerting people on coasts along the Indian Ocean of an impending tsunami. A text message network broadcasting system is currently in place for countries of the Pacific basin, Schwartz adds, and that a text message network is being built at the Netherlands for the North Sea area. Evidently, public announcement and broadcasting in text message format indeed has a broad and essential impact.

While the younger generation today tends to their iPods and smart phones, communication and the information exchange further shifts—this time from the effects of the multi-medium of visual and audio imprint. Studies have shown that deeper relationships are established among text–talkers than presumed, and sharing of the real-self expands via quiet text-based interactions as opposed to face-to-face communication (Grinter & Eldridge, 2001; Jarrell & Freiermuth, 2005; Yuan, 2003).

From the macro-perspective, the incentive exists among all parties involved to enhance and develop real-time text systems. Visual text is displayed in a variety of formats on CNN news, for instance, allowing us to view multiple news pieces simultaneously. These visual texts, including captions, allow what is spoken to be seen and benefit visually monolingual and multilingual youths. Culturally relevant pedagogy (Ladson-Billings, 1995) to young people includes text–talking. Could this be a strategy to blend different worlds, turning structural barriers into boundaries (Phelan, Davidson, & Yu, 1998) and promoting youths' access to the funds of knowledge (Stanton-Salazar, 2001)?

While the text medium benefits all of us, from a micro-perspective our academic discourse space has yet to meet the minimal needs of visual/spatial American Sign Language speakers. We continue to play host passively and actively to a system of oppression by reliance on interpreters, for instance, instead of providing all course participants, deaf and hearing, equal voice opportunities to also communicate directly via a printed language. Furthermore, we are spending much more time signing or speaking as opposed to writing academic English in the classroom (Lane, 1999).

ACADEMIC DISCOURSE SPACE: VISUAL AND AUDITORY CHANNELS

Most often, the academic discourse space is to communicate interactively via the auditory channel, for instance, a spoken language. A common option is to bring in signed language interpreters for deaf and hard-of-hearing students. However, another option would be to communicate directly, engaging in academic discourse via printed language to benefit all students in enhancing their signing/speaking and writing fluencies. Freire emphasized, "Changing language is part of the process of changing the world" (2003). He also pointed out that the relationship, language-thought-world, is a dialectical, processual, contradictory relationship. After all, there are two modes of visual social discourse: (1) signed language and (2) written language (Livingston, 1997).

To elaborate further, begin with the functionalism perspective as identified by the Ochoa Paradigm—where there is a social control to maintain social solidarity through the control of sociopolitical power using a position of preferred social status and privilege (Darder, Baltodano, & Torres, 2003; Stanton-Salazar, 2001). With speaking English via the auditory channel as such an example in the United States—we need to liberate ourselves by exploring other means of academic discourse. We have a total of three social discourse strategies to begin work with: (1) signed language and/or gestures, (2) written language, and (3) spoken language. For some it could begin with (1) gestures and/or signed language, (2) spoken language, and then (3) written language. This is to signify the fact that all of us begin language development with the use of gestures before communicating via a signed or spoken language. Furthermore, many teenagers are becoming text–talkers engaging in real-time pragmatic discourse (Yuan, 2003).

Thus, instead of a gap between developing signing/speaking and writing standards, classroom students could spend more time as real-time text–talkers while acquiring world knowledge as we construct and reconstruct them. The focus here is on using text as a motivational social discourse tool. Interactive computer gaming is an example of utilizing this learning space. We have the responsibility to raise our social consciousness by continually revisiting and redefining social discourse strategies if we are to consider ourselves as equals (Darder, 1991).

Darder (1991), Freire (2003a,b), and Stanton-Salazar (2001) clearly emphasized that the path toward cultural democracy is to understand the rules and the roles of the system and how we all practice "-isms". An example of practicing -isms is when deaf students are placed in public school systems learning alongside their nonsigning hearing peers. Often they continue to be placed in separate but "equal" environments where they sit next to classmates with minimal communication and without engaging in critical academic discourse. Communication might be transacted via interpreters. Direct communication via a written language would be better.

Tatum (1997) emphasized the importance of discovering one's voice and entering into modes of bicultural dialogue so that diverse individuals can become active social agents and transform their worlds. From that stage, negotiation strategies, for example, could be extrapolated, applied, and fine-tuned through ongoing mediation among themselves and others (Stanton-Salazar, 2001). Critical thinking is the key to bicultural affirmation. After all, each individual has the right to be educated in her or his own language and learning style, as well as the right to understand the very rules and roles of the system that is defined by the dominant culture (Darder, 1991).

Everyone is engaged in ongoing analysis of their own values, experiences, fears, concerns, biases, and prejudices—both in theory and in practice, as highlighted by Phelan and colleagues (1998). One way to do this is to document ongoing experiences, conflicts, questions, area of improvement, and actions. The focus is on personal and social responsibilities with the premise that we all are social agents within the classroom and within the community (Darder, 1991). An underlining theme that Darder painted was the importance of entering the stage of bicultural dialogue and that it is ok to feel lost and confused. It is through that very process, Darder (1991) points out, that one learns to understand and confront the conflicts and contradictions that function to interfere with his or her process of empowerment as an individual to this society.

WHO ARE WE AS WRITERS?

How often do we hear individuals say "I am not a writer"? Those words echo among school-age children and college students. Even some classroom teachers dread the writing process. It could be that they internalized such an oppressive perspective of "who is a writer and who is not" when in actuality we all are writers. Indeed, we do need to see ourselves as writers in this literate society. After all, further education attainment begins with positive language attitudes.

Visualize entering a seminar meeting or a K-12 classroom spending at least one-third of the course time as a text–talker each time the class meets. With the daily motivational "practice" of being text–talkers, what could our perceptions as writers then be? Is there a relationship between increased experiences of text–talking and a positive perception of the self as a writer? If we were to watch a film and then text–talk about the same film before writing a reaction paper, would we become much more comfortable with writing? Would this speed our academic language discourse acquisition? Such studies could investigate the relationship between academic attainment and social capital (Dika & Singh, 2002).

Furthermore, having positive language attitudes are necessary for the transitions between communicating basic interpersonal skills (BICS) and cognitive academic language proficiency (CALP) as text–talkers as well. Students need opportunities to text–talk critically with their peers at the comprehension input level while expanding their BICS and then CALP (Krashen & Terrell, 1996). The comprehension input level parallels with Vygotsky's (1962) zone of proximal development, while access to CALP means increased access to resources such as funds of knowledge if associated with individuals of power as Stanton-Salazar (2001) pointed out. With whom are the text–talkers networking that may have the culture and social capital needed for an improved academic attainment? Being text–talkers may enhance transitions between different worlds described by Phelan and colleagues (1998), and access to world knowledge is now literally at our fingertips.

Livingston (1997) recognized the importance of interacting with text. Schirmer and Ingram (2003) reported using online chat as a motivational communication tool. If the existing motivation is to speak more than we write—a discourse culture that we have adapted to mainstream patterns of interactions (Phelan et al., 1998)—how about motivating youths in the classroom as text–talkers to enhance language acquisition and development? Synchronous academic discourse could be a bridge between speaking and writing for fluency. It is with the balancing act of signing/speaking, text–talking, and writing within the classrooms that we all can view ourselves as writers. As Phelan and colleagues (1998) may put it, text–talkers respond to the issue of blending aspects of multiple roles, a transformational process of speaking and writing, which is most often the key to further academic attainment. Evidence also indicates that computer and literacy skills become linked due to motivational factors (Jarrell & Freiermuth, 2005; Schein, 2000; Schirmer & Ingram, 2003; Wesely, 2013; Yuan, 2003).

The implication for educators is for students to have positive self-images and to strengthen students' self-confidence as writers (Steele, 2003). The power of feeling has a strong correlation with our cognitive process. Phelan and colleagues (1998) further emphasized the importance of understanding students' perception of self as they navigate through borders, especially those that conflict with how others view them. A closer look at students' transitional patterns could inform us of students' adaptation strategy as writers. Their responses to how teachers see them as writers are worth further investigation via critical dialogue and reflections. For instance, tracking or grouping students may mislead them in their sense of self-identity and self-worth when what the students really need is improved access to cultural and social knowledge that foster further educational opportunities.

RETHINKING OUR SOCIAL AND ACADEMIC LEARNING SPACE

Through the use of verbal discourse, verbal–text discourse, and text discourse, balancing among three multimodal discourses can be predicted to enhance each student's articulation and written skills. The more students talk and text, the potential for improved outcomes increase. Perhaps papers and state test scores are also improved. Furthermore, texting allows us to develop our self-identities as writers, enhancing our academic knowledge as we continue to polish our speaking and writing skills.

Texting via printed English does place Deaf learners on an equal platform with others, with the ability to communicate directly with hearing learners. This would be an example of a least restrictive environment. Nover, Christensen, and Cheng (1998) assert, "As ASL and English are used more effectively in classroom instruction, students will be empowered to take a more active role in their literacy development so that they become independently engaged learners" (p. 69).

In addition, this multimodal approach to instruction could bring more attention to cognitive researchers, further examining the cognitive advantages of being multimodal. Petitto and Dunbar (2004) point to such crucial research: "Importantly, our preliminary results suggest that the bilingual "cognitive advantage" spans linguistic modalities, that is, it is true of bilinguals exposed to two spoken languages as well as bilinguals exposed to one spoken and one signed language" (p. 6).

NARRATIVE RESEARCH AND PEDAGOGY

As part of the narrative research work, the author carried out a qualitative study of "Cultural Transformation Practices and Students' Learning Processes" at a charter school in San Diego. The research included frequent informal class observations, noting that second-grade students enjoyed culturally relevant pedagogy in visual form (Ladson-Billings, 1995). After 6 months of text-writing at least 1 hour a day, three to five times a week, with only pens and paper and/or markers and whiteboards, these students were then videotaped for 1.5 hours on June 22, 2005. Data collection included videotext and written descriptions of visual discourse pedagogy and drawings and written documentations of the second-grade students' experiences. The videotaped documents included students engaging in thematic-based activities where they became text-writers. Immediately after an activity, students were given the opportunity to draw and write about their experience during the interactive visual discourse activity.

After working with and through the second graders and collecting data, I met with their classroom teachers. One of the teachers was African-American and another was Anglo-American. We were engaged in critical dialogue where I functioned as a research participant. Data collection consisted of video text and transcripts of constructive dialogue. During the first session we discussed our research rationale and what the word verbal meant (i.e., signed or spoken). We also shared our historical and educational backgrounds, cultural transformation practices, and their relationships with students' learning processes and shared the "visual discourse pedagogy" experience.

During the second session, the author met with the same teachers individually for approximately 2 hours each. We discussed the following questions critically. (1) What cultural transformation practices have you done in the past that may not fit within recent class dynamics? (2) What cultural transformation practices have you done this year that blend within recent class dynamics? (3) What other visual discourse pedagogy have you incorporated? (4) What are some benefits of visual discourse pedagogy? (5) What other senses have you incorporated? (6) Tell me more about visual discourse centers. (7) In analyzing ways that visual discourse pedagogy experiences benefit students' learning processes/way of knowing, what worked? (8) In continuing with the text-writing activity the next academic year, what would you do differently?

OBSERVATION NOTES OF THE VISUAL DISCOURSE PEDAGOGY

During the visual discourse pedagogy session on June 22, 2005, second-grade students had the opportunity to rotate between thematic centers discussed previously by the classroom teacher. In each of those centers, they could (1) make crowns and swords out of paper, (2) write notes with chocolate chips attached for a future treasure hunt activity, (3) make layered picture frames of kings/queens, and (4) with the use of wooden manipulatives, create a house, a castle, or etc.

Throughout the visual discourse period, all students had the opportunity to interact spontaneously by acting, gesturing, drawing, or writing. Boal (1985) discovered that dramatic actions throw light upon real actions and allow for a "rehearsal of revolution." In other words, students could be empowered to develop their identities as active participants and polish their social capital skills. There was one rule that we all agreed to follow—to not use any American Sign Language or spoken English. Instead, printed English was the target language.

The classroom teacher reported that this pedagogy was in practice for the past 6 months at an average of three times a week, giving the Deaf student opportunities to communicate directly without utilizing an interpreter. The initial goal was for this activity to last for approximately 20 minutes per day. However, often upon students' request, this activity would be extended to approximately 1 hour and 30 minutes daily. Evidently, this direct academic discourse via printed English not only benefitted the Deaf student, it also motivated all students.

After the visual discourse period, students drew and wrote about their experiences and how they felt about them before we engaged in a discussion using their home languages (i.e., ASL or spoken English). A total of 22 students participated during the visual discourse pedagogy centers. However, only 17 drawings/writing samples were collected. Of the 22 students, one was Asian, one was Latino, one was Filipino, and four were African-American. The remainder were white. One student came from a predominantly ASL-speaking family. Another spoke Tagalog at home. The rest of the families spoke mainly English at home.

Eleven out of 17 students included general-to-detailed drawings of the manipulatives they used at a center or two. A few students used one-word labels. Most wrote phrases and sentences. One student wrote, "I like to write on the white board the best. It is my favorite. I like it because it is fun. I love it." Another student wrote, "I had fun writing. There was one part that I did not like. A student kept whispering to me instead of writing on the white board. But all and all I had fun." A student with a happy face drawing wrote, "When I write to communicate, I feel calm and observant. But I also feel like I can't talk at all."

After the students drew and wrote about their experiences, we all sat in a circle. One by one, each student was given the opportunity to talk about his or her experience. They shared their opinions. At least 95% of the students stated repeatedly that they had a whole lot of fun and really enjoyed the hands-on activities. Another common response was how much they enjoyed acting and writing to exchange information or to ask questions. A talkative girl in class stated that at times she would feel the need to talk, yet liked the calm music and acting. She also stated that this strategy made it easier for her to focus on selected tasks. Another student agreed that the visual-based pedagogy felt calm and absorbing with soothing music. One student added that this interactive writing pedagogy was indeed creative, allowing her to become expressive.

SHARING CULTURALLY RELEVANT VISUAL-BASED PEDAGOGY

The two second-grade general education hearing classroom teachers and the author collaborated by sharing some of the visual-based activities implemented with students. The goal was for students to listen with their eyes and to promote their visual intelligence and creativity through engagement in cooperative learning activities. Lyman, Foyle, and Azwell (1993) discussed how cooperative learning holds particular promise for elementary teachers. Lyman et al. (1993) specifically stated that cooperative learning increases individual student motivation, encourages interactive group processes, and rewards successful group participation. Ogbu (2003) also reported that the cooperative learning approach helps improve the school performance of some African-American students.

During critical dialogue, we noticed that students benefitted from activities that were motivating and meaningful to them. In addition, each activity would commonly include manipulatives (i.e., objects and/or actors) while using two or more of their senses. It is also critical to design activities that empower students to make independent decisions (Boal, 1985; Darder, 1991) and interact spontaneously with each other (Lyman et al., 1993; Ogbu 2003). The following includes nine examples of visual-based activities.

1. Visual-based pedagogy can begin with toddlers engaged in interactive prewriting activities. A Deaf mother and her 1-year-old son sat on opposite sides of a closed door. Mother and son

each had a pen and shared one piece of paper. The mother drew a circle on a paper and slid it under the door to her child. The child drew the eyes and slid it back under the door to his mother. The mother added a nose and slipped the paper under the door. The son added a smile before returning the paper back under the door. The mother then wrote "smile" on the paper and slipped it under the door again.

2. Upon a signal to commence, a group of 20 second-grade students, sitting in a full circle, each with pen and paper, began to write a sentence. After writing, each student would crunch the paper into a "snowball" and then throw it to another student across the circle. The snowball receivers would then unfold the paper, read the sentence, add another related sentence, and crunch the paper into "snowballs" again. The process would continue until short stories were created.
3. To enhance students' visual listening skills, a hearing African-American second-grade teacher in a predominantly hearing classroom had students chant nonverbally using their hands in synchronized motion. All students were required to follow each other's motions in speed and pace, even as the speed and pace would increase over time. A Deaf researcher shared similar practices, increasing the speed and pace of motion faster and faster until "we all fall out of sync."
4. A hearing Anglo-American English-speaking classroom teacher would encourage students to first create a silent play followed by classroom discussion. After the silent actors performed a skit, they would facilitate class discussions, giving the audience the opportunity to guess who the characters were and their relationships with each other, the story plot, and etc. Next, the silent actors would perform their part again with use of a signed or spoken language. The second-grade teacher or another student would then document the verbal dialogue for all to read.
5. A hearing African-American classroom teacher demonstrated a four-step scientific process using exaggerated actions without using speaking or signing. Then the teacher repeated the

process through an inquiry approach (i.e., What happened first? What did I do secondly?). Students then had the opportunity to discuss each process verbally in sequential order while the English-speaking second-grade teacher would write down each descriptive process on the whiteboard. Selections of scientific key terms were often negotiated. Finally, students were divided into groups and were ready to begin their experiment. They referred to directions written on the whiteboard as needed.

6. A hearing African-American teacher shared her struggle with learning hip-hop dance from various instructors until she met the one that fit with her learning preference. Instead of demonstrating each dance move while talking about it simultaneously, an instructor first demonstrated each move and then talked about the specific moves.
7. An advanced mathematic Deaf student struggled with learning specific mathematical concepts for the first time in a seventh-grade mainstreamed classroom. The challenge was watching the interpreter while the classroom teacher gave direct instruction and was solving each math problem on the board while talking quickly. Moving the interpreter closer to the teacher and the whiteboard did not help. Upon learning that the student learned best visually, the teacher modeled solving a problem without talking, giving the student opportunity to directly see and visualize on the board solutions to mathematical problems without having to glance or gaze at the interpreter. Once this was done, the teacher would then talk about the problem and solution, and the interpreter would sign. This was successful for the student. As a result, the classroom teacher altered her pedagogy by problem solving visually first before talking about each solution.
8. With a classroom of 20 students, students would be split in fives and four rows would be created while sitting down. The first person in each row would then step up to review the chart that the teacher drew or wrote. Usually this chart would begin with a simple symbol. While four students stepped up to the teacher, everyone else behind would move a seat forward. At this point,

those seated in the front row each had an erasable marker and a small whiteboard, and waited for the messenger behind him/her. The four students that reviewed the chart would then move back in line, seating themselves behind the fourth-row students and begin, with their fingers, to trace the symbol they saw on the chart on the backs of these students. These students would then attempt to duplicate and trace the same symbol on the backs of the students seated in front of them. The process was repeated, and the front-row students then drew the symbol onto paper.

9. As a former fourth/fifth-grade classroom teacher in a bilingual classroom, I would act out the story of a Native American legend by visualizing story concepts with and through the children. While watching their nonverbal cues to check for comprehension, I would elaborate by continuing to act out specific story concepts. The story would be retold daily with an increased use of sign language and student participation. I retold the story, codeswitching between giving students minimal eye contact while narrating to inform the students to freeze their actions and, with direct eye contact, bring students into the story so that they can act with their imagination. By the third day of retelling the same story, I become less of a narrator while more students would be acting. Their use of imagination fine-tuning the sensory and descriptive imagery continued to increase as they role-played interactively among themselves. On the fourth and fifth days, the same story would be retold demonstrating connections with story concepts written on the board. We then went onward to drawing and writing about the same legend. This writing activity was done spontaneously and interactively using pen and paper to draw and ask questions about the story (i.e., story texting). Eventually, we would move onward to reading the legends before each student become engaged in videotaped storytelling and story writing activities. If the plan was to "publish" and/or demonstrate their stories and writings, we would also then go through storytelling and writing editing processes.

INTERPRETATIONS AND LIMITATIONS OF CULTURALLY RELEVANT VISUAL DISCOURSE PEDAGOGY

The observational notes of visual discourse pedagogy tie in well with other research findings where students prefer to write (Jarrell & Freiermuth, 2005; Schein, 2000; Schirmer & Ingram, 2003; Yuan, 2003), which allow them to reconsider and/or reflect before they text via a written language. Twenty of the 22 research participants stated that they really enjoyed the interactive writing thematic activity.

The second major finding was that the quiet students of color in class became even more expressive and were engaged in visual discourse activities, whereas the same students were less expressive when the spoken form dominated (Jarrell & Freiermuth, 2005). This finding of "passive" speaking students of color becoming "assertive" text–talking students also occurred when I gave a "Culturally Relevant Visual Discourse Pedagogy" presentation in a teacher education graduate seminar at Claremont Graduate University.

Future studies could also learn more about the benefits of being text–talkers for those who love to talk verbally. For instance, a second-grade student who was a class talker stated that she found herself having to stop and think before text–talking. She felt that the process of thinking before one talks does not usually apply when she talks in spoken form. Another interesting observation that needed further investigation was that a student of Filipino descent who was the least talkative when participating via spoken English class discussions yet was the most expressive of all when participating via printed English discourse.

The classroom teachers reported that not only the Deaf student's but all hearing students' use of written language flourished greatly that year. Evidently the motivating factor there (Jarrell & Freiermuth, 2005; Schein, 2000; Schirmer & Ingram, 2003; Yuan, 2003) is in communicating academic concepts directly via a printed language. It is recommended that several longitudinal studies or cross-grade level studies be carried out to examine the relationship between texting and students' language attitude as writers and in language acquisition development. This includes comparison of students' state test language scores.

Yuan (2003) reported that on-line chatting provided the participants a unique opportunity to put their grammatical knowledge to practice through meaningful communication.

The critical dialogue with the second-grade classroom teachers revealed that we all had a similar language attitude and ideology. Each of us valued critical dialogue where students could call learning their own, and all students were given opportunities to communicate directly with each other, as well as to choose what they would like to construct and/or reconstruct. Furthermore, we incorporated music, dance, art, and theatre as part of students' learning processes. Evidently, and due to our backgrounds, we value visual and spatial activities, which supports Ladson-Billings' (1995) case for culturally relevant pedagogy and Ogbu's (2003) theory of culturally responsive pedagogy to benefit diverse students' learning processes.

CONCLUSION

If the best way to acquire a language is to use it, what opportunities do ASL and non-ASL students have with engaging in printed English discourse in classrooms? Instead of facing a gap between developing speaking and writing standards, classroom students could traverse the bridge between these two standards and spend more time as real-time text–talkers as they construct and reconstruct new knowledge. With the goal of enhancing students' articulation skills, the focus here is on using text as a motivational social discourse tool.

Studies have taught us that underrepresented students of color become much more expressive via text-written language. They became active participants exchanging information through the simple use of pen and paper much more than they would have if they communicated verbally. The hearing privileged often demonstrate and share the need to communicate verbally while engaged in typed or written discourses. Thus, both types of learners, the underrepresented and the hearing privileged, will benefit from engaging in balanced discourse between communicating verbally and via text:

> We speculate that young people's tweeting practices may open up opportunities for their development of standard language proficiencies in several ways: (1) improving students' motivation and engagement with course content; (2) increasing student–student or student–instructor interactions, which create more opportunities for feedback and mentoring; and (3) offering lower barriers to publishing and a more "relaxed" writing style, which can encourage self-expression, creativity, playfulness, and risk-taking (Greenhow & Gleason, 2012, p. 472).

Research studies that include the "art" of texting and engaging in interactive text discourses are emerging. However, deaf school-age students today are scattered widely and sporadically across the nation with minimal communication access to sign language. Also minimal for these students are access to real-time texting and socio-academic dialogue.

As Lawrence Siegel, attorney, (2006) asserts, "there is not a hearing child in this nation who must think, even for a second, that each day and year she goes to school, she must secure anew her right and need to communicate." Deaf "students are confronted with the essence that these issues are unavoidable and learn how they can be a part of the solution or a part of the larger system that continues to oppress without power and privilege" (Eckert & Rowley, 2013, p. 123).

With the use of text to communicate synchronously, opportunities for valuable direct communication in a visual learning space that brought together deaf and hearing learners, including ethnically and linguistically diverse students (Feinberg & Soltis, 2004), in developing their academic language proficiency and critical thinking skills (Vygotsky, 1962) increased. Learning via a printed language across cultures is one way to "enable students to view concepts, issues, themes and problems from several ethnic perspectives and points of view" (Banks, 2008, p. 141), embracing chaos and changes (Fullan, 1999).

RECOMMENDATIONS

Given that texting at school is the beginning of civic engagement and transformative education embracing social justice pedagogy, this new practice of socioeconomic literacy needs further research. The following are a few research questions to consider:

- What are the cognitive benefits of engaging in well-balanced academic discourse utilizing these multimodal communication acts: (1) verbal, (2) verbal–text, and (3) text?
- While the multimodal discourse model is designed to be implemented within monolingual or multilingual classrooms for students of all ages, in what ways could English-only students, ASL and English-speaking students, and Spanish and English-speaking students, for instance, benefit from the use of multimodal academic discourse space?
- What is the relationship among storytelling, story texting, and story writing?

> "If there is no struggle, there is no progress. Those who profess to favor freedom, and yet depreciate agitation, want crops without plowing the ground. They want rain without thunder and lightning. They want the ocean without the awful roar of its many waters."
>
> –Fredrick Douglass.

ACKNOWLEDGMENTS

I sincerely appreciate Dr. Kathee Christensen, Dr. Alberto M. Ochoa and Frank B. Amann's ongoing support with their eagle-eye editing work.

REFERENCES

Banks, J. (2008). *An introduction to multicultural education.* Boston, MA: Allyn and Bacon.

Boal, A. (1985). *Theatre of the oppressed.* New York: Theatre Communications Group.

Bourdieu, P. (1973). Cultural reproduction and social reproduction. In R. Brown (Ed.), *Knowledge education and cultural change* (pp. 71–112). London: Tavistock.

Bowels, S., & Gintis, H. (1976). *Schooling in capitalist America: Educational reform and contradictions of economic life.* New York: Basic Books.

Coleman, J.S. (1988). Social capital in the creation of human capital. *American Journal of Sociology, 94* supplement, S95-S120.

Coleman, J.S. (1990). Social capital. In *Foundations of social theory* (pp. 300–321). Cambridge, MA: Belknap Press of Harvard University Press.

Darder, A. (1991). *Culture and power in the classroom: A critical foundation for bicultural education.* Connecticut: Bergin & Garvey.

Darder, A. (2002). Reinventing *Paulo Freire: A pedagogy of love.* Oxford: Westview Press.

Darder, A., Baltodano, M., & Torres, R.D. (2003). *The critical pedagogyreader.* New York: Routledge Falmer.

Dika, S.L., & Singh, K. (2002). Applications of social capital in educational literature: A critical synthesis. *Review of Educational Research, 72*(1), 31–60.

Eckert, R.C., & Rowley, A.J. (2013). Audism: A theory and practice of audiocentric privilege. *Humanity & Society, 37*(2), 101–130.

Feinberg, W., & Soltis, J. (2004). *School and society.* New York: Teachers College Press.

Freire, P. (2002). *Pedagogy of oppressed* (30th anniversary ed.). New York: The Continuum International Publishing Group Inc.

Freire, P. (2003a). *Teachers as cultural workers: Letters to those who dare teach.* Oxford: Westview Press.

Freire, P. (2003b). *Pedagogy of hope.* New York: The Continuum International Publishing Group Inc.

Fullan, M. (1999). *Change forces: The sequel.* Philadelphia, PA: Falmer Press.

Greenhow, C., & Gleason, B. (2012). Twitteracy: Tweeting as a new literacy practice. *The Educational Form, 76,* 463–477.

Grinter, R., & Eldridge, M. (2001). 'y do tngrs luv 2 text msg?' In W. Prinz, M. Jarke, Y.

Jarrell, D., & Freiermuth, M.R. (2005). The motivational power of internet chat. *Regional Language Centre Journal, 36*(1), 59–72.

Krashen, S., & Terrell, T. (1996). *The natural approach: Language acquisition in the classroom.* Bloodaxe Books Ltd.

Ladson-Billings, G. (1995). But that's just good teaching! The case for culturally relevant pedagogy. *Theory Into Practice, 34*(3), 159–165.

Lane, H. (1999). *The mask of benevolence: Disabling the Deaf community.* San Diego, CA: DawnSignPress.

Livingston, S. (1997). *Rethinking the education of deaf students: Theory and practice from a teacher's perspective.* Portsmouth, NH: Heinemann.

Lyman, L., Foyle, H.C., & Azwell, T.S. (1993). *Cooperative learning in the elementary classroom: Developments in classroom instruction.* Washington, DC: National Education Association.

Nover, S.N., Christensen, K.M., & Cheng L.L. (1998). Development of ASL and English competence for learners who are deaf. *Topics in Language Disorders,* August.

Ochoa, A. (2003). *Ochoa Paradigm: Models of cultural pluralism.* Working paper, San Diego State University, CA.

Ogbu, J.U. (2003). *Black American students in an affluent suburb: A study of academic disengagement.* Mahwah, NJ: Lawrence Erlbaum Associates.

Petitto, L.A., & Dunbar, K. (2004). New findings from educational neuroscience on bilingual brains, scientific brains, and the educated mind. *Building Usable Knowledge in Mind, Brain, & Education.* Cambridge University Press.

Phelan, P., Davidson, A., & Yu, H. (1998). *Adolescents worlds: Negotiating family, peers, and school.* New York: Teachers College Press.

Putnam, R.D. (1993). The prosperous community: Social capital and public life. *The American Prospect, 13,* 35–42.

Rogers, K. Schmidt, & V. Wulf (Eds.), *Proceedings of the Seventh European Conference on Computer-Supported Cooperative Work ECSCW '01* (pp. 219–238). Bonn, Germany/Dordrecht, Netherlands: Kluwer Academic Publishers.

Schein, J.D. (2000). Reading, writing and rehabilitation. *American Rehabilitation, 25*(4), 32–35.

Schirmer, B., & Ingram, A. (2003). Using online chat to foster the written language development of students who are deaf. *Reading Online*; July, pp. 2–21.

Schwartz, J. (2004). Text messaging pushed for use as disaster warning systems. *The New York Times,* Dec. 31, pA12 col 03 (19 col in).

Siegel, L. (2006). The argument for a constitutional right to communication and language. *Sign Language Studies, 6*(3), 255–272.

Spring, J. (2001). *Deculturalization and the struggle for equality: A brief history of the education of dominated cultures in the United States* (3rd ed.). New York: McGraw Hill.

Stanton-Salazar, R.D. (2001). *Manufacturing hope and despair: The school and kin support networks of U.S.-Mexican youth.* New York: Teachers College Press.

Steele, C. (2003). Stereotype threat and African American student achievement. In T. Perry, C. Steele, & A. Hilliard (Eds.), *Young, gifted, and Black: Promoting high achievement among African-American students.* Beacon Press.

Tatum, B.D. (1997). *Why are all the Black kids sitting together in the cafeteria?* New York: Basic Books.
U.S. Department of Education (2013). For Each and Every Child—A Strategy for Education Equity and Excellence, Washington, DC.
Vygotsky, L. (1962). *Thought and language.* Cambridge, MA: MIT Press.
Wesely, P.M. (2013). Investigating the community of practice of world language educators on Twitter. *Journal of Teacher Education, 64*(4), 305–318.
Yuan, Y. (2003). *The use of chat rooms in an ESL setting.* National University of Singapore, Singapore.

Chapter 14

"I Absorbed the Teacher's Mind, Mannerisms and Storytelling Skills and Transformed Them Inside Myself to Retell the Story Perfectly Using ASL.": A Case Study of Juan

LEONARD S. GRANDA, Ed.D.
Assistant Professor, Bloomsburg University

PATRICIA STOUDT, Ed.D.
Educational Consultant, HIS Homeschool Center

INTRODUCTION

The number of English Language Learners (ELLs) is increasing in American schools. There is a demand for schools to provide more English as a Second Language (ESL) services. These statements are true for general education classrooms, but are also true in deaf education. This chapter explores the interaction between a Deaf teacher and a deaf immigrant youth, given the pseudonym Juan, during paired-reading ELL sessions where both teacher and student engaged in the reading of continuous texts using picture storybooks based on culturally relevant themes. Granda (2014) explored the use of three tools to support the learning of English reading. The first tool was the use of picture books written in English but based on Mexican or Latino culture. The second was the use of the repeated reading technique with modeling and scaffolding. Finally, the third tool was the use of select American Sign Language (ASL)–English bilingual strategies.

DEFINITION OF READING

Reading comprehension is the act of getting meaning from print (Goodman, 1973). Having a strong language base is fundamental to learning to read. The process of learning to read is a social-cognitive activity. According to the still influential report, *Becoming a Nation of Readers* (Anderson, Hiebert, Scott, & Wilkinson, 1985), skilled reading is constructive, fluent, strategic, motivated, and a lifelong pursuit.

Deaf immigrant youths from non-English-speaking families may experience difficulty in learning to read because they do not have a strong language foundation in their native language (i.e., Spanish), in a sign language, or in English. These youths are often subjected to tedious instruction based on word study rather than engaging in reading continuous texts, simply because their English vocabulary is limited. In addition, teachers may not be familiar with the deaf youths' language and culture and how they may bring their languages and culture (e.g., Latino) to the reading experience.

ROLE OF THE DEAF TEACHER IN THE READING CLASSROOM

The important role of the Deaf teacher in the classroom has been well documented (Andrews & Franklin, 1997; Shantie & Hoffmeister, 2000; Simms, Rusher, Andrews, & Coryell, 2008; Vernon, 1970). Furthermore, in intervention studies teaching signing deaf children how to read, the Deaf teacher has played a pivotal role in teaching reading, particularly with participating in reading and translating stories into sign language (Bailes, 1998; Cannon & Guardino, 2012; Gallimore, 2000; Herbold, 2008; Kuntze, 2004; Whitesell, 1992). Using qualitative research, including classroom ethnographies and case studies, these researchers documented how Deaf teachers of reading use ASL–English bilingual strategies such as translation and codeswitching between ASL and English print. The unique aspect of Granda's (2014) study was that the researcher was a Deaf teacher providing the intervention for improving reading comprehension with one deaf immigrant youth. One of the advantages of a single subject study is that Granda (2014) had the opportunity to observe Juan closely over time. He was able to focus on what he learned from observing Juan, modify his approach, and test a number of strategies to see what worked best.

DEMOGRAPHICS

The majority of deaf immigrant youths in the United States are from Latin America. The Gallaudet Research Institute (GRI, 2011) reported in 2009–2010 demographics data that 30.4% of the Deaf population surveyed in the United States identify themselves at Hispanic or Latino. Furthermore, data from GRI (2011) revealed that 22.8% of the total population identify themselves as ELL.

THE LITERACY CHALLENGE

Literacy learning is conceptualized as social and cognitive skills that take into account the learner's languages and culture (Purcell-Gates, 2007). Literacy learning also incorporates Vygotsky's (1978) sociocultural language and learning theory. This theory has been applied in teaching literacy. The teacher must determine the student's *zone of proximal development* (ZPD), which is the area where the student cannot quite accomplish a task independently and must depend on a teacher or mentor's support to complete the task. The teacher or mentor provides support while the student is trying to complete the task, such as reading a passage. The teacher must observe and intervene continually until the child is able to accomplish the task on his or her own (Vygotsky, 1978).

Reading comprehension is a complex skill that combines and interrelates perceptual, cognitive, social, linguistic, cultural processes, and neurobiological processes all at once for the reader (Vacca et al., 2012). Readers use bottom-up processes (letter, to word, to phrase, to sentence) but also use mental or cognitive and top-down processes where they tap into their memories of prior experiences or background knowledge about the topic in the text. Moreover, the reader must understand the semantics or word and phrase meanings, including multiple meanings of words. The reader must understand the syntax or grammar of the language. Most hearing children have mastered these aspects of the English language naturally by 4 years of age, whereas deaf children may experience delays depending on their home and school language exposure and comprehensibility (Andrews, Leigh, & Weiner, 2004).

Because the learning of English is relatively new for immigrant deaf youths and their access to English is limited due to their hearing loss, these youths are in need of repetition embedded in instruction with a knowledgeable person who can communicate with them fluently and who scaffolds the interaction. Thus, scaffold literacy instruction can be used concurrently with another strategy—repeated readings. Repeated readings is a practice in which the students read and reread a text or passage before they achieve fluency, accuracy, and reading comprehension (Samuels, 1979). The teacher or mentor intervenes and models the reading of the text for the struggling reader. A teacher can take observation notes or take a running record to identify areas that are proving to be obstacles for the struggling student (Clay, 2000).

Having deaf immigrant youths read culturally relevant picture books may be a promising approach to help improve their reading (Barrera & Quiroa, 2003). This could tap into their background knowledge and prior experiences. An additional approach is to provide modeling of the reading process. A mentor could present the books while sitting beside the student and modeling the reading of the storybook (Samuels, 1979). Neither of these practices has been explored with immigrant deaf youths. In Granda's (2014) case study, the researcher explored reading intervention strategies that could be beneficial to one deaf immigrant youth from Mexico who had only basic communication skills in Mexican Sign Language or Lengua de Señas Mexicana (LSM), gestures, ASL, Spanish, and English.

MULTILINGUALISM AND BILINGUALISM

A deaf immigrant youth must use all of these processes at the same time if he is to be a successful reader. Understanding a deaf immigrant youth's multicultural and multilingual background is important in understanding how he learns to read (Purcell-Gates, 2007). The organization Teachers of English to Speakers of Other Languages International Association (TESOL, 2012) considers all Deaf learners to be ELL because of the linguistic differences between ASL and English. However, a growing number of deaf immigrants arrive in the United States with an impoverished native language base. Granted, some deaf immigrants are fortunate to receive some form of education in their native countries, a form of language learning readiness (TESOL, 2012). This readiness provides the first language foundation for the student in preparation to learn another language.

BILINGUAL EDUCATION

The goals of bilingual education are twofold: (a) to develop academic English literacy and (b) to maintain and develop one's first heritage language (Krashen, 2002). Cummins (1979) theorized that bilingual learners must learn a social or conversational language as well as an academic or written language. Cummins (1979) called the social language Basic Interpersonal Communication Skills. He called the academic language Cognitive Academic Language Proficiency. Cummins (1979) noted that developing academic or written language takes from 7 to 9 years after social language is learned. Teachers of Deaf students (TODs) often question how deaf children can learn English if they are taught in their L1, ASL. Quality ASL–English bilingual instruction aims to do just that (Nover & Andrews, 1998). As Krashen (2002) noted, the teachers provide quality instruction in the child's L1, then teach the English language that has been made comprehensible by using the L1 foundation.

Cummins (1979) stated that learning subsequent languages is easier if the L1 is solidly formed in the learner's mind. With a strong L1 foundation, the learner can readily transfer his L1 skills to his second language (L2) skills. The important point is that a strong L1 must be established first. Unfortunately, many deaf youths, particularly deaf immigrant youths, are at risk for not developing a strong L1, which may impede their development of an L2. Most deaf youths in the United States are learning two languages simultaneously—ASL and the mainstream culture's English. Immigrant deaf youths who are bringing some language influence from their home country must learn both ASL and English on top of their heritage language and often the sign language of their home country. Yet spoken and sign language are frequently inaccessible to immigrant deaf students, particularly those coming from developing countries lacking services to the deaf.

Although these students coming into the United States have access to a visual language such as ASL, it often occurs when the student is at an age near or past the critical language learning window (Emmorey, 2002). Therefore, the deaf child is at a disadvantage for developing a strong L1 foundation (Humphries & Allen, 2008). Lacking a strong L1 impedes the full development of an L2, not to mention an L3 and L4, as is the case with many deaf immigrant youths.

Two studies of deaf students enrolled in bilingual programs showed that early exposure to ASL resulted in higher reading comprehension scores (Geeslin, 2007; Myers, 2011). Furthermore, visual strategies, such as pictures, signs, fingerscanning, and fingerspelling, have been found to be useful with deaf children cross-culturally and cross-linguistically (Jones, 2013). Granda's (2014) study involved a Deaf teacher utilizing all of these visual strategies to teach reading to one deaf immigrant youth.

ASL–ENGLISH BILINGUAL STRATEGIES AND DEAF STUDENTS

Nover, Christensen, and Cheng (1998) were the first to suggest a language model that addresses the teaching of ASL and English to deaf learners. They devised a language planning model specifically for deaf students using a three-pronged approach with literacy, oracy, and signacy. *Literacy* referred to the deaf student's act of reading and writing, as well as the use of fingerspelling, and typing. *Oracy* referred to the deaf student's use of lipreading, speaking, and listening skills. Finally, *signacy* referred to the deaf student's use of signing, as well as attending to or watching signs. Work by Nover and Andrews (1998, 1999, 2000, 2002) expanded this model in the Star Schools project. Nover and Andrews worked with more than 50 teachers at schools for the deaf in the United States and developed a curriculum for preservice and in-service teachers to use in the teaching of two languages for deaf students.

Some of the bilingual strategies developed by Nover and Andrews (1998, 1999, 2000, 2002) are the following: preview-view-review (PVR), chunking, and the use of chaining. Granda (2014) included these along with several other strategies in his study, as follows: PVR, codeswitching, mediating/dialogic inquiry, ASL expansion, chunking or bridging, shared reading, repeated readings, and the use of finger-spelling with chaining and sandwiching.

Preview-view-review involves alternating languages for previewing, viewing, and reviewing lessons. For example, a topic is introduced (pre-viewed) in the student's L1, then considered in-depth (viewed) in the student's L2, and finally reviewed in the student's L1. The sequence can also occur in the opposite order, i.e., L2 for preview, L1 for view, L2 for review (Li, 2006).

Codeswitching, another strategy, is a change by the speaker from one language or dialect to another. Codeswitching can vary according to the nature of the audience, the subject matter, and the situation in which the conversation is taking place. Codeswitching can take place in a conversation when one speaker uses one language and the other speaker answers in another language. Codeswitching can occur at the one- or two-word level, at the sentence level, at the paragraph level, or even at a broader level (Andrews & Rusher, 2010; Nover et al., 1998).

With the strategy of mediating/dialogic inquiry, the teacher engages the student in dialogue and meaningful question-and-answer exchanges related to the reading material (Evans, 2004; Mayer, Akamatsu, & Stewart, 2002). This interaction allows the teacher to connect the material more effectively with the student's background and experiences.

ASL expansion is still another strategy using specific linguistic and visual techniques that support explanation for a clear comprehension of English text. Humphrey and Alcorn (1995) identified seven expansion types for ASL used to convey information effectively: (a) creating contrast with negation, (b) adding sign synonyms, (c) reiterating, (d) role shifting and selecting signs to maximize three-dimensional space, (e) explanation by examples, (f) couching/nesting information, and (g) describing then doing.

Creating contrast with negation is used when the signer is juxtaposing two ideas that form the negative and positive of the same statement (Lawrence, 1994; Livingston, Singer, & Abramson, 1994). For example, MY CAR NOT WORKING. BROKEN IT. However, adding sign synonyms, also known as *faceting*, is used when the signer is expressing or stressing certain concepts by the use of several synonyms to express an idea or piece of information (Lawrence, 1994; Livingston et al., 1994). For example, *I cleaned the house. It is spic-n-span, squeaky clean, shiny, CLEAN*!

Reiterating, another ASL expansion type, is used when the signer occasionally repeats the sign within the same utterance for clarity or emphasis (Lawrence, 1994; Livingston et al., 1994). For example, I CAN'T GO PARTY. CAN'T I! Moreover, role shifting and selecting signs to maximize three-dimensional space are two techniques by which the signer "enters the scene" of an event being conveyed, taking advantage of the 360 degree space surrounding the signer. This results in a more image-based pictorial and dynamic means of using visual communication. Using body agreement (head, trunk movement; eye indexing and other visual grammatical features), locatives, and directional verbs, the signer literally sets up people and objects within the signing area according to real space and location. The signer typically steps into the role of the individuals involved in the communication exchange being discussed—a technique known as role shifting or character assumption (Lawrence, 1994; Livingston et al., 1994).

Still another ASL expansion type, explanation by example, is used by a signer providing a list of examples after the introduction of a term that clarifies the use of that term (Lawrence, 1994; Livingston et al.,

1994). For example, THIS YEAR I WANT PLANT VEGETABLES: CORN, CARROTS, BROCCOLI, SPINACH, SO-FORTH. The next expansion technique, couching/nesting, is used by the signer with an introductory expansion making the key point or comment understandable (Lawrence, 1994; Livingston et al., 1994). For example, CEMETERY. YOU KNOW? PEOPLE DIE, GO WHERE? BURY IN-GROUND, HAVE HEADSTONE. THAT CALLED-BY-NAME CEMETERY. Describe then do, another expansion technique, is when the signer states what he will do or say from a narrator position, then via role shift, does or says what was described from the perspective of the person or thing doing the action (Lawrence, 1994; Livingston et al., 1994). For example, I CLEANED HOUSE – *role-shift, becoming the person mopping, dusting, vacuuming, etc.*

Chunking and chaining are other strategies employed in bilingual instruction. Chunking is a visual strategy that involves identification of the grouping of words or groups of words that represent one unit of meaning, or in this case one equivalent sign in ASL, as well as a discussion of the appropriate translation (Rusher, Schimmel, & Edwards, 2012). For example, the words *let it go* would be used as one sign LET-GO. Chaining, however, is a bilingual technique for supporting vocabulary acquisition by adding fingerspelling. A sequence in no particular order of equivalent-meaning concepts using sign, fingerspelling, writing, pictures, and gestures is used to introduce or emphasize that specific concept or term (Padden & Ramsey, 1998). For example, the teacher would point to the word *art* then immediately give the sign ART.

Sandwiching is another bilingual technique similar to chaining, yet differing in that a purposeful and specific sequence is essential. This sequence of equivalent-meaning concepts using sign, fingerspelling, writing, pictures, and gestures is used to introduce or emphasize a specific concept or term. With this sequence the first and third expressions are the same and an equivalent is *sandwiched* between them. Examples of sandwiching included sign, word, sign or sign, fingerspelling, and sign (Haptonstall-Nykaza & Schick, 2007; Humphries & MacDougall, 1999). See Table 1 for a definition for each of these ASL–English bilingual strategies.

Table 1. Evidence-Based ASL–English Bilingual Teaching Strategies and Methods

Strategies and methods	Definition	Source
Chaining	Chaining is a bilingual technique used to support vocabulary acquisition. A sequence of equivalent meaning using sign, fingerspelling, writing, pictures, and gestures is used to introduce or emphasize a specific concept or term. With chaining there is no specific order or sequence.	Haptonstall-Nykaza & Schick (2007), Humphries & MacDougall (1999), Padden & Ramsey (1998)
Sandwiching	Sandwiching is similar to using chaining; however, in this case a purposeful and specific sequence of equivalent meaning using sign, fingerspelling, writing, pictures, and gestures is used to introduce or emphasize a specific concept or term. With this sequence the first and third expression are the same and an equivalent is "sandwiched" between them. For example sign, word, sign or sign, fingerspelling, sign, etc.	Haptonstall-Nykaza & Schick (2007), Humphries & MacDougall (1999), Padden & Ramsey (1998)
Chunking/ bridging	This strategy involves the identification of words or groups of words that represent one unit of meaning or one sign in ASL and following a discussion of appropriate translation.	Atwell (2013), Rusher, Schimmel, & Edwards (2012)

(continued)

Table 1. Evidence-Based ASL–English Bilingual Teaching Strategies and Methods *(continued)*

Strategies and methods	Definition	Source
Preview-view-review (PVR)	PVR involves the alternating of languages for previewing, viewing, and reviewing lessons.	Li (2006)
Codeswitching	A change by the speaker from one language to another. Codeswitching can take place in a conversation when one speaker uses one language and the other speaker answers in another language.	Andrews & Rusher (2010), Nover et al. (1998)
Mediating/dialogic inquiry	The teacher engages students in interactions that were meaningful and encouraged knowledge building. This can involve the student's first language and cultural understanding.	Evans (2004), Mayer et al. (2002)
ASL expansion	The seven expansion types that ASL uses to convey information effectively: creating contrast with negation; adding sign synonyms (faceting); reiterating; role shifting and selecting signs to maximize three-dimensional space; explanation by examples; couching/nesting; and describe then do.	Humphrey & Alcorn (1995), Lawrence (1994), Livingston et al. (1994)
Repeated readings	Reading technique in which the student rereads a short and meaningful passage until a criterion level of fluency is achieved.	Rasinski & Padak (2008), Samuels (1979), Schirmer, Therrien, Schaffer, & Schirmer (2009)

OVERVIEW OF THE STUDY

As stated earlier in this chapter, the purpose of Granda's (2014) study was to explore the interaction between a Deaf teacher and a deaf immigrant youth during paired reading sessions where both teacher and student engaged in the reading of continuous texts using picture storybooks based on culturally relevant themes. Granda (2014) investigated two research questions. The first research question asked how visual strategies such as culturally relevant picture books, ASL–English bilingual strategies, and repeated readings of storybooks increase word recognition skills of a deaf immigrant youth reader. The second question addressed the frequency and type of ASL–English bilingual strategies for improving comprehension used by the Deaf teacher during guided and repeated readings sessions. The ASL–English bilingual strategies used are as follow: (a) chaining, (b) sandwiching, (c) chunking/bridging, (d) PVR, (e) codeswitching, (f) mediating/dialogic inquiry, (g) ASL expansion, and (h) repeated readings. A question not asked directly, but observed as an outcome of the study, is whether a deaf student, well past the "critical age" for language acquisition, can increase his reading ability significantly using the strategies suggested.

The Deaf teacher met with the deaf immigrant youth for 18 sessions over 6 weeks. During these sessions, they worked through three culturally relevant picture storybooks, each increasing in reading difficulty from the previous book. The sessions were videotaped and later transcribed. The teacher recorded errors or miscues on running records forms to monitor progress. Before discussing the results, it is important to become more familiar with the participants.

PARTICIPANTS

The deaf immigrant youth. The subject of this case study was a profoundly deaf youth, referred to as Juan, who had immigrated to the United States from Mexico at age 7. In the United States, Juan had to learn both ASL and English. Juan brought with him a limited foundation in a L1, Mexican Sign Language or LSM, combined with limited speech in Spanish and home signs and gestures he learned as a young child.

Juan was born two and a half months prematurely, which is the suspected cause of his deafness. He was not actually identified until age 2 as having a profound bilateral sensorineural hearing loss when he failed to acquire spoken Spanish. Juan's first word was in Spanish around the age of one and a half years. Members of the family household spoke Spanish and used gestures and home signs along with expecting Juan to lipread.

At the age of 2, Juan began attending an early intervention preschool program at a special school in Mexico. Juan then attended another special school for kindergarten and first grade. This Mexican school focused on using LSM and spoken Spanish as a bilingual approach for learning to read and write Spanish.

Although Juan completed first grade in the Mexican school system, on arriving in the United States he repeated first grade in a mainstreamed program for deaf and hard-of-hearing (Deaf/HH) students that mainly used sign language such as Pidgin Signed English (PSE) and some ASL. Juan's educational records indicated average intelligence, yet significant language and academic delays.

At the time of the study, Juan was 20 years old and had been using ASL for 13 years. He had 3 years of direct ASL instruction in high school with a Deaf, native ASL teacher for most of those ASL classes. These classes allowed Juan to establish a more solid language base upon which he could build the rest of his education. At the time of the study, Juan was in a mainstreamed program for academic classes as well as a technical training program with the use of an ASL interpreter and support from a TOD.

Juan reported that his communication preference was using ASL to communicate with his Deaf friends and with the staff at school. At home, he used ASL along with home signs or gestures with his family, due to the family's limited ASL skills. Juan noted that he felt that both ASL and English are valuable, with English having a slight priority over ASL. Juan explained that English skills are needed to function in the general society, especially with people who are not fluent in ASL. Thus, Juan was highly motivated to participate in this study.

The Deaf reading teacher. The important role of the Deaf adult as a reading teacher has been documented (Bailes, 1998; Gallimore, 2000; Shantie & Hoffmeister, 2000). The Deaf reading teacher in Granda's (2014) study played an important role as a reading model for the deaf ELL student. Juan was able to observe the Deaf teacher as he modeled the process of reading a continuous text. Here are Juan's words (translated from ASL to English) about this modeling of the reading process: "I absorbed the teacher's mind, mannerisms, and storytelling skills and transformed them inside myself to retell the story perfectly using ASL."

Juan's comment was the goal of the study—to have him act as a reader of authentic text and be able to translate the text, but also to think about the text and retell segments of the text to show that he was comprehending it fully. For the teacher, this raised the question of whether Juan was simply remembering the teacher's signed translation or depending too much on the pictures. In reality, Juan's comprehension of the printed English was a combination of all factors. Following the models proposed by Goodman (1973) and Vacca et al. (2012) about how reading comprehension is a process that entails cognitive, linguistic, social, and discourse processes, Juan's reliance on ASL and picture support combined to support his learning of reading print. In other words, Juan utilized his knowledge of ASL, as well as information from pictures with the support of his teacher, an expert signer and reader, to strengthen his reading of English print. The repeated readings strategy allowed him to practice his reading skills as vocabulary reoccurred across storybooks. The visual prompts of the pictures also supported his background knowledge and concept development.

MATERIALS

Granda (2014) utilized three picture books, each increasing in reading difficulty level from the previous book and each written in English yet relevant to Latino or Mayan culture. These books connected with Juan's background and prior experiences, such as corn, baking bread, the Day of the Dead festival, and hummingbirds. Based on

Juan's reading comprehension level, Granda determined that these three books were challenging enough without overwhelming the participant's limited abilities in reading. The first book, *Corn Is Maize: The Gift of the Indians* (Brandenberg, 1976), nonfiction, was about the history, scientific background, and significance of corn in Mayan culture.

The other two cultural stories were fictional Mayan folk tales. The first of the two folktales, *The Sleeping Bread* (Czernecki & Rhodes, 1992), was based in Guatemala and involved a baker who, when faced with the dilemma of not having his bread rise, befriended a beggar who helped solve the mystery. The other Mayan folktale, *The Hummingbird's Gift* (Czernecki & Rhodes, 1994), was about a story of a Mexican wheat farmer and his family who endured a drought and helped the hummingbirds stay alive in the drought. In return the hummingbirds helped the family devise a plan to salvage their dried crops by weaving straw figures to sell at the annual Day of the Dead festival.

These three picture books had food, holidays, and cultural connections that were familiar to Juan based on his prior experiences and cultural background. All three books had pictures that could assist as a visualization tool in helping Juan read the passages. All books encouraged Juan to think, make predictions, and see outcomes of problem situations.

DATA COLLECTION

Granda (2014) conducted reading intervention sessions approximately 1 hour long, three times a week for 6 weeks. All sessions were videotaped and were utilized to record and measure Juan's reading miscues while he was exposed to repeated readings of storybooks (Clay, 2000). A miscue was recorded in the running records when Juan omitted a word in his read aloud, signed the word incorrectly, or used a sign that might be decoded correctly but represented the wrong concept. In this study the term *read aloud* refers to signing the story to the other participant. The videotapes also were later transcribed into ASL gloss, an informal way to represent ASL concepts in writing indicated by the use of all capital letters (Valli, Lucas, Mulroney, & Villanueva, 2011) and then transcribed into English to help in data analysis. Granda made adjustments for linguistic differences between English and ASL. For example, miscue scores were calculated based on total word count within a given story. As English contains articles, *a*, *an*, and *the*, whereas ASL does not, Granda eliminated articles from the total word count to accommodate that linguistic difference.

DESCRIPTION OF INTERVENTION

After reviewing the literature, Granda (2014) developed a plan of intervention based on studies for students who are learning English as a second or third language (ELLs) and based on reading pedagogy in reading comprehension (Vacca et al., 2012). Because Juan was deaf, ELL, and showed evidence of language delays, Granda chose to use visual materials and visual language learning strategies. These included the use of culturally relevant picture books, guided reading lessons (Gallimore, 2000), read alouds (Schleper, 1997), visual tactile strategies such as finger scanning (Gallimore, 2000), and finger pointing (Jones, 2013), as well as ASL–English bilingual strategies during the reading lessons (Bailes, 2004; Gallimore, 2000; Simms, Andrews, & Smith, 2005).

Intervention occurred through dialogic reading sessions when Granda translated each storybook into ASL. Then he and Juan engaged in a dialogic, or back and forth, reading of each sentence. When Juan did not understand a word, Granda intervened using eye gaze, turn taking, and visual strategies for engaging with the deaf youth as they discussed the text.

Procedures for the First Book

For the first book, *Corn Is Maize* (Brandenberg, 1976), Granda started with modeling how to hold and read a book. He showed Juan the book and gave him time to look at the pictures or diagrams. Granda proceeded to fingerscan the English sentences or phrases, and immediately thereafter, he signed the equivalent meaning using ASL. Various ASL–English bilingual strategies were utilized for words that Juan could not read.

Next Granda used guided reading, where Juan read each English sentence or passage and then retold it using ASL. When Juan stumbled on a word or encountered phrases he did not understand, Granda provided support through ASL–English bilingual strategies or used visual support strategies. This continued for the second, third, and fourth sessions until fluency increased and mistakes were reduced. For the fifth and final session focusing on this book, Juan read independently, without intervention strategies, and Granda recorded Juan's miscues in the running record.

Interestingly, Granda (2014) discovered a unique aspect of conducting research such as this with all deaf participants. Granda noted that the nature of this study involving deaf individuals presented visual constraints preventing the researcher from looking at Juan and at the running records at the same time. Both participants relied on visual communication rather than auditory communication. Traditional use of running records requires a teacher to glance down to record data while listening to the student continuing through his task. He realized the challenge of keeping running records without either missing visual information as Juan signed or interrupting him continuously to pause while data were recorded. Consequently, Granda made a decision for subsequent sessions to use video recordings and fill out the running records later, allowing his focus to be on Juan and the interventions during the sessions.

Procedures for the Second Book

For the next book, *The Sleeping Bread* (Czernecki & Rhodes, 1992), Granda altered the sequence of steps taken with the first book. The first session with the second book, which was actually Session 6 in the study, started with guided reading rather than with the researcher modeling the story in ASL. As Juan read, he received immediate support with ASL–English bilingual or visual support strategies when he stumbled on words or phrases he did not understand. After the guided reading, Granda modeled reading the story out loud using ASL. This reversed sequence was done to provide data of the participant's comprehension and miscues without having any prior guided or modeled reading from the researcher. After modeling the second story in ASL, Granda then encouraged Juan to read a phrase or paragraph silently first before retelling it to help him utilize contextual clues and to see if miscues would be reduced using this method.

Procedures for the Third Book

The procedures for the third book, *The Hummingbird's Gift* (Czernecki & Rhodes, 1994), were similar to the procedures for the second book. However, during the last session with this book, Juan first read aloud the story to the researcher. Granda then asked Juan to summarize the story using Juan's own words in ASL. Granda attempted to see if Juan had enough comprehension to express the story in his own words.

A DESCRIPTION OF READING BEHAVIORS

Research Question One

How do visual strategies such as culturally relevant picture books, ASL–English bilingual strategies, and repeated readings of storybooks increase word recognition skills of a deaf immigrant youth reader?

Increasing reading comprehension skills is the inverse of decreasing miscues when reading. Intervention led to decreases in miscues because the researcher provided instant feedback when Juan did not understand the words during the repeated reading sessions. Instead of reporting minute details from each of the 18 sessions, a summary of the observations, strategies, adaptations, and even some researcher notes and conclusions are presented here. Session numbers refer to their order in 18 total sessions. To show an increase in word recognition, running record data from the first session with each storybook were compared with the final session running record results for that storybook. The researcher determined that a criterion of at least an 80% accuracy would be used for Juan to move on to the next storybook.

Storybook one: *Corn Is Maize.* In the first reading session of five, Juan omitted many English words or concepts when retelling the story using ASL, which differs in structure from English. For example, the very first English passage of the book is *This is a kernel of corn. It is a corn seed. Kernels of corn are planted in a small hill of good earth.* For that passage, Juan signed, CORN CL: 5 (as a corn plant) CHOOSE CL: G (pluck a corn seed, puts in ground) IN. NOW CORN CL: open B (covers and pats with a small amount of soil) COVER WILL GROW. In this ASL reading passage, Juan did not specify *kernel*, *seed*, or *good earth*. Instead, Juan opted to create a more visual description using the power of the visual–gestural aspects of ASL to express his understanding of the passage.

When encountering the first few pages, Juan simply looked at the pictures and scanned the passage quickly. Juan signed his retelling using more ASL structure and grammar similar to the first sentence. However, when Granda started to fingerscan the English passage for Juan on page three, Juan immediately switched signing modes and signed using more English structure and grammar. It was noted that after the third page, most of Juan's retellings seemed to adhere to English structure rather than ASL structure. In his retelling Juan used some ASL along with some Manual Coded English (MCE) signs such as *the* or *it*, even though the teacher had modeled the ASL structure previously. This session revealed the tension of working between two languages and the conflict of adhering to structure or to grasping the meaning. Juan and the teacher often utilized the pictures in the book to connect to the English passage with fingerscanning, which also helped clarify meaning using one of the ASL–English bilingual strategies.

Granda also noticed that whenever Juan stumbled upon a word he did not understand, he would do one of the following things: (a) stop signing, point to the word, and then look at the teacher with a puzzled look; (b) stop signing, look at the teacher with a puzzled look, and then point to the word in need of attention; (c) sign something that he was not sure of, repeat the sign, and look at the teacher with a puzzled look; (d) fingerspell a word with a puzzled look, point to the word, and look at the teacher; or (e) fingerspell a partial word and look at the teacher with a puzzled look. It was interesting to note that all inquiries were done via nonmanual markers with a puzzled look rather than with actual signs asking for assistance. Juan never signed WHAT THAT MEAN? or WHAT WORD MEAN?

After Juan indicated uncertainty about a specific word or phrase, Granda often provided a sign; a sign and fingerspelling; fingerscan the word then sign; or fingerscan, fingerspell, then sign. Most of the time ASL expansion techniques followed after giving the sign or Granda followed up with a dialogic or mediating inquiry to make sure that Juan understood the meaning of the sign/word. In addition to intervening after those nonmanual inquiry signals, Granda often intervened if Juan omitted or signed important concepts or words incorrectly. In those cases, Granda asked Juan to repeat a missed word or concept, asked Juan what that word meant directly, and pointed to the word in the book.

Granda also intervened when Juan gave a sign that matched the signed word the way the word was spelled, but did not match the meaning of the sentence or passage. Two examples of this mismatch of print and concept are (a) *at last* and (b) *ground.* Juan signed the first example as LAST, meaning the opposite of being first. Granda then gave Juan the appropriate sign PAH meaning *finally!* For the second example, Juan signed *ground* incorrectly as LAND, when it should have been signed as GRIND in the following passage: *The rest they ground into meal on a flat stone called metate.* Granda explained after correcting Juan that some words have multiple meanings, such as *ground.* Sometimes that can be confusing, and readers need to rely on the whole sentence for context and for correct meaning.

In addition to intervention at the single word level, Granda took the opportunity to point out examples of chunking and bridging, when phrases in one language could be represented by single words in the other language, or vice versa. For example, Juan gave a single sign SUN (signed directionally from the sky down to the people) for the passage *The sun shines down on them.*

Session two: Corn Is Maize. In the second session, while Juan was reading and retelling using ASL, Granda continued to support Juan with ASL–English bilingual strategies whenever Juan did not understand a word or passage. Because Juan continued to have difficulty describing the various parts of the corn plant with specific terminology such as *tassels*, *silk*, *fertilization*, and *kernels*, Granda made the decision to use a computer to locate those terms and bring up real pictures of a corn plant demonstrating specific terminology for parts of a corn plant. Granda followed up by discussing and showing the signs for each part using ASL. This strategy seemed to help Juan identify the specific parts of the corn plant. Juan was able to better describe the fertilization process after seeing photographs and diagrams on the Internet.

Granda also showed other concepts that Juan had difficulty understanding, such as showing how corn is ground into corn meal. Immediately, Juan was able to connect and share his prior experience of grinding corn with a large round device that had a handle to stir around and grind the corn into meal. Other prior experiences with which Juan connected after seeing pictures and brief explanations were an old red mill such as the one near his home, his mother making tomales, and the idea of a kernel of corn functioning as a seed. This session exemplified the importance of connecting reading materials with real situations and past experiences.

***Session five:** Corn Is Maize.* At the end of session five, which was the last session with the book *Corn Is Maize*, Juan's miscues were reduced greatly. His fluency and reading speed were noticeably quicker than at the first session retelling of the story. The teacher did not provide any ASL–English bilingual intervention during this session, but simply recorded Juan's miscues.

Granda noticed that even though Juan had reduced the miscues in the fifth session, it seemed like Juan was favoring following English grammar and structure rather than ASL grammar or structure except for descriptions that required using the visual–spatial aspects of ASL. The following English passage provides a good example: *Not long ago they found some. It was in a cave in Mexico where people once lived. They found scraps of plants and tiny ears of ancient corn, more than 5,000 years old. It was not like any the scientist had ever seen.* Juan signed the following in ASL: NOT LONG AGO FOUND SOME IT fs-WAS HIDDEN IN MEXICO WHERE PEOPLE ONCE LIVE THEY FOUND INSIDE LITTLE PLANTS SMALL EARS LONG-TIME-AGO MORE THAN 5 THOUSANDS YEARS AGO IT fs-WAS NOT LIKE SCIENTIST NOT SEEN SINCE.

Comparing Juan's final ASL rendering in the fifth session to how the researcher signed during the guided reading retelling in the first session can be insightful. The researcher initially signed the following: RECENTLY NOT LONG-AGO RECENTLY SCIENTIST FOUND SOME OLD CORN CL: F (kernels) fs-KERNELS WHERE? MEXICO IN fs-CAVE CL:1 (deep down in ground) FOUND CL:C (jar) CL:C (opening lid of jar) NEVER SEEN BEFORE. FIRST TIME. ASL most commonly follows a topic-comment structure in which the main idea or concept is signed and then additional details are given after that (Valli et al., 2011). For example, Granda's description of finding corn kernels in the caves of Mexico focused on the topic of kernels and added details such as location as a comment expanding the topic. Juan, however, followed the English structure using ASL signs by explaining the location first and then describing the finding of the corn in the caves. This is a specific skill that most fluent bilinguals possess by having the ability to change the content and idea from one language's grammatical structure to another (Cummins, 1979; Valli et al., 2011).

Consequently, Granda made a decision for the next two storybooks to encourage Juan to first read the whole passage or paragraph on a page without retelling and then to go back to the first sentence on the page to start retelling in ASL. Granda wanted to see if Juan would improve his use of ASL grammar and structure with summarizing rather than transliterating using English structure and grammar. Juan continued to make a few sign concept mistakes. For example, Juan signed the word *saved* as STORED like *saved money* instead of *rescued* in the following English sentence example: *When the Pilgrims landed in America, maize saved their lives.* Again Granda speculated that having Juan read the whole passage for context clues might help reduce these types of miscues in the next two storybooks.

Storybook two: *The Sleeping Bread.* The next storybook, *The Sleeping Bread*, had eight sessions (Czernecki & Rhodes, 1992). For the first session with this book (the sixth session), Granda wanted to see how much Juan knew first before modeling the story in ASL for introducing *The Sleeping Bread* so Granda fingerscanned the story while Juan signed the passage in ASL. According to Gallimore (2000), fingerscanning is a technique that signals to the deaf reader that a translation is about to occur. Similar to the first book, whenever Juan got stuck on signing a word, Granda provided ASL–English bilingual support. He again noticed that Juan confused similar-looking familiar words throughout the second book, indicating that he did not have mastery. For example, Juan signed the English word *baker* as BAKE, so Granda intervened and, using ASL, explained that the English root word is *bake* and the suffix *–er* means a person, so combining together both words is signed as BAKE + PERSON. Juan also signed *greet* as GREEN and *huge* as HUG incorrectly, confusing words spelled with similar letters, yet vastly different in meaning. Another behavior that Granda observed was that Juan relied heavily on fingerspelling, especially for words with which he was not familiar.

Furthermore, the second book had many higher level words that Juan did not first recognize. Granda used ASL–English bilingual strategies to help explain the meaning of each word. For example, in the following English passage, *As the bread baked, its sweet aroma wafted through the little town, and every morning the villagers awoke to the wonderful smell of fresh bread*, for the word *wafted*, Granda used dialogical and mediating inquiry by asking Juan of his experience of smelling baked bread. Granda asked Juan what happens when the bread is baked inside a house. Juan replied that the smell tends to spread throughout the room and the house. Granda was able to connect Juan's experience to the word *wafted*.

Session eight: The Sleeping Bread. For this session, Granda modeled and signed the whole story by fingerscanning the passage for each page and then signing the story in ASL. Because the researcher was signing, no ASL–English bilingual strategy intervention was given; however, many of the ASL expansion skills and chaining/sandwiching techniques were incorporated into the ASL storytelling. With the book having several characters, the ASL expansion of role shifting and selecting signs to maximize three-dimensional space was the most heavily strategy used for this storybook.

Session 10: The Sleeping Bread. For the 10th session, Granda introduced a new procedure for Juan to first read the passage on one page and then try to sign in ASL while avoiding English order or structure. After

Juan signed the passage on one page, Granda modeled the same passage in ASL. Then Juan signed the passage again in ASL while expanding more ASL structure and grammar. Juan improved his ASL retelling of the story, utilizing the appropriate ASL structure and grammar. Later, for the first passage on page eight of *The Sleeping Bread*, Juan signed the English passage with a perfect ASL translation. Granda did not even have to model a better ASL retelling nor provide any intervention.

Session 13: The Sleeping Bread. During the final session of *The Sleeping Bread*, Granda instructed Juan to first read the whole passage on the page without signing and then go back up to the first sentence in the passage to begin retelling the passage in ASL. For the first page, Juan read it and then summarized what he had read without going back to the first sentence on the page. With his first attempt he omitted many key words and concepts. For the second page of the storybook, Granda reminded Juan again to first read the whole passage and then go back and read aloud the first sentence of the passage at the top of the page. After this, Juan reduced his miscues for each page.

Storybook three: *The Hummingbird's Gift.* In the final storybook, *The Hummingbird's Gift* (Czernecki & Rhodes, 1994), Granda asked Juan to retell the English passage using ASL, with Granda providing ASL–English bilingual intervention when needed. The first intervention was dialogical inquiry. When Juan read the title of the book, Granda asked questions regarding Juan's prior experience and background knowledge of hummingbirds. Initially Juan did not recognize or find meaning in the print word *hummingbird.* After Granda used the ASL expansion describe then do technique, Juan was able to confirm that he had seen a hummingbird. Juan asked how *hummingbird* was signed or fingerspelled. Granda explained that first it is fingerspelled *humming* with the sign BIRD added.

For the 14th session, visual support in *The Hummingbird's Gift* was used more than in *The Sleeping Bread*. Similarly to *The Sleeping Bread*, *The Hummingbird's Gift* also had several characters in the story, which meant that ASL expansion role shifting and maximizing three-dimensional space were often used in this storybook. Two other strategies used frequently were ASL expansion describe then do and ASL expansion couching/nesting.

Session 17: The Hummingbird's Gift. For this session, Granda instructed Juan to follow the usual procedures of reading a passage and then retelling it in ASL. However, the researcher added one new request that Juan should first read the entire story before summarizing it in ASL. The purpose of this was not only to encourage Juan to utilize the pictures and context supports, but to see if Juan could comprehend the story enough to retell it using his own words or, in this case, his own signs. This time Juan had more time to attend to the text to read for context cues within the whole passage before summarizing it in ASL.

Session 18: The Hummingbird's Gift. In the final session of *The Hummingbird's Gift*, Granda asked Juan to retell segments of the story in his own words using ASL. Granda continued to give ASL–English bilingual support as needed. Juan's accuracy rate was much better than the accuracy rate from the second storybook *The Sleeping Bread*. In this session, Juan used more ASL structure and grammar than English structure and grammar.

Granda noted that Juan often decoded words correctly in the story, but still used signs representing the incorrect concept. For example, in the English sentence *Tassels grow like a hat at the top of the stalk*, Juan signed the word LIKE as showing fondness rather than the correct sign concept SIMILAR or SAME.

Research Question Two

What are the frequency and type of ASL–English bilingual strategies used by the Deaf teacher during guided and repeated readings sessions to improve comprehension?

Various types of ASL–English bilingual strategies were used by the Deaf teacher during the reading sessions to improve comprehension. In addition to the repeated readings strategy, codeswitching was used throughout all sessions. Codeswitching is the bilingual approach of having a speaker (or reader or writer) from one language or language dialect change his language use to another language (Andrews & Rusher, 2010; Nover et al., 1998). In this case, Juan was looking at the English print, reading in English, and then translating and expressing it using ASL.

Another bilingual strategy, the PVR approach, was utilized. PVR involves the alternating of languages for previewing, viewing, and reviewing lessons (Li, 2006). For example, Granda introduced the topic and gave directions in ASL (L1) as a preview, then English (L2) was used during the reading, and finally the discussion and reviewing of what was viewed occurred in ASL. Both Juan and Granda used the PVR approach.

The most frequently used ASL–English bilingual strategy was the chaining–sandwiching strategy (see Figure 1). The next most frequently used ASL–English bilingual strategy was ASL expansion role shifting and selecting signs to maximize three-dimensional space. The third most-used ASL–English bilingual strategy was ASL expansion reiterating. The least used ASL–English bilingual strategy was ASL expansion creating contrast with negation—with only 31 occurrences throughout the study.

Granda selected examples from the actual ASL gloss transcript for each of the ASL–English bilingual strategies presented in Figure 1. These examples are presented as follows corresponding in order with Figure 1, but separating the first category—chaining and sandwiching—for clarity:

Chaining. Juan pointed to print word *wander.* The researcher's response is shown in ASL gloss: MEANS WALK CL:1 (wandering around).

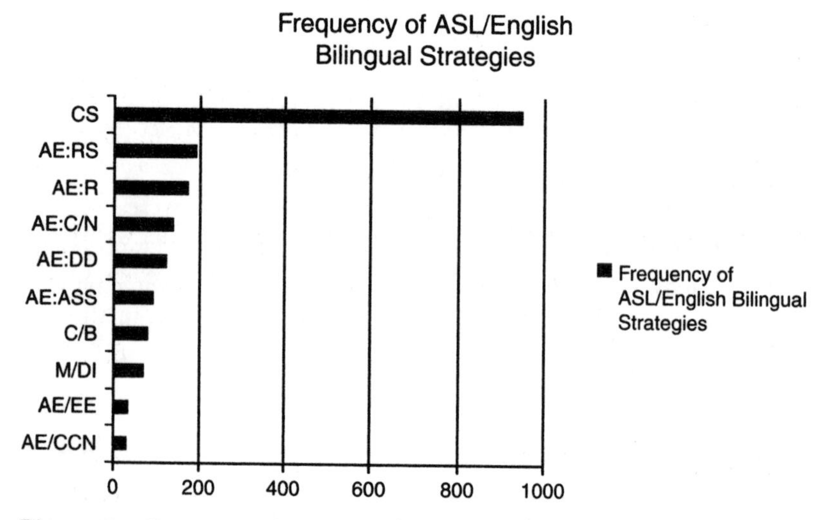

Figure 1. Frequency of ASL–English bilingual strategies.

Sandwiching. Juan pointed to print word *fellow* and then fingerspelled (fs) FELLOW with a puzzled look. The researcher's response in ASL gloss was fs-FELLOW MEANS PERSON OTHER WORD FOR PERSON fs-FELLOW.

ASL expansion: Role shifting and selecting signs to maximize three-dimensional space. CORN fs-HUSK GROW INSIDE WRAPPED HUNDREDS fs-KERNELS KNOW CL:C (ear of corn) CL:S (husks corn) ONE CL:G (picks a kernel out of a corn ear) SMALL IX-that one SMALL CORN YELLOW fs-KERNELS.

In another example involving role shifting with the researcher: fs-ZAFIRO (as Zafiro) KNOCK-ON DOOR LIGHTLY fs-TIMIDLY KNOCK DOOR, DOOR-OPEN, fs-BENTO (as Bento) WELCOME! COME-IN....

ASL expansion: Reiterating. The following is an example of how the researcher reiterated the concept of absence for emphasis. Researcher: LOOK-UP NONE CLOUDS NONE.

ASL expansion: Couching/nesting. YOU KNOW fs-BLUR? MEANS CL:5 (blurry) YOU KNOW DRIVE YOU-KNOW DRIVE FAST CL:4 (indicating trees passing by side window blurry) THAT-ONE

ASL expansion: Describe then do. Researcher: FS-HUMMING BIRD YOU KNOW BIRD SMALL CL:C (small body), CL: G (small beak) SEE BEFORE? FLAPPING-WINGS CL:1 (flying as a hummingbird in zigzag pattern) FAST FLAP-WINGS, FLOWER CL:5 (as a flower blossom) CL:1 (as hummingbird hovers and sips nectar in flower) BIRD YOU KNOW?

ASL expansion: Adding sign synonyms. Researcher: fs-BRITTLE MEANS EASY BREAK KNOW CL:flat C (like breaking hard flat bread or cracker)...SUPPOSE GREEN (points to a picture of catcti) CL: flat C (cactus bends) HARD BREAK BUT DRY BROWN CL:flat C (breaks easily).

Chunking and bridging. For the printed phrase ...*have shown us*..., the researcher signed SHOW-ME. This is an example of taking the chunk of words *have shown us* and bridging them to one concept sign in ASL.

Mediating and dialogical inquiry. The interaction was based on the following English text: *On the first Thanksgiving, the Pilgrims and the Indians together gave thanks for the corn harvest, as the Indians had done long before.* The following dialogue ensued. Researcher: THANKSGIVING, YOU KNOW? THANKSGIVING, fs-NOV? Juan: (nods head). fs-NOV (nods head). Researcher: fs-NOV (nods head). Juan: 26... SOMETHING...THANKSGIVING. Researcher: YES, TEND. PILGRIMS GIVE THANKS-TO INDIANS IX-they (Indians) TEACH-TO (Pilgrims) GROW CORN...THAT WHY THANKSGIVING, INDIANS, PILGRIMS CL:C (group of Pilgrims) THANKS-TO-INDIANS, THANKS (upward to God) GOD MAKE CORN. Juan: (nods head) THANKSGIVING.

ASL expansion: Explanation by example. ...CORN BEAT OTHER PLANTS SAME-AS (points to word "beans") BEANS fs-BEANS YOU KNOW GREEN BEANS, fs-SQUASH YOU KNOW SAME-AS YELLOW fs-OR GREEN CL:C (shape of long yellow squash or zucchini) CUT fs-OR PUMPKIN CL:C (pumpkin shape) ORANGE CL:C (pumpkin)

ASL expansion: Creating contrast with negation. Researcher: fs-SCRUFFY MEAN CL:4/C (describing dirty long messy hair, messy beard) DIRTY NOT CLEAN NOT SHAVEN (points to word "fellow") PERSON

SUMMARY OF FINDINGS

Overall the ASL–English Bilingual strategies for reading intervention used by the teacher resulted in reduced miscues during Juan's retelling of the English passages. Visual pictures, along with culturally related readings, also assisted Juan in improving his understanding of the text. The following strategies were used in joint reading with Juan.

Sign-Based Strategies

Granda signed the whole storybook to Juan and then returned to the first page and signed again to Juan. He used ASL–English strategies as listed previously throughout the joint reading of the three storybooks. He encouraged Juan to not transliterate the passage into English or read word for word, but instead to read the passage silently, then using ASL, to summarize or retell segments of the story back to the researcher.

Picture-Based Strategies

Granda also used picture-based strategies with Juan. He pointed to the picture in the text and provided background knowledge support to Juan. When Juan had difficulty with a passage or page of print because of a concept, Granda found supporting pictures on the Internet such as the stages of growth of corn.

Effective and Ineffective Strategies

When Juan was asked to summarize or retell in his own signs, Granda was able to determine if Juan comprehended the text or not. This also enabled Granda to intervene and provide ASL expansions with vocabulary that Juan did not know. Juan benefited from the use of repeated readings. For example, when similar words came up such as *harvest*, he was able to recall the meaning of the word from a previous book.

Granda also noted that Juan used ineffective strategies. For example, Juan had difficulty with multiple-meaning words. He often made mistakes or miscues with words that had similar letters. He also fingerspelled words that he did not know. He transliterated a text (sign word for word) but then was not able to tell Granda what the meaning of text was.

DISCUSSION OF DATA

Granda (2014) found that repeated readings, along with other confirmed strategies, did help improve fluency. Running records data for each of the three storybooks from the first and last reading sessions for each book showed a reduction in the miscues for each book, indicating improved fluency. Juan showed improvement in recognition of vocabulary, as well.

In the beginning of the first few reading sessions, it was noted in the running records and videotaped observations that Juan tended to read aloud the English sentences word for word using ASL signs in English word order. Miscues were low compared to the middle and later reading sessions. This word-for-word decoding comes at the expense of comprehension of the text. Just because a student can sign individual words in English word order does not show that he truly understands the meaning of the passage. A better indicator of reading comprehension is when he is able to read the English print and then express the meaning in ASL structure, showing a true translation of meaning from one language to another.

Additionally, in the later sessions Juan showed great comprehension using ASL summary and using appropriate ASL translation, thus using less word-for-word translation of English sentences. Juan improved his use of ASL retelling of segments of the story using the appropriate ASL structure near the end of the last intervention sessions compared with the first sessions of the study. When Juan decoded English words to MCE, he did not fully comprehend the appropriate meaning. When Juan was able to summarize in ASL in his own words, then comprehension occurred while he was reading the English passage. The importance of having a qualified TOD who has fluency in both English and ASL and has training in second language acquisition cannot be stressed enough (Humphries & Allen, 2008). One suggestion Granda (2014) had is to pair a TOD teacher who has weaker ASL sign skills with a fluent ASL model, for example, a certified deaf interpreter, to help map ASL language with English print (Andrews & Franklin, 1997; Shantie & Hoffmeister, 2000).

Pairing ASL and English bilingual strategies with repeated readings helped improve comprehension as data suggested by having a fluent bilingual model with the knowledge, experience, and training to map and bridge the two languages effortlessly. Juan had a background using sign language in various forms: LSM, PSE, MCE, and ASL. During the early reading sessions Juan tried to sign each word that was read, including using MCE signs for articles. Many of the English signs that Juan used seemed to be correct for decoding the word; however, often the meaning was lost in transition. Throughout his scholastic career, Juan had many TODs but never a Deaf teacher nor a child of a Deaf adult who could provide an effective ASL linguistic model to provide a foundation for his first language, which in turn could have been transferred to a second language, in this case written English (Bialystok & Hakuta, 1999; Emmorey, 2002; Johnson & Newport, 1989; Snow & Hoefnagel-Höhle, 1978).

Granda (2014) observed that deaf readers tend to use more visual mapping rather than audiological or sound mapping to connect languages and comprehension. For example, Juan used mostly grapheme clues, visual clues, and top-down approach using ASL to decode the English print language. Hearing readers rely on audiological clues and sound mapping to connect to print.

SUGGESTIONS FOR READING WITH DEAF ELL READERS

1. The teacher should model reading of a whole storybook, making sure the student understands by questioning.
2. The teacher should fingerscan the text as he reads to signal to the deaf reader that a translation of a text is about to occur (Gallimore, 2000).
3. The teacher should frequently point to pictures and pair those pictures with signing, fingerspelling, and print (Jones, 2013).
4. The student should read a passage silently and then summarize or retell the passage.
5. When the student stumbles upon a vocabulary word or phrase that he does not understand, then the teacher should provide intervention with bilingual strategies.
6. The teacher should connect prior knowledge by asking the reader about his or her experiences or build background knowledge utilizing the Internet for visual resources.
7. The teacher should use the running records assessment for detailed analysis, watching for a decrease in errors.
8. The teacher and the student should reread the story multiple times.

SUMMARY

During one of the reading sessions, Juan read and signed a passage perfectly, requiring no intervention from the researcher. Granda informed Juan that his retelling was perfect. Immediately Juan remarked that he had personally absorbed the researcher's mind, mannerisms, and storytelling skills and transformed them inside himself to retell the story perfectly using ASL. This result was made possible by many aspects, including the Deaf teacher's knowledge, training, experience, instincts, fluent ASL skills, and cultural knowledge. More important, perhaps, is the strong bond, relationship, and respect that the teacher and student developed for each other. This should be the aim for all teachers who want to teach reading or any aspect of language arts effectively. Reading is, after all, a form of human communication.

TERMINOLOGY

American Sign Language. ASL is the language used by the American Deaf community. It has its own grammar, syntax, phonology, and structure and is a visual–gestural language expressed through the hands, face, and other movements (Stokoe, 1970).

ASL gloss. Currently there is no formal writing system for ASL; however, there have been methods of transcribing ASL into a written form that has been developed, a process called *glossing*. The written product is called *ASL gloss*, with most of the sign concepts written in all capital letters (Valli et al., 2011). For example, a sign for *cat* would be written in ASL gloss as CAT.

Bilingual. This term refers to "…those people who use two (or more) languages (or dialects) in their everyday lives…Despite the great diversity that exists among people, all share a common feature: they lead their lives with two (or more) languages" (Grosjean, 1998, p. 21).

Chaining. Chaining is a bilingual technique used to support vocabulary acquisition. A sequence of equivalent meanings using sign, fingerspelling, writing, pictures, or drama is used to introduce or emphasize a specific term or concept. No specific order is required for the chain (Padden & Ramsey, 1998).

Codeswitching. In a bilingual approach for deaf children, codeswitching is defined as a change by a speaker or writer from one language to another. "Codeswitching can take place in a conversation when one speaker uses one language and the other speaker answers in a different language" (Nover et al., 1998, p. 60). Code switching is also sometimes referred to as *translanguaging.*

deaf. This term, with a lowercase *d*, refers to "any person with a hearing loss that is serious enough to impede educational progress" (Stewart & Kluwin, 2001). This is a general term that encompasses all deaf people, regardless of their cultural identity.

Deaf. This term, with a capital *D*, refers to people who have some degree of hearing loss, use American Sign Language as their primary mode of communication, are members of the American Deaf community, and use this term as a cultural identity (Padden & Humphries, 1988). In contrast, deaf people who do not identify themselves with the Deaf culture use the word *deaf*, with a lowercase *d.*

English Language Learners. These individuals are learning English as a second language. Many ELLs already have a strong first language from their native culture and are building upon that to learn English.

Literacy. This term "involves the skills of reading and writing" (Nover et al., 1998, p. 66). Literacy is a primary goal of education.

Oracy. This term "involves the skills of speaking and listening" (Nover et al., 1998, p. 66). The emphasis is on communication in the spoken and audible mode, often not accessible to deaf individuals.

Read aloud. For this study *read aloud*, rather than referring to reading audibly, means reading to another person in sign language. This could involve a student reading and signing to a teacher or the teacher modeling appropriate ASL language in retelling a story passage to another person using a bilingual approach.

Repeated readings. Samuels (1979) defines repeated readings as having a student read a story multiple times until he or she attains a 90% accuracy of reading the words. Repeated reading is a strategy used in literacy training.

Sandwiching. Sandwiching is a bilingual technique used to support vocabulary acquisition. A sequence of equivalent meaning using sign, fingerspelling, writing, picture, or drama is used to introduce or emphasize a specific term or concept. With this sequence, the first and third expressions are the same and an equivalent is *sandwiched* between them (Haptonstall-Nykaza & Schick, 2007; Humphries & MacDougall, 1999). Examples: sign+fingerspelling+sign; fingerspelling+sign+fingerspelling; printed word+sign+printed word; sign+printed word+sign; fingerspelling+printed word+fingerspelling; printed word+fingerspelling+printed word.

Signancy. This term indicates "the skills of watching or attending and signing. In its narrow sense, signacy is used as a skill involving the ability to control the visual/signing medium of linguistic transmission in the form of signing and watching skills" (Nover et al., 1998, p. 66).

Zone of proximal development. According to Vygotsky (1978), the ZPD is the area where the student cannot quite accomplish a task independently and must depend on a teacher or mentor's support to complete the task. Identifying a student's ZPD can help teachers determine how to help that student learn and develop to the next level.

REFERENCES

Anderson, R.C., Hiebert, E., Scott, J., & Wilkinson, I. (1985). *Becoming a nation of readers.* Washington, DC: National Institute of Education.

Andrews, J., & Franklin, T.C. (1997, March). Why hire deaf teachers? *Texas Journal of Speech and Hearing (TEJAS), 22*(1), 12013.

Andrews, J.F., Leigh, I.W., & Weiner, M.T. (2004). *Deaf people: Evolving perspectives from psychology, education and sociology*. Boston: Allyn & Bacon.

Andrews, J.F., & Rusher, M. (2010). Codeswitching techniques: Evidence-based instructional practices for the ASL-English bilingual classroom. *American Annals of the Deaf, 155*(4), 407–424. PMid:21305977

Atwell, W.R. (2013). *Deaf readers and phrasal verbs: Instructional efficacy of chunking as a visual tool* (Doctoral dissertation). Retrieved from ProQuest. (UMI 3593363)

Bailes, C.N. (1998). *Primary-grade teachers' strategic use of ASL in teaching English literacy in a bilingual setting.* University of Maryland, College Park, MD: Unpublished doctoral dissertation.

Bailes, C.N. (2004). Bridging literacy: Integrating ASL and English into the language arts. In D. Power & G. Leigh (Eds.), *Educating deaf students* (pp. 127–138). Washington, DC: Gallaudet University Press.

Barrera, R.B., & Quiroa, R.E. (2003). The use of Spanish in Latino children's literature in English: What makes for cultural authenticity? In D. L. Fox & K. G. Short (Eds.), *Stories matter: The complexity of cultural authenticity in children's literature.* Urbana, IL: National Council of Teacher of English.

Bialystok, E., & Hakuta, K. (1999). Confounded age: Linguistic and cognitive factors in age differences for second language acquisition. In *Second language acquisition and the critical period hypothesis* (pp. 161–180). Mahwah, NJ: Lawrence Erlbaum Associates.

Brandenberg, A. (1976). *Corn is maize: The gift of the Indians.* New York: HarperCollins Children's Books.

Cannon, J.E., & Guardino, C. (2012). Literacy strategies for Deaf/hard-of-hearing English language learners: Where do we begin? *Deafness & Education International, 14*(2), 78–99. http://dx.doi.org/10.1179/1557069X12Y.0000000006

Clay, M.M. (2000). *Running records for classroom teachers.* Auckland: Heinimann.

Cummins, J. (1979). Linguistic interdependence and the educational development of bilingual children. *Review of Educational Research, 49*(2), 222–251. http://dx.doi.org/10.3102/00346543049002222

Czernecki, S., & Rhodes, T. (1992). *The sleeping bread.* New York: Hyperion Books for Children.

Czernecki, S., & Rhodes, T. (1994). *The hummingbird's gift.* New York: Hyperion Books for Children.

Emmorey, K. (2002). The critical period hypothesis and the effects of late language acquisition. In K. Emmorey (Ed.), *Language, cognition, and the brain* (pp. 205–226). Mahwah, NJ: Lawrence Erlbaum Associates.

Evans, C. (2004). Learning with inquiring minds. *The Science Teacher.* 71, 27–30.

Gallaudet Research Institute (GRI)(2011, April). *Regional and national summary report of data from the 2009–10 annual survey of Deaf and hard of hearing children and youth.* Washington, DC: GRI, Gallaudet University. Retrieved from http://research.gallaudet.edu/Demographics/2010_National_Summary.pdf

Gallimore, L.E. (2000). *Teachers' stories: Teaching American Sign Language and English literacy* (Doctoral dissertation). Retrieved from ProQuest. (UMI 9983855)

Geeslin, J.D. (2007). *Deaf bilingual education: A comparison of the academic performance of deaf children of deaf parents and deaf children of hearing parents*. Indiana University, Bloomington, IN: Unpublished doctoral dissertation.

Goodman, K.S. (1973). Psycholinguistic universals in the reading process. In F. Smith (Ed.), *Psycholinguistics and reading* (pp. 21–27). Austin, TX: Holt, Rinehart & Winston.

Granda, L.S. (2014). *Increasing English reading comprehension of a deaf English language learner (ELL) youth: A case study* (Doctoral dissertation). Retrieved from Proust. (UMI 3623016).

Grosjean, F. (1998). Transfer and language mode. *Bilingualism: Language and Cognition*, *1*(03), 175–176. http://dx.doi.org/10.1017/S1366728998000285

Haptonstall-Nykaza, T.S., & Schick, B. (2007). The transition from fingerspelling to English print: Facilitating English decoding. *Journal of Deaf Studies and Deaf Education*, *12*(2), 172–183. http://dx.doi.org/10.1093/deafed/enm003

Herbold, J. (2008). *Emergent literacy development: Case studies of four Deaf ASL-English bilinguals*. University of Arizona, Tuscon, AZ: Unpublished doctoral dissertation.

Humphrey, J.H., & Alcorn, B.J. (1995). *So you want to be an interpreter?: An introduction to sign language interpreting*. Renton, WA: H & H Publishing Company.

Humphries, T., & Allen, B.M. (2008). Reorganizing teacher preparation in deaf education. *Sign Language Studies*, *8*(2), 160–180. http://dx.doi.org/10.1353/sls.2008.0000

Humphries, T., & MacDougall, F. (1999). "Chaining" and other links: Making connections between American Sign Language and English in two types of school settings. *Visual Anthropology Review*, *15*(2), 84–94. http://dx.doi.org/10.1525/var.2000.15.2.84

Johnson, J.S., & Newport, E.L. (1989). Critical period effects in second language learning: The influence of maturational state on the acquisition of English as a second language. *Cognitive Psychology*, *21*, 60–99. http://dx.doi.org/10.1016/0010-0285(89)90003-0

Jones, G.A. (2013). *A cross-cultural and cross-linguistic analysis of deaf reading practices in China: Case studies using teacher interviews and classroom observations*. University of Illinois, Urbana-Champaign, IL: Unpublished doctoral dissertation.

Krashen, S. (2002). *Explorations in language acquisition and use: The Taipei lectures*. Taipei: Crane Publishing Company.

Kuntze, M. (2004). *Literacy acquisition and deaf children: A study of the interaction between ASL and English* (Doctoral dissertation). Retrieved from ProQuest. (UMI 3128664)

Lawrence, S. (1994). *Interpreter discourse: English to ASL expansion.* Presentation made at the 1994 Conference of Interpreter Trainers, Charlotte, NC.

Li, Y. (2006). *The effects of the bilingual strategy—preview-view-review—on the comprehension of science concepts by deaf ASL-English and hearing Mexican-American Spanish/English bilingual students.* Lamar University, Beaumont, TX: Unpublished doctoral dissertation.

Livingston, S., Singer, B., & Abramson, T. (1994). Effectiveness compared: ASL interpretation vs. transliteration. *Sign Language Studies, 82,* 1–54. http://dx.doi.org/10.1353/sls.1994.0008

Mayer, C., Akamatsu, C., & Stewart, D. (2002). A model for effective practice: Dialogic inquiry with students who are Deaf. *Exceptional Children, 68*(4), 485.

Myers, M.R. (2011). *The relationship between English reading comprehension scores and years enrolled at a residential school for the deaf.* Lamar University, Beaumont, TX: Unpublished doctoral dissertation.

Nover, S., & Andrews, J. (1998, 1999, 2000, 2001, 2002). *Critical pedagogy in Deaf education: Bilingual methodology and staff development.* Year 1, 2, 3, and 5 Reports. USDLC Star Schools Project, U.S. Department of Education, First Year report. New Mexico School for the Deaf, Santa Fe, NM (www.starschools.org/nmsd).

Nover, S.M., Christensen, K.M., & Cheng, L.R.L. (1998). Development of ASL and English competence for learners who are deaf. *Topics in Language Disorders, 18*(4), 61. http://dx.doi.org/10.1097/00011363-199808000-00007

Padden, C., & Humphries, T. (1988). *Deaf in America: Voices from a culture.* Cambridge, MA: Harvard University Press.

Padden, C., & Ramsey, C. (1998). Reading ability in signing deaf children. *Topics in Language Disorders, 18,* 30–46. http://dx.doi.org/10.1097/00011363-199808000-00005

Purcell-Gates, V. (2007). *Cultural practices of literacy: Case studies of language, literacy, social practice, and power.* Mahwah, NJ: Lawrence Erlbaum Associates.

Rasinski, T.V., & Padak, N. (2008). *From phonics to fluency: Effective teaching of decoding and reading fluency in the elementary school.* Boston, MA: Allyn & Bacon.

Rusher, M., Schimmel, C., & Edwards, S. (2012). Utilizing Fairview as a bilingual response to intervention (RTI): Comprehensive curriculum review with supporting data. *Theory and Practice in Language Studies, 2*(7), 1317–1329. http://dx.doi.org/10.4304/tpls.2.7.1317–1329

Samuels, S.J. (1979, January). The method of repeated readings. *The Reading Teacher, 32*(4), 403–408.

Schirmer, B.R., Therrien, W.J., Schaffer, L., & Schirmer, T.N. (2009). Repeated reading as an instructional intervention with deaf readers: Effect on fluency and reading achievement. *Reading Improvement, 46*(3), 168–177.

Schleper, D.R. (1997). *Reading to deaf children: Learning from deaf adults*. Washington, DC: Gallaudet University Press.

Shantie, C., & Hoffmeister, R.J. (2000). Why schools for Deaf children should hire Deaf teachers: A preschool issue. *Journal of Education*, *182*(3), 37–47.

Simms, L, Andrews, J., & Smith, A. (2005). A balanced approach to literacy instruction for deaf signing students. *Balanced Reading Instruction*, *12*, 39–54.

Simms, L., Rusher, M., Andrews, J.F., & Coryell, J. (2008, Fall). Apartheid in deaf education: Examining workforce diversity. *American Annals of the Deaf*, *153*(4), 384–95. PMid:19146075

Snow, C.E., & Hoefnagel-Höhle, M. (1978, December). The critical period for language acquisition: Evidence from second language learning. *Child Development*, *49*(4), 1114–1128. http://dx.doi.org/10.2307/1128751

Stewart, D.A., & Kluwin, T.N. (2001). *Teaching deaf and hard of hearing students: Content, strategies and curriculum*. Boston, MA: Allyn & Bacon.

Stokoe, W.C. (1970). Sign language diglossia. *Studies in Linguistics*, *21*, 27–41 Reprinted in W.C. Stokoe, Jr. (1972), *Semiotics and human sign languages* (pp. 154–167). The Hague, Netherlands: Mouton & Co. N.V.

TESOL (2012, December 7). *TESOL mission and values*. Retrieved from http://www.tesol.org/about-tesol/association-governance/mission-and-values

Vacca, J.A.L., Vacca, R.T., Gove, M.K., Burkey, L.C., Lenhart, L.C., & McKeon, C.A. (2012). *Reading and learning to read* (8th ed.). New York: Pearson.

Valli, C., Lucas, C., Mulrooney, K.J., & Villanueva, M. (2011). *Linguistics of American Sign Language: An introduction* (5th ed.). Washington, DC: Gallaudet University Press.

Vernon, M. (1970). The role of the Deaf teacher. *The Deaf American*, *22*, 17–20.

Vygotsky, L.S. (1978). Interaction between learning and development. In L.S. Vygotsky (Ed.), *Mind and society* (pp. 79–91). Cambridge, MA: Harvard University Press.

Whitesell, K.M. (1992). *Reading between the lines: How one deaf teacher demonstrates the reading process* (Doctoral dissertation). Retrieved from ProQuest (UMI 304016721).

CHAPTER 15

Reframing Social Justice for All Deaf Learners

DORALYNN FOLSÉ
MICHELE BERKE
California School for the Deaf

INTRODUCTION

The United States is experiencing a demographic shift in the population as it "becomes a richer and thicker mélange of races, ethnicities, and identities" (Fullwood, 2013). Recent data show that youth of color who are under the age of 18 comprise 47% of the population (Census Bureau, 2012). In addition to race/ethnicity, there are other ways that students and teachers are culturally diverse. The multitude of differences includes religion, gender, sexual orientation, disability, home language, socioeconomic status, hearing status, and other distinct influences. In order to create an optimal learning environment that equitably serves students from all kinds of backgrounds in our classrooms and in our communities, it is the responsibility of teachers and administrators to develop curricula and pedagogical practices based on social justice principles.

SOCIAL JUSTICE EDUCATION

The intention of social justice education is to "challenge, confront, and disrupt misconceptions, untruths, and stereotypes that lead to structural inequality and discrimination based on race, social class, gender, and other social and human differences" (Nieto & Bode, 2008, p. 11). Social justice includes a "vision of society that is equitable" (Adams, Bell, & Griffin, 2007, p. 1) and treats all people with fairness, respect, and dignity (Nieto & Bode, 2008). In addition to preparing students for the world academically, schools also prepare students to live in a pluralistic society successfully. The front line people who carry this out are the classroom teachers.

One of the first steps in becoming a social justice educator is to examine and clarify one's own cultural identity. It is the responsibility of teachers and administrators to recognize and acknowledge the differences between themselves and their students. Teachers have to recognize the diversity that exists in their classroom and acknowledge that every teacher brings to the classroom their "own way of believing, thinking, and acting that evolved from one's own culture and experience. All of these may vary greatly from that of the students in the classroom" (Gollnick & Chin, 2009, p. 376). Therefore, teachers that make a commitment to educate themselves will be in a better position to create a learning environment that promotes critical thinking. In doing so, they often consciously include topics that focus on inequality (Nieto & Bode, 2008). This includes acknowledging the privileges they have. By making a commitment to explore their privileges (i.e., hearing, white, male), teachers can begin the work that Peggy McIntosh (1988) calls unpacking. By doing this work with their students, the classroom becomes a safe and supportive environment for all. When a teacher incorporates social justice in the classroom, the students are better prepared to go out in the world, interact effectively with groups that are different from themselves, and become agents of social change.

However, teachers often need support to be able to incorporate social justice in the classroom. Likewise, many school systems may find it challenging to incorporate social justice approaches in their curriculum. California School for the Deaf is no different.

As evidence of its commitment to social justice education, the California School for the Deaf–Fremont (CSD) recently announced the seven new Expected Schoolwide Learning Results (ESLRs) that form the educational expectations for each student upon graduation. One of the ESLRs includes the following: Students will contribute to their community as advocates for rights and social justice.

CSD'S JOURNEY: STAFF DEVELOPMENT

> "Never doubt that a small group of thoughtful, committed citizens can change the world: Indeed it's the only thing that ever has."
>
> –Margaret Mead

Incorporating social justice education in schools is not something that can happen immediately. At CSD, the shift toward an inclusive and equitable education, which includes a social justice perspective, did not happen overnight. Over the years, many people contributed to this historical journey to become a school that works actively toward infusing social justice as an ongoing practice in the classroom as well as an institutional goal. This chapter describes CSD's journey at two levels: staff development and student development. To begin, we will trace the staff development with the establishment of the first multicultural committee, the emergence of bilingual–bicultural (Bi-Bi) education, the incorporation of Deafhood teachings, the development of cultural proficiency training, the implementation of an anti-bias teacher learning community, and the formation of the lesbian, gay, bisexual, and transgender (LGBT) curriculum committee. We then will present CSD's journey in empowering students through a social justice lens. The focus will be limited to early childhood education and middle school because this is where the authors of this chapter have worked primarily. We also include feedback from a survey that was sent to teachers who incorporate social justice in their current educational practice. The survey had eight questions and asked about how educator training has impacted their views and experiences related to teaching social justice (see Appendix A for survey questions).

CSD's Multicultural Committee

In the mid-1990s, CSD established the first multicultural committee, which included representatives from each department on campus. The committee was established to better support the culturally diverse student population that was in contrast to the predominantly white teaching staff. The explicit goal of this committee was to bring awareness on multicultural issues to the campus and to examine school practices with regards to people of color. One of the committee's projects was to support family weekend workshops. The Black Family weekend, Latino Family weekend, and Asian Family workshops brought together families with Deaf[1] students of color and provided them with an opportunity to learn about resources and network, and to support each other as they shared their experiences and challenges of raising a Deaf child.

The multicultural committee also assumed the role of coordinating several staff development days focusing on this topic. CSD reached out to Dr. Harry Edwards and Hugh Vasquez of the Todos Institute to provide consultation and training on creating respectful multicultural environments. During this process, there was a realization that, while it was valuable to provide teachers with multicultural training, students were also in need of education, direct intervention, validation, and support. CSD then provided age-appropriate half and full-day workshops for students in every department. The workshops, which were entitled "Respect Days," focused on analyzing personal and family identities, embracing differences, and becoming an ally. This was a catalyst for students to begin to explore the many social identity and cultural groups of which they were members. Eventually, the students established student-led affinity groups such as the Deaf African-American Leadership Council and later, the Gay Straight Alliance (GSA), Latin@ Deaf Club, and Asian/Pacific Deaf Club. The multicultural committee was eventually phased out as the school's priorities shifted toward the STAR schools project, focusing on bilingual–bicultural approaches to educating deaf children.

[1] For the purpose of this chapter, the use of the word Deaf includes those who identify as D/deaf and hard of hearing.

Bilingual–Bicultural Committee

Within the next few years, CSD organized a Bi-Bi committee with the task of establishing a model bilingual program. The basic tenet was to improve education for Deaf children by supporting equal respect for American Sign Language (ASL) and English in its written form as well as to recognize that the students and staff are members of both Deaf and hearing communities. Through this bilingual lens, the journey toward a deeper understanding of Deaf culture for both staff and students began at CSD. This led to the establishment of an ASL/ Deaf Studies teacher specialist whose responsibility was to provide curricular support to teachers and create awareness among the entire CSD community about issues related to Deaf studies.

Deafhood

In 2003–2004, CSD was introduced to the concept of Deafhood with the release of Paddy Ladd's groundbreaking book, *Understanding Deaf Culture: In Search of Deafhood* (2003). In line with social justice education, Deafhood is a way of framing the Deaf experience in order to "move beyond present Deaf cultural limitations resulting from the colonialism of Sign Language Peoples" (Deafhood Foundation, n.d.). Furthermore, Deafhood asserts that all Deaf people "embark on a journey towards deepening and refining their Deaf selves. Many are content to reside within the "boundaries" of existing Deaf cultures, yet some press on to stretch those boundaries" (Deafhood Foundation, n.d.). Workshops and classes were offered for CSD staff with the goal of moving beyond a Bi-Bi approach to education. Although a large percentage of CSD's staff was Deaf, there were few opportunities at that time to have structured conversations about the Deaf experience. The Deafhood discussions prompted a deeper level of analysis. As one survey respondent stated:

> Deafhood training allowed me to analyze Deaf people's collective history of struggle and resistance against the pathological view of Deaf people. I learned about the ideology of normalcy that has devastated many Deaf children's lives

> in the past and will continue to hurt many in the future. I learned about the value of embracing our journey toward having a healthy Deaf identity in midst of an oppressive and non-accepting society.

However, it appeared that the focus on diversity and the focus on Deafhood were viewed as separate, unrelated issues. A survey respondent who participated in the Deafhood class stated that the premise of Deafhood is that "we are all Deaf first and everything else is second" (survey respondent, June 2013), which implies that being Deaf supersedes any of the numerous identities to which one subscribes. While some Deaf people may feel that being Deaf should be one's primary identity, this attitude overlooks the multiple intersectional identities that exist within the Deaf community. As civil rights activist Audre Lorde states, "There is no thing as a single-issue struggle because we do not live single-issue lives" (2007, p. 138).

Cultural Proficiency Training

Around the same time that the Deafhood movement was introduced to CSD, the state Superintendent of Public Instruction Jack O'Connell made a bold commitment to address the educational needs of certain students by announcing the Closing the Achievement Gap Initiative. The California Department of Education defines the achievement gap as the "disparity between white students and other ethnic groups, between English learners and native English speakers, between socio-economically disadvantaged and non-disadvantaged, and between students with disabilities as compared to students without disabilities" (WestEd, n.d., B1).

This mandate of "Closing the Achievement Gap" dovetailed with CSD, which established a diversity teacher specialist position. One of the goals of this position was to address the educational needs and academic achievement of Deaf students of color at school. This had been documented in CSD's action plan as a critical need during the accreditation process for the Western Association of Schools and Colleges and the Conference of Educational Administrators for the Deaf. Along the lines of meeting the needs of Deaf students of color, the diversity committee was established. Similar to its multicultural committee predecessor, the committee continued to support staff development in promoting social justice education for the CSD community, both students and staff alike. However, one significant difference in the training was the incorporation of **cultural** diversity through the Deafhood lens. Topics discussed included Cultural Capitals, White and Hearing Privilege for Educators, Are Nice People Like Us Racially Biased? and Deafhood and People of Color. These topics were a critical preliminary step in self-exploration and created the potential for a broader and more inclusive understanding of social justice.

Because of time constraints and staff resistance, further staff development on these topics did not take place nor were there sufficient opportunities for ongoing dialogue and follow-up. In retrospect, structured opportunities should have been provided for motivated staff to continue the conversation on a regular basis. This follow-up is critical, as research has found that superficial discussion and episodic one-time events are not effective (Lindstrom & Speck, 2004). More specifically, such events make it difficult to retain the information and do not allow for ongoing deep reflection and personal transformation. What is needed is a long-term commitment from a group of people in order to open themselves up to a transformative process (Elmore, 2002; Sparks, 2002) so they can inform practice, sustain, and integrate strategies that make a difference for student achievement (Lindstrom & Speck, 2004). As such, a teacher learning community, which relies on a community-centered perspective to promote professional learning (Bransford, Brown, & Cocking, 2000), was needed. This kind of community encourages participants to engage in critical dialogue that leads them to building authentic relationships and supporting one another through the process of learning, growth, and transformation.

Because the episodic one-time staff development approach was not entirely effective, the diversity specialist recognized that if transformation was to happen on an institutional level, it had to start with individuals. To begin to address this situation, the diversity specialist conducted a 2-year monthly training session for the counseling department staff. Because of the nature of their field of study, the counseling staff was able to delve deeply into self-reflection and recognize the importance of understanding how to work with students from a variety of backgrounds and cultures.

The next step in creating an equitable and social justice education community at CSD was to conduct monthly culturally proficient coaching seminars with the teacher specialists who provide support and mentoring to classroom teachers. This 2-year monthly training grew into a teacher learning community facilitated by the student diversity teacher specialist. A critical facet of the training was that teacher specialists began the introspective process of examining their own backgrounds and family histories by following Glenn Singleton's *Courageous Conversations about Race—A Field Guide for Achieving Equity in Schools* racial/ethnic autobiography model. They began to explore their personal histories; examine their learned biases, inherent privileges, and cultural identities; and ponder how all of these impact their personal, professional, and social beliefs. The shift in the teacher specialists' perspective was immediate and profound. Several individuals commented that their lens had shifted significantly and that viewing the world through a culturally proficient lens not only increased their awareness of the privileges and injustices in the world around them, but also highlighted the fact that multiple perspectives have now added to their view of the world. As one's awareness is heightened and the transformative work has begun, one becomes more acutely aware of the need to seek support from allies or like-minded individuals.

Using Terry Cross' cultural proficiency model, which defines cultural proficiency as a "paradigm shift *from* viewing cultural difference as problematic *to* learning how to interact effectively with other cultures" (Lindsey, Robins, & Terrell, 2009, p. 4), teacher specialists began to analyze their role in the bigger context of the school system. This continuum provides a "context or frame of reference, by which you can describe organizations and individuals" (Lindsey et al., p. 79). Visualize a continuum where each point—cultural destructiveness, cultural incapacity, cultural blindness, cultural precompetence, cultural competence, and cultural proficiency—is depicted in Figure 1.

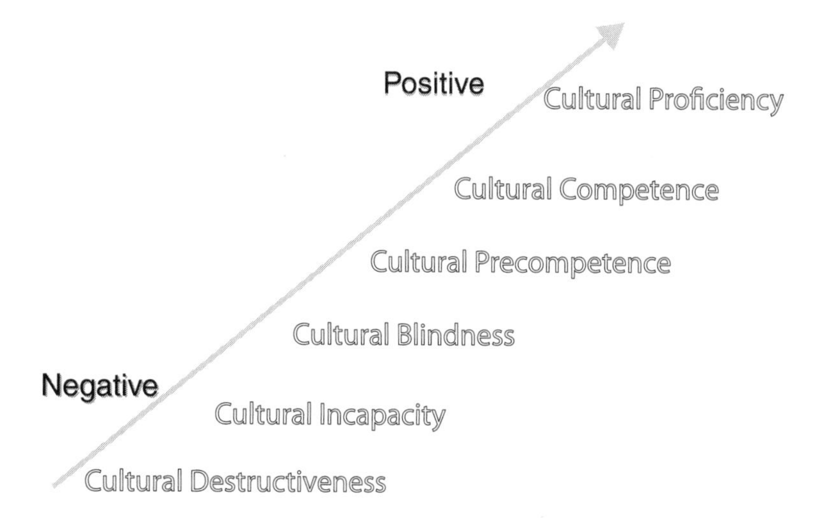

Figure 1. Positive and negative continuum.

A description for each point is given here:

- Cultural destructiveness is any policy, practice, or behavior that effectively eliminates all vestiges of other people's cultures.
- Cultural incapacity is any policy, practice, or behavior that presumes one culture is superior to others.
- Cultural blindness is any policy, practice, or behavior that ignores existing cultural differences or that considers such differences inconsequential.
- Cultural precompetence recognizes that their skills and practices are limited when interacting with other cultural groups.
- Cultural competence is any policy, practice, or behavior that uses the essential elements of cultural proficiency as the standard for the individual or the organization.
- Cultural proficiency is manifest in organizations and people who esteem culture, who know how to learn about individual and organizational cultures, and who interact effectively with a variety of cultural groups (Robins, Lindsey, Lindsey, & Terrell, 2006, p. 80).

Teacher specialists practiced using the continuum as a tool to identify where a policy or instructional practice fit within the continuum. This elicited discussions of how to move along the continuum toward culturally proficient and transformative practices. One of the issues the teacher specialists explored is the concept of the color-blind[2] teacher, where they may be "proud of not seeing color, just seeing human beings" (Robins et al., p. 89). By not seeing differences and treating everyone alike, it is presumed that the dominant cultural norms are equally beneficial for all. Moreover, when members of a dominant group value cultural "blindness," they cause further unintended harm by contributing to the sense of invisibility experienced by members of nondominant groups. This, in fact, diminishes respect for students of color or any student that is different from the teacher. Using the cultural proficiency continuum as a frame for analysis created a small group of individuals who recognized that the status quo of being "color blind" and not recognizing was insufficient for meeting the needs of our highly diverse student population.

Anti-Bias Learning Community

In an effort to move along on the path toward cultural proficiency, the Early Childhood Education (ECE) Department took the lead in establishing an anti-bias teacher learning community emphasizing social justice education. In addition to Singleton's racial autobiography work that the teacher specialists were guided through self-analysis, the ECE department used Derman-Sparks and Olsen Edwards' (2010) framework, "Anti-Bias Education for Young Children and Ourselves," as their guide. The following four goals of the anti-bias framework became the guiding principles of the department:

> Goal One: Each child will demonstrate self-awareness, confidence, family pride, and positive social (group) identities.

[2] This specific terminology was coined and used by the original authors of the continuum framework. However, the authors of this chapter want to recognize how this term is not sensitive toward Blind, DeafBlind, or low-vision individuals and populations, given that it equates "blind" with "ignorance."

Goal Two: Each child will express comfort and joy with human diversity, accurate language for human differences, and deep, caring human connections.

Goal Three: Each child will increasingly recognize unfairness, have language to describe unfairness, and understand that unfairness hurts.

Goal Four: Each child shall demonstrate empowerment and the skills to act with others or alone against prejudice and/or discriminatory actions (p. 4).

Some may question the appropriateness of exposing these concepts to children at a young age. However, Gorski (2010) states that educators should teach about issues such as racism, sexism, poverty, and heterosexism because children at the youngest ages from disenfranchised communities have already experienced them or have witnessed their parents or guardians experiencing them. According to Derman-Sparks and Olsen Edwards (2010), the intentions of anti-bias education are "to support children's full development in our multiracial, multilingual, multicultural world and to give them the tools to stand up to prejudice, stereotyping, bias, and eventually to institutional "isms" (p. vii). Although CSD's ECE staff is typical, where the teachers are predominantly white, they committed themselves to the work and agreed to prioritize the commitment to social justice for themselves, the students, and their families. As one teacher stated, "It was the anti-bias classroom training that made the most influence on my desire to change personally and professionally" (survey respondent, 2013).

LGBT Curriculum Committee

While the achievement gap mandate by the state brings heightened awareness of racial inequities that need to be addressed in school systems, other inequities had not been addressed adequately. Passage of the Fair, Accurate, Inclusive and Respectful (FAIR) Education Act in California in 2011 (LegiScan, 2011) attempted to ensure that schools are fully inclusive of all underrepresented and marginalized groups, including the lesbian, gay, bisexual, transgender, queer community.

The FAIR Education Act led to formation of the LGBT curriculum committee at CSD, which immediately organized CSD's first school-wide LGBT history month during October 2011. An LGBT timeline was posted in the school library, and posters showing Deaf LGBT individuals were displayed prominently on campus. In addition, two forms of professional development were offered during the month. They included LGBT ally training and a weekly film series and panel discussions with the goal of raising consciousness among faculty and staff regarding LGBT individuals and issues. Each is described here.

The Gay, Lesbian, and Straight Education Network (GLSEN's) Safe Space Kit: Guide to Being an Ally to LGBT Students (GLSEN, 2011) was selected as the training tool for interested allies. This kit was designed as a guide for schools to become safer places for LGBT students. The guide is easy to follow and includes outlines for sample presentations. The four main sections include (1) *know the issues*, which gives background information about the experiences of LGBT students and anti-LGBT bias; (2) *support*, which describes specific actions you can take to support LGBT students effectively; (3) *educate*, which discusses ways to teach students and inform school staff about combating anti-LGBT bias and behavior; and (4) *advocate*, which provides strategies that can be used to promote change within a school. The last section includes additional materials, including definitions of LGBT-related terms and a comprehensive list of resources and referral sources for LGBT youth.

Onc e the training was completed, the participants received a certificate and a 'Safe Space' sticker (GLSEN, 2011) to display on their classroom or office door or window showing they are a visible ally of LGBT students, staff, and families in the CSD school community. By participating in the ally training, these supportive staff members made a commitment to ensure that CSD is a safe and welcoming place for all, including the LGBT community.

Other staff enrichment activity included weekly film documentaries followed by a postscreening panel discussion. This provided an opportunity for the viewers to experience the lives of LGBT individuals from their unique perspective and personal stories. Each captioned film began with an ASL public service announcement (PSA) or a brief film clip made within the Deaf community related specifically to the documentary topic. The four documentaries shown were Bullied: A Student, a School and a Case That Made History (Cohen, R. Producer, Brummel, B., & Sharp, G., Directors, 2010), It's Elementary—Talking About Gay Issues in School (Cohen & Chasnoff, Chasnoff, 1996), My (Extra) Ordinary Family: Inside the Transgender World (Nightline Primetime, 2011), and Daddy & Papa (Symons & Sablosky, Symons, 2002). The feedback from the staff participants was mostly positive. They include:

> Thank you for all the hard work it took to made such an important step forward in our educational endeavor—and thank you for creating relevant tools we can use to help change attitudes and foster acceptance of all diversity.
>
> This workshop helped so much by demystifying the culture of transgendered individuals and by giving the entire transgender community a human face.
>
> We learned a lot about embracing our students and their LGBT families. Unfortunately, students begin to use negative gay-slurs in pre-kindergarten and kindergarten. When teachers are silent about LGBT people and families, students learn that the words "gay" and "lesbian" are words used to degrade others rather than words to be used with respect. We learned that we must not just teach tolerance, but also embrace all kinds of families by designing a non [anti] bias curriculum.

CSD's Journey: Student Development

Banks (1998) proposed that there are four approaches to integrating multicultural content in the curriculum. Level 1 is the contributions approach, which focuses on heroes and holidays. This is also referred to as a tourist curriculum (Derman-Sparks & Olsen Edwards, 2010), which does not necessarily refer to any curricular change, but enables educators to claim a level of multiculturalism. Level 2 is the additive approach, where content or concepts may be added but do not alter the structure of the curriculum. Level 3 is the transformation approach, which actually changes the structure of the curriculum to "enable students to view concepts, issues, events, and themes from the perspectives of diverse ethnic and cultural groups." Level 4 is the social action approach, which incorporates the transformation approach and empowers students to address important social issues.

Expanding on the four levels, there are teachers who consciously integrate cultural diversity and social justice concepts in their instruction. There are teachers that teach in a more traditional manner by adhering to their curriculum, including bits of diversity by celebrating heritage months. This would be Banks' Level 1, contributions approach. This is where the content focuses on specific ethnic groups and is limited to heroes and holidays (e.g., Martin Luther King, Jr. and Cinco de Mayo). Other teachers may incorporate books and materials or have specific units that provide another perspective. An example of this additive approach is that they may add a week-long unit on Fred Korematsu during Asian-American and Pacific Islander heritage month in May. Still other teachers expose and teach students to different viewpoints. Those who are at the transformation level create opportunities to examine the influence of multiple perspectives and can incorporate the experience of other oppressed groups. For example, when teaching about Rosa Parks and her taking a stand for equal rights, teachers can include a discussion about Cesar Chavez's nonviolent fight to support farm workers rights, as well as refer to the Deaf experience and how the Deaf President Now protest was similar or different. Culturally responsive curriculum dictates that teachers who are at the social action level will encourage students to "investigate the status quo and generate actions that combat or improve equity within the school or local community" (NCCREST, 2008, p. 21). These teachers infuse this model throughout the curriculum and empower their students to be agents of change.

Lessons Learned from Middle School

> "Once social change begins, it cannot be reversed. You cannot uneducate the person who has learned to read. You cannot humiliate the person who feels pride. You cannot oppress the people who are not afraid anymore..."
>
> – Cesar Chavez

In an effort to take the social action approach (Level 4), CSD's middle school offered formal social justice classes and adopted the four-step model of inclusive classrooms as discussed by Schniedewind and Davidson (2006):

Step A. Create an inclusive, trusting community where students appreciate diversity in the classroom
Step B: Enable students to empathize with others' life experiences and explore why and how inequality based on difference exists
Step C: Help students examine discrimination in the institutions in their lives and see how it has affected them
Step D: Empower students to envision and create changes to foster greater equality

These 8-week courses were required of all sixth- and seventh-grade students using the curricula adapted from *Making Allies, Making Friends* (Vasquez, Myhand, & Creighton, 2003). Students in middle school were introduced to understanding and analyzing the "-isms" (ableism, ageism, audism, classism, ethnocentrism, heterosexism, lingucism, nativism, racism, religious oppression, including anti-Semitism and islamaphobia, sexism, xenophobia), domestic violence, anti-bullying and becoming an ally, learning and appreciating how we are part of a multicultural society, and questioning what has been taught throughout their educational experience, including so-called "facts" that have historically been written from the hearing, Eurocentric, and patriarchal perspective. These activities allowed students a growing awareness of how these issues are interconnected.

An example of an exercise that covered a range of issues and exposed the larger complex and interconnected structure of these topics is one where students were asked to look at their educational materials with an analytical eye. Students researched traditional American holidays such as Columbus Day and Thanksgiving and compared different sources of information from multiple perspectives. One excellent resource utilized was *The Young People's History of the United States* (Zinn, 2009), which presents facts and the perspective of oppressed groups not typically included in traditional textbooks. This exercise also opened up the discussion to a variety of topics, including immigration and xenophobia, and the reality that almost everyone's ethnic identities originated in another country. By seeing history through the eyes and stories of Native Americans, students brought a deeper and more informed view to the discussion of the inaccurate representation of indigenous peoples as mascots and the Native appropriations of Halloween costumes.

Reteaching history is a critical part of social justice education. A social justice class cannot be taught in the context of historical events or understanding history from multiple perspectives alone. The middle school social justice teachers also took great advantage of the current events happening around the world and allowed these events to guide instruction. For example, when LGBT youth suicides commanded national attention in 2012, schools around the country responded with anti-LGBT bullying campaigns. CSD students did the same by promoting Spirit Day activities at CSD, interviewing staff and students who were signifying their support by wearing purple, and later developing a PSA for LGBT history month that noted the alarming statistics related to bullying specifically with middle school students. They also participated in No Name Calling Week, an annual week of educational activities sponsored by the GLSEN aimed at ending name calling of all kinds and providing schools with the tools and inspiration to launch an ongoing dialogue about ways to eliminate bullying in their communities.

Another important theme in the social justice classes was recognizing the "-isms" that exist in our society. When addressing social justice issues through the lens of "-isms", it is important to also explore the intersecting privileges and oppressions that one may experience because of the multiple identities with which they affiliate (e.g., a Deaf Latina lesbian) in our society. *Making Allies, Making Friends* (Vasquez et al., 2003) provided a framework that helped students understand that what underlies oppression is the need for a person or group of people to have power and control over other individuals or groups of people. In addition to the curriculum, it is critical to include the rich resources available within the school, as well as from the larger Deaf community, so that students are able to gain a deeper understanding of the multiple ways of viewing the world. Through the stories from people that are from cultures different from their own, students are better able to dismantle stereotypes that they have about those in our classrooms, schools, and communities.

Lessons learned from Early Childhood Education

> "Keep in mind always the present you are constructing—it should be the future you want."
>
> –Alice Walker

As stated earlier, the ECE staff benefited from ongoing anti-bias education training and pedagogy, which resulted in a more equitable learning environment for young children regardless of their backgrounds. One important task was to become more conscious about the use of materials. As one survey respondent stated, "In some cases, it was being mindful of the materials that were used in the classroom of the very youngest children such as making sure that dolls and books represented a variety of ethnicities, cultures, languages and were a true reflection of the diversity of the classroom and the world around them." One challenge many teachers face is the discussion about skin color. This is unfortunate because it can be an opportunity to teach accurate vocabulary, labels, and debunk the false stereotypes that abound. At CSD, kindergarten teachers provided a learning activity that centered on matching the accurate skin color for each student. With this activity, students were able to see how many of us have underlying similarities in our skin color. Students mixed the combination of paints to find each unique color. This de-emphasized the notion that children of European descent have skin color that matches white paint or those of African descent matches black paint. The process of mixing many colors empowered the students to discover how equally unique everyone's skin color was. Another example is that teachers can be cognizant of the paper they use when printing and duplicating pictures of people signing. While most copying paper is white, teachers can make an effort to copy on different shades of paper that are more reflective of the various skin tones in our community. If that type of paper is not available, the teachers can take the responsibility to color-in using crayons that represent a variety of shades of skin color.

The commitment to create an inclusive environment was reinforced by the Anti-Defamation League, which states:

> What is present and absent in the school classroom provides children with important information about who and what is important. Every effort should be made to create a setting that is rich in possibilities for exploring cultural diversity. Such an environment assists children in developing their ideas about themselves and others, creates the conditions under which children initiate conversations about differences and provides teachers with a setting for introducing activities about diversity. It also fosters children's positive self-concept and attitudes (Anti-Defamation League, n.d.).

Families and community members can be valuable resources for ensuring that our classroom environments are inclusive. A conscientious effort ECE made was to invite individuals who represented a variety of family structures, racial, ethnic, and cultural identities to participate in activities such as storytelling, developing ASL corpus materials, and volunteering in the classroom.

Another valuable resource to ensure that children are provided with equitable learning environments was the Checklist for Assessing the Visual Material Environment (Derman-Sparks & Olsen Edwards, 2010, p. 161–162), which serves as a reminder that "what children do not see in the classroom teaches children as much as what they do see" (p. 161). All of these strategies create a setting that is rich in possibilities for exploring cultural diversity (ADL, n.d.).

For all learning environments, teaching and learning vocabulary is essential to understanding the content. A teacher in ECE stated, "I've also seen my students use more social justice vocabulary, such as fairness, equality, support, bystander, bully, etc. Knowing these terms and what they mean can empower my students to stand up for not only themselves but also the rights and equality of others" (survey respondent, May 2013).

Clearly, social justice goes beyond people of color and members of the LGBT community. Gender, religious diversity, economic class, and people with other social and human differences, including individuals with different abilities, also need to be addressed. In following the social action approach (Level 4 of Banks' model), ECE students were introduced to a Deaf Little Person who uses a wheelchair to engage in a dialogue about accessibility. Following the discussion, students explored the campus and found only one electric door and very few ramps. This prompted them to take action and write a letter to the superintendent requesting electronic doors and ramps to improve accessibility for people who use wheelchairs. The superintendent then invited them to address the issue before the CSD's Community Advisory Council. The teacher who accompanied them commented, "Seeing our students stand before the Community Advisory Council and 'fighting for change' was inspiring. They stood there and shared their ideas with confidence because they knew it was important to fight for what was right" (survey respondent, May 2013). This supports the social action model and the importance of social justice education at a very young age. Young people can and do internalize the goals of anti-bias education and are poised to become social justice advocates as they navigate the world around them.

Lessons Learned from High School

The emphasis of this chapter has been on social justice and anti-bias education in ECE and the middle school. It's not to imply that other departments at CSD have not addressed social justice education. The high school department has included social justice in their curriculum. One example was the Senior English Slice of Life course. Within this project, students studied their own identities and learned accurate information about various cultural groups. By understanding the values and beliefs of various communities, they were better able to analyze stereotypes and biases that exist on an individual and institutional level. English elective courses are also offered in LGBT Literature and Latin@ Literature. In addition, at the beginning of each school year, the diversity specialist presented a workshop on "-isms" in the media" for high school students enrolled in the yearbook class, the instructional television class that produces a weekly news show, and the class that develops the school website. Each class developed their own guidelines to ensure that they do not perpetuate biases and stereotypes but instead promote an accurate and positive portrayal of all people.

Lessons Learned from Elementary School

The elementary school at CSD has not only been a longtime advocate of social justice work through the Character Counts Educational program, but also has been proactively immersing students in facilitating their monthly cultural diversity assemblies. This reflects one of the many components of the department's curriculum toward embracing diversity. An extraordinary example of infusing social justice education was the way the teachers presented the LGBT history month to their students. They established learning centers where all students participated, within their grade level, in five rotating workshops facilitated by elementary staff. The centers focused on the Stonewall Riots, Harvey Milk, the rainbow "Pride" flag, gender identity/ expression via the book *My Princess Boy* (Kilodavis, 2010), and workplace discrimination based on sexual orientation. The elementary students engaged in age-appropriate activities that supported their ability to recognize and understand the injustice that has been experienced by the LGBT community. These activities promoted the development of critical thinking skills and helped them understand they all share the responsibility to keep the classroom and school community a safe, respectful, and inclusive place for all students, staff, and families.

SUMMARY

Starting with the first multicultural committee, CSD's journey continued through the adoption of a bilingual–bicultural educational program, establishing student affinity groups, understanding of Deafhood, and receiving anti-bias education and culturally proficient training. However, this does not mean that the journey is over nor should CSD be complacent with the progress that has been made. For instance, it is expected that staff will not always be in the same place in terms of doing the work. At CSD, as at other schools, there are a range of people who are clearly committed and incorporate anti-bias and social justice teachings as well as those who have not.

Fortunately, valuable lessons have been learned along this journey, and we would like to share the following reflections for you as an individual, for your curriculum, for your department, or for your school. In addition, there are a number of resources available in Appendix B.

For you as an individual:

- The journey can be challenging. The first step is to learn about yourself and others. Keep a journal for self-reflection and identify areas in which you want to grow and plan ways to do so. Learning about others can be done by reading authors from diverse backgrounds or watching documentaries that can give one an authentic glimpse into the experiences of people whose lives are different than one's own. Visit your students' home/neighborhood as well as areas that may be unfamiliar. Try shopping at a different market than you normally would.
- Finding a trusted friend and/or colleague is extremely important because this type of work is difficult to do in isolation. Ongoing support and time are needed to process this experience.

For curricular considerations:

- Check your curriculum, materials, and classroom environment to make sure they are sensitive to and inclusive of diverse populations. Ask yourself if they reflect primarily the dominant white, male, hearing, straight culture or do they reflect the diversity represented in society and the multiple identities that the students represent? Also, seek materials that represent multiple perspectives on events and are not one-sided.

- Recognize "-ism's" and confront students (and colleagues) when inaccurate or potentially offensive terminology is used. If you choose to ignore them, you are perpetruating the problem or even condoning inappropriate statements and actions.
- Reanalyze who you invite or ask to come to school (grad, career day, guest presenters). Are students only exposed to people who reflect the dominant culture? Be sure to include people from diverse backgrounds, including race/ethnicity, gender, sexual orientation, religion, and class (people who reflect the identities of your students), and do not limit them to a specific month based on their cultural identity.

For schoolwide and/or departmental practices:

- Ideally, staff development should be a continuous process over a period of time rather than taking place once or twice a year. Making a long-term commitment provides staff the opportunity to engage in the self-reflective process on a deeper level. What is equally important is structuring staff development to allow for a small group process. This would allow for an authentic analysis of one's own biases, existing social systems, and constant reflections on how we each can contribute and become better educators. It is critical to allow time for informal or formal small group discussion and follow-up meetings for those interested in continuing the conversation.

An optimal teaching environment that promotes social justice education provides Deaf students with the tools to better understand their own identities and how they fit in the multicultural world around them. With better knowledge of themsleves, they are better equipped to recognize the inequities that exist and can then learn how work to effect positive change to create a just society. As exemplified in this chapter, infusing social justice education in the classroom is an ongoing process. Social justice educators and administrators must commit to further learning about themselves and the multitude of identities in our society. Successful social justice educators collaborate with other like-minded colleagues within the school and involve the families and the greater community. Teaching social justice classes in middle school and providing early childhood anti-bias education, along with activities in high school and elementary school departments at the California School for the Deaf, exist because of the contributions of many people since the mid-1990s.

REFERENCES

Adams, M., Bell, L., & Griffin, P. (2007). *Teaching for diversity and social justice.* New York: Routledge.

Anti-Defamation League (n.d.). Creating an anti-bias learning environment. Retrieved 30 June 2013 from http://www.adl.org/education-outreach/curriculum-resources/c/creating-an-anti-bias-learning-environment.html#.UdHHsq6veRk

Banks, J. (1998). Approaches to multicultural curriculum reform. In E. Lee, D. Menkart, & M. Okazawa-Rey (Eds.), *Beyond heroes and holidays* (pp. 73–75). Washington, DC: AK Press.

Bransford, J.D., Brown, A.L., & Cocking, R.R. (2000). *How people learn: Brain, mind, experience and school.* Washington, DC: National Academy Press.

Cohen, H. (Producer), & Chasnoff, D., & Cohen, H. (Directors)(1996). *It's elementary: Talking about gay issues in school* [Documentary film]. United States: GroundSpark.

Cohen, R. (Producer), & Brummel, B., & Sharp, G. (Directors)(2010). *Bullied: A student, a school and a case that made history* [Documentary film]. United States: Southern Poverty Law Center.

Deafhood Foundation (n.d.). What is Deafhood? Retrieved 30 June 2013 from http://www.deafhoodfoundation.org/Deafhood/Deafhood.html

Derman-Sparks, L., & Olsen Edwards, J. (2010). *Anti-bias education for young children and ourselves.* Washington, DC: National Association for the Education of Young Children.

Elmore, R. (2002). *Bridging the gap between standards and achievement: The imperative for professional development in education.* Washington, DC: Albert Shanker Institute.

Fullwood, S., III (2013, July 30). Race and beyond: It's time to go all in. Retrieved 6 August 2013 from http://www.americanprogress.org/issues/race/news/2013/07/30/70888/its-time-to-go-all-in/

Gay, Lesbian, & Straight Education Network (2011). *Safe Space Kit.* New York: GLSEN.

Gollnick, D., & Chinn, P. (2009). *Multicultural education in a pluralistic society*. New Jersey: Pearson Education, Inc.

Gorski, P. (2010, September). *Beyond celebrating diversity: Twenty things I can do to be a better multicultural educator*. Retrieved 8 August 2013 from http://www.edchange.org/handouts/20things.pdf

Kids Count Data Center (2012). *Child population by race.* Retrieved 9 August 2013 from http://datacenter.kidscount.org/data/tables/103-child-population-by-race?loc=1&loct=2#detailed/1/any/false/867,133,38,35,18/66,67,68,69,70,71,12,72/423,424

Kilodavis, C. (2010). *My princess boy*. New York: Alladin.

Ladd, P. (2003). *Understanding Deaf culture: In search of Deafhood*. Bristol, UK: Multilingual Matters.

LegiScan (2011). *CA SB48*. Retrieved 9 August 2013 from http://legiscan.com/CA/text/SB48/id/74798

Lindsey, R., Robins, K., & Terrell, R. (2009). *Cultural proficiency: A manual for school leaders*. Thousand Oaks, CA: Corwin.

Lindstrom, P., & Speck, M. (2004). *The principal as professional development leader.* Thousand Oaks, CA: Corwin.

Lorde, A. (2007). *Sister outsider*. Berkeley, CA: Crossing Press.

McIntosh, P. (1988). White privilege: Unpacking the invisible knapsack. Retrieved 9 August 2013 from http://www.nymbp.org/reference/WhitePrivilege.pdf

Nightline Primetime (2011). *My (extra) ordinary family: Inside the transgender world* [Television broadcast]. New York: American Broadcasting Company.

National Center for Culturally Responsive Educational Systems (NCCREST) (2008). *Culturally responsive pedagogy and practice—Academy 3*. Retrieved 10 August from http://www.equityallianceatasu.org/pl/modules

Nieto, S., & Bode, P. (2008). *Affirming diversity: The sociopolitical context of multicultural education.* Boston, MA: Pearson Education, Inc.

Robins, K., Lindsey, R., Lindsey, D., & Terrell, R. (2006). *Culturally proficient instruction: A guide for people who teach.* Thousand Oaks, CA: Corwin Press.

Schniedewind, N., & Davidson, E. (2006). *Open minds to equality: A sourcebook of learning activities to affirm diversity and promote equity.* Milwaukee, WI: Rethinking Schools, Ltd.

Singleton, G.E., & Linton, C. (2006). *Courageous conversations about race: A field guide for achieving equity in schools*. Thousand Oaks, CA: Corwin Press.

Sparks, D. (2002). *Designing powerful professional development for teachers and principals.* Oxford, OH: National Staff Development Council.

Symons, J. (Producer/Director), & Sablosky, L., & Symons, J. (Directors)(2002). *Daddy & papa* [Documentary film]. United States: Persistent Films, LLC.

Vasquez, H., Myhand, M.N., & Creighton, A. (2003). *Making allies, making friends: A curriculum for making the peace in middle school.* Todos Institute: Oakland, CA.

WestEd (n.d.). *Workbook for improving school climate & closing the achievement gap.* Retrieved 9 August 2013 from http://www.wested.org/online_pubs/WB_1221_allv5.pdf

Zinn, H. (2009). *A young people's history of the United States.* New York: Seven Stories Press.

APPENDIX A

Survey Questions

1. How do you incorporate SJ in your curriculum/lessons/conversations with your students? When did this begin?
2. What is your experience with Deafhood training?
3. If you participated in DH training, did this influence your desire to incorporate SJ in your classroom activities?
4. Have you had opportunities to collaborate with colleagues on SJ pedagogy?
5. What changes, if any, have you seen in students? For example, sharing what they have learned, aha moments, changing their perspectives, becoming involved, and effecting change in their world.
6. Where have you acquired your teaching materials?
7. Since you have been here at CSD what changes have you seen in the area of
   a. Professional development
   b. Administrative support–Institutional/Departmental
   c. Family consideration
   d. Students materials
8. What are the next steps as a teacher, as a department, as a school, as a community member, and as a member of society?

APPENDIX B

Tools

5+ Ways to Make Our World More Trans*-Friendly: http://itspronouncedmetrosexual.com/2012/04/list-of-ways-to-make-world-trans-friendl/

10 Myths About Immigrants: http://www.tolerance.org/immigration-myths

28 Common Racist Attitudes & Behaviors: http://www.stcloudstate.edu/affirmativeaction/resources/insights/pdf/28ToolsChange.pdf

Are you Challenging Sexism and Male Supremacy by Paul Kivel: http://www.paulkivel.com/component/jdownloads/finish/1/13/0?Itemid=31

Assessing Yourself & Your School Checklist: http://www.adl.org/assets/pdf/education-outreach/Assessing-Yourself-Your-School-Checklist.pdf

AWARE Anti-Oppression Principles and Guidelines: http://awarela.org/wp-content/uploads/2010/04/AWARE_Chapter_Packet1.pdf

Beyond Celebrating Diversity: 20 Things I Can Do to Be a Better Multicultural Educator: http://www.edchange.org/handouts/20things.pdf

Checklist for Allies Against Racism: http://johnraible.files.wordpress.com/2007/05/revised-2009-checklist-for-allies.pdf

Checking Your Privilege 101: http://www.feminish.com/wp-content/uploads/2012/08/privilege101.pdf

Dos & Don'ts of LGBT Ally Assumptions: http://www.iwu.edu/multicultural/SafeZone/ally_dos_donts_2010.pdf

Eleven Things YOU Can Do to Bring Class Equity to School: http://www.edchange.org/handouts/class-equity.pdf

Five Approaches to Social Justice Activism: http://www.edchange.org/handouts/approaches-activism.pdf

Male Privilege Checklist: http://sap.mit.edu/content/pdf/male_privilege.pdf

So You Think You're an Anti-Racist? Six Shifts of Consciousness for Well-Intentioned White Folks: http://www.edchange.org/handouts/paradigmshifts_race.pdf

Websites

Anti-Defamation League:
www.adl.org/education-outreach
Audism: A Theory and Practice of Audiocentric Privilege:
http://www.aslta.org/sites/default/files/images/Audism%20handout.pdf
Audism Free America:
http://audismfreeamerica.blogspot.com/
CEASE Concerned Educators Allied for a Safe Environment:
http://www.peaceeducators.org/
Center for Multicultural Education–Resources:
http://education.washington.edu/cme/resources.htm
Center for Research on Education, Diversity, and Excellence (CREDE):
http://www.cal.org/crede
Culture of Pedagogy:
www.cultofpedagogy.com/social-justice-resources/nti
Deafhood Foundation:
http://www.deafhoodfoundation.org/Deafhood/Video_Welcome.html-
EdChange Critical Multicultural Pavilion:
http://www.edchange.org/multicultural/
Education World:
http://www.educationworld.com/a_lesson/lesson/lesson294.shtml
Everyday Feminism:
www.everydayfeminism.com
Facing the Future:
http://www.facingthefuture.org/TakeAction/TakeAction/tabid/124/Default.aspx#.UeD_cTHhdXd
IndyKids! A Free Paper for Free Kids:
http://indykids.net/main/
National Association of the Education of Young Children:
http://www.naeyc.org/
Oyate (Publisher and reviewer of books about Native Americans, particularly those aimed at schoolchildren.):
www.oyate.org
Peace Library:
www.childpeacebooks.org
Race Forward: The Center for Racial Justice Innovation:
https://www.raceforward.org

Rethinking Schools:
http://www.rethinkingschools.org/index.shtml
Social Justice Leadership (Deaf history Included):
https://sojustlead.org/
Teachers for Social Justice:
http://www.teachersforjustice.org/ -
Teachers for Social Justice: Deaf Learners:
www.tsjdl.org
Teaching for Change: Building Social Justice Starting in the Classroom:
http://www.teachingforchange.org/
Teaching Tolerance:
http://www.tolerance.org/
West Ed:
www.wested.org
Zinn Education Project:
http://zinnedproject.org/

Curriculum

Perspectives for a Diverse America—a literacy-based, k-12 antibias curriculum:
http://www.tolerance.org/sites/default/files/general/Perpectives_for_a_Diverse_America.pdf
Challenging Homophobia and Heterosexism: A K-12 Curriculum Resource Guide:
http://sexedcentral.com/wp-content/uploads/2011/10/Challenging-Homophobia-and-Heterosexism-Final-2011.pdf
Dos and Don'ts with Special Diversity Events:
http://www.adl.org/assets/pdf/education-outreach/Dos-and-Don-ts-with-Special-Diversity-Events.pdf
The Safe Space Kit: Guide to Being an Ally to LGBT Students, Gay, Lesbian and Straight Education Network 2009:
http://glsen.org/sites/default/files/Safe%20Space%20Kit.pdf
GSA Network: Empowering Youth Activists to Fight Homophobia and Transphobia in Schools:
http://gsanetwork.org/get-involved/change-your-school/campaigns/lgbtq-inclusive-curriculum
Ready, Set, Respect: GLSEN's Elementary Tool Kit:
http://glsen-cloud.mediapolis.com/cgi-bin/iowa/all/news/record/2833.html

Films

Are You a Sexist?: Deafhope (ASL and English captions): http://www.youtube.com/watch?v=wMaXJ46GBXU Audism Unveiled

Bullied: A Student, a School and a Case That Made History: http://www.tolerance.org/kit/bullied-student-school-and-case-made-history (CC available on purchased order)

Cracking the Codes—The System of Racial Inequity (CC available): http://world-trust.org/cracking-the-codes-understanding-the-system-of-inequity/

DYUSA—Community Accountability (ASL and English captions): https://www.youtube.com/watch?v=btEbUhYti10

DYUSA—Privilege (ASL and English captions): https://www.youtube.com/watch?v=0PE2iTOVrcA

DYUSA—Systematic Oppression and Social Justice (ASL and English captions): https://www.youtube.com/watch?v=fnLqJpf_gLc

It's Elementary—Talking about Gay Issues in School (CC available): http://www.newdaydigital.com/It-s-Elementary%E2%80%94Talking-About-Gay-Issues-In-School.html

It's Still Elementary (CC available): http://groundspark.org/our-films-and-campaigns/stillelementary

Marlee Matlin Message of Acceptance/GLAAD.org (ASL and English captions): https://www.youtube.com/watch?v=SVvZDV5vr_A

Mirrors of Privilege: Making Whiteness Visible (CC available): http://world-trust.org/mirrors-of-privilege-making-whiteness-visible/

Social Justice Project Lecture Series (ASL and voiced in Spoken English): http://info.texasdhhresources.org/pdf/Lesson_Plans/Social%20Justice/SJPLS%20Announcement.pdf

The Unequal Opportunity Race (captions inserted): http://www.youtube.com/watch?v=vX_Vzl-r8NY

Chapter 16

Poco a poco, se va lejos: Is That Fast Enough?

KATHEE MANGAN CHRISTENSEN, Ph.D.
Professor Emerita, San Diego State University

> "A person may cause evil to others not only by his actions but by his inaction, and, in either case, he is justly accountable to them for the injury."
>
> –John Stuart Mill, Philosopher and Economist (1806–1873)

> "…I will act, says Don Quixote, as if the world were what I would have it to be, as if the ideal were real…"
>
> – Miguel de Cervantes (1547–1616), "Don Quixote de la Mancha"

No doubt we are all familiar with the old adages that encourage us to take our time. "The road to success begins with one step." "Haste makes waste." "Rome wasn't built in a day" or, in Spanish, *Poco a poco, se va lejos* (Little by little, one goes far.) And, no doubt, we all have felt frustration when our goals are not achieved rapidly or within the time frame that we expect and desire. It is helpful to stop occasionally and take stock of what progress has been made as we work toward future goals—assess the "attainability" factor, make a plan, and move forward.

A question that has been raised throughout the chapters of this book is: How does a Deaf or Deafblind person from underrepresented ethnic and racial groups achieve success despite the odds? What obstacles must they overcome? How can educators and other leaders maintain high expectations and assist ALL students along their chosen paths?

Here are some thoughts on the subject.

CREATE A (CULTURALLY) WELCOMING SCHOOL ENVIRONMENT

Students feel more comfortable with teachers who look like them—teachers who can communicate with them. The Global Coalition of Parents of Children who are Deaf and Hard of Hearing makes it clear, in their 2010 position statement, that cultural considerations can and should be incorporated into all early intervention systems. Fischgrund (2012) studied the demographic data of teachers in schools for Deaf students in the United States. He found that of 1175 teachers of Deaf students who responded to his survey, 28 (2.4%) were African-American, 41 (3.5%) were Latino, and 446 (38%) were Deaf. The number of Latino and African-American teachers is well below the number of Deaf children of color in schools for Deaf learners across the United States. In 2008, 37% of the teachers were Deaf. Although it is encouraging to see that more than one-third of the teachers are themselves Deaf, the majority of these Deaf teachers (57%) are assigned to high school and co-curricular classrooms. Only 19 (4.3%) worked in early intervention programs. Clearly, teachers of color must be recruited and prepared to work with the growing number of Deaf children of color, especially in parent intervention/early intervention and preschool programs. In addition, more Deaf teachers must be prepared to work in early intervention. It is the responsibility of college and university programs to prepare professionals to meet these needs. A concern is that courses in multicultural issues in education of Deaf students were required in only 29% of teacher preparation programs in 2008 (Dolman, 2008). More courses of this nature, along with an infusion of multicultural issues across the curriculum, will be a step toward helping prepare teachers and related professionals to meet the diverse needs of an increasingly diverse school population.

Deaf culture is a relatively new field of study within multicultural education. The study of multicultural issues within the Deaf community is even newer. Research efforts within communities of color in the Deaf population move toward theories that bring these smaller communities of color into relevant interaction with the larger Deaf community. Consider the following questions:

- Which aspects of Deaf culture are new, evolving, and emerging?
- What do you know, from personal experience, about these aspects of Deaf culture?

Let's consider the core of Deaf culture, the state residential school.

The state residential school (center school) has for generations existed as the foundation of Deaf culture, the place for transmission of signed language and cultural behavior, the place for early identity formation. Currently, there is a growing attitude within educational administration that mainstreaming is the best placement for *all* so-called special education programs, including programs for learners who are Deaf. This educational placement is a less expensive option when compared with the financial support required to maintain large residential schools. Cuts in special education budgets have a significant impact on expensive, low incidence programs, such as programs for Deaf and Deafblind children. Closure of many dynamic residential programs across the United States has been a result of budget cuts. What will replace these cultural meeting grounds? What new resources will be found that can build cultural identity and self-actualization for Deaf individuals, including Deaf people from diverse ethnic/cultural backgrounds? And, beyond that, how will all Deaf individuals learn the skills to navigate cultural boundaries (usually modeled by Deaf mentors, often in residential schools) and connect positively and beneficially with the larger environment? These are important considerations that affect the quality of life for Deaf children in school and in the community.

Recruit and Prepare Interpreters from Diverse Ethnic, Racial, and Linguistic Backgrounds

Remarkable gains have been made by the Registry of Interpreters of the Deaf (RID) since its inception in 1964. In the formative years, individuals could become members of RID with just two recommendations from the originators of the organization—and a handshake. I know, because I was one of those early members. Emil Ladner, a Deaf teacher, recruited me while we were playing chess in the teachers' lounge at the California School for the Deaf in Berkeley in 1965. If memory serves, Ralph Neesam, a CODA and pioneer in the field of interpreting, was the second signature on my application. The organization made rapid gains during the next few years, so that by 1969 an effective evaluation of applicants was in place. I know about that, also, because I went through the evaluation (recorded film clips and personal interviews with Deaf teachers) at the Illinois School for the Deaf in 1969. As I recall, I was petrified, hands shaking, in the throes of test anxiety. In fact, I was so nervous that I forgot to look at the first few seconds of the film and totally missed the topic of the presentation. There was no stopping, so I soldiered on, eventually figured out the topic, and was given a respectable score, thanks to Robert R. Anderson, an outstanding Deaf teacher and President of the National Fraternal Society of the Deaf from 1984 to 1993. Bob understood my anxiety! Why am I dropping names here? I am hoping to establish a bridge between the past and the present. Any outstanding achievement can be traced back to its roots, and the success of RID is no different. Deaf and Hearing pioneers worked diligently to establish the profession of sign language interpreting, even before American Sign Language (ASL) had a legitimate academic name.

As for the future, again RID is taking a leadership role for the entire Deaf world. The year 2014 marked the development of a Trilingual Standard Practice Paper that dealt with best practice in Spanish–ASL–English interpreting environments. Much earlier, in 2007, RID designed Standard Practice for interpreting for individuals who are Deafblind. Interpreters continue to be a valuable resource for all Deaf people and all settings where Deaf people live, work, and are educated. Recruitment of qualified interpreters of color remains a goal to be attained. Perhaps international connections can be developed to achieve this goal. For example, an article by Zach Dyer in the Costa Rican "Tico Times" reported that a Costa Rican CODA, Estefania Carvajal, has been hired to work in the office of the president of Costa Rica. She will use Costa Rican sign language, LEngua de Senas COstarricense (LESCO), to bridge the communication gap between the government and the Deaf community. In addition to being a native signer of LESCO, Estefania is fluent in American, Brazilian, and International Sign Language. She speaks Spanish and English (Dyer, 2015). The identification of and collaboration with individuals such as Ms. Carvajal on a worldwide basis are possible through innovative uses of technology. Recruitment and preparation of multicultural interpreters could benefit from these connections.

Create More Cross-Cultural Arts Programs That Appeal Equally to Diverse Deaf and Hearing Audiences

An example of a successful program that reaches beyond cultural boundaries is the National Theatre of the Deaf (NTD). NTD was founded in 1967, under the leadership of Broadway set and lighting designer David Hays and internationally respected Deaf actor Bernard Bragg. Over the years, the NTD has been a platform for Deaf actors, directors, and others to showcase their talent and culture through the theatre, all the while breaking down stereotypes. The performers and the performances reflected diversity from the very beginning. Deaf and Hearing audiences were simultaneously captivated and educated about cross-cultural communication through the arts!

Visual arts programs are another way in which both Deaf and Hearing audiences can benefit. More and more museums of art in metropolitan areas are including ASL-interpreted tours as a part of their community outreach programs.

Support Legislation That Views Deaf and Deafblind Learners as "Able" Instead of "Disabled"

Words, particularly words that are used to describe groups of young children, are important to the development of self-esteem, cognition, and decision making. Negative "labels" that focus on loss or disability can have far-reaching effects on Deaf children. Dr. Martin Paulus, a psychiatrist and professor at the University of California–San Diego Medical School, has done extensive research into ways in which negative words affect the brain. He found that the amygdala and the medial prefrontal cortex work harder when processing criticism and keep the brain from doing much else while this processing is happening. In other words, criticism "sticks" in the mind. Along with other neuroscientists, Paulus examines the question of which neurological processes help people perform optimally in difficult situations (Winkielman, Knutson, Paulus, & Trujillo, 2007). The work of Paulus and his colleagues does not address the population of Deaf individuals per se; however, educators would do well to consider the implications of this research in the case of children who live with negative educational labels such as "hearing impaired."

No Child Left Behind (NCLB) legislation was touted as a positive move forward for all children, including those labeled with negative terms such as disability, hearing loss, or impairment and/or special needs, as well as those students for whom English was a second language. These labels placed emphasis on what was missing or lacking in the child. Standardized tests measured the areas in which these children had the greatest challenge. Their strengths were left unmeasured—unnoticed. Unfortunately, NCLB, a revision of the Elementary and Secondary Education Act (ESEA) of 1965, proposed standardized test-based school reform. Passed in 2002, the results of NCLB have fallen short of its promise. In a study 10 years after authorization, NCLB was deemed a policy failure. It was reported that the NCLB failed badly both in terms of its own goals and more broadly. It neither significantly increased academic performance nor significantly reduced achievement gaps, even as measured by standardized exams (Guisbond, Neill, & Schaeffer, 2012).

Because Congress did not reauthorize ESEA, in 2010 the Obama administration offered states a plan that allowed the flexibility to develop and implement standards that ensure students to be college and/or career ready. More than 40 states, to date, have been approved for state-developed accountability plans. In other words, each state can decide what is important and necessary for educational programs. Consistency and consensus, at the national level, will be difficult to achieve, as each state has independent authority. Imagine a presentation at a national conference that might begin with "Here's how we do it in my state!"

Senator Tom Harkin, who has a Deaf brother, proposed an overhaul of NCLB. In 2013, Harkin was instrumental in preparing a reauthorization of the Elementary and Secondary Education Act to include support for English language learners (ELL) and students with disabilities in an attempt to move toward closing the achievement gap. We have yet to see Congress reauthorize ESEA and are left with the question: Will the promises of the original ESEA of 1965 and the NCLB of 2002 be fulfilled by a strong reauthorization in 2015 and beyond? Educators and parents express concern. The President of the National Education Association and the President of the National Parent Teacher Association assert that No Child Left Behind has failed. In an article in the *Washington Post*, they agree that we have a chance to fix the law by refocusing on the proper federal role: equal opportunity. They propose that we change the way we think about accountability (Eskelsen & Thornton, 2015).

No Child Left Behind is defined by Cristian Solorza, Bank Street College of Education, as No Child Left Bilingual (2007). His work focuses on Hearing students in New York City schools who, due to lack of exposure to English, are designated ELL. These students are assessed with English Language Arts measures after as little as a year in school, and for a variety of reasons, are determined to be "failures." This research has implications for the education of Deaf children, who may benefit from early exposure to a visually accessible signed language such as ASL but, similarly to the Hearing students that Solorza studies, are assessed only in English. Bilingual ASL–English educational programs are growing throughout the United States; however, there are gaps in both teacher preparation, instruction, and assessment practices that interfere with effective acquisition and the use of both languages. We have had data for several decades that demonstrate the effectiveness of bilingual education for Hearing children. The research of Krashen (2003) and others has found that a meaningful curriculum presented consistently, over time, using comprehensible input and a lowered affective filter, results in successful bilingual students. Assessment in these programs is viewed as a tool to inform teachers rather than to diminish or view as below par those students who do not achieve within "norms" on standardized tests. Studies of

Deaf children who learn ASL at home from their Deaf parents, or learn ASL in early educational programs, reveal the positive impact of early and consistent ASL/English bilingualism on English literacy (Strong & Prinz, 1997).

A paramount principle of assessment was not factored into NCLB; that is, the need to include observational assessment practices that inform teachers rather than demean students. Observational assessment, often called qualitative or ethnographic assessment, was entirely overlooked. Deaf children and youth, especially those born Deaf, need **both quantitative and qualitative** measures, which take into account and value nonverbal, visual communicative strengths (Christensen & Regan, 1995) and all aspects of Multiple Intelligence theory (Gardner, 1983).

Ensure Culturally Unbiased Educational Assessment

Qualitative assessment is especially important in viewing the strengths of Deaf children who immigrate to the United States from other countries. For example, Deaf children from Asian countries where tonal languages are used face an added communicative challenge. This became apparent to me during my first visit to Taiwan in 1985 where I participated in the first national symposium on speech, hearing, and language in Taipei. I met with teachers, spoke with university professors, and observed programs for Deaf children. Deaf children were underrepresented in college preparatory classes and were more commonly encouraged to learn a trade. This was due to their low literacy skills. They simply could not pass the battery of tests used to determine college entrance. I found that the primary language used in schools for the Deaf was spoken Mandarin, a tonal language. Meaning was made and communicated by means of the clear perception of four distinct auditory tones. Literacy, following acquisition of spoken language, was closely associated with tonal perception, as well. Although Taiwanese Sign Language (TSL) was a complete signed language and used in some schools for the Deaf, TSL was not linked directly to Mandarin in the same way that ASL is not linked directly to English. Signed and spoken languages are discreet and separate. In that first symposium, we talked about the situation of profoundly Deaf children and what could be done to provide tactile, kinesthetic, and visual supplements to spoken language so that salient visual and tactile programs could be designed for the literacy curriculum. To date, this is an ongoing concern; however, there are some new and exciting Taiwanese research projects on the horizon. In a recent visit to Taiwan, I learned that a newly adapted form of Cued Speech has been found useful in some programs to provide visual support for tone differentiation. Cued Speech, invented by R. Orin Cornett in 1966, is a system that uses hand shapes and positions synchronized with mouth movements to make speech visible. The original purpose of Cued Speech was to help Deaf individuals develop and understand spoken language and dialects (Cornett, 1992). Recent work at Chung Shan Medical University in Taichung, Taiwan holds promise for solutions to the task of providing comprehensible linguistic input to Deaf children whose heritage language is tonal (Liu, Andrews, & Liu, 2014). This research can provide a model for programs in the United States that welcome Deaf children from Asian countries. Fortunately, Liu and her colleagues are active in sharing their research at annual meetings of the Association of College Educators of the Deaf and Hard-of-Hearing. I am hopeful that their findings will become part of a multilingual–multicultural emphasis in teacher preparation programs.

Identify and Eradicate Racism

Over the years, I have observed some comparisons between diverse groups of Deaf people and Hearing members of underrepresented ethnic/cultural groups. A Deaf member of an underrepresented cultural/racial group may, in effect, be estranged from two cultures. Consider just a few parallels:

1. Parent–child identity and expectation "mismatch" as seen with parents of LGBT children and hearing parents of Deaf children.
2. Men who feel the need to "speak for women" and hearing or hard-of-hearing persons who do the same for persons who are Deaf.

3. Overrepresentation of children of color in the least productive public school programs and overrepresentation of Hispanic Deaf immigrant children in classes for children with additional special needs.
4. Isolation of an ELL in groups separate from general education and isolation of a Deaf child, with minimal support, in a mainstream placement. (It has been noted that even with an ASL interpreter, Deaf children feel that they are swimming upstream against the mainstream with few opportunities to develop healthy social networks.)
5. Use of volunteers as language interpreters in meetings where important decisions are made about a child's education. This can happen with "other than English speaking" parents of Deaf or Hearing children (e.g., when a certified trilingual interpreter is not available, due to budget constraints or other reasons, it is not unusual to ask a hearing sibling to interpret for his/her parents in teacher conferences in general or special education settings).
6. Reduction in the number of bilingual education classrooms and loss of special day classes for Deaf children.

The biases and examples of discrimination just listed have been part of the history of the United States for decades. Slight advances have been made in some cases, but, for the most part, these barriers still exist. The December 2011 issue of the *American Annals of the Deaf* listed only four doctoral dissertations on Hispanic topics and one on Japanese Sign Language. In the 2012 December issue, just one dissertation on multicultural issues was listed—a study involving Black Deaf Women. Clearly, more attention to research in diversity in the Deaf community is needed in order to provide exposure to new realities and allow for the building of new and lasting understandings. Research in areas of diversity will help recast educational experiences into thought forms of contemporary society.

Frey (2014) predicted that by the year 2020, 40+% of the population in the United States will be other than White and that more than half of the people under age 30 will be people of color. Younger ethnic groups are growing rapidly and creating what Frey called a "cultural generation gap." Members of the White culture are uncomfortable with the growing population of people of color. The older White population is dying off, and racial/ethnic intermarriage is increasing in the younger generation. We must consider how these changing demographics will affect the Deaf community. Will Deaf people of color comprise a "new minority" that invigorates our ever-changing society? We know that cultures are naturally designed to grow. It is our responsibility to provide conditions to nurture and ensure positive growth and resilience (Young, Rogers, Green, & Daniels, 2011).

Build a Culture of Inquiry through Research and Teaching

Some recent studies point the way toward a greater awareness of cultural and linguistic strengths within the Deaf community. At the forefront of ASL/English bilingual education is the Visual Language & Visual Learning Center at Gallaudet University. Known as VL2, this center studies behavioral and neurological mechanisms of learning primarily through vision and visual processes. The work informs the Department of Education at Gallaudet, which prepares professionals to interact and communicate fluently with Deaf individuals with diverse family backgrounds and learning characteristics (Garate, 2012). Some VL2 research briefs are available in Mandarin and Spanish. Although trilingual education does not appear to be a primary focus of VL2 at this time, Chapter 14 in this book describes the application of VL2 strategies to literacy intervention with a Deaf youth from a Spanish-speaking family. I am hopeful that VL2 eventually will expand to incorporate research, which leads to the development of strategies for use with trilingual (ASL+English+heritage language) Deaf learners.

Mayberry (2015) has done in-depth research on American Sign Language and Deaf children as she examines language acquisition and its effect on the brain. She has found that comprehensible language exposure and acquisition are critical during early brain growth to establish typical brain language processing and to achieve full linguistic capabilities. Work of this nature can inform the curricula of all programs for Deaf children in the future as we provide greater opportunities for *all* Deaf children to maximize inherent cognitive and communicative potential.

Cross-cultural research can enhance the understanding of Deaf individuals from tricultural or multicultural backgrounds. For example, an article in the *American Annals of the Deaf* provided recommendations for working with Deaf Hispanic women (Feist, Saladin, & Hansmann, 2013). More recently, Mann and Haug (2015) reviewed a book on the assessment of bilinguals and applied the findings to the assessment of Deaf bilinguals. More work of this nature is needed to bring multicultural issues to the forefront of research and practice.

Consider American Sign Language as a Heritage/Community Language

Heritage language has been broadly defined by the Center for Applied Linguistics as a language other than the dominant language(s) in a given social context. English is the primary language used in government, education, and public communication in the United States. Any language, other than English, acquired and used at home in the family, can be considered a heritage language (Kelleher, 2010). Although the term heritage language has been applied traditionally to spoken languages, Compton (2014) makes a convincing case for the designation of ASL as a heritage language for groups of signers in the United States. Deaf children of Deaf parents and Hearing children of Deaf parents (CODAs) comprise two groups that could be considered heritage language signers. I would add a small group of Hearing children of Hearing parents who grow up in the Deaf community, as I did when my family lived in a house on the campus of the Michigan School for the Deaf where my parents worked. I acquired both spoken English and ASL more or less simultaneously, and that experience influenced my world view, as well as my identity. Furthermore, Compton (2014) observed that "today there are almost as many deaf and hard-of-hearing students from homes in which minority spoken languages are used (47%) as from monolingual English-speaking ones" (p. 280). This complicates the situation in interesting ways. For example, is a congenitally Deaf child from a monolingual Spanish-speaking family living in the United States a candidate for Spanish, Spanish Sign Language, or American Sign Language as their heritage language? Or does that child count all three languages as part of his/her heritage? Obviously, it will depend on the individual child and the surrounding circumstances, but, in my opinion, this is a fascinating topic for further research and discussion.

On the horizon is an exciting new technological advance that can enhance communication on a global level among Deaf and Hearing people. Microsoft Research Connections Asia is working on experimental real-time technology that "reads" the hand and body movements of signed languages and translates them automatically into spoken languages and vice versa. Microsoft **Kinect** technology has global potential. It could allow access to communication for Deaf people internationally and promote comprehensible communication among Deaf people and Hearing nonsigners within a broad scope of signed and spoken languages worldwide. Still in the beginning stages of development, the Kinect project involves collaboration with the Chinese Deaf community and a research laboratory at Beijing Union University. Microsoft Kinect technology, when available to consumers around the world, has the potential to make communication accessible for Deaf cultures and communities globally.

The 21st International Congress in Vancouver, British Columbia, July 2010, approved a global statement of principle (Sinclair, 2010). The statement, "A New Era: Deaf Participation and Collaboration":

– Rejected all resolutions passed at the Second International Congress on Education of the Deaf in Milan, Italy, 1880, that denied the inclusion of sign language in educational programs for Deaf students

– Acknowledged with regret the detrimental effects of the Milan Congress

– Called upon all nations to ensure that educational programs for the Deaf accept and respect all languages and all forms of communication

This statement represents a giant step forward in global education of individuals who are Deaf. I am hopeful that the next International Congress will add one more line:

– Accept and respect the heritage of all ethnic, cultural, and racial groups within the global Deaf community.

As editor, I have chosen to have the "last word," and I want to end on a positive note! Several chapters in this book have challenged us to look at culture through the eyes of a Deaf child and ask ourselves if equal justice is being served. Where does racism come from? What are the intergenerational consequences of avoiding confrontation with discriminatory practices in the education of Deaf children? Where can we, as people concerned about social justice, work to remove injustice?

One place to make an impact is in teacher preparation. Another place is in educational programs at all ages and stages. Ultimately, the most important place is in our hearts and minds. After all, as Maya Angelou stated so eloquently, we all belong to the same "human family."

Human Family by Maya Angelou

I note the obvious differences
in the human family.
Some of us are serious,
some thrive on comedy.
. . . .

The variety of our skin tones
can confuse, bemuse, delight,
brown and pink and beige and purple,
tan and blue and white.

I've sailed upon the seven seas
and stopped in every land,
I've seen the wonders of the world,
not yet one common man.
. . . .

I note the obvious differences
between each sort and type,

but we are more alike, my friends,
than we are unalike.

We are more alike, my friends,
than we are unalike.

We are more alike, my friends,
than we are unalike.

REFERENCES

Angelou, M. (1994). *The complete collected poems of Maya Angelou.* New York: Random House.

Christensen, K., & Reagan, J. (1995). *Nonverbal and verbal communication analysis.* San Diego: SDSU Press.

Compton, S. (2014). American Sign Language as a heritage language. *Handbook of heritage, community, and Native American languages in the United States: Research, policy, and educational practice.* In Wiley, Peyton, Christian, Moore, & Liu (Eds.). New York: Routledge and the Center for Applied Linguistics.

Cornett, R.O. (1992). *The cued speech resource book for parents of Deaf children.* Raleigh, NC: The National Cued Speech Association, Inc.

Dolman, D. (2008). College and university requirements for teachers of the deaf at the undergraduate level: A twenty-year comparison. *American Annals of the Deaf, 153*(3), 322–327.

Dyer, Z. (2015). *Costa Rica's first official sign language interpreter has long history of bridging the communication gap.* http://www/ticotimes.net/2015/04/20/costa-ricas-first-official-sign-language-interpreter-has-long-history-of-bridging-communication-gap

Eskelsen, L., & Thornton, O. (2015). No Child Left Behind has failed. *Washington Post,* www.washingtonpost.com/opinions/no-child-has-failed/2015/02/13

Feist, A., Saladin, S., & Hansmann, S. (2013). Working with Hispanic women who are Deaf: Recommendations from the literature. *American Annals of the Deaf, 157,* January.

Fischgrund, J. (2011). *Preparing teachers for schools for the Deaf: New realities and new opportunities for teacher preparation programs.* Annual meeting: American College Educators-Deaf and Hard of Hearing, February 16, Jacksonville, Florida.

Frey, W. (2014). *Diversity explosion: How new racial demographics are remaking America.* Washington, DC: Brookings Institution Press.

Garate, M. (2012). ASL/English bilingual education: Models, methodologies and strategies. *Visual languge & visual learning science of learning center: Research brief #8: June.* Washington, DC: Gallaudet University.

Gardner, H. (1983). *Frames of mind: The theory of multiple intelligences.* New York: Basic Books.

Global Coalition of Parents of Children who are Deaf and Hard of hearing (2010). *Position statement.* www.gpodhh.org

Guisbond, L., Neill, M., & Schaeffer, B. (2012). NCLB's lost decade for educational progress: What can we learn from this policy failure? *National Center for Fair and Open Testing.* http://fairtest.org/NCLB-lost-decade-report-home

Kelleher, A. (2010). What is a heritage language? *Heritage Briefs.* Washington, DC: Center for Applied Linguistics.

Krashen, S. (2003). *Explorations in language acquisition and use.* Portsmouth, NH: Heineman.

Liu, H., Andrews, J., & Liu, C. (2014). Literacy and Deaf students in Taiwan: Issues, practices and directions for future research: Part I & Part II. *Deafness Education International.* http://www.maneyonline.com/loi/dei

Mann, W., & Haug, T. (2015). Facing the daunting task of assessing (Deaf) bilinguals: Book review. *American Annals of the Deaf, 159*(5), 484–486.

Mayberry, R. (2015). How the environment shapes language in the brain. *CARTA Symposium: How language evolves.* University of California–San Diego, April 27.

Menken, K., & Solorza, C. (2012). No child left bilingual: Accountability and the elimination of bilingual education programs in New York City schools. *Education Policy, 28*(1), 96–125.

Sinclair, W. (2010). We did it! The rejection of Milan resolutions. *Deaf History International Newsletter*, Nos. 42 & 43, Summer and Fall, pp. 6–9.

Strong, M., & Prinz, P. (1997). A study of the relationship between American Sign Language and English literacy. *JDSDE, 2*(1), 37–46.

Winkielman, P., Knutson, B., Paulus, M., & Trujillo, J. (2007). Affective influence on judgments and decisions: Moving toward core mechanisms. *Review of General Psychology, 11*(2), 179–192.

Young, A., Rogers, K., Green, L., & Daniels, S. (2011). Critical issues in the application of resilience frameworks to the experiences of Deaf children and young people. In D. Zand & K. Pierce (Eds.), *Resilience in Deaf* children: Adaptation through emerging adulthood (pp. 3–24). New York: Springer.